The Koreans

THE KOREANS

*Contemporary Politics
and Society*

THIRD EDITION

DONALD STONE MACDONALD

Edited and Revised by

DONALD N. CLARK
Trinity University

WestviewPress
A Division of HarperCollinsPublishers

Frontispiece: Satellite view of the Korean Peninsula (photo courtesy of Korea Overseas Information Service)

Published in 1996 in the United States of America by Westview Press, 5500 Central Avenue, Boulder, Colorado 80301-2877, and in the United Kingdom by Westview Press, 12 Hid's Copse Road, Cumnor Hill, Oxford OX2 9JJ

Library of Congress Cataloging-in-Publication Data
Macdonald, Donald Stone.
 The Koreans: contemporary politics and society / by Donald Stone
Macdonald; revised and edited by Donald N. Clark.—3rd. ed.
  p. cm.
 ISBN 0-8133-2888-8 (pb)
 1. Korea—History. 2. Korea (South)—Politics and government.
 3. Korea (North)—Politics and government. 4. Korean reunification
question (1945–) I. Clark, Donald N. II. Title.
DS907.18.M33 1996
951.9′04—dc20   96-13297
                                                                         CIP

10   9   8   7   6   5   4   3   2

Contents

Tables and Figures

Preface to Third Edition

Donald Stone Macdonald's survey of modern Korea has been a mainstay of Korean studies courses in the West since it was first published in 1988. Written from the point of view of a senior American scholar-official, it reflects both his experience as a Foreign Service officer and government Korea specialist and his disciplinary training as a political scientist. The book is based on a truly distinguished career. Macdonald first saw Korea as a young army officer with the U.S. military occupation forces in 1946. He was on the scene as a third secretary in the American Embassy when the Korean War broke out in 1950. As Korea desk officer in the State Department in 1960–1961 he had a front-row seat for the transition from the Rhee regime to Park Chung-hee's military rule. Later he contributed to U.S. Korea policy in positions in Washington and Seoul. After retirement from government service he earned his Ph.D. in political science at George Washington University with a dissertation on the military government period. He taught at East Stroudsburg State College in Pennsylvania and then at Georgetown University, where he was Research Professor of Korean Studies and one of the founders of Georgetown's Korean studies program. Throughout all those years he dedicated his energies and leadership to fostering better relations between the United States and Korea and won the respect and affection of fellow officials, academic colleagues, and students alike.

When Macdonald died in 1993 he was contemplating a third edition of *The Koreans* but had not yet begun work on it. He was familiar with the phenomenon of rapid change in Korea and recognized that there would have to be considerable revision of the manuscript to reflect the changes since the second edition in 1990. The preceding December, south Korea had elected its first civilian president since 1963. A year before that, north and south Korea had signed a series of agreements that seemed to promise progress on the perennial problem of reunification but were clouded by north Korea's apparent determination to develop nuclear weapons. North Korea and the international community barely averted a major confrontation in June 1993. At the time of his death a few weeks later Macdonald was persuaded more than ever that the West needed to take Korea seriously and study it systematically.

Donald Macdonald was an optimist about Korea. He was quick to praise the performance of the south Korean economy—and he was tolerant of the stern military regimes that directed it. His career in Korean affairs had been shaped during the most violent phase of modern Korean history, and his experience with the devastation of the Korean War and the Herculean efforts that were required to reconstruct the country persuaded him that the ultimate foe was the danger of renewed warfare on the peninsula. Like most Korea specialists of his time, he never had a chance to visit north Korea and saw the Kim Il-sung government mainly as a threat. Yet he tried hard to understand north Korea on its own terms and not merely in terms of the Cold War. Had he lived, he surely would have played the role of senior adviser in the unfolding drama of gradual U.S. engagement with the north.

In taking charge of the project of revising Macdonald's third edition, I wanted to preserve Macdonald's voice and viewpoint on Korean affairs. However, I knew him well enough to believe that he would have seen the changes taking place in the early 1990s as an opportunity to adjust some of his earlier views. Like the Korean people themselves, he would have been shocked at the scale of corruption in the regimes of Chun Doo-hwan and Roh Tae-woo that was uncovered over the winter of 1995 and brought to light in the trials of 1996. He also would have been fascinated by north Korea as it practiced Kimilsungism without Kim Il-sung, struggling to deal with massive internal problems while pursuing engagement with the outside world on its own terms. He would have been more admiring than ever of south Korea's economic influence in the world and the revolutionary potential of telecommunications and open markets for Korean society. Revising *The Koreans* therefore meant revising Macdonald on these points, in addition to updating facts and figures throughout the volume. I believe the result is a volume that speaks a subtler language about the U.S. role in shaping contemporary Korea and that takes account of the political reckoning that Koreans are facing, both in "righting the wrongs of the past," as President Kim Young-sam has termed it, and in the ultimate goal of peaceful and mutually charitable reunification between the south and north.

Donald N. Clark

Preface to First Edition

Among its foreign residents, Korea is known as "the best-kept secret" because living there is so much better than they had expected. This gap between expectation and reality is only one of many indications that the West—particularly the United States—does not know Korea. Such ignorance is grossly out of proportion to the real importance of Korea to the rest of the world. It also overlooks the fascinating history of the Korean people, who have preserved their own distinctive identity and culture despite hundreds of invasions over the centuries by their neighbors.

Since World War II, Korea has undergone a dramatic transformation from a sleepy and poverty-stricken nation of landlord-ridden peasants to become a vital, expanding modern economy. Tragically divided since 1945 by ideology, superpower rivalry, and civil war, both Koreas have nevertheless led the developing world in economic progress. In fierce competition with each other, the two Korean states have become major factors in the security, stability, and progress of East Asia.

This book is intended as an attack upon Western ignorance about Korea. In brief summary form, it endeavors to explain why Korea is important—strategically, economically, and culturally. It traces the historical roots of the Korean people, the development of their culture as a blend of native heritage and foreign influence, and the problems of national development under the conflicting pressures of Confucian tradition, U.S. democratic capitalism, and Soviet communism. It tries to convey something of the fascination that Korea has for people who, like the author, have studied its problems and sought to understand its delightful but fractious people.

Korea should be understood as a single nation, even though it was divided into two states by superpower rivalry and ideological differences. (To emphasize the point, *north* and *south* are not capitalized in this book when referring to the two halves of Korea.) The Democratic People's Republic of Korea (north Korea) deserves full attention, along with the Republic of Korea (south Korea). Yet I have given north Korea far less space than south Korea. The reason is that reliable detailed information about the north is exceedingly difficult to obtain because of the self-isolation and secretiveness of its government and the virtual absence of relations between that government and the United States. In the future, perhaps, the doors to the north may be further opened to outside inquiry and knowledge.

It is my hope that this introductory survey will help to stimulate much-needed general awareness and understanding of Korea. One test of its usefulness will be the interest it creates in reading the growing number of English-language books available on various aspects of Korean affairs. Appendix C has suggestions for further reading.

Most Western readers have difficulty with East Asian names and terms. This is due partly to the strangeness of the foreign words. A glossary (Appendix A) is provided to assist the reader in dealing with Korean terms. In addition, it is difficult to write the East Asian languages phonetically in Latin letters (a difficulty that applies to Korean, Chinese, and Vietnamese words, but not Japanese). The Koreans have one of the world's best alphabets for their own language, but few non-Koreans can read it.

There is no really satisfactory way of writing Korean words in the Latin alphabet. The best available system, devised in 1939 by George M. McCune and Edwin O. Reischauer along the lines of the Wade-Giles system for romanizing Chinese, has been adopted by the U.S. government and most English-speaking scholars. It recently became the official romanization system of the Republic of Korea (south Korea). North Korea uses a somewhat different system, apparently modeled after the pinyin romanization system for Chinese, which was developed by the People's Republic of China.

The McCune-Reischauer system is used in this book for all pre-1945 Korean names, places, and terms and for those of post-1945 south Korea (except that the diacritical marks over "o" and "u" that distinguish certain vowel sounds are omitted to facilitate printing). However, where other spellings are preferred by individuals or in common use, they have been used here (the city of Seoul, for example would be *Soul* in McCune-Reischauer spelling). The north Korean spellings, insofar as known, are used for post-1945 north Korean names, places, and terms. A few facts about the Korean language and the McCune-Reischauer system are presented in Appendix B.

Donald Stone Macdonald
1988

Acknowledgments

In preparing the manuscript, I have had the advice and support of many friends, colleagues, and associates. Their names appear alphabetically below. Literally dozens of them have read all or a portion of the draft manuscript and made valuable criticisms and suggestions. (Some family names come first, in the East Asian order; see A Note on Korean Names. Romanization of Korean names is according to the individuals' preference, where this is known; otherwise, it is according to the McCune-Reischauer system.) The list does not include many other people who shared their knowledge and insights with me in the course of conversation and whose ideas are reflected, explicitly or implicitly, in these pages. The final product is my responsibility, but whatever merit it may have comes in greater part from these many contributions.

- Chung Shil Adams, Seoul International Publishing House, Seoul
- Dr. Ahn Young Sop, Director for Political Studies, Korea Institute for Policy Studies
- Dr. Vincent S.R. Brandt, Center for East Asian Studies, Harvard University
- Dr. Ardath W. Burks, Professor Emeritus of Asian Studies, Rutgers University
- Dr. Choi Jang Jip, Professor of Political Science, Korea University
- Dr. Choi Young, Director, Division of National Security and Strategy Affairs, Institute of Foreign Affairs and National Security, Ministry of Foreign Affairs, Republic of Korea
- Dr. Paul S. Crane, M.D., Director, Health Ministries, Presbyterian Church (U.S.A.)
- Sophie Montgomery Crane, former missionary and writer
- Thomas P.H. Dunlop, Counselor for Political Affairs, U.S. Embassy, Seoul
- Col. Kerry G. Herron, Office of the Assistant Chief of Staff, J-3, ROK-U.S. Combined Forces Command
- Dr. Hong Sung-Chick, Director, Asiatic Research Center, and Professor of Sociology, Korea University
- Dr. Dong Joon Hwang, Research Director, Korea Institute for Defense Analysis
- Dr. Lim Hy-Sop, Professor of Sociology, Korea University
- H.E. Kim Chung Yul, former Minister of National Defense and Prime Minister of the Republic of Korea
- Kim Jin-Hyun, Chief Editorial Writer, *Dong A Ilbo,* Seoul

- Gen. Frederick C. Krause, U.S. Army, retired, former Executive Vice President, American Chamber of Commerce in Korea
- Dr. Ku Young Nok, Professor of Political Science, Seoul National University
- Dr. Paul Kuznets, Professor of Economics, Indiana University
- Kwak So Jin, United States Information Service, U.S. Embassy, Seoul (retired)
- Dr. Yung-hwan Jo, Professor of Political Science, Arizona State University
- Dr. Lee Hahn-Been, former Deputy Prime Minister, Republic of Korea
- Dr. Lee On-Jook, Visiting Professor of Sociology, The Johns Hopkins University
- Dr. Dennis McNamara, S.J., Professor of Sociology, Georgetown University
- Paik Syeung Gil, Director, Dept. of Culture and Information, Korean National Commission for UNESCO
- Dr. Eul Y. Park, International Bank for Reconstruction and Development
- Park Kwon Sang, former Editor, *Dong A Ilbo,* and Visiting Fellow, Institute of Sino-Soviet Studies, The George Washington University
- Hon. Park Sang Yong, Vice Minister and former Director, Institute of Foreign Affairs and National Security, Ministry of Foreign Affairs, Republic of Korea
- Fr. Basil M. Price, S.J., Chairman of the Board, Institute for Labor and Management, Sogang University, Seoul
- Hon. Shin Byung Hyun, former Deputy Prime Minister, Republic of Korea
- Dr. Dae Sook Suh, Director, Institute of Korean Studies, University of Hawaii
- Sul Kuk-hwan, Chairman of the Board, Korea Tourist Bureau, Ltd.
- Dr. George Viksnins, Professor of Economics, Georgetown University
- Dr. Yi Myong-yong, Professor of Political Science, Songgyun'gwan University, Seoul

Apart from the foregoing contributions, my efforts would have come to naught without the support I received from many institutions and individuals. A generous grant from the U.S. Department of Education provided time and opportunity to complete the manuscript in Korea during the first half of 1986. Gratitude is particularly due to Georgetown University's Asian Studies Program and its director, Professor Matthew M. Gardner, Jr.; to the Asiatic Research Center of Korea University and its then director, Professor Sungjoo Han; and the Yongsan Library of United States Forces, Korea, directed by Sunny Murphy and Arlene Hahn.

About seventy participants at a Yongsan Library lecture series based on the manuscript provided helpful criticism of style and substance. The Korea Research Foundation provided support for Korean courses at Georgetown University that provided the testing ground for the material presented here. Kim Chin-ki, in Seoul, and Gregory O'Connor, in Washington, provided valuable research assistance.

Wongi Sul, a New York artist, created the illustrations for the chapter headings. Dr. Paul S. Crane provided the photograph of his ancient screen depicting the sixteenth-century Battle of Pyongyang, which appears in Figure 1.3. Edward B. Adams, headmaster of Seoul International School, and the Korea Overseas Information Service of the Republic of Korea's Ministry of Culture and Information kindly provided several of the illustrations. Park Shinil, Cultural Service director in New York, Park Young-Gil, Information Office director in Washington, and Clyde Hess, consultant to the Cultural Office, were particularly helpful.

I wish to acknowledge with profound gratitude my debt to the many scholars and associates who have helped me over the years to understand something of Korea's fascinating nature and spirit. Among them are the late Professor George M. McCune, the late Shin Chung Kiun, Sul Kuk-hwan, Professor Suh Doo Soo, Dr. Min Kwan-sik, Dr. Lee Hahn-Been, Suh Kwang-soon, Key P. Yang, Kim Yong-song, Hong In-pyo, Kwak So-jin, and many members of the Republic of Korea diplomatic service, including ambassadors Hahn Pil Wook, Park Sang Yong, Oh Jay Hee, and Minister Lee Sang-kon. Finally, no words can convey adequate recognition of the contribution to this and many other projects by my wife, Jean Carroll Macdonald, in time, energy, and loving support.

In this new edition, I want to reaffirm my debt to all those who helped to make the first edition possible. To their names I would add Susan McEachern and Libby Barstow of Westview Press, who patiently worked on my initial manuscript; Phil Klein, who edited the revision; Fr. Clifford Smart and Dr. Arthur McTaggart, who helped to keep me informed at long distance about events in Korea; and Carl Mehler, who provided the cartography for the improved physical-political map of Korea and locator map of East Asia in Chapter 1 of this edition.

D.S.M.
1988

A Note on Korean Names

Most Korean names in this book are given in the Korean order, with the family name first, and most given names consist of two syllables written with a hyphen between them. However, some names are given in a different form or order to reflect common usage in the literature (e.g., Syngman Rhee) or to respect an individual's own preferred usage.

D.S.M.

1

Introduction:
Land, People, Problems

Storm Center of East Asia

The Korean peninsula is fated by geography and history to be the storm center of East Asia. For centuries, it has been both bridge and battleground among its neighbors. Three of the world's greatest nations—Russia, China, and Japan—surround Korea. Each of them considers the peninsula to be of major importance to its own security and each, in the past century, has sought to dominate it. Since 1945, the United States has also had a major security interest in Korea. Thus, far more than most of the U.S. and European public realize, Korea is of vital importance to the peace and progress of this dynamic region.

The Korean people have virtually no record of aggressive ambition outside their peninsula. More than a thousand years ago, Korea was a major, but wholly peaceful, influence on the growth of Japanese culture. Yet it has endured many invasions, great and small, in its two thousand years of recorded history. It has suffered five major occupations by foreign powers. Four wars in the past hundred years were fought in and around Korea.

Despite these trials, Korea had a history of well over a millennium as a unified, autonomous nation until Japan took it as a colony in 1910. The victors in World War II, who drove out the Japanese, divided the country for military convenience in 1945. The Soviet and U.S. occupiers then proceeded to create two mutually hostile states that were based on existing divisions between left-wing and right-wing Koreans and which aligned themselves with the opposing sides in the Cold War. By the time the occupying superpowers withdrew their forces in 1948 and 1949, a low-level conflict was already under way between communist and anti-communist Koreans in the south, and in June 1950, when communist-led north Korea attempted to liberate the south by military means, the conflict erupted into the three-year-long Korean War. The Korean War, with its enormous human and material costs, was never formally declared and has never formally been concluded. The shooting stopped with an armistice in July 1953, which established a cease-fire line roughly along the 38th parallel where the fighting started in 1950. The warring armies were separated by a "demilitarized" strip across the peninsula, and today, more than forty years later, 1.5 million soldiers (including 37,000 from the United States) still face each other, armed to the teeth, across that strip.

The existing rivalry between left and right within Korea thus played into the rivalry between the superpowers in the Cold War, who undertook to support and develop the rival Korean states as part of the worldwide competition between communism and democratic capitalism. The longevity of the Cold War overcame early hopes for Korean reunification and established powerful vested interests in the military confrontation between north and south Korea. These interests, added to the bitter experience of the Korean people during the Korean War era, created an almost insoluble problem for the Korean people. By 1996, though there had been numerous hopeful turns, there was little indication of how, and on what terms, Korea could ever be reunited, in spite of what could be gained if reunification were to occur. Even in their tense and divided condition, the two Korean states have made impressive progress toward the realization of a modern industrial society. A reunited Korea would be among the twenty most populous countries in the world. Its people would already be known as some of the hardest-working, most productive people in the world. Their economy would rank in the world's top twelve and their military forces would establish them as a top regional power, leaving behind as a distant memory the time when Korea was known as a "shrimp among whales."

Though the Cold War has dominated the circumstances of recent Korean history, another kind of confrontation has been working itself out: the clash between modernity and tradition, between a new urban industrialized society and an old rural agrarian one, between the new demands for political participation and social justice and the old hierarchical, authoritarian order. Understanding this problem in all its complexity, as well as appreciating Korea's progress, requires some knowledge of Korean history and social and political background.

This introductory chapter briefly reviews the geography, resources, and people of the Korean peninsula. It then touches upon the problems arising out of Korean history, culture, politics, economics, and international relations—topics that are examined in greater detail in the rest of the book.

Basic Geographic Facts

The Korean peninsula juts southward from the Eurasian land mass between Russian Siberia and Chinese Manchuria. As nineteenth-century strategists used to say, it points "like a dagger at the heart of Japan" (Figure 1.1). The national territory, now as for many centuries past, includes a slice of the Asian mainland—a reminder of ancient Korean domains in parts of Manchuria (see frontispiece).[1]

Korea's shape has been compared by Korean scholars to a rabbit, whose ears touch Siberia at the 43d parallel in the northeast; whose legs paddle in the Yellow Sea on the west, and whose backbone is the great T'aebaek mountain range along the east coast (Figure 1.2). The semitropical, volcanic Cheju Island, which is just above the 33d parallel south of the peninsula, could be regarded as the rabbit's slightly misplaced cottontail.

The 1,025-kilometer (636-mile) Korean boundary with China is formed by two rivers, the Yalu to the west and the Tumen to the east; they rise near the fabled 9,000-foot Mt. Paektu ("White-Head Mountain" in Korean; "Changpai-shan," or "Ever-White Mountain" in Chinese), the highest point in Korea, and flow through rugged mountains into the seas on either side of the peninsula. The last 16 kilometers (about 11 miles) of the Tumen's course separate Korea from Russia's Mar-

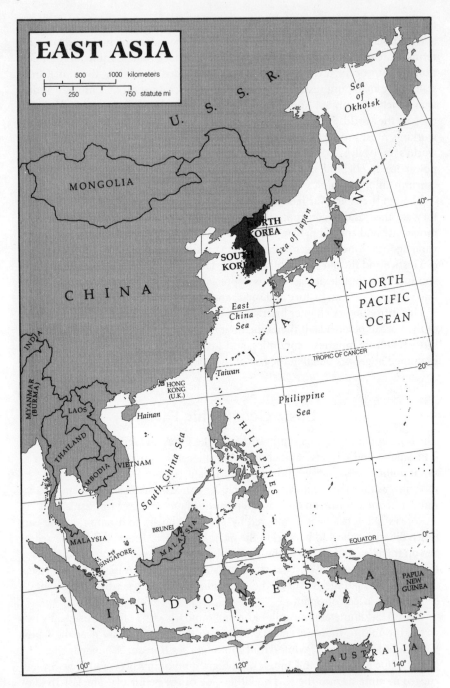

FIGURE 1.1 Korea in its East Asian setting (map by Carl Mehler)

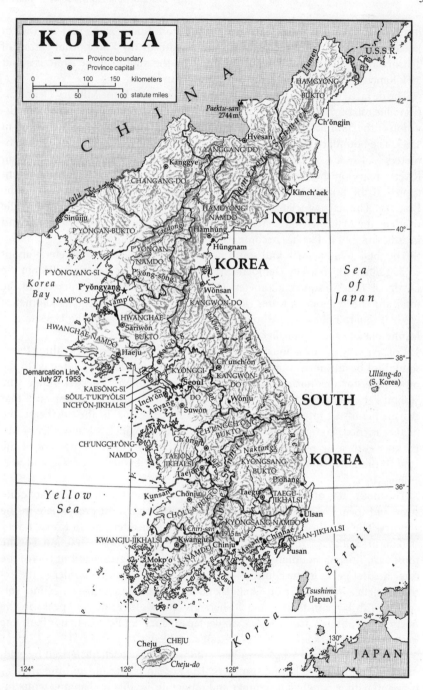

FIGURE 1.2　Physical-political map of Korea (map by Carl Mehler)

itime Province. Japan, to the east, is separated from Korea by the East Sea (Sea of Japan) and by the 100-kilometer (60-mile) width of the Korea Strait (Strait of Tsushima). The Japanese island of Tsushima, in the middle of the strait, is about 35 kilometers (20 miles) from the nearest point in Korea.

The de facto boundary between the two Korean states is the Military Demarcation Line established by the Armistice Agreement of 1953, which replaced the division at the 38th parallel agreed to by the United States and the Soviet Union in 1945. The boundary lies in the middle of the Demilitarized Zone (DMZ), 4 kilometers (2.4 miles) wide.[2] Traced from west to east, the line begins in the Han River estuary on the west coast, runs just south of the city of Kaesong (ancient capital of the Koryo Dynasty), and then extends generally east-northeast to the East Sea. The narrow triangular area above the 38th parallel thus added to the south by the Armistice Agreement is technically under United Nations Command jurisdiction, but in fact has become part of south Korea.

The total area of north and south Korea is 220,847 square kilometers (about 85,300 square miles). The Democratic People's Republic of Korea (DPRK) in the north has 122,370 square kilometers (47,300 square miles), or 55 percent of the total, and the Republic of Korea (ROK) in the south has 98,477 square kilometers (38,000 square miles). The whole of Korea is about as large as the U.S. state of Minnesota and slightly smaller than the United Kingdom.

Korea is very mountainous; the Koreans themselves speak of their "three thousand *ri*[3] of beautiful rivers and mountains" in song and story and often go to the mountains for meditation or enjoyment. The dominant T'aebaek range (the "rabbit's" backbone) has a series of spurs, mostly running southwestward, that cut the peninsula into narrow valleys and alluvial plains. In the northeast, the picture is more complicated; it includes a range of extinct volcanoes from Mt. Paektu southeastward to the East Sea (Sea of Japan). About 16 percent of the land in the north and 20 percent in the south is flat enough for grain and vegetable crops.

The mountains of Korea are not very high for the most part, but they are quite steep and form a dominant feature of the landscape almost everywhere in the country. The so-called Diamond Mountains in southeastern north Korea, a very striking area of sharp, rocky pinnacles, have long been a tourist attraction. For the most part, Korean mountains are nonvolcanic granite of great age, but two of the three highest peaks in the country—Paektu on the Manchurian border in the extreme north and Mt. Halla on Cheju Island in the extreme south—are extinct volcanoes with lakes in their craters. There are a few other volcanic peaks in the north, none of them active. Korea, unlike Japan, does not lie on a major fault line in the earth's crust, so earthquakes are not a problem.

Like the rest of East Asia, Korea has a monsoon climate characterized by cold, dry winters and warm, humid summers. The Korean spring and autumn are very pleasant, with generally fair weather and moderate, gradually changing temperatures. Rainfall varies between 76 and 102 centimeters (30 and 40 inches) per year in the south (somewhat less in the north) of which about half comes in June, July, and August. For comparison, in the continental United States, annual rainfall is 107 centimeters (42 inches) in New York City, 79 centimeters (31 inches) in Oklahoma City, and 51 centimeters (20 inches) in San Francisco.

Southern Korea is warmed by the Japan Current, somewhat as the eastern U.S. seaboard is warmed by the Gulf Stream; for this and other reasons, southwestern Korea and the adjacent island-province of Cheju are semitropical and have more rainfall. Mean daily temperatures in the extreme north range between −18° Celsius (0° Fahrenheit) in January and 20°C (68°F) in August; in the extreme south (Cheju Island), between 3°C (34°F) in January and 27°C (81°F) in August. In Seoul, near the center of the peninsula, the range is from −6°C (21°F) to 26°C (79°F). Considerably higher and lower temperatures are not uncommon. For comparison, average New York City temperature in January is 0°C (32°F); in July, 25°C (76°F).

Korea's rivers—except for the Yalu on the border with China and the Taedong River near Pyongyang, capital of north Korea—are generally too small, silted, and variable in flow to be practical for navigation. Some of them—particularly in north Korea—have hydroelectric potential; but for this purpose, too, their variation in flow, because of the concentration of rainfall in the summer months, reduces their utility. Most of them rise in the eastern mountain chain and flow west to the Yellow Sea or south to the Korea Strait. The Yalu, with a length of 790 kilometers (490 miles), is Korea's longest river and is navigable for most of its length. Other north Korean rivers are the Tumen (exceptional in flowing northeast and southeast), 521 kilometers (323 miles) long, of which only the seaward one-sixth is navigable; and the Taedong, 397 kilometers (246 miles), which flows through the capital city of Pyongyang and is navigable for about three-fifths of its length.

South Korean rivers include the Naktong (defense line of the beleaguered UN forces in the summer of 1950), 521 kilometers (323 miles) long, and the Somjin 203 kilometers (126 miles), both of which flow south to the Korea Strait; the Han, 514 kilometers (319 miles), which flows past Seoul; and the Kum, 401 kilometers (249 miles). Other, shorter rivers are the Yongsan, flowing southwest into the Yellow Sea at the southwestern port of Mokp'o; a tributary of the Han, the Pukhan, which rises in north Korea; and the Imjin, also rising in north Korea, which flows for part of its length along the Demilitarized Zone separating the two Korean states.

On Korea's east coast, the mountains rise almost directly from the sea. There is a narrow coastal strip in some areas, and there are a few harbors at north Korean cities such as Chongjin, Kimchaek, Hamhung, and Wonsan and south Korean cities like Kangnung and Ulsan. Pusan, perhaps the best port on the peninsula, marks the eastern beginning of the southern coastline along the Korea Strait. On the west, the coastline is deeply indented, with hundreds of islands and islets; a nine-meter (thirty-foot) differential between high and low tide causes mud flats, treacherous currents, and other navigational problems. The ports of Sinuiju and Namp'o, in north Korea, and Inch'on, Kunsan, and Mokp'o, in south Korea, are at or near the mouths of rivers (the Yalu, Taedong, Han, Kum, and Yongsan, respectively); at Namp'o, in north Korea, and Inch'on, in south Korea, giant locks maintain a constant water level within the port area. Along the south coast there are ports at Yosu, Chinju, and Masan.

From the strategic point of view, Korean geography offers something of the same defensive advantage against ground forces as does Switzerland.

The majority of the boundary is seacoast, much of which is not practical for landing large ships. The land boundary with China is mostly in difficult, mountainous terrain, and the flatter coastal approaches are cut by the wide Yalu River. A similar coastal approach from the Soviet Union is cut by the somewhat narrower Tumen River. Roads within Korea wind between mountains and over passes, where defensive action is relatively easy. However, there are three major invasion corridors across central Korea: one near Ch'orwon in the middle of the peninsula, the other two in the west, where the bulk of the south Korean defense is concentrated.

From the air, Korea is as vulnerable as any country, and its internal communication lines, concentrated as they are in narrow valleys and often bounded (in summer) by soggy rice fields, could be readily interdicted by bombardment. South Korea's greatest geographical vulnerability is the difficulty of supply from any source other than the two hostile neighboring continental powers, China and the Soviet Union. The sea lanes are open to attack from either air or water.

Resources

Although Korea was essentially self-sufficient as an agrarian subsistence economy until the twentieth century, its development prospects as an independent state depend upon world trade. This is even more true of the two present divided states—particularly south Korea. The peninsula as a whole is only moderately endowed with natural resources; in both north and south, the principal asset is an educated, motivated, and able work force. The north has far more natural resources than the south; the rugged northern mountains contain coal (chiefly a poor grade of anthracite), iron ore, and a variety of nonferrous minerals, including tungsten, lead, copper, zinc, gold, silver, and manganese. Other ores include graphite, apatite, fluorite, barite, limestone, and talc. There are extensive hydroelectric power resources, particularly along the Yalu, Tumen, and Taedong rivers, as well as smaller streams. (Since the Yalu and Tumen rivers are on Korea's northern border, their resources must be shared with China.) Only about one-sixth of the mountainous north Korean terrain is suitable for cultivated crops, and the climate is relatively harsh. Nevertheless, coastal lowlands, particularly in the west, produce rice as well as other grains; elsewhere, corn, wheat, millet, and soybeans are grown. There are rich timber reserves and extensive orchards. Livestock grazing is also possible in the upland areas.

The south is the traditional rice bowl of Korea, with somewhat greater rainfall, warmer climate, and a slightly larger expanse of flat terrain than the north. These same factors make for a higher population density in the south—much increased by in-migration since World War II—which offsets the agricultural advantage. There are some of the same kinds of minerals as in the north but in less desirable deposits and smaller quantities, coming nowhere near the requirements of an industrial economy. The only significant reserves are tungsten, graphite, and limestone. Offshore oil possibilities in the Yellow Sea and on the continental shelf between Korea and Japan have so far yielded nothing but are being explored by south Korea, to the extent that the competing interests of Japan and China permit. By the 1950s, south Korea was virtually deforested; a vigorous reforestation program has brought a surprising recovery, but indigenous timber resources can never approach consumption requirements.

People

In 1994, south Korea's population stood at 44,453,000, an increase of 2.7 percent since the census of 1990 at an annual rate of 0.9 percent. The Republic of Korea was thus the third most densely populated country in the world, with 447 persons per square kilometer (1,176 per square mile). The capital city, Seoul, accounted for almost a quarter of this number (10,925,000), with a staggering density of 18,933 people per square kilometer (47,500 per square mile, equivalent to a square of land 7.4 meters [23 feet] on a side per person). Aside from Seoul, there were five other cities with over 1 million people: Pusan, the major southeastern port, with 3,798,000; Taegu, in the southeastern agricultural region, with 2,229,000; Inch'on, the major west-coast port near Seoul, with 1,817,000; Kwangju, in the southwest, with 1,139,000, and Taejon, in central south Korea, with 1,049,000 (population figures from the 1990 census). Cities of more than 50,000 people accounted for 75 percent of the total population.[4]

North Korea's population, according to United Nations statistics, was 22,627,000 in 1992, corresponding to a population density of 187 persons per square kilometer (494 per square mile), about two-fifths that of the south. The capital city is Pyongyang, with a population of 2.3 million in 1987; the second largest urban center is the twin-city area of Hamhung-Hungnam, on the east coast, with 701,000. Other major cities are Chongjin (520,000) on the east coast, and Namp'o (370,000) and Sinuiju (289,000) on the west coast. In 1990, 67 percent of the north Korean people lived in cities, a 10 percent increase in urbanization since 1980.[5]

Although the Koreans bear some physical resemblance to the Chinese, their language is totally unlike Chinese; it has similarities with Turkish, Mongolian, Japanese, and other Central Asian languages, which are sometimes considered to be related to Hungarian and Finnish. (However, both the Koreans and the Japanese borrowed the Chinese writing system and many Chinese words; about half the words in a standard Korean dictionary are of Chinese derivation.)[6] The Koreans, then, may trace their ancient origin to the Central Asian area whose tribes burst out of their steppe and desert habitat from time to time to conquer much of the known world—the Golden Horde of the Mongols, the Seljuk and Ottoman Turks, and to a much more limited degree the Jurchen, or Manchu.

The south Koreans enjoy an average life expectancy of sixty-six years for males and seventy-three years for females. Literacy is estimated at 93 percent. Education is a high priority for all Koreans. Elementary education has been universal and compulsory for more than thirty years; over four-fifths of the school-age population complete high school, and over a quarter of the corresponding age group receive some postsecondary education. Vigorous efforts have been made to provide supplementary schooling through military training, adult and night classes, and literacy programs. North Korea has a similar record, with a literacy rate of 90 percent.

The Korean people today are culturally and genetically homogeneous (although differences may grow over time if the political division of the peninsula persists). They are taller, on the average, than most other East Asians and are sufficiently distinctive in appearance so that a trained observer can often identify them—as one can sometimes distinguish between French and Germans, for example. Nevertheless, there are readily visible differences in physiognomy among Koreans. Distinctive provincial dialects, stereotypes, and prejudices have been strong and still persist. There are few permanent foreign residents in Korea; the largest minority are the Chinese, of whom there are some 40,000 in the south.

The total number of ethnic Koreans in the world in 1996 is around 71 million. In addition to the approximately 67 million in south and north Korea, there are at least 4 million in other countries: 1.8 million in China, 1 million in the United States, 0.7 million in Japan, 0.4 million in the former Soviet Union, and the remainder in many other countries in Asia, Europe, and the Americas.[7]

History

Since their ancestors entered the peninsula five or more thousand years ago, the Koreans have been influenced by their own indigenous tradition, by their close contact with China, and by the impact of Japan and the West. The first recorded Korean state was exterminated in 108 B.C. by the Chinese, who established an imperial outpost under direct Chinese rule. Three Korean kingdoms emerged—one of them taking over the Chinese domain. By A.D. 668 Silla, one of the three kingdoms, had conquered the other two, with Chinese support. An autonomous, united Korea and a special relationship with China endured for over a millennium thereafter.

United Korea was ruled by three royal dynasties, each of them long-lived by world standards. Silla gave way to Koryo in 936, and Koryo to Choson (reviving the ancient kingdom's name) in 1392. Choson endured for over 500 years, until the rapidly modernizing Japanese occupied Korea in 1905 and annexed it to their empire in 1910. Each of the three dynasties in turn had its days of glory and decline and of invasion from outside.

Buddhism flourished in the Silla and Koryo dynasties; Confucianism became the state philosophy of Choson, which evolved a political and social structure transcending in some respects its Chinese model. Each dynasty brought forth cultural and aesthetic accomplishments: Silla, for example, had its distinctive pottery, gold and silver ornamentation, and architecture; Koryo, the beautiful celadon ware that has never been fully reproduced; Choson, a scientifically correct phonetic alphabet to replace the ill-fitting Chinese ideographs.

Khitan[8] and Japanese raiders menaced Silla and Koryo; the Mongols invaded Korea and maintained hegemony over it for a hundred years in Koryo times; the Japanese ravaged Korea for six years in the middle of the Choson dynasty and were followed hardly more than a generation later by Manchu invaders (see Figure 1.3). These invasions weakened the ability of the leaders of the Choson dynasty to rule, and despite the reassertion of central government authority in the eighteenth century and a certain cultural reinvigoration, the propensity of aristocratic landholders to resist central control and taxation brought troubles to the kingdom and contributed to eventual dynastic collapse.

Throughout most of its history, the kingdom of Korea maintained foreign relations primarily with China and its neighbors to the north and had relatively few contacts with the peoples of the West. However, in the nineteenth century, Western influence made itself felt and Korea was affected by global forces including imperialism. Rivalry among a reawakening China, a modernizing Japan, and an expanding Russia for hegemony over Korea led to two wars fought in and around the peninsula. Japan, having beaten China in 1895 and Russia in 1905, became Korea's master, with the blessing of the Western powers. The Japanese brought modern industry, transportation, communications, and government administration to Korea and improved Korean agricultural productivity. The world was impressed, but the Koreans benefited little from the process. The people resisted Japanese attempts to assimilate them into the Japanese culture. They rose up in nationwide unarmed protest in 1919, reacting against Japanese military repression and responding to the idealism of the Versailles Conference, the Russian Revolution, and the May Fourth Movement in China, but to no avail. However, the identity of Korea was maintained by nationalists both within Korea and in exile throughout the period of Japanese domination, and in World War II the Allies pledged to restore the country's independence.

Japan's defeat in World War II ended its control of Korea, but Korean independence was deferred by three years of U.S. and Soviet military occupation, during which no agreement was reached as to how independence would be arranged. In the end, two independent states emerged out of the respective occupation zones, each reflecting the political complexion of the occupier, and each committed to reunification by any means. The Korean War was the result. The Koreans, their entry into the modern world delayed first by their own policy of isolation, then by Japanese domination, now had to deal with the complex problems of modernization in a telescoped time frame. It is against this background that Korea's recent development and its problems must be viewed.

FIGURE 1.3   Depiction of the Battle of Pyongyang, 1592, between the Chinese and the Japanese, showing the muskets of the Japanese, the bows and arrows of the Chinese, and the Chinese three-barrel cannon (photo of eight-panel screen loaned by Dr. Paul S. Crane to the Hannam University Museum, Taejon, Republic of Korea)

The Cultural Heritage

Korea, in contrast to many developing countries and even some developed ones, has a well-established national tradition reaching back at least 2,000 years. For two-thirds of that time, the Koreans have lived in a unified, autonomous state. They share a sense of ethnic identity, a language intelligible everywhere in the country, and a common culture. The culture (not the language or the sense of identity) has been strongly influenced over the centuries by China and the philosophy of Confucius, somewhat as the culture of the United States has been strongly influenced by Greece, Rome, and Europe; but Korean culture is no more identical with Chinese culture than U.S. culture is with that of England, France, or Germany. In recent decades, Western influence, industrialization, and urbaniza-

tion have induced changes. Korean values and behavior patterns—for better or worse—are moving in the direction of the world's industrialized societies. Yet the Korean mix of old and new, native and foreign, remains distinctive, as it has always been. An understanding of the tradition helps one to appreciate the present.[9]

In the Confucian-oriented Korean society, people have thought of themselves as part of an organic whole that includes human society and the world around it, hierarchically arranged, related in a family-like pattern with eternally ordained responsibilities for everyone. Individuals found their identity not as much in themselves as in their relationships and mutual obligations within their extended families (out to the eighth degree of relationship) and, above all, in their relationships with their parents. Families have been a key element of society. Order and harmony, rather than competition and adversarial relations, have been supreme values, to be upheld by the conduct and example of superior men. Government officials were expected to be such men, with superior benevolence and wisdom derived from study of the classics and tested by state examinations. The king, at the pinnacle of government, ruled by authority of the Mandate of Heaven, which he might forfeit if he failed to rule correctly. These attitudes toward government have carried over to some extent to the present day.

Human affairs being part of a larger whole, a person's capacity to control his or her fate was traditionally seen as small. Social change was cyclical within limits that forever remained the same. An idealized past, rather than a golden future, was the goal and norm. The model of conduct and behavior laid down by the sages of old was to be studied, understood, and emulated. Form was of importance equal to substance. Right interpersonal relations were more important than contractual or legal obligations. Family duty and obedience took precedence over personal aspirations or the interests of the nation. Political contention and faction, though common in practice, were considered unseemly or heretical. Government and scholarship were the highest callings; industry and commerce were looked down upon. Yet at the same time, Koreans had an individualistic, ambitious element that clashed with the Confucian norms.

In the Chinese international system, the Chinese emperor was at the center of the universe. Neighboring civilized people had a subordinate status, like younger brothers; they acknowledged their status by sending periodic tribute missions to the Chinese emperor. Peoples who did not acknowledge Chinese supremacy or accept Chinese values were barbarians—a category that included the Europeans—to be dealt with by exclusion, by playing one against another, and if need be, by force. The Koreans, close as they were to China, evolved an attitude of acquiescence in the Chinese-centered social order. In recent times, the Koreans have condemned themselves for this attitude, which they call *sadaejuui*—respect for, or subservience to, greater status. However, at the time it was the established order for relations between peoples in East Asia and entirely proper in the view of the people who belonged to it. Indeed, by paying tribute to the Chinese emperor, the Koreans actually guaranteed their autonomy from Chinese interference.

Korean culture thus evolved along very different lines from that of Europe and the United States. The West valued mastery over nature, not blending with it; equality of men, rather than hierarchy; individual dignity and freedom, rather than a web of reciprocal duties and responsibilities; subordination of rulers to the will of the ruled and subordination of all to an impersonal law, rather than benevolent personal rule by superior men; sovereignty deriving from the people, not from Heaven; change and progress, rather than a static, past-oriented order; supremacy of rational thought, rather than feeling and intuition; dignity of labor and commerce, rather than scholarship. The West extolled, in theory, the virtue of struggling for the right, rather than acquiescence to superior power; yet at the same time it saw virtue in compromise, in contrast to the Asian priority for loyalty and steadfastness. Only in matters of religion did the West compel uniformity and exclusivity, as opposed to East Asian eclecticism and tolerance; but the West saw political, economic, and social aspects of life as separate, whereas Confucianism saw them all as part of a whole.

As we shall see in subsequent chapters, Western philosophy and thought patterns have nonetheless had a tremendous effect in Korea and East Asia in the century and a half since the Opium War between Great Britain and China demonstrated Western power. The Western impact irreparably tore the Confucian fabric and left Korea—like other East Asian nations—groping for values to guide society and politics. Korea is engaged in a search for new directions, to which Christianity has made an important contribution. However, Western values are not uncritically accepted; indeed, there is something of a backlash against them in some quarters. In south Korea, the Chinese and indigenous tradition is being given renewed attention, but only in the context of an industrializing society and the new imperatives that industrial organization imposes.

The process of accommodation has taken very different directions in north and south Korea. The whole body of classical Chinese philosophy has been explicitly rejected in the north since 1945. The philosophy of Marxism-Leninism has been imposed on the people since the Soviet occupation of 1945–1948 through education, propaganda, and "agitation." In recent years, Marxist-Leninist principles have been integrated with a system of political philosophy called *juch'e* (self-reliance), which is represented as a higher stage of thought to deal with the problems of national development. Toward the end of his life in 1994, Kim Il-sung, the supreme leader in north Korea since 1948, shaped a total political ideology that was aptly termed "Kimilsungism" by his son and successor, Kim Jong-il. Kimilsungism reverberates with ideas from neo-Confucianism (loyalty and the familial succession), Marxism-Leninism (socialism and anti-imperialism), and the *juch'e* idea (as seen in north Korea's determined pursuit of a self-reliant nuclear program). Thus after fifty years it is clear that the north Korean system, not surprisingly, is a hybrid of tradition and modernity.

In the south, the United States endeavored to encourage Western social, educational, economic, and political ideas during its three-year occupation and in the formative years of the Republic, building upon foundations laid by missionaries and Korean modernizers; but the democratic belief system, by its own nature, prevented its imposition in the way that the Soviet Union and Kim Il-sung could impose Marxism-Leninism in the north. Instead, there has been an ongoing search for a system of indigenous values that will provide answers to the problems of a modern industrializing state.

Politics

Like other developing countries, Korea (both north and south) has experienced serious political growing pains—more evident in the relatively open south than in the closed north. Its problems arise from the clash between the deep-rooted attitudes and values of a traditional agricultural society, on the one hand, and the requirements of an urban industrial economy on the other.

There was a deep gulf in political thinking between the Koreans and the Western world on the eve of their liberation from Japanese rule in 1945 and between the Korean left and right. Notwithstanding some exposure to Western political ideology in the brief and traumatic period from 1876 (when the Japanese concluded the first Western-style treaty with Korea) to the Japanese annexation in 1910, most Koreans had had little opportunity to test political ideas under Japanese rule.

Since 1945, the two halves of Korea have followed different paths of political development, separated by the gulf between competing political ideologies of democratic capitalism and communism. The Republic of Korea, in the south, was legitimized by elections under United Nations observation in 1948, followed by adoption of a Western-style constitution. Since then, the Republic has been experimenting with a succession of constitutional forms (the present 1987 constitution is the sixth version since 1948, not counting several other amendments). At the same time, south Korea's political system has shown remarkable continuity and durability as well as increasing effectiveness; but it has functioned more nearly in accord with traditional political norms than with the Western concepts expressed in the successive constitutions.

As already noted, the Confucian ethic—still accepted in south Korea and surviving in the north—makes the individual a part of a family collectivity, whose collective goals and interests are his or her own. Family responsibility has traditionally taken precedence over all other responsibilities, including duty to the ruler and the state. Interpersonal responsibilities within other nonfamily groupings, such as relations between a scholar and his disciples, have also been important. In today's Korea, alumni associations are one modern equivalent of such groups. Political communication still flows largely through informal family and group connections.

The Confucian ethic also imposes a hierarchical pattern of relationships in which people are superior or inferior to one another but rarely equal. It calls for modesty and restraint and for behavior motivated by principle, not by hope of material gain. Governmental position has traditionally been high in the hierarchy, while business and industry have been low. Moreover, harmony and consensus, rather than competition, are valued; Western-style adversary relations in courts, legislatures, political campaigns—even elections—have been uncomfortable or absent.

Nevertheless, despite the outward Confucian discipline, Koreans seem to contain within themselves a second person who is assertive, eager for material gain and for recognition, and impatient with family and group restraints on individual freedom of action. This duality has undoubtedly been encouraged during modernization, but it is not new. It may help to explain the success of some Koreans as entrepreneurs. It also makes Koreans competitive and even fractious in their political behavior. In south Korea's evolving democratic system, the Confucian-based habit of resisting compromise on principle reveals itself in the form of factionalism and rivalry in open political competition.

Western political ideas followed Western military, technical, and economic ideas into Korea. The present south Korean constitution, like its five preceding versions, nominally sets up a modern Western system of government under popular sovereignty, with separate executive, legislative, and judicial branches and a bill of rights. The north Korean constitution is similarly modern in Communist terms. Despite the attractiveness of Western concepts of individual liberty, equality, and basic rights, however, Western institutions (except in such areas as administrative organization and industrial production) have thus far been respected more in form than in substance. The part played in Korean politics by the large military establishments since the Korean War (including the conditioning of millions of young draftees over the years on both sides) has reinforced the authoritarian strain in Korean political behavior.

For many years these circumstances kept south Korea's political progress from keeping pace with economic development and, in north Korea, have come to interfere with economic progress as well. In the south, the continuation of authoritarian, paternalistic policies and behavior was proved to be increasingly out of phase with the expectations of a literate and sophisticated population exposed to the outside world. In the closed society of the north, however, where the population has been conditioned over a fifty-year period to the totalitarian style of Kimilsungist Communism, there have been few signs of mass dissatisfaction; yet the north's system, stressed as it is, hardly seems a model for the future.

The political systems of both south and north have maintained, in their separate ways, a high degree of stability and continuity. In the anticommunist south, income distribution is more equitable than in most developing countries; tax collection is efficient and reaches both rich and poor; and despite headlines in the Western press, the extent of violence and loss of life has been relatively small.[10] No facts are available to make such judgments about the north, especially regarding the costs of several political purges, although the system has functioned well enough to outlive all but a very few of the former Communist nations.

Charges continue to be made, by both foreign and domestic critics, of press controls, imprisonment for political dissent, overly coercive action against dissidents—particularly college students—and use of torture by security agencies. Such charges are easier to document against the south, because of its relative openness, than against the north, where such abuses may well be far more widespread and repression more severe. Yet, in the south, except for direct criticism of the government or support for Marxist ideas, personal liberty of speech, action, and movement is not seriously restricted, particularly since the establishment of the Sixth Republic in 1988. Controls still apply to "subversive" or pro–north Korean ideas.

South Korean political problems are the result of Korea's historical experience and developing status. They include the occasionally shaky performance of the present government in the public eye; the dislike of what the people see as a disproportionate military influence in politics; the lingering nervousness about an orderly succession to political power especially as it applies to the transfer of power between generations; the shallowness of experience with successful representative institutions and a stable constitution; and the growing demands of the south Korean population, with students and intellectuals in the forefront, for more freedom, equity, and voice in political decisions.

North Korea also faces problems, particularly the consolidation of the position of Kim Jong-il. The death of President Kim Il-sung in July 1994 at the age of eighty-two came as a shock to the north Korean people, as was predictable in the case of leader who had been in power for forty-eight years, longer than any other ruler on earth at the time. Kim's death also happened at a most inopportune moment for the world, while north Korea was engaged in a tricky diplomatic duel with the international community over its nuclear program. The significance of these issues for the world masked the internal maneuvering among factions within the Pyongyang government as it struggled too with the passing of the Korean War generation and the nearly mortal consequences of the death of Communism in Europe, which cut north Korea loose from its economic support system. These problems, added to the continuing burdens of military posturing vis-à-vis the south, have left the Kim Jong-il government fighting for its very survival. Kim Jong-il's likely ascension to the post of president, though long delayed, will end the period of mourning following the death of the supreme leader; however, it will not solve any of Kim's problems, not the least of which is his own lack of revolutionary credentials for his father's post. His one great asset must be the loyalty of his people and the players in the north Korean political system, based on his incarnation as an extension of his father. Without this element of the Kim-ilsungist system, he cannot rule for long.

Economics

In recent years, south Korea has been universally acclaimed as an economic success story. It has one of the longest-sustained and highest national economic growth rates in history; in 1994 it continued to keep the inflation rate down to 5.7 percent; it has successfully coped with international economic crises, such as the "oil shocks" of 1973 and 1979 (although it suffered a serious recession in 1980); it has achieved, by the standards of developing countries generally, a reasonably equitable distribution of the benefits of economic growth; and it expects, not without reason, to sustain an annual real economic growth rate of around 7 percent or more until the year 2000, with exports of increasingly sophisticated technology including automobiles, computer chips, and electronic products. Its principal economic problems stem from its very success: Expanding Korean exports are exciting protectionist reactions in the United States and Europe; growing income levels at home are making Korea vulnerable to competition from other developing countries; and its more affluent workers can turn from former worries about their next meal to new concerns about distribution of wealth and political freedom.

It is easy to forget that in the 1960s north Korea was the success story, impressing the newly independent Third World countries of Asia and Africa with its burgeoning economic growth, while south Korea was viewed as an economic "basket case"—a black hole for vast quantities of U.S. grant aid.

In their different ways, both north and south Korea have made impressive economic gains. In recent years, however, the north's inflexible central planning and lack of incentives, together with its inward-looking stance of self-reliance, have seriously damped its growth curve and even caused contraction, while the south's outward-looking, export-oriented economy, driven by an effective relationship between government and private enterprise, is ever more outdistancing its northern rival.

Until the end of World War II, Korea was essentially a traditional agrarian economy, based primarily on rice and other grains. During their forty-year occupation, the Japanese installed an industrial superstructure geared to their own imperial needs, but this was of little benefit to most Koreans, whose standard of living did not improve and whose dietary intake actually fell. Koreans had little role in managing the modern sector, economic or administrative. However, the beginnings of a trained labor force emerged, a few Koreans established themselves as entrepreneurs, and a transport and communication infrastructure was put in place.

Liberation in 1945 left to the Koreans the shell of the economy built by the Japanese. The plant they inherited was heavily depreciated from wartime overexploitation and partly irrelevant to their own needs. The Japanese market was cut off, and division of the country separated the mineral resources and heavy industry of the north from the light industry and agricultural surplus of the south. Moreover, the Koreans lacked the necessary managerial and technical skills, as well as the capital, for an industrial economy.

Development after liberation proceeded in very different ways in north and south. South Korea, under U.S. guidance, had the semblance of capitalism and private enterprise. It did, however, complete a thoroughgoing land reform, which subsequently meant that the farming population would support the political regime. After a slow start, economic progress began to be visible in 1950, but the war destroyed most of what had been accomplished. In the north, land had been redistributed to the tillers more promptly than in the south, and all large industry was nationalized. The single-minded zeal of the northern leaders under Soviet guidance and their centralized direction of the economy made up for lack of experience, and the north achieved more rapid progress than the south. War damage, however, was even greater in the north, obliterating almost all the industrial plant.

By mid-1951 the fighting was chiefly limited to the line between the two halves. South Korea could then begin its reconstruction effort, assisted by the United States, the United Nations, and private American relief donations; but the economy was plagued by inflation, mismanagement, and the costs of the positional warfare that continued for another two years. Prewar consumption levels were not reestablished until the late 1950s. In north Korea, U.S. saturation bombing continued until the armistice; the years from 1953 to 1955 were devoted to reconstruction, followed by multiyear economic plans that at first resulted in truly extraordinary rates of growth. Well-publicized north Korean economic progress probably added to the growing popular discontent in the south, based on both political repression and lack of economic progress, that led to the overthrow of the Syngman Rhee government in 1960. Continued economic stagnation was also a factor in the military seizure of power in 1961.

Rapid development in the south began under military leadership. General Park Chung-hee, later elected president, recognized that rapid economic improvement would justify a regime that had been established by force and therefore lacked legitimacy. Applying discipline and managerial skill, the military leaders utilized the human abilities and economic infrastructure that had been accumulating in earlier years. Continued external economic aid from the United States and new aid from Japan after normalization of relations in 1965 provided capital investment and technology. Emphasis was shifted from import substitution to export-led growth, beginning with traditional labor-intensive consumer goods (south Korea has never had significant amounts of exportable raw materials except for graphite and tungsten).

Despite some early mistakes, the new south Korean leadership achieved an economic takeoff by 1965. For the next twenty years, annual real growth of gross national product ranged from a high of over 15 percent (1975) to a low of 5 percent (1983), with one year of unaccustomed negative growth (1980) resulting from the second oil crisis and internal problems. From the 1970s on, south Korean export moved increasingly into shipbuilding, iron and steel, machinery, electronics, and more recently, highly technical items like computers and computer chips. Automobile export began in the 1980s. In 1982, inflation rates were brought to single-digit figures and ranged below 5 percent in the mid-1980s. In 1986, with a real growth of 12.2 percent in gross national product, the Republic showed a surplus on its balance-of-payments account and began paying off its foreign debt.

However, south Korea faced serious problems of adjustment. The United States, Japan, and other principal export markets kept putting up protectionist barriers and demanding more access to protected Korean markets. Other developing countries entered into competition with Korean textiles and other traditional exports. Falling oil prices reduced south Korea's import bill, but they ended the Middle East construction boom that had carried the economy through two oil crises and brought both companies and workers back home in search of employment. Domestically, the growing concentration of economic power in a few giant combines (called *chaebol*) and disparities in earnings between rich and poor, as well as the failure of some highly leveraged and overly ambitious corporations, aroused concern. Labor unrest in the freer political environment after 1987 resulted in wage increases totaling about 60 percent over three years, causing worry about future competitiveness. The south Korean economy met all these tests, however, and continued to grow at an impressive rate. By 1994 the gross national product stood at more than US$355 billion, nearly triple the 1987 figure of $133.3 billion.

Economic projections remain guardedly optimistic, sustained by south Korea's thirty-year record of performance and its flexible, pragmatic response to changing circumstances. "Globalization" (*segyehwa*), the watchword of the administration of south Korean President Kim Young-sam, has meant ever more aggressive pursuit of trading partners and world markets, sustaining the generation-long pattern of export-led growth. The domestic market, meanwhile, has expanded dramatically, affording south Koreans an unheard-of living standard. Though environmental pollution and the spectacular traffic jams around Seoul are among the dividends, the future appears to promise continued growth, controlled inflation, low unemployment, and decreasing vulnerability to international shocks such as the Mexican liquidity crisis of 1994.

In north Korea, for the first twenty years after the Korean War, the centrally planned Communist economy progressed very well, continuing to grow faster than that of the south. At first, the north benefited from considerable sums of Soviet and Chinese aid. This aid dried up in the 1960s, however, accounting in part for the failure to fulfill the First Seven-Year Plan on schedule in 1967. In the early 1970s, the north tried to hasten progress by importing entire industrial plants from Western European nations and Japan, but because of the 1973 oil crisis and perhaps faulty planning, north Korea could not repay the massive foreign-currency bills for the equipment it bought. This debt remains, despite several attempts at renegotiation, and has complicated subsequent attempts to deal with the outside world. The north Korean economy continues to suffer from bottlenecks in transportation, electric power, and raw materials, as well as from problems with outdated technology and low worker productivity.

Through the late 1980s, north Korean economic growth was estimated variously at 2 to 6 percent annually. With military expenditures amounting to 20 percent of its gross national product and a slightly higher population growth rate than the south, the economy labored to expand. There were fitful approaches to more trade with the outside, particularly with Japan. Even the south Koreans explored investments with the north. Each step forward, however, was followed by one backward. In 1989, following the Summer Olympics in Seoul, the north Koreans staged a world youth festival in Pyongyang that reportedly consumed US$4 billion in aid from the Soviet Union. In 1991, following the fall of the Soviet Union, Russia started demanding payment in convertible currency for exports to north Korea, ending a system of barter-trading that had compensated for north Korea's meager foreign-exchange earnings. In 1992 China did the same. North Korea's energy imports fell and its economy appeared about to implode. In the early 1990s north Korea experienced negative economic growth. While precise figures are not available, international estimates are that the northern economy has contracted by nearly 30 percent since 1990, requiring heroic sacrifices from the people.

International Relations and Security

Korean international relations since 1948 have been overshadowed by the hostility between the two Korean states—a hostility hugely magnified by the war. Each state has regarded itself as properly sovereign over all Korea and the other as illegitimate. Since hostilities ended with the Armistice Agreement of 1953 (which south Korea never signed), the two Korean states have been in competition with each other for international recognition and support, while beefing up their huge armed forces along the so-called Demilitarized Zone that separates them. The continuing presence of 37,000 U.S. soldiers close to the front line and a Combined Forces Command headed by a U.S. general serves as a deterrent to the renewal of hostilities by either state.

Security has been the dominant foreign-policy concern of both Koreas since their establishment. South Korea looks primarily to the United States as its protector under the Mutual Defense Treaty of 1953. It faces over 800,000 heavily armed and offensively deployed north Korean forces, many of them within fifty kilometers (thirty miles) of the south's capital city, potentially supported by huge Chinese forces nearby. Recalling that the withdrawal of U.S. forces in 1949 was followed by a north Korean invasion, the Republic has opposed all subsequent U.S. withdrawal initiatives, particularly that of President Jimmy Carter in 1977. North Korea, which retains its defense treaty with China (though it lost its Soviet backing in 1991), insists on the withdrawal of U.S. forces, often as a precondition for any other step toward reduction of tensions on the peninsula. Its fear of U.S.-Korean invasion, voiced constantly but particularly at times of annual joint south Korean–U.S. maneuvers, was a major obstacle to progress in the negotiations over its nuclear program in the 1992–1994 period. At the same time that it professes peaceful intentions, the north continues to talk of popular revolution in the south, which it would support, and still attempts infiltration of the south by armed special warfare teams and agents. A vague United Nations umbrella over the armistice still exists in the form of a skeleton United Nations Command that staffs the south side of the Military Armistice Commission; however, the talks themselves and most other arrangements that were part of the 1953 armistice have broken down, replaced by much higher-level contacts between Pyongyang and Seoul, Washington, and the United Nations.

Economic relations are a growing part of south Korea's foreign-policy concerns, since exports account for about a quarter of its national product and it must import most of its industrial raw materials. For many years, the south's largest markets have been the United States and Japan, with the United States taking one-fourth of south Korea's exports and Japan taking one-eighth; but increasing protectionism in both countries and in other industrial nations and competition from other developing countries have turned south Korea's attention toward the People's Republic of China and Southeast Asia. The United States and Japan have also been south Korea's principal sources of capital investment, in both loan and equity form, and of technology; capital induction from abroad will be needed for some years to come, but technology will be needed even more.

North Korea, with greater natural resources and a policy of self-reliance, spent the Cold War years concerned with trade mainly with other socialist countries. Having lost this matrix, it has turned to improving trade ties with Japan and the West. Its most significant trade is still with China; but it depends for capital especially upon the Korean community in Japan. It has significant earnings from weapons exports, notably missiles, to the Middle East, an aspect of its trade that has serious implications when coupled with its suspected production of plutonium in the early 1990s. Creating a friendlier trading environment for north Korea is one of the issues confronting south Korea and the industrialized nations as they try to coax the Kim Jong-il regime out of its isolation.

Both Koreas cultivate the Third World for reasons of prestige, ideology, and economics. North Korea has supported its policies with military aid, including training in unconventional warfare, to a number of left-oriented developing countries. North Korea gained considerable Third World support in the 1950s and 1960s by its economic success and its strong anti-Americanism, playing a leading role in the nonaligned movement with such other radical nations as Cuba. At that time, south Korea suffered in its Third World relations both from an indifferent economic performance and from its conservatism and close alliance with the United States. This picture began to change in the 1970s. North Korea no longer appeared as an economic leader; its shrill radicalism started to backfire; and its initiatives in the nonaligned movement no longer gained majority support. The north's attempt to blow up the south Korean president and his party in Rangoon in 1983 and the bombing of a south Korean passenger airplane over the Andaman Sea near Burma in 1987 were costly in international-relations terms. Even the massive effort to stage the 1989 International Youth Festival in Pyongyang created mixed impressions because of the north Koreans' aversion to decadent influences like rock music.

Reunification of Korea remains a supreme desire of all the Korean people, both north and south. No Korean government could avoid doing something about it. Both states have repeatedly advanced proposals for reunification since 1960, but little real progress has been made because of the hostility and distrust between the two sides. In 1972, driven by the uncertainty that followed the U.S. withdrawal from Vietnam and opening toward the People's Republic of China, the two states issued a joint declaration pledging peaceful negotiations on a basis of grand national unity without outside interference; but attempts at negotiations soon fell apart. In 1985, fifty citizens of each Korean state were admitted to the other state for meetings with separated family members. Several sets of preliminary talks on north-south relations broke down soon thereafter; and although there was a hopeful period from 1990 to 1992 when the two sides negotiated and concluded a number of potentially important agreements, the deep ideological rift between them reasserted itself in 1992, and there had been no progress by the mid-1990s (see Chapter 8).

Notes

1. For detailed discussion of Korean geography, see Patricia Bartz, *South Korea* (Oxford: Oxford University Press, 1972); Shannon B. McCune, *Korea's Heritage: A Regional and Social Geography* (Rutland, Vt.: Charles E. Tuttle Co., 1956); Andrea Matles Savada, ed., *North Korea: A Country Study,* 4th ed. (Washington, D.C.: U.S. Government Printing Office, 1994); Andrea Matles Savada and William R. Shaw, eds., *South Korea: A Country Study,* 4th ed. (Washington, D.C.: U.S. Government Printing Office, 1992).

2. The Demilitarized Zone has in fact been heavily militarized on both sides. See Chapter 7.

3. A *ri* (also romanized as *li*) is a traditional Korean unit of distance, equivalent to about one-half of a kilometer (one-third of a mile). The initial consonant is one of the most confusing Korean sounds for foreigners, pronounced like "l," "n," or "r," depending upon its location in a phrase or word. The sounds of the Korean language are briefly discussed in Appendix B.

4. Population figures are based on *Korea Annual 1994* (Seoul: Yonhap News Agency, 1994), p. 245, and Savada and Shaw, *South Korea: A Country Study,* pp. 77–81.

5. Savada, *North Korea: A Country Study,* p. 59.

6. The Korean language is discussed in Appendix B.

7. For a discussion of Korean minorities overseas, see Chapter 7.

8. The Khitan were a nomadic people of East Central Asia, contending with other peoples such as the Jurchen (Manchu) and Mongols for control in the region. As the Liao Dynasty, they ruled part of China in the tenth to the twelfth centuries. They may be related to the Koreans; their language (like Mongolian and Japanese) is structurally similar.

9. An excellent brief discussion of the changes in modern Korean society is contained in a pamphlet by Vincent S.R. Brandt, *South Korean Society in Transition* (Elkins Park, Pa.: Philip Jaisohn Memorial Foundation, 1983). Also see Hagen Koo, ed., *State and Society in Contemporary Korea* (Ithaca: Cornell University Press, 1993).

10. The most serious incidents of political violence in south Korea since 1945 (excluding the Korean War period, 1950–1953) include the October 1946 riots in the Taegu area during the American occupation, in which perhaps 100 people were killed; the "student revolution" of April 1960, in which 203 students were killed or subsequently died; and the Kwangju uprising of May 1980, for which the official report shows 193 deaths but for which unofficial sources claim considerably more. In the military seizure of power on May 16, 1961, one person was shot; there was virtually no other damage or casualty. There were several suicides and accidental deaths of students, workers, and riot police in the demonstrations of 1986 and 1987 and in subsequent years.

2
Historical Background

Westerners have a tendency to view all East Asians alike and to think of East Asian nations as having similar backgrounds. It is important to counteract this tendency by considering the countries' ethnic and cultural diversity and the variety of their historical experiences, which far exceed those of Europe. Far from being similar, each nation is the product of its own experience over many millennia.

Understanding Koreans, therefore, comes from looking at their historical and cultural roots. The Koreans began as small tribes entering the peninsula thousands of years ago from the north. They gradually came together—first into small collections of villages; then into three good-sized states; and finally into a single homogeneous nation that has kept its identity despite repeated invasions by surrounding peoples.

In this process, Korea has been shaped by four main influences:

- the tradition of its own people, reaching back into the Siberian steppes of five thousand or more years ago;
- the power and culture of neighboring China;
- the impact of Japan, particularly since the late nineteenth century;
- the economic and cultural inroads of the West.

It is important to note that the Western influence has come to Korea in two conflicting forms: the capitalist, liberal-democratic tradition of Western Europe and the United States, and the Marxism-Leninism of the Soviet Union. This conflict between Western influences contributed to the separation of Korea into two states.

Although Korea has been classified as a developing country (or two developing countries), it differs from most other developing nations in three important ways. It was an autonomous, unified state with a sophisticated central government for over thirteen hundred years. Its people all speak the same language and share the same culture (the largest minority in a population of 60 million is about 40,000 Chinese). The Korean colonial experience was under an Asian power (Japan), not a Western one. As we shall see, all three factors help to explain Korea's condition today.

It is impossible in one short chapter to do justice to Korea's long, rich history. The best that can be done is a gallop through thousands of years, in which the passing scenery is blurred—particularly in the earlier periods. Many readers will undoubtedly want to know more; they are encouraged to consult the English-language histories in the list of suggested readings in Appendix C.[1] A chronological summary of Korean history appears at the end of this chapter in Table 2.1.

Origins

People have lived in the Korean peninsula since the Paleolithic period (about 60,000 years ago), but the origins of the first settlers have not been clearly established. Around the fifth millenium B.C., a Neolithic people entered the peninsula or nearby Manchuria. Korean tradition calls them Yemaek and regards them as the ancestors of present-day Korea. They must have come from the north and west, in small tribal groups, probably from the Yenisei river valley of Siberia. Such movement of related peoples continued into historic times. Links with Central Asia are suggested by the structural similarity of the Korean language to those spoken by Turkic, Mongolian, Tungusic, and other peoples who originated in East Asia north of China.[2] There are also similarities between Neolithic Korean pottery and other remains, such as stone dolmens, and those found in Central Asia. The stylized fir-tree and reindeer motifs on ancient gold crowns found in Korean royal burial mounds also point to Central Asian origins.

The most popular Korean origin myth holds that the founder of the nation was Tan'gun, a man born of a bear at the bidding of a god. A tiger, also offered the opportunity, lacked the patience to wait the prescribed gestation period. The animals probably represented ancient tribal totem symbols. This event is dated 2333 B.C. and is celebrated in south Korea as Foundation Day (*Kaech'onjol*) on October 3. Another myth, with some basis in Chinese records, holds that Kija, a Chinese prince (Chinese: Qize), established Ancient Choson in 1122 B.C. In both myths, people are already present when the founder arrives.

By Neolithic times, the Koreans lived in small communities both by the sea and inland, fishing, hunting, and gathering fruits for their livelihood. Rice cultivation entered from China in the first millenium B.C. Chinese records establish that by the third century B.C., as China itself was becoming a unified empire under the Qin (232–208 B.C.) and Han (208 B.C.–A.D. 220) dynasties, tribes were moving from Siberia and Manchuria into Korea, bringing knowledge of bronze and iron. At the same time, Chinese influence expanded into the northwestern part of the peninsula, bringing with it new agricultural techniques and the use of metal. Partly in response to these pressures, the state known as Ancient Choson (Chinese: Chaoxian) emerged.

The nomadic peoples of Central Asia were a constant challenge to the Chinese empire from earliest times. Determined to crush their threat, the Han Emperor Wudi in 109 B.C. undertook a campaign to outflank them by conquering Ancient Choson. (This was about the time that Rome was demolishing Carthage in the West.) By the following year, he had destroyed Choson and replaced it with four military commands over large territories in the northern half of the Korean peninsula and southern Manchuria. However, the Chinese could not long maintain their hold on so much distant alien territory. A generation later, only one of the commanderies remained, known as Nangnang (Chinese: Lelang), with its capital at Pyongyang (now the capital of north Korea).

Controlling the northwestern part of the Korean peninsula, Nangnang endured four centuries, outlasting by one hundred years its parent Han Dynasty. Its ruling class was Chinese, and its culture was a replica of that at the Chinese capital; some of the finest remains of Han Dynasty culture have been found near Pyongyang. Nangnang was finally overwhelmed by the resurgent Koreans in A.D. 313 (roughly at the same time that the Roman Emperor Constantine established Constantinople as his capital). By that time, it had assured a permanent place for Chinese cultural influence in the Korean peninsula.

Three Kingdoms Period

Outside the Chinese commanderies, the Koreans gradually came together into three kingdoms, Koguryo, Silla, and Paekche—a process doubtless helped by the influence of Nangnang. The Koguryo people were a hunting tribe that had settled the mountainous regions of Manchuria and northern Korea. They asserted their independence as the Chinese relinquished three of their four Korean commanderies and drew back into Nangnang in the first century B.C. Three hundred years later, Koguryo conquered Nangnang to complete its control of the northern part of the peninsula and part of Manchuria as well.

In the southern part of the peninsula, where conditions were more favorable for settled agriculture, the process of nation-building took longer. The tribal people there, called Han (not to be confused with the Han Dynasty), belonged to three broad groups, Mahan, Chinhan, and Pyonhan, which had no central authority. The divisions among the Han may have been the result of geography: A rugged mountain range, the Sobaek, isolates the southeast.

By the middle of the fourth century A.D., however, two states had arisen in the south: Silla in the east, and Paekche in the west. Paekche was probably dominated by a branch of the Puyo tribe that, like other peoples entering Korea, had come from the area of the Yenisei River in Siberia.[3] The fluctuating division between Koguryo in the north and Silla and Paekche in the south was in the general vicinity of the 38th parallel—the line along which Korea was divided in 1945.

The Three Kingdoms period is traditionally dated from about the time of Christ to A.D. 668 (roughly contemporaneous with the rise and fall of the Roman Empire), but in actuality it probably covered no more than three to four centuries. It was characterized at first by Koguryo ascendency and by repeated wars between a militant Koguryo and its less warlike and less well organized southern neighbors. Nevertheless, Paekche was a prosperous and cultured state in the fourth century, trading with both China and Japan and calling upon Japan as an ally against Koguryo. Influenced extensively by Chinese culture, Paekche first encountered Buddhism, brought by a Chinese monk, in A.D. 384 (Koguryo was probably ahead of Paekche, both in Chinese influence and the adoption of Buddhism). Later, Paekche transmitted Buddhism as well as Chinese scholarship to Japan—which was then just beginning its own national development.

The kingdom of Silla, less affected by Chinese culture or outside conquest because of its geographic isolation, was at first weak and backward in comparison to the other two Korean states. It had a confederal rather than an autocratic political structure. The six major constituent tribes had an elite leadership strictly separated into hereditary classes known as "bone ranks." Silla also had groups of young warriors, known as *hwarang;* accounts of their training and esprit de corps are reminiscent of feudal Japanese or European fighting men. Their tradition, *hwarangdo,* is a source of patriotic inspiration for the modern Republic of Korea as well as a school of martial art.[4]

As Silla matured in political organization, Chinese influence increased and may have been a factor in Silla's growing power. In the mid–sixth century, Silla and Paekche together crushed a smaller confederation of Han tribes in the south, known as Kaya (called Mimana by the Japanese, with whom Kaya had close relations); then Silla extended its territory at Paekche's expense. Meanwhile, China was reunited under the Sui Dynasty after three hundred years of internal division. As in previous periods of Chinese strength, the Sui emperors undertook campaigns to control the northern barbarians and again threatened Korea. This time, however, the Koreans were a match for the Chinese. Koguryo's defeat of the second Sui emperor's invasion attempt contributed to his overthrow by the succeeding Tang Dynasty in China. The hero of this campaign was General Ulchi Mundok, who is still acclaimed as a Korean national hero.

China, however, tried to take advantage of the rivalries among the three Korean kingdoms as they sought allies in their struggles for hegemony. In 660, allied with Silla, a Chinese naval assault crushed Paekche. The victors then turned on Koguryo, and by 668 Silla alone remained to rule a united Korea; but it took eight years to push the Chinese out of the territories they had conquered and intended to hold.

Unified Korea

By the end of the seventh century, most of the Korean peninsula was thus brought under a single government.[5] The leaders in the unification effort, Silla Prince Kim Ch'un-ch'u (later King Muyol) and General Kim Yu-sin, brought many of the Koguryo and Paekche leaders into their ruling elite. Once it had rid the peninsula of Chinese power, Silla accepted a tributary relationship to China and utilized the Chinese political model in consolidating its own control. This was a brilliant period for East Asia, with China flourishing under the Tang Dynasty and Japan becoming a nation-state—while Europe was in the depths of the Dark Ages.

Notwithstanding Chinese influence on Silla, distinctive Korean characteristics endured. Notable among these were the "bone-rank" system of inheritance of political power, in preference to the Chinese merit examinations, and the survival of rigid class distinctions, with virtual serfdom among the peasants; some were slaves. Buddhism had more influence than Confucianism. Great Buddhist temples and shrines were erected with official patronage. One of the finer examples of the

Buddhist art and architecture of the time is an artificial stone grotto on a mountaintop near the Silla capital of Kyongju, with a magnificent stone image of the Buddha (see Figure 3.2 in the next chapter).

The kingdom of Silla fell in 936. Internal decay, encouraged by the tension between the indigenous culture and transplanted Chinese institutions, had set in by the late eighth century. The cohesiveness of the ruling groups broke down; a king was killed, and members of collateral lines succeeded to the throne in rapid succession as various factions gained ascendency by force or guile. The peasantry rose in revolt or retreated into banditry. Inevitably rival leaders rose, carving out domains for themselves called "Latter Koguryo" and "Latter Paekche." A Latter Koguryo general named Wang Kon, from a trader family in the west-central port city of Kaesong, emerged supreme. Overthrowing the Silla Dynasty, but treating the fallen ruling class kindly, he proclaimed himself founder of the Koryo Dynasty, moving the capital to Kaesong (then called Songdo). Wang Kon's accession to the Korean throne thus followed Charlemagne's in the West by a little more than a century.

The new dynasty again drew from the Chinese model in organizing its political institutions, even modeling its capital city after the Chinese capital of Changan. However, it still differed from the Chinese in its aristocratic distinctions and in its patronage of Buddhism as a state religion. The status of women appears to have been higher in Koryo than in China. The Chinese examination system for entry into the bureaucracy existed, but in practice it was open only to members of the aristocracy. The extended family system was even stronger than in China. As time went on, the aristocracy gained more and more independent control over its landholdings, thus weakening the central government.

During its first century, Koryo successfully repelled invasion by a Tungusic Khitan tribe from the north and then pushed the northern frontier to approximately its present location (along the Amnok [Yalu] and Tumen rivers).[6] Peace came a decade later, to be followed by thriving commercial, intellectual, and artistic activity. Then, like Chinese dynasties and like Silla before it, Koryo began to decay internally through weakness at the top, rivalry among court factions, growth of tax-exempt aristocratic landholdings, and indifference to the problems of the masses.

Koryo military officials, perceiving themselves discriminated against by civil officials, seized power in 1170, Korea's first military coup d'état.[7] Three decades of civil war and revolt followed, ending with the assertion of power by a self-proclaimed administrator, Ch'oe Ch'ung-hon, reminiscent of the shoguns of Japan.[8] His family held power for sixty years under impotent kings.

In addition to its internal troubles, the dynasty was constantly under external military threat from northern tribes. One of these, the Khitan, captured the Koryo capital in 1011 before being expelled. Such threats reached their peak in the Mongol invasion of 1231—Korea's share of the Mongol sweep through most of the known world. After a quarter century of struggle, the Koreans submitted; their kings, with titles and privileges reduced, were married off to Mongol princesses, and the sons were held hostage at the Mongol court at what is now Beijing. Mongol officials watched over the Korean administration, and Mongol culture strongly influenced the ruling class. Surviving elements of this influence can be seen in Korean cuisine and traditional military costume. The Koreans were mobilized to support the Mongols' unsuccessful attempts to invade Japan; meanwhile, the Koreans suffered repeated attacks by Japanese pirates.

The Koryo period was the zenith of Buddhism in Korea but also saw the growth of Confucian influence. Buddhism was, in effect, the state religion. The temples and clergy were powerful and often wealthy; some temples had large landholdings and private armies. The oldest remaining wooden temple buildings in Korea date from the thirteenth century; many stone pagodas also survive from the Koryo period. The entire Buddhist scripture was codified and carved on wooden blocks early in the dynasty, though the blocks were destroyed by the Mongols. A second set of some 80,000 blocks, prepared as a penance early in the period of struggle against the Mongols, is still preserved at Haeinsa, a temple in southeastern Korea.

Graphic art and poetry flourished, particularly among the emerging Confucian literati, who often expressed themselves in Chinese-language poetry. The peasantry, also, had their *changga* (long poems) with accompanying song. Two important historical works date from Koryo: the *Samguk Sagi* (History of the Three Kingdoms), by Kim Yu-sin, and *Samguk Yusa* (Records of the Three Kingdoms), a more anecdotal writing by the Buddhist monk Iryon. Internationally best known of Koryo's cultural achievements are the beautiful celadon bowls and vases. Printing with moveable metal type was developed (according to Korean sources) in 1240; a Paris museum houses an example of Koryo printing dated to 1377, greatly antedating Gutenberg's invention in the West.

With all its political and economic problems, the Koryo Dynasty could not long survive the collapse of the Mongol Empire in the mid–fourteenth century. The final blow came when a Korean general, sent by the Koryo court against the advancing armies of the new Ming Dynasty in China, realized the folly of the mission. Making his peace with the Ming, General Yi Song-gye turned on his own government, seized control of it, and in 1392 proclaimed a new dynasty. He moved the capital to its present location, Seoul, and readopted the old name of Choson for the dynasty and the nation.

Medieval Korea: The Choson (Yi) Dynasty

The new Yi monarch (known by the posthumous title T'aejo, "Great Progenitor") promptly sought confirmation of his status by the Chinese court and eventually received it. T'aejo consolidated his power with great skill. He granted extensive privileges to his supporters ("merit subjects") but nonetheless established a governmental system closely modeled after the Chinese, including merit examinations for public service. He redistributed the land to ease the lot of the peasants. To dispose of the heavy Buddhist hand on the court, he banished the Buddhist priests to the hills, confiscated much Buddhist property, and established the neo-

Confucianism of Ming China as a state philosophy. He made Choson a far more perfect embodiment of Chinese philosophy and politics than any previous Korean regime, adopting, among other Chinese institutions, the Ming administrative code. After six years on the throne, he wearied of the power struggles in his family, and abdicated in favor of one of his eight sons. Another son seized the throne four months later, setting the stage for the constant power struggles that characterized the dynasty thereafter.

The Korean adoption of the Chinese political system extended to society and culture. Within one to two centuries, Korea became recognized as a more perfect Confucian state than China itself. Court records were kept in Chinese; scholars composed excellent Chinese prose and poetry and were learned in the Chinese classics. The behavior of even the common people was governed by Confucian ethics.

Yet differences from China persisted. These differences included the strong aristocratic tradition, which limited examination takers to sons of the aristocracy; a marked tendency toward collective power at the expense of the king's authority; and a high incidence of factionalism, in which family, clan, and regional connections were factors. The Chinese institution of the Censorate, intended as a check on official misconduct and inefficiency, became in Korea an instrument for attack on the administration. The Korean state, smaller and less secure, was more strongly centralized than in China. Moreover, the Korean king was not the Son of Heaven but rather the vassal or licensee of the Chinese emperor.[9]

The first century of Choson was one of notable cultural as well as political achievement. The fourth king, the great Sejong (1418–1450) (Figure 2.1) and his court academy created a phonetic alphabet, *han'gul*, which is considered to be one of the best writing systems ever devised (see Appendix B on the Korean language). Numerous works of literature and music were created by court-sponsored scholars. Rain and wind gauges were devised, as well as clocks, sundials, and surveying instruments.

Toward the end of the fifteenth century, however, disagreements over the royal succession and other political and ethical points led to struggles for power and position among cliques of *yangban* (scholar-officials) at court. The struggles were bitter and bloody and they even ruined kings. For example, Yonsan'gun (1494–1506) lost his reputation during one wave of purges and was dishonored after his death.[10] After the first series of purges around the year 1500, factional rivalries became a major motif of Korean politics, often taking precedence over the general welfare.[11] By the late seventeenth century, the *yangban* were divided among four major factions and their adherents had their own economic base in agricultural estates, lived in separate areas of the capital, and jockeyed constantly to gain power.

In 1592, Hideyoshi, second of three great leaders who reunified Japan after a century of civil war, decided to invade the Asian continent through Korea. (This was fifteen years before the first permanent English settlement was established at Jamestown in what was to become the United States.) He was initially successful

FIGURE 2.1   Statue in Seoul of Sejong, fourth king of the Choson Dynasty (reigned A.D. 1418–1450) (photo by Edward Adams)

against weak and faction-ridden Korean government forces. However, he suffered a severe naval defeat at the hands of Korean Admiral Yi Sun-sin, who invented an armored ship (the famed "turtle ship") and used a flotilla of them to devastating effect. Volunteer bands called *Uibyongdae* (Righteous Armies), and even armed Buddhist monks, offered significant resistance.

In the end, the Japanese were made to abandon their adventure in 1598 by Chinese intervention and the death of Hideyoshi. Six years of devastation, however, had dealt Korea a heavy blow. Adding insult to injury, the retreating Japanese took with them many of Korea's best artisans and craftsmen. The Japanese ceramic and lacquer industries, for instance, owe their start in large part to the imported Koreans. The resentment of the Korean people that resulted from the war has never ceased. Nevertheless, peaceful relations were established with the leaders who succeeded Hideyoshi.[12] The Japanese were given limited access and residence rights in a small area near the southeastern port city of Pusan, an arrangement that continued into the nineteenth century.

The strain of countering the Japanese invasion of Korea weakened China as well as Korea and facilitated the Manchu conquest of both countries. The Jurchen, or Manchus, descendants of the barbarian tribes that had conquered north China in the twelfth century, reestablished a Manchurian empire of their own in the sixteenth century. Before invading China and founding the Ch'ing dynasty, they invaded Korea in 1636 and forced the Koreans to pay them tribute and break off relations with the Ming. Submitting bitterly, the Koreans also instituted a rigid exclusion policy, authorizing no visitors except for officials from China and Manchuria, and traders from Japan at their enclave near Pusan.

The Japanese and Manchu assaults, together with continuing factional strife, weakened the Korean political and economic structure. The aristocratic class entrenched itself in privileged political and economic positions at the expense of the throne and the common people, upholding the rigid neo-Confucian order inherited from China against all attempts at social change.

In other areas, however, there were significant reforms. One of these was the philosophical movement now referred to as *Sirhak* (Practical Learning), which arose among aristocrats out of power in the seventeenth century. It was inspired in part by deteriorating social conditions and in part by new currents of thought in China, including Christian ideas, brought by young members of the official tribute missions to China. At the same time, new agricultural techniques brought about the growth and concentration of wealth and the beginnings of a commercial economy, despite continuing aristocratic disdain for such activity. During the reigns of kings Yongjo and Chongjo (1724–1800), factional strife was brought under control by a policy of equal distribution of posts.[13]

However, there was further decline in the nineteenth century. There were significant uprisings of peasants. At court, rival families jostled each other for power through their women relatives (reigning and previous queens, subsidiary wives, concubines), while a succession of boy-kings were put on the throne. Midcentury reform efforts by the regent T'aewon'gun (father of the boy-king Kojong, who ascended to the throne in 1863) failed to meet the country's needs. On the contrary, the T'aewon'gun's rigid enforcement of the long-standing policy of excluding all foreigners made Korea all the more vulnerable when the nineteenth-century imperialists commenced their penetration of Korea. The ensuing struggle for hegemony ended with Japanese annexation in 1910.

The Choson Dynasty thus perished, but its long rule of 518 years had left a deep impression upon national attitudes and behavior that is still important. Chinese philosophy, ethics, and politics had become accepted as part of Korean culture. The process was similar to the European assimilation of Greek and Roman culture, but perhaps even more complete. A brief summary of the traditional political and social order, which endured into the late nineteenth century, will show the foundation upon which modern Korea has been built.

At the apex stood the king, with theoretically absolute power within Korea, although acknowledging the overlordship of the Chinese emperor. A bureaucracy of scholar-officials controlled the central government functions and extended into the eight provinces (increased to thirteen in 1895 by subdivision) down to the county level. There was a large royal household, not clearly differentiated from the government until the 1880s. A censorate was charged with criticizing malfeasance and error, even by the king himself. A distinct but subordinate military hierarchy staffed the Five Commands into which the country was divided; the military also performed police functions. Officials were named on the basis of examination, inheritance, or otherwise demonstrated merit (such as supporting the king against rivals). The *yangban,* together with the royal family, were the social aristocracy of the country. They preferred to live in the capital city but also lived in provincial towns and country estates. Many *yangban* were not in government office, either because they were out of favor or because there were no vacancies. Those without government position lived as scholars (often critical of the administration), teachers, or agrarian landlords; many of them hoped to resume office, individually or through factional struggle.

The *yangban* were both artists and art patrons (but not artisans or manual workers); their taste set the standard for artifacts such as ceramics and lacquerware, produced during the first part of the dynasty by government-employed artisans. Because of the Confucian emphasis on proper form in social activity, rites and ceremonies were as important for the *yangban* as the substance of government. In Korea, as in China, one of the six major government ministries specialized in Rites (which in the Confucian view included relations with foreign states).

The common people lived in their own separate world of agricultural villages, clustered in the midst of the fields they tilled. (Only social or economic outcasts lived outside villages.) The villages were largely self-governing and self-sustaining. Political and social authority rested in a council of elders of the leading local families. One or more of the elders were recognized by the government as titular leaders and served as the linkage to higher governmental levels. County magistrates had advisory councils of local dignitaries. Decisions were reached through discussion and consensus, rather than Western-style voting. Families were expected to provide for themselves and settle their own quarrels; those that could not be contained within the family were settled by the village elders and only in exceptional cases referred to county magistrates. If things got out of hand, the provincial police and military units might be called in.

The central government protected the villagers from foreign invasion and domestic disorder. It provided the critically important agricultural calendar, received annually from Beijing.[14] It sometimes afforded relief from natural calamities. It levied taxes in money and kind on grain crops and on individuals and mandated labor on public works and military service (exemption from which amounted to a kind of tax). The central government was accepted by the people—with fear and awe, rather than love, sometimes mingled with resentment—as part of the natural universe, along with the heavens, the spirits, the winds, and natural calamities. Since county magistrates and other officials were reassigned frequently to prevent corruption, essential linkage and continuity were provided by locally appointed functionaries, called *ajon*. Not included in the civil service structure, these men often inherited their posts and served for life. They played an important liaison role in dealing with the agricultural villages where the bulk of the population lived.

In the late nineteenth century, the picture of Korean government commonly drawn by Western observers, and largely corroborated by Korean folklore, is one of a tremendously swollen bureaucracy, preoccupied with ceremony and status and jockeying for power. The office-holders were supported by constantly growing taxes and rents exacted from those of the peasantry who could not evade them. Tenants or laborers on the estates of absentee landlords made up a growing proportion of the farming population. Many of the landlords had managed to assure themselves tax-exempt status, thus adding to the people's burden. The resulting poverty, discontent, and injustice, coupled with a conservative and unyielding aristocracy, made Korea a tinderbox for social upheaval.

The Imperialist and Colonial Period

The period from 1876 (when Japan forced the signing of Korea's first modern treaty) to 1945 (the end of World War II) marked a great divide in the history of Korea. Before 1876, Korea had been wholly within a China-centered international order.[15] Then began a transition, as Western diplomacy and culture upset the traditional order. In Korea—unlike most Asian countries—much of this influence was indirect, through Japan. It was Japan, itself rapidly modernizing in response to Western influence, that emerged as the winner among imperialist contenders for control of Korea and that monopolized control until the end of World War II. Other significant external influences on Korea came from the United States and the Soviet Union.

European countries began their march to the East in the late fifteenth century. By the nineteenth century, they had reduced much of Asia and Africa to colonial possessions and were rapidly penetrating and manipulating the countries that had remained independent. Until the 1860s, however, Korea was virtually untouched because it was not perceived as important enough, and little was known about it.[16] French missionaries had been martyred, and the crew of a U.S. trading ship had been killed on the Taedong River near Pyongyang because of a misunderstanding. Both France and the United States sent small punitive naval expeditions in retribution, but their small scale and quick withdrawal left the Koreans with the illusion that they had defeated the West. They had little incentive to seek further contact.

Japan, however, saw Korea as a prime area for control and expansion. Early in the Meiji period, aggressive factions in the new Japanese government began demanding that their leaders remove Korea from Chinese suzerainty and establish control over the peninsula. In 1876, following the example of Commodore Matthew Perry and the U.S. naval squadron that had "opened" Japan in 1853, the Japanese sent a naval force to Korea and forced the signing of Korea's first Western-style treaty as an independent sovereign state. A Japanese legation was set up in Seoul. The Chinese, fearful of Japanese penetration of their borders, dispatched a representative to Korea to extend Chinese political influence. They also encouraged the Koreans to sign treaties of friendship, commerce, and navigation with a number of Western states, beginning with the United States in 1882.

The circumstances of Korea's "opening" make for an interesting study in the differing methods and motives of diplomacy East and West. The Korean kingdom was satisfied with the status quo; the Chinese wanted to preserve their historic tributary relationship with Korea; the Japanese wanted to replace China as hegemon in Korea; and the West was looking for trade opportunities—though when they found that there was little in the way of commercial opportunity in Korea, most Westerners soon lost interest, and the symbolic and political motives of China and Japan continued to shape events. In the 1890s, however, Korea became the object of a new kind of imperial interest. Czarist Russia took an interest in Korea as part of its heightened activity in the northeast Asian region, touching off reactions from Great Britain, which felt threatened by Russian expansion, and by Japan, which felt threatened by Russian commercial and military competition in Manchuria. By this series of external developments between 1876 and 1900, Korea came to be caught in a cockpit of contention between external empires. At the same time its domestic politics were embroiled in struggles between traditionalists and reformers.

The reformers, some of whom were familiar with the rapid changes then taking place in Japan, China, and the West, wanted Korea to learn from the rapid reform program of the Meiji government in Japan. In 1884, a faction of young Korean aristocrats attempted a coup d'état with the support of the Japanese in an attempt to put their government on the road to modernization. The modernizers' bid for power failed; the traditionalists, backed by China, retained control. The Japanese minister, who had supported the coup, fled the capital to escape angry crowds. War between China and Japan over the incident was averted with an agreement that each nation would withdraw its troops from Korea and give advance notice to the other before sending troops back in.[17]

Ten years later, a major popular rebellion in southwestern Korea against deteriorating economic and social conditions brought a new crisis. Some years previously, in 1860, a frustrated local *yangban* named Ch'oe Che-u had founded a new religion known as *Tonghak* (Eastern Learning). The *Tonghak* movement was a product of both the frustrations of the era (which had led to other rebellions in various parts of Korea) and a hostile reaction to Western and Christian influence; it was somewhat similar to the *Taiping* movement in China at roughly the same time. *Tonghak* gained growing support from the oppressed peasantry. On their behalf, the movement's leaders demanded reforms from the central government, which temporized and then ignored them. Rebuffed, the growing *Tonghak* movement became a rebellion in 1894, gaining control of considerable territory.[18]

The Korean court, under Chinese influence, asked for help in suppressing the rebellion. The Chinese sent troops without prior notification to Japan, although the rebellion actually was suppressed by Korean forces before the Chinese went into action. Japan also sent troops; the Japanese and Chinese forces engaged each other, and Japan declared war on China. To the world's surprise, Japan emerged victorious. The 1895 Treaty of Shimonoseki, which ended the war, declared Korea an independent sovereign state. Korea was thus separated from her centuries-old political link with China and entered an uneasy decade of nominal independence while Russia and Japan jockeyed for preeminence.[19]

After their victory over China, the Japanese overplayed their hand in Korea by forcing reforms against the still-conservative opinions of the people and by murdering the Korean queen, whom they viewed as an enemy of their interests. As a result, the Russians temporarily gained a dominant position. The Korean king fled from Japanese confinement in his palace, took refuge in the Russian legation, and ruled the country from there for a year (1896–1897). However, the Russians in their turn went too far. The Russo-Japanese contest for hegemony continued for a decade, with the Western powers playing minor roles. Korea, militarily and economically weak, was almost helpless; in fact, certain Korean factions sought advantage by seeking the backing of one great power or the other.[20]

Emboldened by the Anglo-Japanese alliance of 1902, Japan went to war with Russia in 1904, driving it out of Korea and Manchuria and establishing a protectorate over Korea. (The Treaty of Portsmouth, which ended the war in 1905, was mediated by U.S. President Theodore Roosevelt.) Five years later, with the acquiescence of the Western powers—including the United States—Japan annexed Korea. The Korean people, except for a small opportunistic minority, were deeply resentful of Japanese control, but the nation was totally unequipped to resist. A number of guerrilla bands (called Righteous Armies, like those that had resisted Hideyoshi's forces three centuries before) nevertheless fought the Japanese occupiers for several years.

As colonial masters of Korea, the Japanese had an advantage over Western colonizers: They shared much of the same Chinese tradition and utilized the same Chinese writing system. However, Korean hostility toward Japan was traditional; memory of the devastation wreaked by Hideyoshi's forces in the sixteenth century was still vivid. Moreover, the Koreans did not consider the Japanese to be superior, as some colonial peoples had considered their foreign rulers. On the contrary, the Koreans thought of themselves as culturally superior. Furthermore, the legitimacy of imperialism itself was beginning to be challenged. For these reasons, as well as from sheer assertiveness, the Japanese relied extensively on force to maintain their control. Their regime was never regarded as legitimate by the Korean people.

Though a good deal of Western opinion subscribed to the idea that the Japanese were making significant improvements in Korea, the objective of the Japanese administration always was to rule and exploit the colony to serve Japanese interests. The traditional Confucian-ordered agrarian society was preserved, but a colonial administration and economic system replaced the political structure of the Choson Dynasty. Heading the Japanese colonial administration was a governor-general, always a senior military leader, who reported directly to the emperor of Japan. Virtually all key positions both in government and in major business and financial enterprises were staffed by Japanese. Landholding was drastically reformed, and the Japanese appropriated large agricultural tracts for themselves; yet the old gentry were largely confirmed in their landholdings, so long as they did not obstruct the new order. Both agricultural and industrial production were directed to serve the needs of Japan, while the Korean standard of living—except for those who were co-opted by the Japanese or acquiesced in their rule—was actually reduced.[21]

Under these circumstances, business, education, and the surprisingly successful Christian church organizations offered the only opportunities for most Koreans to rise to responsible positions in the modern sector. In 1942, Koreans accounted for 18 percent of the 442 senior government officials, 32 percent of the 15,479 junior officials, and 57 percent of the 30,000 in lower ranks. There was an advisory council of sixty-five Korean members, but they were little more than window dressing.[22]

Elections for provincial, city, and town councils were held at intervals beginning in 1921, but Japanese candidates and voters had the advantage (property requirements for voter eligibility gave disproportionate weight to Japanese). Villages and towns were more closely linked to government than in pre-annexation times, and police were omnipresent. Nevertheless, most village and town chiefs were Korean. As in the Choson Dynasty, the lowest career official was the county magistrate.

Nine years after annexation, the Koreans rose up in a remarkable nationwide nonviolent demonstration for independence, known as the March First Movement (*Samil undong*) after the month and day of the event—March 1, 1919. This action, an expression of the deep Korean resentment of Japanese overlordship, followed the death of former King and Emperor Kojong (reigned 1863–1907), who had been forced by the Japanese to abdicate because he sought international support for Korean independence. His approaching funeral had drawn thousands of Koreans from the countryside to Seoul. The movement was stimulated by Korean students in Japan who had been sensitized to the meaning of Korean nationalism, by ideas emanating from the Russian revolution of 1917, and by Woodrow Wilson's doctrine of self-determination, which had been put forward at the Versailles Peace Conference then in session to end World War I. Wilson himself, however, refused to support the Koreans against the Japanese, who were World War I allies.

The harsh suppression of the uprising—reported in Japan and the West primarily through Western missionary channels—caused strong international criticism. In Japan there was a review of colonial policies and the appointment of a new, less authoritarian figure as governor-general in Seoul. The Japanese did moderate their rule somewhat in the 1920s, among other things permitting some Korean groups to meet and to publish in their own language. Nevertheless, resistance continued, with the March First Movement as a major symbol of Korean nationalist aspirations. Within Korea, nationalists constantly sought expression through the media and the few Korean groups the Japanese permitted. The Japanese even allowed the Koreans to form a political organization called the *Shin'-ganhoe* (New Korea Society), which broke up in quarrels between left and right wings. The left wing included communists; the right included "cultural nationalists," persons who believed that after the violent experience of March First, the Korean people should devote themselves to self-strengthening through education and the affirmation of their Korean identity through preservation and study of their history, art, and literature.

Many nationalist leaders left Korea after 1919 and continued their activities in China, the United States, and the Soviet Union. Foremost among exile groups was the Provisional Government established in Shanghai, China, by prominent nationalist leaders following the Japanese suppression of the March First Movement of 1919 in Korea. It was headed first by Syngman Rhee, but Rhee soon returned to his activities in Hawaii as teacher, preacher, and propagandist. He and his Korean Commission in the United States maintained a tenuous link with the Provisional Government, which, for most of the time thereafter, was headed by Kim Ku. The Provisional Government, however, was weakened by the difficulty of maintaining contact with the homeland, by the lack of significant international support, and above all by the ideological left-right split among nationalists that had been fueled by the Bolshevik Revolution of 1917 in Russia (see below).[23]

As Japan moved toward domestic autocracy and external aggression in the mid-1930s, liberal policy toward Korea was reversed, and a policy of assimilation took its place. Expressions of nationalism within Korea were severely punished. One example was the Seoul newspaper photograph of Son Ki-jong, who won a gold medal as a member of the Japanese track team at the 1936 Berlin Olympics. The newspaper staff retouched the photograph to erase the Japanese Rising Sun on the runner's uniform. The newspaper was suppressed. Attempts by Christians to avoid paying homage to the Japanese emperor at Shinto shrines on grounds of religion were punished with imprisonment and torture. In 1938, exclusive use of the Japanese language was ordered. Koreans were "encouraged" to take Japanese names; schoolchildren had to make ritual obeisance to the Japanese emperor. Korean versions of Japanese patriotic associations were organized.

Pressures intensified as war in China expanded into world war. Koreans were mobilized on a large scale as both soldiers and civilians for labor in Japan and throughout the Pacific. Women were drafted into service with the Japanese armed forces as sex slaves in military brothels. Large numbers of Koreans, mainly from the southern provinces, were encouraged or forced to move into Manchuria as laborers or farmers (these people and their descendants constitute an autonomous region in China today). By the end of World War II, more than 2.5 million Koreans had been sent abroad. As a token palliative, the governor-general was put under the authority of the Japanese home minister in 1942, and two representatives were elected from Korea to the Japanese Diet.

Although the Japanese regime benefited the Japanese disproportionately and diminished rather than improved Korean living standards, it nonetheless played some role in Korea's modernization. It gave the Koreans greater expectations as they observed the affluent Japanese community in their midst. Industrialization led to urbanization and the beginning of a modern labor force. Japanese education, limited as it was for Koreans, increased literacy and put Korean intellectuals in touch with international currents of thought. Some young Koreans, principally the children of those who worked with the Japanese, went on to Japanese universities. Though quite a few Koreans gained experience or competence in middle management, those who entered the Japanese system or conducted successful business under it were later branded by their compatriots as collaborators.

The Western Impact

Western religious and philosophical ideas had seeped into Korea since the seventeenth century, by way of the tribute missions to Peking. These ideas played a role in the *Sirhak* reform movement. At the end of the eighteenth century, Catholic converts clandestinely entered the country. They were followed by a few French priests. A translation of the New Testament into Korean by a Scottish Protestant missionary was also influential. The government swung from toleration to persecution of the converts, but virtually wiped them out in 1866 when it discovered a Korean priest's letter asking for French military intervention to protect the Christians. It was not until 1885 that missionary activity resumed, although the Presbyterian medical missionary Dr. Horace Allen entered in the guise of a U.S. legation physician in 1884. The attempt by young Korean progressives to modernize by coup d'état was inspired, in the immediate sense, by Japanese influence, but that influence was ultimately traceable to the West. The *Tonghak* movement was also, in part, a reaction against Western influence.

From 1884 to 1905, several Westerners occupied influential advisory and even administrative roles in the Korean government. Trade expanded; although it was still dominated by Chinese and Japanese, there was some European and U.S. investment (U.S. citizens owned and operated a profitable gold mine in north Korea from the 1890s until 1939 and built the first streetcar line, electric plant, and railroad). Korean officials traveled in Europe and the United States. The king confided in U.S. diplomatic representatives, particularly the first naval attaché, Lieutenant George Foulk, and Dr. Allen, who later became U.S. Minister. Missionaries were freely admitted from 1885. Led by Presbyterians and Methodists from the United States, they not only established churches but also started Western-style schools and hospitals all over the country. A retired U.S. general, William Dye, became the first modern Western military adviser. But the old Confucian patterns still held fast.

Although Western powers maintained diplomatic and consular establishments in Korea until 1905, and consulates thereafter, they played peripheral roles in Korean affairs. Attempts by U.S. diplomats to help Korea in dealings with Russia and Japan were vetoed by Washington. (Minister Allen and General Dye were involved in attempts to break the Japanese house arrest of the king in 1895.) By the time of the Russo-Japanese War, Westerners were disenchanted with the decadent and backward Korean scene and were content—except for the missionaries—to leave the country to Japan.

After 1905, the Japanese themselves became the chief instruments of modernization in Korea. Even after annexation, the Japanese permitted Western missionary, educational, and business activity as long as it did not involve politics. Young people continued to study in Western countries, and many of the students returned to Korea to spread new ideas. Some of these ideas (including Marxism) also entered by way of the Japanese educational system and through contacts with intellectuals in China, notably in Shanghai, where "Mr. Democracy" and "Mr. Science" were under intense discussion. Thus a small but growing number of Korean intellectuals learned something about Western ideas of government and society.

Until the end of the Japanese occupation, the great majority of the Korean people were still only superficially touched by Western ideas; their attitudes were basically shaped by the long Confucian tradition and by antipathy toward their Japanese overlords. Nevertheless, the growth of industry and a money economy and the spread of Western ideas—especially through the growing Christian community—were gradually planting the seeds of social change.

The clearest manifestation of Western influence was the nationwide Korean uprising of 1919. Woodrow Wilson's enunciation of support for self-determination and the mood of the talks at the Versailles Peace Conference encouraged the Korean will to resist. The language of the Korean Declaration of Independence—proclaimed in a public park in Seoul as the Japanese police arrested the thirty-three signers—was reminiscent of the U.S. declaration and the French Declaration of the Rights of Man and Citizen. The Provisional Government-in-exile, established in China following the uprising, adopted a Western-style parliamentary constitution and the form of an elective legislature. The Provisional Government, despite its weakness and its infighting, was regarded by the Koreans as the principal legitimate expression of their aspirations for freedom.

By the end of World War I, the Russian Revolution was stirring attention throughout East Asia with its dramatic overthrow of the old despotic order and its appeal to the impoverished and oppressed workers and peasants of the world. Many nationalists, especially intellectuals, were drawn to socialist and communist ideas as a better solution to political and economic oppression than the conservative capitalist doctrines that had failed to bring desired improvement in the quality of life for the masses. Moreover, geography as well as ideology enabled the Soviet Union to help East Asian nationalists in organizing their struggle.

In contrast, conservative and propertied people and many Christians (some of whom had been educated in Western Europe and the United States), though their nationalist feelings might have been equally strong, could not accept radical programs for social change and economic and social leveling; they feared communism as their Western counterparts did.

Thus, both in exile and within the country, Korean nationalists were divided by the influence of two antithetical Western doctrines, as well as by their own factional rivalries and personal differences, into left and right camps. Korean communist groups were organized in Manchuria and in the Soviet Union and generally competed rather than cooperated with the Provisional Government. Elements in both camps resisted the Japanese by terror and guerrilla action, sometimes in association with the Chinese Nationalists or Communists, but they were rarely united. Both camps received a modicum of external support: from the Soviet Union for the communists, from Chiang Kai-shek's Nationalist China for the noncommunists (with some tacit moral support from the churches and foreign missionaries), but no U.S. or Western European backing or endorsement.

Liberation and Divided Independence

The United States and the Soviet Union, after forty years of near indifference to Korean affairs, renewed their involvement through the Cairo Declaration of November 1943 as a part of the plan for post–World War II dismembering of the Japanese empire. President Franklin D. Roosevelt, Chinese generalissimo Chiang Kai-shek, and British Prime Minister Winston Churchill pledged, "mindful of the enslavement of the people of Korea, [the Allies] are determined that in due course Korea shall become free and independent." Marshal Joseph Stalin associated himself with the declaration soon afterward at a conference in Tehran.

Little specific thought was given to the implementation of these ringing phrases until after the end of the war. Roosevelt proposed a forty-year international trusteeship (based on the U.S. experience in the Philippines), which at Soviet insistence was shortened to five years. He paid no attention to detailed planning documents. It would seem that the Soviets, also, gave Korea low priority in their plans.

The end of the war came sooner than expected, on August 15, 1945, without the anticipated U.S. invasion of the Japanese home islands. The United States hastily proposed a temporary military occupation of Korea in zones divided at the 38th parallel. The Soviets (who had advanced into the peninsula upon their declaration of war against Japan in early August) agreed. The division, by U.S. design, put the national capital on the American side.[24]

Word of the Cairo Declaration filtered into Korea, and as it became evident that the Japanese would lose the war, clandestine nationalist activity within the country intensified. At war's end, the Japanese felt obliged to turn to a Korean leader to maintain order, pending arrival of Allied forces. Spurned by conservatives, who feared being typed as collaborators, the governor-general finally called on a left-leaning nationalist leader—Yo Un-hyong, a missionary-educated journalist and middle-school teacher.[25] Yo posed five stiff conditions, including release of political prisoners. The Japanese accepted and designated him to head an organization to maintain public order. Promptly exceeding his mandate, Yo organized a Preparatory Committee for Korean Independence. With its encouragement, local notables organized people's committees throughout the country, with associated volunteer police forces, and in many places displaced the Japanese in de facto functions of government. The arrangement maintained order; there was no serious violence against the Japanese, notwithstanding their forty years of oppression.

The Preparatory Committee called a national convention, which included delegates representing the local People's Committees and claimed to be elected by them. On September 7, 1945, the day before U.S. occupation forces arrived, the convention proclaimed a People's Republic of Korea, with a cabinet that included distinguished nationalist names of all political persuasions, right and left. Syngman Rhee, conservative nationalist leader in exile in the United States and probably the best known among Koreans, was named president without his knowledge or consent; but the whole was clearly influenced by the left, with communists playing important roles.[26]

The U.S. occupation forces had to be brought from Okinawa, because General Douglas MacArthur did not want to weaken his relatively thin force for the occupation of Japan. Upon the arrival of the U.S. forces, three representatives of the nascent People's Republic went to Inch'on to greet the U.S. commander, Lieutenant General John R. Hodge, but were refused access. Confused by the naive and faction-ridden clamorings of Korean nationalist exiles before and during World War II, the United States had adopted a policy of refusing to recognize the governmental claims of any Korean group until the Korean people themselves could make a choice.

In ignorance of Korean conditions and without any plan of action, the U.S. command at first directed the Japanese governor-general to govern the country until other arrangements could be made. The Korean outcry forced hasty abandonment of this tactic. To the Americans it seemed that the only remaining option was direct U.S. military government of the zone south of the 38th parallel. In occupied south Korea, territory seen by many Americans as former enemy territory, it was easy to lump Koreans together with Japanese as the conquered people. For example, the story is told that a community group in one provincial city approached the U.S. military mayor, a major, with a nomination for civilian mayor. The major drew himself up to his full 162 centimeters (65 inches) and exclaimed, "Mayor! We came here to kill all you people."[27] Not all of the U.S. command had such prejudices, but the story illustrates the ignorance in which the United States and its representatives undertook the administration of a proud and cultured nation.

U.S. authorities nevertheless tried to stimulate dialogue with representative Koreans and began to recruit into the government those they considered qualified—qualifications usually including conservative political views and knowledge of English, which gave the landed gentry and the business community a leading role. The U.S. authorities also brought Syngman Rhee from the United States and the leaders of the Korean Provisional Government (as individuals) from China. Rhee and the Provisional Government leaders were given preferential treatment and promptly set about building a political base.

Meanwhile, the Soviets in the northern zone assembled an administration based on the indigenous people's committees and established a central Five Provinces People's Committee at Pyongyang, the ancient Koguryo capital and the largest north Korean city.[28] To head this administration, they called upon a highly respected Christian leader, Cho Man-sik—the only noted nationalist figure who had remained within the country throughout the Japanese regime. For administrative skills, they relied on several thousand ethnic Koreans brought from the Soviet Union. They also introduced as a war hero an ethnic Korean who had served in the Soviet Red Army during the war, Kim Il-sung, who was destined to become the ruler of north Korea for almost fifty years.

In December 1945 the foreign ministers of the United States, the Soviet Union, and Great Britain met in Moscow. They reaffirmed the proposal for a five-year trusteeship by their three states plus China, renewable if necessary for an additional five years. The United States and the Soviet Union were to establish a joint commission for establishment of an interim Korean administration, in consultation with the Korean people. Although rumors of such a policy had already circulated, its publication profoundly shocked the Korean people. They saw in the trusteeship proposal a renewal of the foreign interference that liberation was supposed to end. Demonstrations began all over Korea but were immediately suppressed in the Soviet zone. Communist and sympathetic leftist groups in the south, as well, were ordered to support trusteeship. In the U.S. zone, Provisional Government leaders seized upon the issue as a means of increasing their political power and called a general strike (which the U.S. command hastily converted into a New Year holiday). Uninformed of the background, General Hodge blamed the Russians for the trusteeship proposal, only to be corrected publicly by the Soviet newspaper *Izvestia* and privately by the U.S. State Department.

Preliminary talks between the two commands began in January 1946. Each side was deeply suspicious of the other, and apart from agreement on supply of electricity by the north to the south, only minor matters were settled, such as the exchange of mail. By March, both sides had named delegates to a Joint Commission, which met alternately in Seoul and Pyongyang over several months in 1946 and 1947. However, the Commission never got beyond the preparatory question of whom to consult among the Koreans. The Soviets demanded that only those accepting trusteeship (which the American side took to mean "leftists") be consulted, while the United States (which had allowed many groups to form) insisted that all credible groups (which the Soviet side took to mean "rightists") should have a hearing. With each side trying to exclude legitimate voices from the other and with the few available centrists (e.g., Yo Un-hyong and Kim Kyu-sik) being labeled as unreliable by both extremes, the talks ran into difficulty.

In August 1947 the Commission adjourned for the last time, and the United States referred the Korean question to the United Nations. The Soviets, on valid legal grounds, objected that the UN had no jurisdiction, but the United States in those days had overwhelming majority support. A UN commission was established to oversee elections for a constituent assembly. When the Soviets, acting through their north Korean surrogates, refused to admit the commission, elections were held "in the areas where the Commission was able to observe and report," resulting in the establishment of an independent Republic of Korea south of the 38th parallel on August 15, 1948.[29] Syngman Rhee was duly elected president, under a Western-style constitution that mixed parliamentary and presidential forms. The north Koreans held their own election in Communist style, resulting in the proclamation of the Democratic People's Republic of Korea (DPRK) the following month, headed by Kim Il-sung under a Soviet-style constitution. Neither side recognized the other, and both states claimed exclusive sovereignty over all of Korea.

Within south Korea, the U.S. Army Military Government in Korea (or USAMGIK) during its three-year existence (1945–1948) displayed to the Koreans a confused picture. The U.S. command set up an administration based on the former Japanese colonial structure, installing locally recruited conservatives and moderates in senior posts and retaining many Korean former civil servants of the Japanese, including many of the Japanese-trained police. Although a Korean administration was thus promptly reestablished, it was criticized by many Koreans as a government by collaborators and interpreters. USAMGIK rescinded all Japanese economic controls, an act that led to maldistribution of food and to hunger in the cities despite a bumper harvest in 1945. The controls were, of course, reimposed. Economic problems were complicated by the repatriation of 1.5 million Koreans from former Japanese territories, as well as a growing flow of refugees from north Korea. Industries were paralyzed by lack of electricity, raw materials, markets, and managerial skills. Inflation was rampant.

The conservative landlord and business class, which had organized its own political party in opposition to the People's Republic, dominated senior positions under USAMGIK. Their Han'guk Democratic Party became a sort of pro-government political force. Both this group and the U.S. command were opposed to any moves against private property or anything else that smacked of socialism or, worse, communism. The local people's committees, regarded (not always with cause) as Communist-dominated, were systematically disbanded.[30]

Since U.S. policy until 1948 was to promote the formation of a unified regime in cooperation with the Soviets, the State Department opposed any reforms in the south that might hinder unification prospects. Even the universally desired land reform was delayed. The military governor's initiative to establish a Department of National Defense in January 1946 was rescinded at State Department direction, although a Philippine-style constabulary was inaugurated in 1947. Moreover, no U.S. funds were available for economic development, and the departure of the Japanese had removed most indigenous capital.

The south Korean populace grew increasingly restive, urged on by the South Korean Workers' (Communist) Party and agents from the north.[31] Political activity was increasingly polarized between left and right. A Washington-inspired attempt to build a moderate centrist coalition failed. There were demonstrations, serious strikes, and a major uprising in Taegu in October 1946, which was put down with considerable loss of life. Two leaders of the moderate coalition, Chang Tok-su and Yo Un-hyong, were assassinated. Syngman Rhee—to the discomfiture of the U.S. authorities—campaigned for immediate independence of south Korea while the U.S.-USSR Joint Commission negotiations were still in progress. In doing so, he lost some of his former allies, including Kim Ku, president of the Shanghai-based Korean Provisional Government (who with other Provisional Government leaders had come back to Korea after liberation).

In an effort to allay popular unrest, the United States organized a South Korean Interim Government (SKIG) and held elections in late 1946 for an interim legislative assembly. The election, held mostly under Japanese rules, resulted in a wholly conservative body, which was offset through the U.S. military governor's appointment of an equal number of moderates. The military governor retained final authority and made no bones about it. By 1947, however, the United States wanted to get out of south Korea as gracefully as possible, both to redeploy scarce troops to Europe and to avoid the unpopularity of being a foreign occupier. To the Koreans, the United States seemed to lack a central philosophy or overall plan. In their eyes, this drift contrasted unfavorably with the purposeful reforms in the north.

Despite all its mistakes and its conservative bias, the military government generally acted with diligence and fairness, pragmatically working with very limited resources to meet basic human needs, revive the economy and infrastructure, and expand education. In 1948, as the UN-observed elections approached, the military government distributed all former Japanese agricultural lands to tenants, while leaving the disposition of Korean estates to the future Korean government. Some last-minute reforms of the legal and educational systems were also made.

USAMGIK brought the economy under control with the aid of $300 million in "disease and unrest" funds (spent chiefly for food and clothing). The United States was able to turn over a reasonably stable if poverty-level economy and a debt-free administration to the new Republic of Korea in 1948, with a surplus in the treasury. On the whole, the display of U.S. goodwill outweighed the mistakes of the administration and the individual sins of the foreign occupiers; Koreans continued to admire and respect the United States.

Korean nationalist feeling nonetheless required that President Rhee display his independence and break continuity with the previous U.S. administration of south Korea. On acceding to power, Rhee discharged all but one of the senior Korean officials of USAMGIK, replacing them with his own supporters. The Han'guk Democratic Party got only one cabinet post, despite its support for Rhee's election, and went into opposition. The new government leaders were inexperienced in administration or economics; under their management, budgetary deficits, inflation, maldistribution, and corruption grew.

As the United States began its military withdrawal, two regiments of the fledgling constabulary mutinied, inspired by Communist agents. The mutiny was put down, and a thousand mutineers were executed, but the ensuing guerrilla war took more than a year to bring under control. There were political crises centering on Rhee's suppression of the left, his unwillingness to allow punishment of alleged collaborators (because he depended upon many of them to support him and run the government), and an opposition attempt to gain power through constitutional amendment.

Nevertheless, by the spring of 1950, an era of progress seemed to have begun. Finances were stabilized (in part because of strong U.S. pressure). The economy picked up, with modest U.S. economic development aid and technical assistance and improved government performance. A land-reform law was finally passed, over bitter conservative opposition. Korean estates began to be distributed to the tillers, while landlords were compensated by government bonds. When Rhee endeavored to postpone the scheduled May 1950 parliamentary election, U.S. pressure forced it to be held (under observation of a UN commission). All but a score of the 200 former legislators were replaced with independents who were not necessarily supporters of the president.

During the same three years (1945–1948) of Soviet occupation, north Korea moved promptly toward popular reforms. The Soviet-sponsored regime confiscated large agricultural holdings, distributed land to the peasants without cost, and nationalized all large industry (the Japanese had concentrated heavy industry in the north, where most of the nation's coal and mineral resources were located). The Korean People's Army was formed in 1946, under Soviet tutelage. The Communist Party, known as the North Korean Workers' Party (later renamed Korean Workers' Party when it took in the remnants of its counterpart in the south), became the central organ of control, and the Five Provinces People's Committee became the central government.

The first Committee chairman, as already noted, was the distinguished Korean nationalist and Christian lay leader, Cho Man-sik. He refused to accept trusteeship (and probably other Communist dictates as well); the authorities placed him under house arrest in December 1945, after which he disappeared and was never heard from again. Kim Il-sung, the anti-Japanese guerrilla leader who had joined the Soviet Army, was imported and established as a leader by the Soviet authorities. With their blessing he displaced not only Cho but other leaders as well (such as Kim Tu-bong, who had returned to Korea from service with the Chinese Communists) and became chief of state and party when the Democratic People's Republic of Korea was proclaimed.

Soviet troops were withdrawn from the north by December 1948. Under apparently firm control of Kim Il-sung and the Korean Workers' Party (the division between northern and southern Communist parties having been abolished), Communist-style collectivization and economic development were under way. Christianity, which had previously been stronger in the north than in the south, was suppressed, as were other religions. The results apparently pleased many peasants and workers, as living standards improved and the traditional status and economic privilege were abolished; but well over a million property owners, Christians, former collaborators, and professional and technical people fled to the south. At the same time, with Soviet assistance, the north vigorously built up its military forces. Both north and south castigated each other, and with their respective allies canceled out each other's bid for United Nations membership. Each side talked of military action against the other, although the United States took pains to ensure that the south Koreans had no offensive capability (they were denied an air force, for example). Unification, although universally desired, was perceived on both sides as a zero-sum game.

The Korean War

In January 1950, Secretary of State Dean Acheson made a speech at the National Press Club in Washington. Although it reaffirmed existing U.S. policy on defense of the Pacific area, it stressed United Nations protection for places beyond what Acheson called the U.S. "defense perimeter."[32] This was meant to signal the Communist Chinese that the United States would not intervene further to protect Chiang Kai-shek and the Chinese Nationalists on Taiwan should the Communists undertake to cross the Taiwan Straits, and that there was no need to launch a merciless attack on the exiled Nationalist government there. But it indicated the same for south Korea, which also lay beyond the perimeter. The 1948 south Korean election under UN auspices, the U.S. military withdrawal in 1949, the Acheson speech, and other American actions and statements all conveyed the impression that the United States would not return in force to defend south Korea from a northern attack.

The south Koreans warned the United States of an offensive north Korean military buildup. Although U.S. intelligence had picked up similar indications, the south Korean claims were dismissed as more border probes of the kind that had been going on for a year and as typical belligerent Rhee rhetoric. It was considered unlikely that the Soviets would permit a north Korean attack. The north Koreans opened a peaceful unification offensive, offering to return Cho Man-sik in exchange for three of their agents held in the south and proposing a unification conference.

A certain endemic level of political violence had been plaguing south Korea since early in the American occupation and had erupted into full-scale rebellion on several occasions, most notably on Cheju Island in April 1948 and in the South Cholla Province towns of Yosu and Sunch'on in October of the same year. The north-south Taebaek mountain range permitted considerable surreptitious traffic between north and south Korea, and the porous seacoast permitted landings of guerrillas and material to assist anti–Syngman Rhee rebels. Added to this leftist infiltration from north Korea was a wave of returning Koreans from areas that had been occupied by Japan during the war, as well as from Japan itself, encountering unemployment and frustration in postwar south Korea. These various types of disaffected elements were prime recruiting targets for leftist organizers; and when it became clear that the U.S. military government in the south was going to opt for the creation of a separate, noncommunist regime under Syngman Rhee instead of pressing for a unified Korea with, possibly, more toleration for leftist views, the remnants of the old People's Committees, encouraged by leftist organizers, raised small-scale revolts across the southern tier of the country. The south Korean constabulary and police, both organized and trained by the Americans, set out to crush these uprisings; and though the low-intensity conflict in south Korea was mostly finished by 1949, it should be seen as a prologue to the Korean War that the world knows, from 1950 to 1953. Indeed, the "Korean War" should probably be understood as encompassing an era from 1947 to 1955, with the period 1950–1953 as its hot phase.

The hot phase of the Korean war began on June 25, 1950, when north Korea attacked across the 38th parallel in an attempt to unify the peninsula by blitzkrieg. The attack was an egregious miscalculation by Kim Il-sung, who was insufficiently schooled in international affairs to realize that the United States could not permit the "loss" of south Korea to Communism, despite what Secretary of State Acheson had said earlier in his National Press Club speech. Kim believed that his battle-hardened veterans who had fought with the Chinese Communists in World War II, equipped with Soviet-supplied tanks, could overwhelm the south Korean constabulary and occupy the southern half of the country before the West could react. He almost certainly regarded it as a local conflict, essentially an intra-Korean attempt to end the division of Korea that had been imposed by the Americans and Soviets in 1945. He certainly did not expect a quick or effective American military response. His original premise turned out to be correct—that is, he was easily able to overcome the south Korean constabulary. However, within hours the United States began organizing a defense under United Nations auspices that marshaled American forces in Japan to halt the invasion in a last-ditch campaign to hold an area roughly following the Naktong River in southeastern Korea. There, with UN reinforcements pouring in through the port of Pusan, the north Korean invasion ground to a halt.[33]

The United States chose to reassert itself in Korea for a variety of reasons, some of which would not have been obvious to Kim Il-sung at the time. First, the United States did not see the north Korean invasion as an intra-Korean conflict, but rather as part of an aggressive Soviet pattern similar to Germany's in the 1930s that, if not checked, would likely lead to another world war. This was the "Munich analogy," a variant of the Vietnam-era "domino theory." Second were the strategic calculations—namely, in political terms, the requirement to prove that the United Nations could deal with outright aggression across borders like the 38th parallel, and, in geopolitical terms, the requirement to retain control of the Korea Strait and with it the capability to limit Soviet access to the Sea of Japan. Third, a Communist victory in Korea could not be permitted to encourage the left wing in American-occupied Japan. Nor, indeed, could the Truman administration and the Democratic Party allow the "loss" of any additional territory to Communist control after the "loss of China" in 1949, given Republican accusations of "treason" in American foreign policy. Domestic American politics was thus an important fourth consideration. Fifth, and finally, came the American moral commitment to the Syngman Rhee regime in south Korea. No treaty obliged the United States to defend Rhee, but American sponsorship of his government and the well-grounded view that Communist control over south Korea would cost pro-American elements dearly, compelled an American response. The United States would probably have intervened unilaterally in any case; however, a United Nations "cover" was made possible by the fact that the Soviet Union was boycotting the Security Council at the time, protesting the West's refusal to admit Communist China.

By the end of June, therefore, the United Nations had created an international force under the command of General Douglas MacArthur to respond to the north Korean invasion of south Korea. President Rhee placed his forces under MacArthur's command, and eventually seven U.S. divisions, a British Commonwealth Division (comprising a British brigade and forces from Australia, Canada, and New Zealand), and troops from eleven other countries joined the south Koreans. After holding the small Pusan perimeter through the summer, MacArthur's forces counterattacked with a masterful amphibious landing at the port of Inch'on, west of Seoul. The Inch'on landing led directly to the liberation of the capital and the capture of much of the north Korean invasion force in south Korea.

Following this defeat for north Korea, the United Nations General Assembly acquiesced in a U.S. proposal to occupy north Korea pending elections for a unified government. However, an overly rapid UN advance to the north Korean border brought Communist China to north Korea's support; as many as a million "volunteers"—many of them impressed former Nationalist troops—pushed back the UN forces south of Seoul. A UN counteroffensive begun in March 1951 returned the lines to the 38th parallel and pushed to more defensible terrain slightly north of it.

At this point, in June 1951, the Soviet representative to the United Nations proposed discussions for a cease-fire. While bitter fighting continued for small changes in the battle line, truce negotiations went on for two years. Most issues were settled in the first few months, but the talks then bogged down—principally over the issue of voluntary repatriation of prisoners of war. The United Nations side insisted on this point because of humanitarian concerns and the World War II experience and because, as it maintained, the great majority of the 100,000 prisoners it held did not want to return to north Korea or China and thus represented a propaganda triumph.[34]

In July 1953, an armistice agreement was finally worked out between the United Nations commander, on one side, and the commanders of the (north) Korean People's Army and the Chinese People's Volunteers on the other. A last-minute threat to the agreement was President Rhee's unilateral release of 28,000 prisoners, in a deliberate attempt to torpedo the armistice and compel a fight for UN victory over the entire peninsula. To gain his acquiescence in the armistice—which south Korea has never signed—the United States promised and delivered a mutual defense treaty, US$1 billion in economic aid over three years, and equipment for an army of twenty divisions (about 700,000 soldiers).

Under the 1953 Armistice Agreement, there has been no significant military action for over forty years, although the so-called Demilitarized Zone has been heavily militarized, most sessions of the Military Armistice Commission have been propaganda exercises, and a number of provocations have occurred (such as the north Korean murder, with axes, of two U.S. officers in the Joint Security Area in 1976 and the digging of large tunnels from north to south under the Demilitarized Zone, of which four have so far been found). The U.S. presence was reduced to two divisions plus supporting units, then in 1970 to one, which still remains just behind the front line. All except token representatives of other nations have withdrawn. The bulk of the Korean combat units remains under U.S. operational control; current command arrangements are discussed in Chapter 7.

The Korean War devastated both halves of the country, but particularly the north, where repeated strategic bombing flattened the industrial plant. Up to 4 million lives were lost on both sides (including 33,729 from U.S. units), and millions more were disabled or made refugees.[35] Around 1 million more north Koreans came south with the retreating UN forces. Damage in the south amounted to one year's gross national product. Only the strength of the Korean family and community system and massive American and foreign aid (both governmental and private) permitted south Korea to survive; similarly, north Korea received substantial aid from the Soviet Union and China, although the Soviet Union provided no military support once the north Koreans were defeated.

Korea from the War to 1970

In south Korea, economic reconstruction and development were handicapped by U.S. and UN controversy over priorities, methods, and responsibilities and by economic ignorance and even indifference on the part of President Rhee and his associates. Inflation again grew beyond 100 percent per year. By 1957, the economy had once more been stabilized, and living standards had returned to prewar levels. After 1957, however, politics got in the way of economics. Economic stagnation was a large factor in the fall of the Rhee regime in 1960.

Political infighting in south Korea resumed as soon as the fighting lines stabilized in 1951. In the heat of conflict, Rhee had accepted some capable opposition leaders in a unity cabinet, but unity dissolved in the face of Rhee's determination to succeed himself in office. The National Assembly, which was to elect the president under the 1948 Constitution, was clearly opposed to Rhee. In a crisis period from January to July 1952, Rhee and his lieutenants forced through an amendment for popular election of the president, which he easily won. The decision of the United States not to intervene in this crisis, despite its enormous wartime power and influence in Korea and despite Rhee's autocratic and coercive tactics, was a watershed in the history of Korean-U.S. relations.

Two years later, his Liberal Party having gained a majority in the National Assembly, Rhee forced through another amendment allowing him a third term. This move unified opposition forces, and in the 1956 election the opposition Democratic Party vice presidential candidate, Chang Myon, won the vice presidential contest (the Democratic Party's presidential candidate had died of natural causes two weeks before the election). When in 1958 the opposition increased its representation in the National Assembly, supporters of the rapidly aging President Rhee resorted to naked coercion in their effort to stay in power. Their tactics included a grossly rigged presidential election in March 1960, which was accompanied by riots and police brutality.

On April 19, 1960, students marched on the presidential palace to present their grievances. Guards opened fire; in the ensuing violence, 200 students were killed. In the nationwide demonstrations that followed, the United States played a catalyzing role by publicly acknowledging the "legitimate grievances" of the people. Rhee was persuaded to resign and go into exile in Hawaii, where he died in 1965.

Under an interim government led by Ho Chong, a respected senior statesman, the Constitution was again amended to provide for a European-style parliamentary government. New elections in July 1960 swept the opposition Democratic Party into power. The new bicameral legislature elected Chang Myon (John M. Chang) prime minister and Yun Po-son president. A ten-month period of unprecedented political freedom ensued, in which the governing party split into two nearly equal fractions, respectively headed by the prime minister and the president.

The new regime, weakened by inexperience and political infighting, faced massive challenges. In the absence of firm central control and with an atmosphere of unprecedented freedom among a people accustomed to strong leadership, politics approached anarchy. Economic problems could not be remedied overnight, and they aggravated popular discontent. The north Koreans proposed unification discussions, to which some south Koreans responded positively, leading to fear of subversion. Chang Myon's overtures for relations with Japan, though overdue, were unpopular. Unlike Rhee, who had made a political asset out of resisting U.S. advice, Chang Myon was perceived as too compliant. When he proposed a reduction of 100,000 in the armed forces, and when students took it upon themselves to propose unification talks with north Korean counterparts, a group of military officers moved in.

In the predawn hours of May 16, 1961, a force of about 3,600 men led by Major General Park Chung-hee and Lieutenant Colonel Kim Jong-pil seized control of the government. Despite the unconstitutionality of the action, the people accepted it—not with enthusiasm, but with something like relief. Restoration of strong control, after the confusion of the experiment in parliamentary democracy, was a return to Korean political normality. Moreover, the armed forces, which not only were the symbol of national security but also had refused to support the unpopular Rhee regime in the crisis of 1960, were favorably regarded by the public. The apparent setback to democracy was, however, a problem for the new U.S. administration of John F. Kennedy.

The military leaders established a ruling group of thirty-two military men (the Supreme Council for National Reconstruction), abolished the legislature, suspended the Constitution, and ruled by decree for two years (at first leaving the elected president in place as a cloak of legitimacy). The military leaders enforced law and order vigorously and harshly, sweeping hoodlums and petty criminals from the streets. Hundreds of former civilian political leaders were forbidden political activity for several years. Despite initial mistakes, the military administration moved to revitalize the economy. They co-opted trained civilian economists and administrators and placed military officers in civil government positions both to improve operations and to reward supporters.

Reluctantly at first, but then on a businesslike basis, the U.S. authorities worked with the military government to stabilize the economy and then to help finance the First Five-Year Plan for development (1962–1966). When the military showed unwillingness to return to civilian government, as they had pledged at the beginning, the United States brought its economic and military leverage to bear. A new constitution was put to popular referendum in 1963 and approved by a wide majority. It was generally an improvement over the 1948 document, with extensive guarantees of civil rights. Park Chung-hee (who had resigned his military rank) was elected president. An elected civil government took office in January 1964, with a respected senior journalist and scholar, Ch'oe Tu-son, as prime minister.

President Park's political control in the new order was effective enough by 1965 to bring about acceptance of normalized relations with Japan—a badly needed source of economic support—despite widespread demonstrations of popular anti-

Japanese sentiment, fanned by opposition politicians. Over token objections by the political opposition, Park also acceded to the U.S. request for support of its military forces in Vietnam; two south Korean divisions eventually served there in the period from 1965 to 1971. In contrast to the public's opposition to the normalization treaty with Japan, it generally supported the dispatch of forces to Vietnam, even though it was the first Korean expeditionary force since the fourteenth century,[36] because they saw it as repayment for U.S. support in the Korean War. (The actual south Korean government motives for sending forces were more complex, involving economic advantage and maintenance of U.S. strategic support.)

To ensure continued control of the fractious Korean body politic, the military government, as one of its first actions, had set up a large Korean Central Intelligence Agency (KCIA), whose powers transcended those of the U.S. Central Intelligence Agency and Federal Bureau of Investigation combined. This organization remained after 1963, ensuring autocratic management of the south Korean political scene, in which the legislature and political parties had little real power. Nevertheless, there was some semblance of democracy, which gradually increased. Park Chung-hee was reelected in 1967, by a wider margin than in 1963.

Remarkable economic progress began in the mid-1960s. The gross national product increased by 10 percent or more per year, and population growth was slowed from over 2.5 percent to under 2 percent annually. The consequence was rapidly improving material conditions and social stability for a populace that had long suffered from poverty, inflation, stagnation, and uncertainty. This progress, which far outweighed the burden of autocratic control in the popular mind, gave this regime, called the "Third Republic," something of the legitimacy it sought.

North Korea also faced massive postwar political and economic challenges. Kim Il-sung, his position weakened by failure to achieve his war aims, faced challenges from the factions that had been brought together in the Korean Workers' Party: the "domestic faction" of communists from within Korea, headed by the ex-southerner Pak Hon-yong; the "Yenan faction" of people who had been associated with the Chinese Communists during the civil war, headed by Kim Tu-bong; and the "Soviet faction" of people who had entered Korea with the Soviet forces, headed by Ho Ka-i. Pak was disgraced, then executed; the other leaders were purged and disciplined. By the end of the decade, Kim Il-sung and the "Kapsan faction" of loyalists who had been associated with him in Manchurian guerrilla campaigns had consolidated their political control. This group has maintained it ever since.

The wartime experience greatly diluted Soviet influence in north Korea because it was the Chinese who saved the state from extinction. Moreover, Kim Il-sung, who followed Stalin's example in encouraging a personality cult to bolster his power, was estranged by Khrushchev's policies. For a time, the Soviets sharply reduced their economic support. In these circumstances, Kim elevated the concept of self-reliance, *juch'e,* to a philosophical dogma. *Juch'e,* as elaborated by Kim, was eventually represented as a higher form of communism for the Third World, transcending Marxism-Leninism. Kim also performed a balancing act between the

Soviet Union and China to reinforce his own independence (a feat that south Korea, with a meager natural resource base and no viable alternative to the United States as a support for its security, could not duplicate).

Collectivization of agriculture, which moved through three successive stages, was completed by 1959; all farmers participated in cooperatives, theoretically owned in common, and shared in the product in proportion to their labor input. North Korea's *Ch'ollima* (Thousand-League Horse) Movement, more or less contemporary with China's Great Leap Forward, brought the cooperatives to village size and made them political as well as economic units, administered from county centers. In 1969, in the course of one of his famous "on-the-spot guidances," Kim Il-sung inaugurated the Chongsan-ni work method for agriculture, under which the manager of each cooperative shared policy control with a committee representing the farmers. This system was extended to industry by another "on-the-spot guidance" at the Tae'an steel works the following year. (The use of the Chongsan-ni and Tae'an models somewhat parallels the roughly contemporaneous use by the Chinese of the model Dazhai commune and Daqing oil complex.)

After an initial two-year reconstruction period from 1953 to 1955, north Korea undertook a Six-Year Plan for economic development and completed it ahead of schedule. This was followed by other multiyear plans; the Seventh Five-Year Plan was due to be completed in 1996. Annual economic growth was as high as 20 percent in the first few years but declined thereafter; this is partly explainable by the very small base from which recovery started, given the enormous wartime destruction.

Internationally, north Korea assumed a militant anti-American posture and, in competition with south Korea, successfully cultivated the Third World. North Korea encouraged celebration of the month from June 25 (outbreak of the Korean War) to July 27 (date of the Armistice) each year as Anti-American Month, both at home and abroad, and promoted visits from Third World leaders. It also sought to foment revolution in south Korea through propaganda and the clandestine dispatch of subversive agents, establishing a People's Revolutionary Party for Unification for this purpose. In 1968 it both attempted to assassinate the south Korean president (by means of a hit squad that infiltrated to within 500 yards of the presidential residence) and sought to take advantage of perceived U.S. weakness by capturing the intelligence interception vessel USS *Pueblo* and holding its crew captive for nearly a year. (North Korea also shot down a U.S. intelligence reconnaissance aircraft in 1969.) By 1970 it was at the height of its Third World influence, having been admitted as member of the nonaligned movement and named to the movement's steering group. It gained observer status at the United Nations (a status that had been held by south Korea since 1949).

Developments Since 1970

International developments in the late 1960s and early 1970s had a profound impact on Korea, both north and south. The U.S. quagmire in Vietnam and President Richard Nixon's move to extricate the U.S. forces created the appearance of weakness and withdrawal. This appearance worried south Korea and encouraged the north, which for years had sought to get U.S. forces out of Korea. Nixon's Guam Doctrine of 1969, ruling out direct involvement by U.S. forces in other countries' wars, put in question the role of the U.S. divisions in Korea—one of which was withdrawn soon afterward. Above all, Nixon's opening to China created profound uncertainty in both Korean states.

In consequence, there were changes both in relations between north and south and within the two states. South Korea in 1971 initiated discussions between the Red Cross societies of the two states regarding separated families. Then a secret south Korean feeler in late 1971 led to the Joint North-South Declaration of July 4, 1972, in which both Koreas pledged peaceful unification, independence of outside forces, and "grand national unity" (since referred to by north Korea as the "three great principles of unification"). The two sides also promised cessation of mutual vilification, but it soon resumed. There has been virtually no movement toward unification, although there have been intermittent contacts between the two sides since 1972 and one token visit by members of separated families (see Chapter 8).

Within south Korea, President Park first imposed a state of emergency, then conducted a "coup d'état from within," leading to a new and much more authoritarian regime, the Fourth Republic, under the so-called *Yushin* (Revitalization) Constitution. Some observers believe that Park was genuinely frightened by the power and discipline his representatives had seen in north Korea, as well as worried about diminution of U.S. support. In addition, however, he had nearly lost the 1971 presidential election to a charismatic opposition figure, Kim Dae-jung, whose capacity to govern the country under such circumstances was distrusted by the military. The election was preceded by amendment of the Constitution to permit Park a third term—evoking memories of Rhee's controversial 1954 amendment for the same purpose.

Under the *Yushin* regime, the president had sweeping powers to rule by decree and used them aggressively to control political activity. For example, criticism of the Constitution itself was made a punishable offense. The legislature and the political parties represented in it were narrowly circumscribed, and although debate within the legislative hall was supposedly protected, it often was not reported to the public. Kim Dae-jung, the opposition challenger of 1971, was abducted from a Tokyo hotel in 1973 by the KCIA and imprisoned in Seoul. The press was self-censored within guidelines provided by the government. A critical declaration by opposition leaders, read from the pulpit of the Catholic cathedral in Seoul on March 1, 1976 (fifty-seventh anniversary of the independence uprising), with foreign reporters present, resulted in prison terms for those who signed it.

Although south Korea rode out the oil crisis of 1973 with relatively little difficulty, the 1979 crisis was more serious. Its effects were compounded by overinvestment in heavy and defense industry, another result of the new international uncertainty, and by rising demands for better industrial wages. A leading opposition assemblyman, Kim Young-sam, was expelled from the legislature for his criticism of *Yushin* regime policies. As Park's hard-line advisers clamped down on growing unrest, labor disputes and student demonstrations erupted into street riots. There were sharp disagreements within Park's entourage over how to handle the disturbances. The nation was shocked by the news on the night of October 26, 1979, that President Park himself had been shot and killed in a firefight between quarreling officials within the presidential compound. The assassin, in fact, was Park's own fellow military academy graduate and KCIA director, Kim Chae-kyu.

Park's assassination led to the succession of Prime Minister Ch'oe Kyu-ha as interim president and then, with confirmation by the electoral college, as president. On the night of the assassination martial law was declared. An investigation began under the ROK Army Security Command. The Army Security commander, Major General Chun Doo-hwan, soon emerged as the real center of power within the military. On the night of December 12, 1979, General Chun and his closest military supporters attacked the martial law headquarters and the Ministry of National Defense, arresting the Army chief of staff and taking effective control of the country's defense establishment in what has since been termed a "coup-like incident." From that time forward, though President Ch'oe was nominally in authority, General Chun was south Korea's strongman-ruler.

However, Chun was not yet in a position to act as military dictator. In the early months of 1980, a period known fondly as the "Seoul Spring," after Czechoslovakia's "Prague Spring" in 1968 before the Soviet crackdown, President Ch'oe Kyuha continued to preside and a civilian prime minister continued to administer the government through his cabinet of ministers. The government undertook to stabilize the economy, to take steps toward political liberalization, and to set up a public discussion through the National Assembly toward the development of a new national constitution. The mood of the "Seoul Spring" interlude was one of anticipation of a return to civilian government, and the period was marked by jockeying for electoral position among the "Three Kims": veteran opposition leaders Kim Dae-jung and Kim Young-sam, and Kim Jong-pil, the architect of Park's 1961 military coup, father of both the ruling Democratic Republican Party and the dreaded KCIA, sometime prime minister, and Park's successor-presumptive. The democratic mood also fostered happenings that were anathema to south Korean conservatives, such as workers' strikes and student demonstrations objecting to compulsory military service and police surveillance on campuses.

Meanwhile, the economy languished in recession, both because of political uncertainty and in response to belt-tightening policies; the gross national product fell by over 5 percent in 1980, the first downturn since the early 1950s. Students demonstrated for more freedom, and workers struck in several locations for better wages and working conditions. The north Koreans, as they had in previous times of south Korean political tension, made overtures for unification talks. As in 1961, senior military leaders grew nervous during the "Seoul Spring" and sought a more orderly environment. In his position as military strongman, General Chun spent the interval putting his former military academy classmates and loyalists in key positions. In April he violated the law guaranteeing civilian control of the KCIA by taking over the directorship of the agency, heightening worries that he was on the way to seizing total power. Student demonstrations grew in size and fervor the following month. A National Assembly session scheduled for May 20 posed dangers that opposition assemblymen under the leadership of Kim Dae-jung and Kim Young-sam would fan the flames of dissent against military rule. Apparently to forestall this possibility, General Chun took decisive action on May 17 during a lull in the demonstrations. He imposed full martial law, canceled the forthcoming National Assembly session, and arrested a number of leading dissidents including the Three Kims, journalists who had been critical of his actions, and intellectuals from the literary, religious, and human rights communities.

The arrest of Kim Dae-jung sparked a reaction in South Cholla Province, Kim's home region. In the provincial capital of Kwangju, university students held demonstrations on May 18 in violation of the martial law decree. Chun responded by dispatching quick-reaction Special Warfare Command paratroopers to the city to break up the demonstrations. These soldiers, known as "black berets," were trained for violent guerrilla actions against north Korean infiltrators, and their attack on the students and citizens of Kwangju was brutal and deadly. It brought out very large crowds for demonstrations the following day. Young students and workers raided the police headquarters, took weapons and vehicles from the armory, and, backed by citizens, drove the army from the city by May 22. A period of negotiations followed between the central government and a citizen's committee in Kwangju. The government argued that it could not tolerate a permanent state of insurrection, while the negotiators asked for amnesty for the demonstrators. On May 27 regular army troops entered the city in force and regained control. The uprising cost at least 193 lives (the official government count) and very possibly more—although probably not as many as the 2,000 claimed by some of the citizens involved.

The Kwangju uprising shocked the entire nation and left a bitter memory that permanently damaged General Chun's public image and robbed his presidency of political and moral legitimacy, and cast a shadow over the presidency of his compatriot and successor Roh Tae-woo. Long after the fact, in 1995, Chun went to prison for his actions. However, in 1980 his ruthless repression of dissent, including the willingness to use deadly force against civilians in Kwangju, cowed the population into a grudging tolerance of his rule. In August Chun succeeded Ch'oe Kyu-ha as interim president; in October a new constitution was adopted, creating the Fifth Republic. Martial law was withdrawn, new political parties were allowed to organize, and there were National Assembly elections in January 1981. An electoral college controlled by the ruling party named Chun, recently retired and now a civilian, to a single seven-year term as president.

Thus the Fifth Republic, roughly similar in law and fact to the Third, continued the era of military-backed rule in south Korea. Strong central control was not without benefits: The economy resumed its rapid rate of growth, creating prosperity that helped to make continued military rule easier to accept. Seoul also won a bid to host the 1988 Olympics, fostering a special sense of pride and purpose through most of the 1980s. There were also steps toward political liberalization: The opposition won one-third of the seats in the National Assembly in the 1985 election and used its power to mount an aggressive challenge to the administration, including demands for constitutional amendment.

Chun often repeated his pledge to be the first south Korean president to leave office through a peaceful transfer of power—as specified in the constitution. However, as the event drew near, it seemed obvious that Chun and his backers in the military leadership intended to maintain their hold on power by having former General Roh Tae-woo, the commander of one of the key front-line army units that backed Chun in the December 1979 coup, win the ruling Democratic Justice Party's nomination to succeed Chun. Since the party controlled the electoral college, Roh seemed certain to succeed Chun. The opposition cried foul and demanded a constitutional amendment to open the electoral process so the winner would be chosen by popular vote.

The ensuing public outcry led to massive demonstrations that forced Chun to allow the constitutional change. Ironically, however, because the opposition split its vote during the election, Roh was elected anyway, by a plurality of 36.6 percent.

The constitutional change created the Sixth Republic, and Roh Tae-woo assumed office as its first president in February 1988. In April, a legislative election gave opposition candidates more seats than the government party for the first time in the Republic's history, although the opposition members were divided among three parties.

The five years of the Roh presidency, 1988–1993, were much discussed as a period of "democratization" in south Korea, through a process that dated from June 29, 1987, the day Roh himself came out in support of popular election of the president. Notable were attempts to investigate political abuses and corruption under the Chun regime, and Roh's aggressive pursuit of better relations with the socialist countries including the Soviet Union, which recognized south Korea in 1990, and the People's Republic of China, which recognized south Korea in 1992. This policy of "*nordpolitik*" also appeared to move north-south relations on the peninsula into a new phase of negotiations between the prime ministers of the DPRK and the ROK, raising hopes for progress toward reunification. Within the republic, there were shifts in political alliances and a reconstitution of the ruling party to include longtime opposition leader Kim Young-sam, who eventually emerged as Roh's successor-candidate and then winner in the presidential election of 1992. This restored the former ruling coalition's grip on the National Assembly, but it was bitterly resented by many opposition politicians and intellectuals who regarded Kim's defection to the party of Chun and Roh as an unworthy and opportunistic move.

Unfortunately, Roh succumbed to the temptation to handle political money in secret—and on an unprecedented scale. While he was president his daughter and son-in-law were discovered to have illegally imported nearly $200,000 in cash to the United States but were excused from serious punishment. This was just a hint of what was to be uncovered in October 1995, when it was revealed that Roh had managed a slush fund of around $600 million dollars donated by Korean corporate interests. The scandal, which dwarfed all preceding corruption exposures in the history of the Republic, ruined Roh's reputation and resulted in his imprisonment almost simultaneously with Chun's imprisonment for crimes related to the December 1979 coup and the Kwangju massacre of May 1980.

Compared to the upheavals in south Korea, the political culture of north Korea seemed stable; but there, too, there were changes after 1970. Apparently concerned about the south's rapid economic progress, the evidence of which northern representatives saw on visits to the south for the sporadic north-south talks—and increasingly in foreign countries, where south Korean products appeared in great numbers during the 1980s—the Pyongyang government decided to seek Western technical assistance. However, the 1971 oil crisis upset their plans for paying the costs of importing production facilities from Europe and Japan. As a result of the crisis, and perhaps also of faulty planning, the north Koreans defaulted on their payments to Western and Japanese creditors for over a decade.

In 1972, the north Korean Constitution was changed to emphasize indigenous authority for political philosophy and administration, although the Communist structure was little modified. Minor cosmetic changes reflected the spirit of the July 4 north-south Declaration. The new office of president was established for Kim Il-sung, who by his seventieth birthday in 1982 had been chief of state and government longer than any contemporary national leader.

North Korea's rapid postwar economic progress met increasing obstacles as the economy became more complex and less amenable to centralized planning and direction, and as external aid declined. The south's growth rate exceeded the north's by the mid-1970s. Partly for this reason, and partly because of its radical militancy on the international scene, the north lost much of its early international advantage over the south. These adverse factors contributed to north Korea's halting attempts to open communications with the United States, Japan, and even south Korea; however, the most serious turn of events for the north was the fall of Communism in Europe and the abrupt loss of special economic support from the Soviet Union. Since 1990, north Korea has been struggling for survival, accentuating its policy of *juch'e* self-reliance while trying simultaneously to open urgently needed channels to the West and to cope with the leadership crisis created by the death of Kim Il-sung in 1994.

Conclusion

Korea's long history (see Table 2.1) has been characterized both by persistent assertion of a distinctive Korean identity and by military, political, and cultural assaults from external sources. Given Korea's strategic location and the much greater power, first of China, then of Japan and Russia, it is remarkable that the Korean nation has survived as well as it has. Its weakness at the time of European and U.S. penetration into East Asia and Japan's success at building strength from this penetration led to forty years of subjugation. No sooner was it liberated than ideology and great-power rivalry split it in two. Notwithstanding thirteen hundred years as an autonomous, unified country, Korea is now deeply divided into two hostile states backed by rival external camps. This hostility shows few current signs of receding and deprives the Korean people of the strength they would have as a single state of over 60 million in a good-sized homeland with clear and defensible borders.

Nevertheless, both Koreas have done better than the vast majority of states in the developing world in terms of total economic development and distribution of wealth and income. The north, with its strong ideology and centralized control, economically outdistanced the south in the first twenty years of its separate existence. But from the 1970s on, the south forged ahead with a more flexible, market-oriented system developed out of the confused experimentation of earlier years. In both Koreas, the material welfare of the average citizen has dramatically improved, but the north now lags behind.

The autocratic Korean political tradition, reinforced by north-south hostility and the associated military threat, retarded political development in south Korea until the late 1980s. In the north, the authoritarianism of Marxist-Leninist Communism and Kim Il-sung seems to intensify the old Confucian restraints. Even in the succession of Kim Jong-il to the leadership role of his father, north Korea has so far shown little outward evidence of basic political change.

TABLE 2.1   A Chronological Summary of Korean History

2333 B.C.	Legendary founding of Korea by Tan'gun
1122 B.C.	Legendary arrival of Kija from China to establish Ancient Choson
108 B.C.	Fall of ancient Choson to Chinese; establishment of Chinese commanderies in Korea
313 A.D.	Fall of Nangnang (Chinese Commandery) to Korean Kingdom of Koguryo
4th–7th centuries	Three Kingdoms period (Koguryo, Paekche, Silla)
668	Unification of Korea by Silla
936	Establishment of Koryo Dynasty by Wang Kon
1231	Mongol invasion, leading to Mongol domination
1392	Establishment of Choson Dynasty by Gen. Yi Song-gye
1446	Korean alphabet (*han'gul*) devised by King Sejong
1592–98	Japanese invasion of Korea
1627–37	Manchu invasions
1783	First Christian convert; philosophical reform movement (*Sirhak*) at its height
1876	First Western-style treaty signed with Japan
1882	Treaty of Friendship and Commerce with United States
1884	Failure of modernizers' attempt to seize power

(continues)

TABLE 2.1 (*continued*)

1894	Tonghak Rebellion, starting Sino-Japanese War
1905	Protectorate over Korea after Russo-Japanese War
1910	Annexation of Korea by Japan
1919	Korean independence uprising
1945	Occupation by United States and USSR; division at 38th parallel
1948	North and south Korea become independent states
1950–53	Korean War
1960	Ousting of south Korean President Rhee by "student revolution"; establishment of Second Republic
1961	Coup d'état led by south Korean Gen. Park Chung Hee
1963	Civilian government reestablished as Third Republic
1965	Normalization of relations with Japan
1971	Kim Dae-jung narrowly defeated in south Korean presidential election
1972	North-south Joint Declaration on peaceful unification; establishment of autocratic Fourth (*yusin*) Republic in south Korea; north Korean constitution revised
1979	South Korean President Park assassinated
1980	Seizure of political control in south Korea by Gen. Chun Doo-hwan; Kwangju uprising; Fifth Republic
1983	Attempted assassination of south Korean President by north Korean agents in Rangoon, 17 Koreans killed
1988	Sixth Republic established in South Korea: Roh Tae-woo inaugurated as president
1991–92	North and south Korea hold government-to-government negotiations leading to a nonaggression pact. Both countries join the United Nations
1992–93	North Korea's nuclear program becomes an international problem amid suspicions that it is developing atomic weapons
1993	Longtime opposition leader Kim Young-sam is elected president of the Republic of Korea
1994	Kim Il-Sung, Leader of the Democratic People's Republic of Korea, dies in Pyongyang at the age of 82
1995	Former presidents Chun Doo-hwan and Roh Tae-woo are arrested and charged with corruption and military insurrection in connection with Chun's rise to power in 1979–80

Notes

1. In a short historical summary, it is impossible to note the variations in interpretation by individual historians, among whom there are considerable differences. Such differences are greatest in the earliest and the most recent periods of Korean history. The author is indebted to Professor Dae Sook Suh of the University of Hawaii for making this important point. The account in this book is intended to reflect, as nearly as possible, a coherent consensus of varying schools. Material in this chapter on the pre-Japanese era is based primarily on Ki-baik Lee, *A New History of Korea,* translated by Edward W. Wagner with Edward J. Shultz (Cambridge, Mass.: Harvard University Press, 1985); Professor Lee is generally considered the foremost Korean historian of the postwar era.

2. Cf. Jung-hak Kim, "Ethnological Origins of Korean Nation," *Korea Journal* 3(6) (June 1963):5–8. Some scholars identify these peoples as members of an Altaic family. The term "Tungusic" refers to the basin of the Tunguska rivers in central Siberia (tributaries of the Yenisei River) from which these peoples are believed to have come. The Turkic and Mongol peoples are also considered Altaic.

3. The traditional dates for the founding of the Three Kingdoms are 37 B.C. for Koguryo, 18 B.C. for Paekche, and 57 B.C. for Silla; but if Paekche and Silla existed at that time, they were far smaller and less inclusive than in the Three Kingdoms period. (One still unproven theory holds that the same Puyo people who dominated Paekche, skilled horse-riding warriors, swept on into Japan to become an important component in its national development.)

4. South Korea tends to stress the role of Silla in the formation of the Korean nation, while the Democratic People's Republic of Korea in the north emphasizes the role of Koguryo.

5. A separate Korean-Khitan state called Parhae (Chinese: Pohai) existed in the harsh and rugged northeast, part of old Koguryo, until the tenth century.

6. The Khitan are a Tungusic people like the Koreans. Under the name Jurchen, one part of this people established a kingdom in what is now Manchuria that in 1644 conquered China and ruled it as the Manchu or Ching Dynasty until 1911.

7. The civil and military bureaucracies were parallel but separate in both Koryo and the ensuing Choson (Yi) Dynasty and were collectively termed the *yangban* (literally meaning "both classes"), which became a term for the aristocracy generally.

8. The Japanese *shogun* were men who seized political power and passed it on to their descendants but left the powerless emperors on the throne. There were three successive shogunates, extending from the eleventh to the nineteenth centuries. In form, they resembled European feudalism. Korea's brief experience under the Ch'oe family was at most a rudimentary and faint parallel; Korea never had a similar feudalistic system of government.

9. North Korean scholars' research on the seventeenth- and eighteenth-century literati of the *Sirhak* school also notes the difference between Korean and Chinese culture. See *Progressive Scholars at the Close of the Feudal Age in Korea* (Pyongyang: Ministry of Culture and Propaganda, DPRK, 1955).

10. It is a sign of the institutional weakness of the Choson dynasty monarchy vis-à-vis the *yangban* that two Choson Dynasty kings were denied the posthumous "temple names" that were normally given as a sign of respect. Yonsan'gun was one; the other was Kwanghaegun (1608–1623).

11. The standard work on the early Choson Dynasty purges is Edward W. Wagner, *The Literati Purges: Political Conflict in Early Yi Korea,* Harvard East Asian Monographs No. 58 (Cambridge, Mass.: East Asian Research Center, distributed by Harvard University Press, 1974).

12. Tokugawa Ieyasu succeeded Hideyoshi as leader of Japan under the nominal but powerless emperor. He and his descendants ruled Japan as *shogun* (in effect, regents or chief ministers) from 1600 to 1868, when the emperor's power was restored by a group of rebellious young aristocrats.

13. For the dynamics of the Choson Dynasty's political system, see James B. Palais, *Politics and Policy in Traditional Korea,* Harvard East Asian Series No. 82 (Cambridge, Mass.: Harvard University Press, 1975), especially pp. 1–22. For examples of issues raised by the much-discussed phenomenon of political factionalism in the Choson Dynasty and at-

tempts to control it, see JaHyun Kim Haboush, *A Heritage of Kings: One Man's Monarchy in the Confucian World,* Studies in Oriental Culture No. 21 (New York: Columbia University Press, 1988), especially chapters 3 and 4.

14. The agricultural cycle of planting and harvest, essential to the people's livelihood, depended upon knowledge of when the various tasks should be done to take best advantage of the weather. Preparation of the calendar called for sophisticated mathematics and astronomical observations that were completely beyond a largely illiterate population.

15. For a description of the traditional Chinese international order and the place of Korea in it, see M. Frederick Nelson, *Korea and the Old Orders in Eastern Asia* (Baton Rouge: Louisiana State University Press, 1945).

16. See W. E. Griffis, *Corea, The Hermit Nation* (New York: AMS Press, 1971; reprint of 9th, or 1911, edition), the earliest English-language book on Korea of the nineteenth century and one of a very few.

17. Harold F. Cook, *Korea's 1884 Incident: Its Background and Kim Ok-kyun's Elusive Dream* (Seoul: Royal Asiatic Society, Korea Branch, 1972). See also In K. Hwang, *The Korean Reform Movement of the 1880s: A Study of Transition in Intra-Asian Relations* (Cambridge, Mass.: Schenkman Publishing Co., 1978).

18. Benjamin Weems described the *Tonghak* movement in his book, *Reform, Rebellion, and the Heavenly Way* (Tucson: University of Arizona Press for the Association for Asian Studies, 1964).

19. To symbolize Korea's new sovereignty and equality, the Korean king proclaimed himself emperor in 1897.

20. See Hilary Conroy, *The Japanese Seizure of Korea, 1868–1910: A Study of Realism and Idealism in International Relations* (Philadelphia: University of Pennsylvania Press, 1960), and C. I. Eugene Kim and Han-Kyo Kim, *Korea and the Politics of Imperialism, 1876–1910* (Berkeley: University of California Press, 1967).

21. Regarding the Japanese occupation of Korea, see Ramon H. Myers and Mark R. Peattie, eds., *The Japanese Colonial Empire, 1895–1945* (Princeton: Princeton University Press, 1984); Bruce Cumings, *The Origins of the Korean War,* Vol. 1, *Liberation and the Emergence of Separate Regimes, 1945–1947* (Princeton: Princeton University Press, 1981), chapters 1 and 2; Andrew Grajdanzev, *Modern Korea* (New York: Institute of Pacific Relations; distributed by the John Day Co., 1944); and Andrew C. Nahm, ed., *Korea Under Japanese Colonial Rule: Studies of the Policy and Techniques of Japanese Colonialism,* Korea Study Series 2: Proceedings of the Conference on Korea, November 12–14, 1970 (Kalamazoo: Center for Korean Studies, Western Michigan University, 1973).

22. Han-Kyo Kim, "The Japanese Colonial Administration in Korea—An Opinion," in *Korea Under Japanese Colonial Rule,* pp. 45, 51–52.

23. See Chong-Sik Lee, *The Politics of Korean Nationalism* (Berkeley: University of California Press, 1963).

24. An excellent discussion of the origins of the 38th parallel division is Michael Sandusky's book, *America's Parallel* (Alexandria, Va.: Old Dominion Press, 1983). I have discussed this problem in more detail in Chapter 8.

25. Brief biographies of Yo Un-hyong (Lyuh Woon Hyung) and most other Korean leaders mentioned in this book can be found in Ainslie T. Embree, editor in chief, *Encyclopedia of Asian History* (New York: Charles Scribner's Sons, 1985).

26. For a discussion of the People's Republic and its background, see Bruce Cumings, *The Origins of the Korean War,* pp. 68–100.

27. This incident occurred during my duty in Korea in 1945 and 1946, in the city where I was stationed.

28. The northern occupation zone comprised all or most of five Korean provinces: North and South Hamgyong, North and South Pyongan, and Hwanghae. A portion of the thinly populated and mountainous Kangwon Province also lay north of the 38th parallel. (The provincial boundaries were subsequently redefined by the northern government to add Yanggang and Chagang provinces along the border with China, and Hwanghae has been divided into North and South Hwanghae, thus bringing the total number of provinces, including Kangwon, to nine—the same as in the south.) The southern zone in 1945 included eight provinces: Kyonggi (in which Seoul, the capital, was situated), much of Kangwon, North and South Ch'ungch'ong, North and South Kyongsang, and North and South Cholla. In 1946, Cheju Island was separated from South Cholla and became a ninth province. A small strip of Hwanghae Province lay south of the 38th parallel and was administered as part of the southern zone until the Korean War, although it could be reached by land from the rest of the zone only by passing through the northern zone.

29. *First Report of the United Nations Temporary Commission on Korea,* United Nations General Assembly Official Records, Supplement No. 9, 3d Session (Lake Success, 1948); *Second Part of the Report* (Paris, 1949).

30. See Bruce Cumings, *The Origins of the Korean War,* chapter 9.

31. See, for example, reports by the Political Advisers to the Commanding General, USAFIK (Benninghoff and Langdon) in 1946; *Foreign Relations of the United States, 1946,* Vol. 8, *The Far East,* pp. 615–616, 662, 704–705.

32. Acheson listed the areas that were considered within the U.S. Pacific defense perimeter (not including Korea) and said that other nations should look to the United Nations for their defense. At the time, the failure of the collective-security provisions of the UN Charter was not as clear as it has become since. For the text of his speech, see *U.S. Department of State Bulletin* 22(551) (January 23, 1950):111–118.

33. For accounts of the Korean War, see (among others) Robert Leckie, *Conflict: The History of the Korean War* (New York: G. P. Putnam's Sons, 1962), and Jon Halliday and Bruce Cumings, *Korea: The Unknown War* (New York: Pantheon Books, 1988).

34. See Callum A. MacDonald, *Korea: The War Before Vietnam* (New York: The Free Press, 1986), pp. 249–256.

35. The *Encyclopaedia Britannica* lists U.S. casualties in the Korean War as 33,729 killed, 103,284 wounded, and 10,218 captured. The corresponding figures for south Korean forces were 70,000, 150,000, and 80,000; for other nations, 4,786, 11,297, and 2,769. North Korean and Chinese battle casualties were estimated at 1.6 million, plus 400,000 deaths from disease; around 500,000 south Koreans and 3 million north Koreans are believed to have died from causes related to the war. *Encyclopaedia Britannica,* 14th ed., Vol. 13, 1973, p. 475.

36. Korean troops were pressed into service by the Mongols in 1274 and 1281 for their unsuccessful attempts to invade Japan. In the late fourteenth century, King Kongmin sent an expeditionary force into Manchuria against the then-weakened Mongols. William E. Henthorn, *A History of Korea* (New York: The Free Press, 1971), pp. 121–122, 129.

3
Korean Society and Culture

Introduction

The people of the United States, like people of all countries, are very proud of their national culture and identity. Most of that culture really came from elsewhere. Cultural values, legal traditions, and ideas of democracy from Greece and Rome; religious traditions from Palestine; myths and legends from northern Europe; language from England and France; and art and music from Europe and Africa are examples. In fact, the United States has no indigenous tradition except that of the Native Americans. Any culture that can be uniquely attributed to the United States is recent and peripheral: baseball, rock and roll, blue jeans, fast food. The particular blend of borrowings, and what has been made of them, is what ultimately establishes the U.S. cultural identity.

In somewhat the same way, the modern society and culture of Korea are a blend of historical influences.[1] But this blend is no mere copy, and its roots are ancient. The individuality of the Korean people and their sense of ethnic identity have both survived and accommodated Chinese, Japanese, and Western impact. Despite its thorough integration of Chinese culture over many centuries and despite the traumatic inroads of Japan and the West, Korea keeps its own distinct culture.

Fitting Western values and behavior patterns into Korean tradition is an ongoing process, which began only a century ago (although elements of Western thought had attracted Korean scholars by the eighteenth century). This process, often painful, is an unavoidable part of Korean modernization and industrialization. The Koreans must therefore be understood in terms of both a relatively fixed tradition and a rapidly changing present. Because English-speaking readers are already familiar with Western culture, the emphasis in this chapter is placed upon Korean tradition; but it must be understood that the Koreans themselves are moving away from tradition toward a new cultural synthesis.

The Western cultural impact has been all the stronger because it came at a time when both Chinese and Korean traditional orders were already weakened from internal causes. The consequent rapid change in values and customs has led to uncertainty regarding the basic guidelines of behavior and aspiration, and sometimes personal trauma and social unrest. For a time after World War II, this cultural uncertainty, coupled with Japanese distortions, misled many Koreans into disparaging their own heritage. Among the most poignant memories of U.S. military government officials in the post–World War II years were the expressions of shame and inferiority by many Koreans in speaking of their own history, especially their failure to ward off foreign imperialism.

Since then, the work of both Korean and foreign scholars has rediscovered Korea's proud indigenous tradition and the Korean contribution to the Chinese heritage. For example, the writings of great Korean scholars, such as Yi Yulgok and

Yi T'oegye in the seventeenth century, are now recognized in Japan and China as contributions to the Confucian literature.[2] Contemporary Korean culture is assimilating Western culture as it did the Chinese, and Korean authors and artists are gaining recognition in the West.

Korea's own adaptations to the needs of a modern industrial society—notwithstanding the dramatic differences between traditional and industrialized values and ways of life—are a renewed demonstration of the nation's vitality; they have thus far been fairly successful, albeit unevenly, in spite of the enormous problems involved. Korea's economic and military achievements since the Korean War have given both leaders and public a renewed sense of their own worth. Koreans are now reasserting their identity in both parts of Korea. Cultural borrowings are being critically reexamined for their relevance to current Korean needs and aspirations.

Nevertheless, despite their dramatic progress since 1945, the people in both parts of Korea still have an underlying sense of insecurity. This feeling is engendered not only by their historical experience and the present military confrontation but also by the uncertainties of cultural change. New economic problems have recently added to this insecurity. One reaction to this is Korean criticism of the behavior of other nations. The United States, for example, is often blamed for its effect on Korean culture (as well as for its other sins, including the division of the country), although it is the Koreans themselves who have accepted U.S. movies, music, blue jeans, English slang, and the rest. All this is part of the painful process of cultural accommodation.

Family

The family is basic to the life of every human being. Its importance in Korea has for centuries been greatly reinforced by Confucian philosophy, received from China and fully accepted into Korean culture by the fifteenth century. This philosophy emphasizes family relationships as fundamental to the entire social fabric and includes relatives far beyond the simple parent-children household. Although the nuclear family (father, mother, children) as a living unit is becoming the norm in the big cities, the traditional Confucian view of family relationships and responsibilities continues as a strong influence on individual attitudes and behavior.

In the Confucian view, the family has the central role in society. Three of the traditional five Confucian social relationships deal with family: father to son, husband to wife, and elder brother to younger brother (senior to junior). The fourth relationship, of ruler and minister, extends a family analogy to the entire polity. Moreover, all but the fifth—the relationship between friend and friend—are based on relations of superior to inferior, not of equals.

Accordingly, most social relationships are conceived in terms of hierarchical order between unequal pairs. The senior has responsibility for wise and benevolent direction of behavior, and for the welfare of those in his charge; the junior has the duty of respect and obedience. Filial piety—children's obedience and re-spect toward their parents—is a cardinal Confucian virtue, which the literature extols even to the point of caricature, as when grown men and women are por-trayed as playing like children before their elderly parents to amuse them. Al-though the traditional relationships are changing in both north and south Korea, and obedience within the family is less strict and formalized, respect of juniors for seniors is still strong, as is the seniors' expectation of obedience and decorum.

The Confucian family unit is not only based on junior-senior relations; it is also a collective in both space and time. In the Confucian ethic, individuals think of themselves as part of this collective, which extends (in diminishing intensity) to eight degrees of relationship (illustrated in the diagram, Figure 3.1) and links the living with deceased ancestors. The personal satisfactions of family members are linked with the fortunes and status of their family and relatives (notwith-standing rivalries and tensions within the family group). So-called ancestor wor-ship is simply a continuing relationship with family members who have died. Family genealogies, called *chokpo*, are carefully maintained and preserved.

Feelings of mutual responsibility among family members have traditionally been very strong. They outweigh responsibilities of neighborliness, which in turn

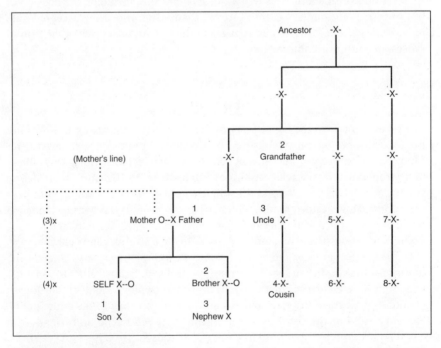

FIGURE 3.1   Chart of family relationships (adapted from Pak Ki-hyuk and Sidney D. Gamble, *The Changing Korean Village,* Seoul: Shin-hung Press for the Royal Asiatic Society, Korea Branch, 1975, pp. 58–59)

outweigh those of citizenship. Providing jobs for one's relatives, condemned as nepotism in Western societies, was—and to a limited extent still is—both a virtue and a matter of course in Korea. In the old days, officials promoted to high office were expected to look after their less fortunate relatives, to the point where the burden made such appointments mixed blessings for their recipients.

It is important to recognize that family responsibility is still the main basis for the individual's social security. Governmental and private responsibility for the welfare of the unrelated individual is a new idea and only beginning to develop, as in south Korea's universal medical insurance and limited pension system. North Korea claims to be more advanced in this area, with elaborate provisions for every human need and loyalty to the leader, the Party, and society as a whole replacing old family loyalties. There is a school of thought in south Korea that holds family responsibility for the welfare of its members to be better, because it is cheaper and more responsive to individual need than governmental welfare programs. The more traditional emphasis on the family and on the virtue of filial piety is consistent with this outlook.

The Confucian ideal of family life was "five generations under one roof." This ideal was not often fulfilled, because of the cost and because the traditional life expectancy was not much over thirty years (it is now around seventy years in both parts of Korea). Moreover, in Korea it was normal for married children other than the oldest son to set up their own households. This process led in former times to whole villages of close relatives. However, three generations (parents, children, and children's children) were, and often still are, frequently under one roof.

In modern cities, the Western-style nuclear family is increasingly common because of the small space and high cost of high-rise apartments as well as the growing desire of young people to form and raise their own families, independent of their parents. Nevertheless, it is still considered normal for parents to live with their eldest son in their old age, and the American practice of packing parents off to nursing homes is abhorrent to Koreans. Reunions of extended families, particularly on three traditional occasions, New Year's and the spring and fall holidays, are common; these may include ceremonies to honor ancestors, who are often buried in a separate family cemetery. Intercity buses and trains are crammed at these times.

Family relationship in Korea exists on four levels. The basic family group comprises the nuclear family and (to a diminishing extent) people within five degrees of relationship (see Figure 3.1), among whom the senior active male member formerly had authority over the whole. The mourning group, which honors deceased ancestors at funerals and subsequent formal occasions, includes eight degrees of relationship. Larger and less well defined is the common descent group, recognizing a noted individual as common ancestor. Finally, there is the clan, comprising all persons descended from an actual or mythical ancient progenitor. Many mourning groups, and even common-ancestor groups, still maintain genealogical records and ceremonial properties.

Marriage, crucial to the continuity of the family, was traditionally too important to be left to the man and woman concerned. It was arranged between the families of the prospective bride and groom for mutual advantage, usually through a go-between who assisted in assuring compatibility by means of a mixture of common sense and astrology. The bride and groom, in theory, had no contact until the wedding; after the wedding, the bride cut her ties with her own family and entered her husband's—often to be mercilessly exploited until she, in her turn, could exploit her own daughter-in-law. A married woman continued to use her own family name for legal purposes and was entered by that name in her husband's family register (to recognize her father's family, rather than her separate identity; her own given name was traditionally not recorded).

From the family's point of view, selection of a wife did not necessarily involve education or talent, so long as she was of good background, could be a good mother, and could perform her assigned household duties. It was perhaps natural, therefore, that men often sought female companionship outside the home. If a man was wealthy enough to support a concubine, there was only weak social opposition to it; the children of the concubine might suffer social disadvantage, but not moral opprobrium. Social gatherings of men outside the home often included the services of professional entertainers, *kisaeng,* who could make intelligent conversation, recite and even compose poetry, sing, dance, and play musical instruments. Sexual services might or might not be involved, although solicitous behavior and physical contact usually were.

Today, many marriages are made by men and women themselves on the basis of emotional attraction and perceived compatibility; but the approval of both families remains important. Marriages are still arranged, but no longer in disregard of the couple's wishes or preferences. There is now more social disapproval of concubinage; it still exists, particularly for the wealthy, but it is increasingly rare.

Until recently, it was both immoral and illegal for a man to marry a woman within the same clan. There are only a few hundred family names in Korea (all but about ten of them monosyllabic, written with one Chinese character),[3] and for many of these names there is only one clan, meaning that persons of the same surname could not marry. However, there are thirty-two Kim clans, and some other surnames also have multiple clans. Since the mid-1950s, easing of the law has been under discussion, but marriage within a clan is still frowned upon by traditionalists.

For centuries it has been the custom to give all children of the same generation within a common-ancestor group a common generation name. This name is selected by a recognized senior relative. Part of the Chinese character used for the generation name usually represents one of five traditional elements—wood, fire, earth, metal, and water, in that order—used in succeeding generations. Thus, each individual has a name composed of three characters (each of one syllable): family name first, then personal and generation names (usually linked by a hyphen when romanized). However, some families give only one personal name, and in families with two-syllable surnames, there may be four characters. This practice became general only during the Choson Dynasty, so that older names (such as Ulchi Mun-dok, defender of Koguryo) do not necessarily follow the rule. (Foreigners should note that among adults there is a strong taboo against addressing people by their personal names, except among very close friends; titles or "pen-names" are used instead.)

In north Korea, Communist social and economic norms have been systematically inculcated for fifty years. It is hard to say how much real change in the people's attitude and behavior has resulted, but personal observations by visitors to the north, and some of the official ideology, suggest that there is considerable continuity with the past. The personality cult of Kim Il-sung was rooted in the old familism. His father, mother, and grandfather were held up as models in official publications, and his son, Kim Jong-il, became his designated successor. Indeed, everything about the way Kim Jong-il behaved after his father's death suggests that filial piety is still a cardinal virtue in the north Korean social system. Within each family, and to some extent in the wider circle of close relatives, the old hierarchical relationships still exist. The collectivism of the Korean political and economic order is akin to the collectivism inherent in the traditional family system.[4]

However, many aspects of north Korean life obviously weaken traditional family solidarity. Decisions affecting people's lives, including place of residence, education, employment, and even marriage are controlled by Party and state authorities rather than by families or individuals. Since private property, other than modest personal possessions, has been eliminated, inheritance is impossible. The cult of Kim Il-sung transferred to the Great Leader at least some of the loyalty and affection traditionally given to parents, and the ostentatious expressions of respect for Kim Jong-il as his father's heir continue the pattern.

Family is important in north Korean social standing, but the traditional status ranking is reversed. Descendants and relatives of former landlords and capitalists are officially discriminated against in education and employment, whereas families of outstanding workers and revolutionaries are favored. Honor is therefore least, under the current ideology, for the ancestors of families who would be most likely to follow the old custom.

Community Life

The rural community was the center of social activity for most Koreans for thousands of years. By the first century of the Choson Dynasty, the community also was guided by Confucian principles; a sixteenth-century scholar, Cho Kwang-jo (1482–1519) institutionalized them in the form of a "village code."[5] Except for taxes, labor on public works, military service, and occasionally the control of major disputes, the villages managed their own affairs. They were largely self-sufficient, with a simple barter economy. Markets held every five days in local centers and itinerant peddlers supplemented village handicrafts. As late as 1960, over 70 percent of the south Korean population lived in centers of fewer than 50,000 people.

Village affairs, including maintenance of social order and propriety, were traditionally governed by an informal council of elders from the constituent families; one of them might be recognized by the central government as village chief, but his authority (except in actions ordered by the state) was subject to the elders' consensus. The process did not originally involve elections or voting.

Industrialization and urbanization began to affect Korean community life in a significant way only in the twentieth century. The Japanese occupation, World War II, the division of Korea, and the Korean War all combined with the industrialization process to uproot traditional agrarian communities. Yet traditions persist to a considerable extent in the shrinking agricultural population and even in the urban consciousness. The continuing strength of family and community bonds was demonstrated by the capacity of refugees during and after the Korean War to move as groups to places of safety and to look out for one another's welfare.

Although attempts were made even during the Japanese period to reform village life, they were resisted as exploitation. In south Korea there was relatively little economic or social change until nearly a generation after liberation. The U.S. military authorities brought in the 4-H movement (an agricultural youth movement sponsored by the Department of Agriculture in the United States), but its impact was limited. However, one dramatic reform in this period, begun by the military government and pushed to completion by the new south Korean government even in wartime, was universal land reform. This program gave ownership of all agricultural land to the tillers, limiting holdings to 3 hectares (about 7.5 acres), with an average of less than 1 hectare (2.5 acres). Although criticized for causing some inefficiency of scale, this measure won the hearts of the farmers as nothing else ever had, and helped, at least in the earlier years of the republic, to maintain consistent rural support for the regime.

In 1971, the New Community Movement (*Saema'ul undong*) was launched throughout south Korea to mobilize villagers in their own service. Thatched roofs gave place to sheet iron and then tile; irrigation was improved; feeder roads and community halls were built; wells were dug; cash crops were planted (some in new plastic hothouses); boundaries among tiny plots were rationalized; techniques were improved, including planting of "green revolution" rice varieties and mechanization. These projects were generally carried out with local labor and resources, with the government providing small amounts of start-up money and some materials, such as cement.[6]

Coupled with other government programs, such as electrification, road construction, grain price supports, subsidized fertilizer, and an agricultural extension program, the movement had dramatic impact. Rural family incomes were brought up to a par with urban incomes by the mid-1970s for the first time in Korean history, while all incomes shared in the rapid national growth. Urban incomes then rose dramatically, leaving farm incomes behind at a level of around 80 percent by the late 1980s. Nearly 40 percent of rural income was from nonfarm activities, and farm households carried considerable debt.

Unlike their U.S. counterparts, Korean farmers live together in hamlets, surrounded by the fields to which they go daily to plant, till, and reap. Farming is a family enterprise; but the major tasks of transplanting and harvesting are shared by the community. Hamlets are made up of one to three dozen families each in its own home, perhaps with one or two small shops. Several hamlets may make up an administrative village unit. Virtually all villages in south Korea are connected to main highways by all-weather feeder roads; the villages have electricity and radios, and most households have television. All children receive at least an elementary education. As a result of wartime dislocation and other factors, villages are often no longer dominated by a few families. Village heads are still named from the local population, but the central government enters into local affairs far more than under the Choson Dynasty. Most villages have their own New Community Movement councils and representatives, in addition to traditional mutual-assistance groups for various purposes, called *kye*. Thus, the traditional decision-making processes are changing, with less automatic authority going with status and seniority, and with less reliance on Confucian tradition. However, there have been no elective local government councils since 1961. Their reestablishment has been under discussion for several years.

In north Korea, after an initial distribution of farmland to individual families in the late 1940s, the traditional villages have been incorporated into collectives of township size, each with its Party committee and administration linking it to the county and thence to the central government. In theory, the farmers collectively own their enterprise, sharing the fruits on the basis of their labor input and supplementing their income with small private plots. Since individuals are frequently moved from one collective to another, community solidarity is probably much less than in pre-Communist days.

The center of gravity of Korean community life has shifted from the rural villages to towns and cities—more so in the south than in the north. According to 1993 estimates, 75 percent of the south Korean population lives in cities of over 50,000—more than 10 million, as already noted, in the capital city and a total of almost that number in three other major cities. Thus the old village life, with its close-knit relationships, its festivals and ceremonies, its folk music, its barter economy and handicrafts—and its grinding poverty—are only a memory for urban Koreans, like the Westerners' illusion of Grandmother's house in the country, "over the river and through the woods." Nevertheless, ties with relatives in native villages persist. For those still living in rural areas, the same cohesive, kinship-centered life continues, and cooperation and barter remain important social features, along with television viewing and some modern conveniences (virtually all villages have electricity, but many still do not have central water systems and fewer have sewerage systems).

Traditional house styles vary in Korea by province and by socioeconomic status, but in many areas the floor plan of the average home has been an L-shape, with the kitchen forming the base, or a U-shape—in either case around a small central courtyard, the whole enclosed by a high wall. (Many new homes have recently been constructed in rectangular designs.) Walls were constructed of clay and straw; the roof, supported by poles and crosspieces, was of straw thatch, replaced every year or two. Windows were small and covered with a special strong paper. A narrow open porch along the front of the house connected the two or three living rooms, which also served for sleeping.

A unique feature of Korean house design was the heating system, called *ondol:* The hot gases from the kitchen fire passed through a serpentine channel, built with large, flat stones, beneath the floors of the rooms, to a chimney at the end of the house. (Sometimes there was one wooden-floored living room without *ondol,* for summer use and entertaining.) The stones, sealed with clay and covered with a special heavy oiled paper, retained the heat after the fire died down, and the warm floors provided efficient radiant heating.

In all but the smallest houses, it was traditional for men and women to sleep in separate rooms, young children with the women. Meals were eaten by the men on small individual tables brought to their rooms; women ate what was left over in the kitchen. Affluent houses had a special room (*sarangbang*) where men met and entertained; women were not supposed to be visible. The toilet was in an outhouse; if bathing was done at home rather than at a bathhouse or in a local stream, a large tub was used (people washed themselves from a bucket before entering it). Such homes had little furniture, except for chests to store bedding and clothing. People lived on the floor, sleeping with a pad (*yo*) below and a quilt (*ibul*) above, eating and studying on low tables. There were no chairs, except in Western-style rooms that were added to homes of the rich in the nineteenth century. Pets and other animals were never allowed in the living rooms.

By the mid-1980s, rapid economic progress had forced many of the traits of industrialized social life on Seoul and to a considerable extent on other large cities as well: fixed-hour employment, commuting long hours to and from work, the pressure for constant, rapid movement and upward striving, heavy use of mass transport and motor vehicles, traffic jams, pollution, noise, mass advertising, and many hours of television viewing.

For about half of the population of Seoul and to a lesser but growing extent in other cities of south Korea, apartments (many of them in large, high-rise buildings) have replaced single houses, although most people still prefer a freestanding home. There has been an acute urban housing shortage since the Korean War, because of war damage, urban in-migration, and the change in family living patterns. According to the 1985 census, the ratio of households to housing units rose from 1.49 in 1980 to 1.53 in 1985 (i.e., there were over three families for every two houses or apartments, although the multiple families might be related). Over the same five years, the number of households grew 20.2 percent, compared with a population growth of 8.1 percent—meaning that the old large families were breaking down into more and smaller families. In 1990 President Roh Tae-woo embarked upon an ambitious program to build 2 million new housing units, 75 percent of which were apartments. The new units raised the housing supply rate to 79.1 percent by 1993—an improvement but still short of the need.[7]

The same trend seems to hold in north Korea as well, although statistics are lacking. The difference in housing between north and south is that in south Korea most housing is obtained through the free market by individual families for whatever price they can afford, but in north Korea housing is assigned and subsidized by the state, according to the political and other qualifications of the families.

Family life in south Korea still shows some of the traditional patterns, but social modernization, growing affluence, and scarcity of space in a densely populated country have brought much change. Some families have adopted Western furniture and lifestyles. For the majority who have not, the most significant change is in the position of women in the home. Women move as freely as men around and outside the home, and modern kitchens and streamlined menus have lessened their burden. Husband and wife of the younger generation usually sleep in the same room, as in the West.

The *ondol* heating system is still preferred, in apartments as in private homes. However, the old wood kitchen fires have been replaced with coal briquettes or with oil or natural gas. In many homes, hot water circulating in pipes does the work of the traditional serpentine flues (there are many deaths each winter from leaks of flue gas from the burning of coal briquettes). Linoleum is replacing oiled paper as floor covering. Windows are of glass, not paper; roofs are tiled. For most people, sitting and sleeping on the floor continues to be the norm, both by custom and for economy of space. Shoes are removed before entering a home, as both tradition and cleanliness demand. Apartments cannot preserve the traditional floor plan; the entrance court, for example, is reduced to a small entryway.

School and workplace have partially displaced the family as social centers in the cities; fast-food restaurants are multiplying, along with high-priced restaurants and bars for business contacts. Nevertheless, traditional family relations continue to be more important than in the West, even among the most urbanized. (The extent to which this remains true in north Korea, with its emphasis on Party-oriented loyalty, is unknown.) Moreover, in the south, the myriad traditional small enterprises—both along streets and alleys and within vast market areas—manage to hold their own against proliferating modern department stores. In both south and north, the state has promoted the organization of "block" groups of residents, somewhat equivalent in size to rural villages.[8] Heads of these groups are expected to maintain local order and provide information to the authorities on local conditions, including suspicious behavior of residents. (Throughout East Asia there is a tradition for this arrangement reaching back to Tang Dynasty China of the seventh century, where five-family groups were organized for the same purpose.)

The Individual and Interpersonal Relations

The Korean individual's view of himself and his place in society traditionally centered on his family, of which he considered himself a part. In the Confucian tradition, the dominance of men was unquestioned in form, although not infrequently the facts were otherwise. The "henpecked" husband is very much a part of Korean folklore. Male children were preferred because only they could carry on the family line.

It was the man's duty before his parents and his ancestors to assure the continuity and prosperity of the family; his success was their success, his failure their failure, his shame their shame. Social responsibility beyond the family extended to the community, and in some measure to the person of the ruler and his officials, but not to society as a whole. Anyone outside the established circles and lines of relationship was viewed as a "nonperson," to whom only the universal courtesy for strangers was due.

In today's Korea, although family ties remain a far more important component of attitudes and behavior than in most Western countries, the sense of family responsibility is diminishing as nuclear family living becomes common. In urban areas, moreover, there is not a strong sense of community responsibility; rather, there is the usual anonymity and isolation of industrialized city life. The hurrying people on the streets of Seoul appear to the foreign visitor to be rude in their pushing and shoving, as though others were inanimate objects; such behavior contrasts sharply with Korean decorum in more controlled situations. In a sense, this is the way Koreans still feel about people, such as casual passersby, with whom they have no established social relationship. The sense of universalized civic responsibility and civility is still weak.

In south Korea, at least, part of the role of family and community has been taken over by groupings based on common local origin, common school experience, and common workplace. People within such groups have a strong sense of shared identity and mutual responsibility. Business firms operate on the same autocratic and somewhat family-style lines found in Japan (and in an earlier era in the United States), although there is more movement among firms than in Japan. Many formal organizations bring together people of common origin and alumni of schools at all levels. These associations function to some extent as mutual-aid institutions, looking out for less fortunate members through the use of influence and connections. In north Korea, the main visible groupings are those based on Party, state, workplace, and place of residence.

The status of women in Korean society has greatly advanced since the Choson Dynasty and is still rapidly evolving in both south and north Korea. Christianity, from its beginnings in Korea, emphasized the equality of all persons under God (although early congregations still seated men and women separately). An American Methodist named Mary B. Scranton founded the first girls' school in Korea in 1886—the nucleus for the noted Ewha Woman's University. This influence, together with the example of modernized societies elsewhere, has had great effect. Women's access to education is virtually the same as for men. Women in considerable numbers pursue high-prestige occupations; there have been women cabinet members, women members of the legislature, and women presidents of universities. Many women leaders are interested in advancing the status of their sex.

Despite women's progress, male dominance continues. Male babies are still preferred; women workers largely fill low-paid factory and household jobs—often to earn a dowry for marriage—and women still do most of the household work. Family law is still based on male superiority in marriage, divorce, household administration, and inheritance. However, revision of the law is under discussion. An increasingly strong women's movement in south Korea is applying pressure for this and other reforms such as remedies for sexual harassment. A government-supported Women's Development Institute encourages further progress.[9] Two-worker families are becoming increasingly common in the cities. (Labor-short north Korea has gone further than the south in this respect. The north has also promoted a high birthrate.)

Children in Korea were traditionally reared by women until, by Confucian precept, boys and girls were separated at the age of seven years (in traditional East Asia, a child was counted one year old at birth). Their early environment was loving and permissive; when outside the house, children were strapped to their mothers' backs, and mothers nursed them for as long as two years or more. The father and male relatives were remote authority figures until the age when sexes were separated. For boys, the transition from a sheltered infancy to the stern discipline of subsequent youth was often traumatic.

Much has been made of this tradition in trying to explain the high level of the average Korean's self-confidence, on the one hand, and his underlying rebelliousness, on the other. In any event, these child-rearing patterns are changing, particularly in the cities: Fathers are sharing in the raising of children, the sexes are no longer separated to the same extent, and all children get the same schooling. Observers differ on how much change in attitudes and values has occurred as a consequence of this and other modern trends; but all agree that in many respects Koreans do not think or react like Westerners.

In interpersonal relations, age and relative status still carry some of their traditional importance: The junior owes respect to the senior, and the senior carries the obligation to look out for the junior. It is still impolite to smoke or cross one's legs before a senior without permission. Koreans bow to superiors; they also shake hands with acquaintances. Calling cards are usually exchanged when introductions are made, partly to establish social relationship. It is still customary for people to call upon their parents, senior relatives, and office or factory superiors at New Year's and at other occasions, such as a death in the family. It is usual in such calls to bring a present—a pleasant custom, but one that has sometimes deteriorated into bribery. Koreans are alert to one another's state of mind, and respect for others' personal dignity and social status ("face") has high prior-

ity in social intercourse. Outspokenness, therefore, is not ordinarily a Korean
virtue.

Attitudes and World View

Korean behavior is the result of three main factors: the traditional Confucian
ethic; an underlying individualism that is somewhat at odds with that ethic; and
an overlay of Western ideas.[10] In the traditional Confucian order, harmony
among men was the supreme goal. Lack of harmony might disrupt the order of
nature; thus a linkage was perceived between social disorder and natural calamities, such as floods or earthquakes. It was the ruler's duty to maintain social order
by his benevolence and superior wisdom and that of his ministers. It was the people's duty to obey the benevolent ruler's commands. Similar relationships applied
to each family.

The standard for just rule was an ancient Golden Age, described in the Confucian classics; the emphasis was on understanding the wisdom of the ancient sages
(although interpretations of that wisdom might differ). Violation of the rules of
right conduct resulted in a sense of personal and family shame before one's superiors or fellows. It was shame before others, rather than a feeling of guilt from an
inner conscience, that regulated behavior. In a relatively static agrarian society,
this past-oriented and situation-oriented approach worked well—indeed, it sustained both China and Korea for over two thousand years.

Two basic characteristics of traditional Korean society followed from these attitudes. First, the whole of human activity was viewed as a seamless web of interpersonal relations; no distinction was necessary between political, economic, social, religious, and artistic endeavors. All were within the ruler's responsibility to
control. (Confucius gave low status to manufacture and commerce; the essential
economic activity was farming, although commercial and industrial activity were
evident in Korea, on a small scale at least, since the mid-seventeenth century.[11]
There was no such thing as free private enterprise, except to the extent that the
ruler chose to permit it.

Second, there was no legitimate room for differing opinions concerning policy
decisions between opposing groups, except for the narrow area of interpretation
of the classics. The ruler gave his command, or discussion among ministers led to
decisions by consensus, which then had total authority. The same pattern prevailed in families and communities. Contending factions existed nonetheless, but
they were not sanctioned by the culture, and usually all but one of them were excluded from power at any one time.

Human nature was also perceived as a continuous whole. The Western separation of body, mind, and spirit did not exist. Western observers have suggested that
in East Asia, for this reason, the region of the navel was traditionally considered
the center of the body, rather than the head. A person's feelings, as well as mental

processes, were an essential part of decision and action. Thus the Western priority for cold logic had no Korean counterpart. Moreover, contemplation—drawing upon one's whole being for guidance—rather than Western-style reasoning was a basis for decision and action. This difference is evident in comparing Korean martial arts with Western-style boxing or wrestling: Contemplation is even more important than physical action and takes more time. Contemporary Koreans have proven themselves in all lines of Western intellectual and scientific endeavor, but their thought processes are nonetheless still influenced by this tradition.

Within the tradition, the individual's attitude toward the self and the self's future was in terms of cultivation rather than improvement—that is, realizing one's innate capacities, rather than transcending them. The ideal to be achieved was true wisdom or sageness. Mastery of the classics, and self-discipline and right conduct, could bring full realization of one's inherent capabilities. For some, self-cultivation might include solitary contemplation and esoteric practices of various kinds, such as breathing exercises—akin to the ideas of Zen Buddhism, but not inherently religious. In seeking to fulfill oneself, of course, each person was conscious of responsibility to the family collective.

Although this Confucian world view is changing in Korea, it still strongly conditions Korean attitudes and behavior. However, now as in previous times, it coexists with a strong, aggressive underlying sense of individual assertiveness and ambition. Often, therefore, men's burning desire for wealth, power, and social recognition tears through the network of Confucian harmony and propriety. Koreans are gamblers for high stakes; they take extraordinary risks to further their ambitions. Success, wealth, and status are flaunted for all to admire. This tendency makes the distribution of wealth in south Korea seem more unequal than it really is.

In viewing the world outside them, the Koreans have seen themselves as "a shrimp among whales." China was the principal whale until the latter part of the nineteenth century, but it was generally a benevolent one. The Koreans accommodated themselves to Chinese cultural and military superiority, accepting younger-brother status in China's world family. The collapse of China, source of so much of their culture and political institutions, had a traumatic effect, adding to Korea's own internal difficulties and external challenges.

Although the Koreans have not accepted the cultural superiority of any other nation in the way they did China's, the relationship of south Korea to the United States after liberation in 1945, or of north Korea to the Soviet Union, was a transference from China of the older-brother–younger-brother relationship. Koreans, both north and south, criticize themselves for their *sadaejuui*—obeisance to power, or over-respect for greatness. This view is, of course, reinforced by Western ideas of individual and national independence. These two attitudes— perception of themselves as a small and weak nation, coupled with rising feelings of independence—confront Koreans with a basic dilemma. As the economic and military power of both Koreas grows, the dilemma becomes less painful; but to some extent it will continue to plague them, at least until reunification can be achieved. This mixture of dependence and independence still complicates the conduct of relations between south Korea and the United States. For example, Korean negotiators have played on their weaknesses in economic discussions concerning protected markets or the need for better Foreign Military Sales credit terms but then argued that U.S. policies do not reflect the new Korean status in the international community.

Today's south Koreans have discarded some of their conscious Confucian heritage because it seems anachronistic. Nevertheless, many of the traditional attitudes continue to influence Korean individual and social behavior, even while alternate values and systems are being borrowed and adapted. In south Korea, there has been renewed recent attention to the positive elements of the Confucian tradition, along with growing nationalist sentiment. The survival of Confucian values makes Korean behavior sometimes incomprehensible and frustrating to Americans.

The continuing influence of Confucianism can be attributed not only to inertia—people do not like to change their basic values—but also to the inherent magnificence of the Confucian philosophical system and the deep roots it established in the Korean consciousness. The ideas of Confucius and of his various disciples in succeeding centuries—notably Mencius and Zhu Xi—emerged in China and spread to all of East Asia, somewhat as the ideas of Plato, Aristotle, and Jesus spread to Europe. Partly because of this heritage, some scholars (including myself) believe that China had ideals, culture, refinement, and power far beyond those of any other part of the world until the nineteenth century. Future Korea is far more likely to arrive at a synthesis of Confucian and other ideas than to abandon its tradition.

Evolution of new values and ideas in south Korea, unlike in north Korea, has been a relatively free process, notwithstanding authoritarian controls. Basic cultural values have been allowed to work themselves out in free interaction with all outside ideas except those of communism (although communism has been the excuse for suppression of a wider spectrum of "progressive" ideas). There have been official attempts to instill patriotism and virtue, particularly through the schools, the New Community Movement, and military training; but such programs lack the coerciveness and single-mindedness of north Korean ideological training. Criticism of south Korean official ideology has focused on governmental repression of subversive ideas through press and media controls and court action. The definition of subversive ideas has fluctuated in scope and at some times has been wide enough to include almost all criticism of government, though this has changed dramatically since the "democratization movement" of 1987.

In north Korea, Confucianism has been officially thrown on the scrap heap, along with all other "-isms" except communism and "Kimilsungism." Yet Confucian influence clearly persists, as already noted, in manifestations of respect for hierarchy and the collective benefit. The cultivation of a father image for Kim Il-sung was another sign of familism in north Korea, as is the succession of power from father to son. At first glance north Korea seems like a model Leninist party dictatorship; but a closer look reveals a commitment to community and ideological orthodoxy that has much deeper roots in the Korean Confucian tradition.

Since the mid-1960s, the official ideology is no longer pure Marxism-Leninism but a new interpretation of communist thought called *juch'e sasang* (the ideology of self-reliance). Beginning in the 1960s, at a time when badly needed support from both China and the Soviet Union was diminishing, Kim Il-sung's writings began to emphasize the idea of self-reliance as a guiding social principle. This concept has been elaborated to include much of the basic doctrine that guides north Korean affairs and is represented as a higher form of Marxism-Leninism, shaped to reflect the needs of a developing nation. A basic aspect of *juch'e* is the idea that man is the master of all things and can accomplish all things, given the necessary will and training. As such it is a variant of Marxist materialism and Mao Zedong's faith in the power of the human will. "Bourgeois" ideas demeaning the dignity and power of the individual are condemned. Other basic ideas include love and obedience for the Leader; loyalty to the Party; the Three Revolutions (ideological, cultural, and technical) for the transformation of the nation; and devotion to practical service, as contrasted with bureaucratic dogmatism and quest for status.

Although north Korea, like other Communist states, has had to modify somewhat its opposition to private profit, the ideal remains unselfish service to society for its own sake, rather than capitalist moneygrubbing. Thus some material incentives have been incorporated in industrial and agricultural operations, but heavy reliance continues to be placed on exhortation of Party, state, and workers on the basis of ideology and duty. Collectivism, "one for all and all for one," is a constant theme of north Korean leaders' exhortations to the people. This concept derives from the Confucian tradition as well as from communist theory. Part of Kim Jong-il's explanation of *juch'e* is included in a discussion of north Korean political culture in Chapter 5.

Education and Students

The enormous importance attached to education in Korea is a principal reason for the nation's rapid development. This attitude, however, is only partly motivated by current realities; it springs from the Confucian tradition, in which entry into government service was by superior merit obtained through years of study of the Confucian classics, proven by examination. Governmental position and scholarship were intimately related; the social ideal was the scholar-official, and scholarship in effect served the state. At a time when government positions were the only way to rise in the world, education thus was the key to fame and fortune.

Education for the masses did not begin in Korea until the end of the nineteenth century. However, schools for the children of the aristocracy to learn the Confucian classics were established in the Koryo Dynasty (936–1392), and the Buddhist temples were also centers of learning. In the Choson Dynasty (1392–1910), with the official adoption of Confucian philosophy and the examination system, education became a major social activity. State schools were established in the capital and the provinces, the highest of which was the *Songgyun'gwan,* the Confucian university. Individual scholars and ex-officials out of favor organized academies of their own, called *sowon,* for the instruction of young people. By the nineteenth century, there were around 300 such academies. They were centers of factional political activity as well as education, and for this reason most of them were abolished a generation before Western influence generated interest in modern schools.

Western missionaries (especially U.S. Protestants), entering Korea in the 1880s, opened elementary and secondary schools and eventually three colleges. These institutions were open to anyone with the requisite ability. They continued to operate during most of the Japanese colonial period, although constrained by Japanese regulation. The Japanese authorities extended primary education through "common schools" throughout the country, which eventually enrolled about half of the eligible age group. Secondary schools and the Keijo [Seoul] Imperial University were primarily for the children of Japanese expatriates, but admitted some Korean students. During their three-year administration of south Korea, the U.S. military authorities encouraged education and sought to introduce U.S. educational principles. However, the traditional and Japanese influence remained strong, with its emphasis on discipline, veneration for ruler and state, and rote learning. It is still strong today.

Education is still regarded by Koreans as the key to success. Until recently, law and government were the preferred college courses in south Korea, because they led to government position. Recent south Korean polls and career choices of college graduates in south Korea show that a significant change has taken place: Business and some of the professions are preferred over a career in government.

South Korea: Elementary and Secondary Education

The south Korean educational system outwardly parallels those of the states in the United States, in providing six years of compulsory primary education, three years of middle school, and three years of high school, followed by two to four or more years of college or technical school. One-quarter of the national budget, as well as some local government revenue, is devoted to education. There are both public and private schools on all levels; private schools charge substantial tuition and include both profit and nonprofit enterprises (some such schools have made substantial profits for their founders).

Overall educational policy is set forth in a 1968 Charter of National Education. The Ministry of Education exercises close control over both public and private schools, approves all textbooks, and prescribes many of them. Curriculum, also controlled by the Ministry of Education, is essentially uniform throughout the country. Appointive educational committees of local citizens exist at provincial and local levels; their functions are mainly advisory, but there is continuing talk about broadening their role. Schools have parent-teacher associations for support. Private schools have legally incorporated foundations but generally have to meet their expenses from students' tuition and fees.

The first six years of school are free and compulsory. Although even state-operated middle schools charge a fee, over 90 percent of children in the eligible ages attend, and 90 percent of those go on to high school. The school year, which begins in March, must have at least 220 school days, or 34 weeks (32 weeks for education above secondary level); school hours range from 782 per year for first grade to 1,088 in sixth grade and 1,224 for ninth grade. (High school requirements are in units of 50 minutes' duration, and range in number from 204 to 216. Some schools operate on two shifts because of classroom shortages.) Teachers must teach 25 hours a week and often do more.[12]

A typical high-school student's school day in Seoul starts at 7:30 A.M. He or she studies until 8:50, then attends classes until 5:00 P.M., with one hour for lunch. After 5:00, specially designated students have another four to five hours of study. Incoming third-year students get only two weeks of summer vacation, because they must take extra courses to prepare for the college entrance examination. Classes are also held on Saturday, although the day is somewhat shorter.

Any given subject of study in Korean schools is spread out over a longer time than in the United States, so that students study more subjects in a single term. Homework requirements are stringent. Students apply themselves diligently because of the emphasis placed on examinations as a measure of academic achievement—especially the crucially important government-administered examinations for admission to college. Instruction emphasizes factual learning, lectures, and memorization. Relatively large classes—averaging over thirty pupils (and often more) at elementary level and up to sixty-five at middle- and high-school levels—require firm discipline, which is made easier by Korean attitudes toward authority, by respect for education, and by supportive family influence.

Elementary-school instruction, according to the Ministry of Education, has seven purposes: to teach the Korean language; to nurture morality, civic spirit, and social responsibility; to observe and analyze natural phenomena; to handle quantitative relationships necessary in life; to "nurture a spirit of industry, perseverance, and self-help"; to appreciate art; and to learn and practice hygiene and sanitation. The regular curriculum includes moral education (including anticommunism), Korean language, social studies, arithmetic, science, physical education, music, fine arts, and crafts. Extracurricular activities begin at third grade.

Middle-school objectives are a continuation of elementary education; occupational opportunities, development of a sense of justice, and physical and emotional development are included. The regular curriculum includes twelve courses: moral education, Korean language, Korean history, social studies, mathematics, sciences, physical education, music, fine arts, classical Chinese (from which the characters used with Korean phonetic script are derived), foreign languages, vocational skills, and home economics. Students must pay tuition, but fees in public schools are moderate, and some poor families receive an education subsidy; thus, nearly all children get a middle-school education.

High schools are classified into general, vocational, and other (art, physical education, science) types. Their objective, continuing from middle school, is to

> impart the necessary qualifications and capabilities [of] a solid citizenry; to foster understanding and a sense of judgment regarding the Korean country and society; and to provide education in general education and specialized subjects in order to instill a correct understanding of the mission of the Korean nation, to upgrade physical standards, and to enable students to properly choose their future course and direction in life.[13]

The regular curriculum consists of thirteen general subjects and several specialized subjects, both divided between required and elective courses. General subjects are the same as for middle school, with the addition of military training. Specialized subjects include agriculture, engineering, commerce, fishery and marine industry, home economics, and other related subjects. Students pay tuition, except for those in agricultural schools; nevertheless, 88 percent of middle school graduates go on to high school. To equalize access to top-class schools, students in some areas have been assigned by lot on the basis of scores in an examination given to all middle-school students (high scorers being thus distributed over a number of schools).

South Korea: Higher Education

College and university education has been a major focus of social and political attention in south Korea since 1945 and remains so today. In 1992, there were 1,753,727 students at 628 institutions of higher education, representing more than one-quarter of high-school graduates (1,092,464 at 127 colleges and universities; the remainder at 350 graduate schools, 128 junior colleges, and various specialized schools). In 1993, 45.2 percent of students were enrolled in natural sciences, 24.7 percent in social sciences (including business), 11.4 percent in the humanities, 5.3 percent in education, and the remainder in the arts, medical science, and agriculture.[14]

Admission to colleges and universities historically has depended upon a student's score in a highly competitive, state-administered entrance examination. This standardized test, administered in August and November, is something like the American Scholastic Assessment Test (SAT), but there are important differences. First, it is administered by the state, which controls the rules for college admission through the Ministry of Education. Second, until 1995, a student could only apply to a particular university, and within that university to a particular major. For example, a student with good grades in high school but borderline chances for admission to a top university such as Yonsei, might take the test and have the score forwarded to a less desirable major department at the highly desirable Yonsei, in hopes that the competition would be less. Intricate calculations about admission chances therefore have driven many students' choices of school and major even before matriculation. This system in turn has generated intense pressure to score well on the tests, including fortunes spent on private tutoring and cram schools (called *hagwon*) during high school. This is Korea's "examination hell," and students who do not score well enough to win a place on the acceptance list at their chosen university are left to try again the next year.

There have been various attempts over the years to alleviate Korea's examination hell. Officials, as do sociologists, recognize the deleterious effects of the competitive atmosphere on students. This, added to the inordinate importance placed upon admission to a top school by Korean society in general has placed unbearable pressure on applicants and upon the colleges, whose officials have been embroiled in admissions bribery scandals from time to time. During the early 1980s, the government experimented by ordering a vastly increased admission quota—coupled with a requirement to eliminate the lowest 30 percent of the freshman class by the time of graduation. Professors accordingly were required, in effect, to flunk the lowest third of their classes. The practice was short-lived; however, the universities remained overburdened with many more students than before, in classes of unwieldy size, with facilities stretched far beyond capacity. At Yonsei University, for example, the large new library with its capacious reading rooms was suddenly the scene of fierce competition for sitting space: Students lined up to get in the door at 7:00 A.M. to claim chairs. Other schools with smaller facilities were even harder pressed. Most state-run institutions charged easily affordable tuition, which meant that they were slow to respond to the increased demand. Private colleges and universities, charging tuition at a level that reflected the actual cost of education, were much quicker to expand and deal with the increased numbers.

In 1995 Yonsei pioneered a change, offering early admission to highly qualified high school seniors. The government also allowed students to apply to more than one school at a time, causing confusion for admissions officers but permitting students to apply to "safe" schools as well as "reach" schools and lessening the chances that a young person would have to sit out a year waiting for the next admissions cycle.

Once in college, the mass nature of Korean higher education promotes a certain relaxation. Completion of 140 credits is required for the bachelor's degree, and students who find congenial intellectual homes in their major departments often go on to graduate school. Others join clubs and work considerably less hard than they did in high school, creating social ties that will serve them well through life. Before 1990 few Korean students could study abroad because of currency restrictions. Male students had an additional restriction: They had to take compulsory military officer training and serve in the armed forces before they could get a passport. Since 1990 both kinds of strictures have been eased, and Korean students are often found abroad on holiday and as undergraduates in overseas institutions. Indeed, some students who do not get into top Korean universities are sent to study abroad where a certain prestige accrues, at least, from attending a foreign institution.

North Korean Education

In north Korea, scholarship still serves the state, in ways reminiscent of the Confucian tradition, although Confucianism as such is proscribed. Academic institutions, from kindergartens to Kim Il-sung University, are part of the state and Party hierarchy. Major essays on many subjects have been written by, or in the name of, the late President Kim Il-sung and by his son and successor, Kim Jong-il. These writings enjoy great authority, reading of them is enjoined upon the people, and they form a part of educational curricula. Critical thought is encouraged as part of "social education," but it must conform to the broad principles that govern the state and Party and must serve state and Party purposes.

North Korean education is administered by the state at national, provincial, and local levels, under the general supervision of parallel Party organizations. It is free, compulsory, and universal through the equivalent of tenth grade. There are also Party schools, and there are training institutes within large factories and some government ministries. The curriculum is balanced between academics and politics. Subjects such as mathematics, science, language, and music are supplemented with classes in political ideology including the Kimilsungist *juch'e* creed and the history of the Korean Workers' Party and its exploits. Politics suffuses the curriculum further through political songs in music class and stories of Kim Il-sung's life and accomplishments in language class.

In 1987, 1.49 million children were in primary school and 2.66 million were in secondary school, representing an enrollment rate of 96 percent of the age group six to fifteen years. There are no precise recent figures on postsecondary enrollments, but as of 1988, 13.7 percent of the population was attending, or had graduated from, institutions of higher learning, and the Kim Il-sung regime was well on its way to realizing its oft-proclaimed goal of the "intellectualization of the whole society."[15]

College Students: Life, Attitudes, Activities

In south Korea, most college students behave like their counterparts in other countries. They spend from fifteen to twenty-one hours a week in fifty-minute classes during the school term. Some clues to student life outside the classroom can be drawn from surveys of students conducted at Korea University in 1983 and 1985.[16] Nearly half of the students said they spent their free time at school with fellow course members and classmates; one-third spent it alone, mostly for study.

Only 2 percent spent it with members of the opposite sex. A little more than one-quarter of the students said they spent their after-school time with friends and classmates; nearly the same number studied in the library; about one in eight went home, and about the same number went to "circle" (equivalent to club or society) gatherings or activities on campus.

Among student worries, military service was highest for juniors and second-highest for sophomores. Problems of values and ideals were foremost worries among sophomores and freshmen. Almost half of the students said they preferred to discuss their problems with friends, about one-quarter with classmates, one-eighth with parents, a few with older brothers.

Students reported spending an average of 40,000 to 50,000 won per month ($44 to $55, at 1986 exchange rates) for daily living. One-fifth of this amount went for books; about one-sixth each for travel, food, drink, and cigarettes; about one-quarter for hobbies and amusements (including dates). One-third of the students said they drank *soju* (a strong rice liquor something like vodka) because it was cheap; one-quarter drank *makkoli* (a weaker, cruder drink brewed from rice, traditional in the countryside) for fellowship; and about one in five drank beer "for its taste." About one in nine said they did not drink. Respondents reported that they spent an average of five to six hours per week outside school in reading books (21 percent of the books were novels), and fifty minutes per day reading newspapers (6 percent said they did not read newspapers). They watched television 1.4 hours a day (mostly news and sports) and listened to radio nearly two hours.

Although only a small proportion (most observers suggest around 5 percent) of south Korean college students are actively involved in planning and carrying out the political demonstrations that make for such dramatic (and stereotypical) news coverage worldwide, students generally are much more conscious of their status as the nation's future leaders than are their U.S. counterparts. They consider themselves to be at the leading edge of political and social criticism and reform. In a time of rapid and painful social change, there is no lack of problems for them to criticize, and they do so with youthful idealism and rigid black-and-white moral standards. Moreover, students enjoy relatively high social status, deriving from the tradition of the Choson Dynasty (when scholarship and government were closely related). Students were a major factor in the 1919 independence movement against Japan, and students led the uprising in 1960 that ended the Rhee regime. Since that time, they have been a significant factor in south Korean politics. Indeed, it was again students who led the national wave of protest that led to "democratization" in 1987; and it was students' refusing to drop the Kwangju issue that led, after many years, to a reassessment of the Chun Doo-hwan regime's role in the December 1979 coup and the Kwangju massacre and led, consequently, to Chun's arrest in 1995.

In addition to a traditional sense of political responsibility and a critical view of the Korean political scene, other factors have fostered student political activism.

Universities operated until the mid-1960s on the European system: Class attendance was not required as long as students could pass the examinations. After years of intense concentration in secondary school to pass the college entrance examinations, students tended to treat much of their college as a sort of vacation between test periods. The didactic and authoritarian attitudes of some professors, whose offerings were often anachronistic and unstimulating, did little to promote attendance. Thus there was ample time to meditate on the evils of society and to listen to dissident intellectuals.

Moreover, in 1960, unemployment was high among college graduates. Demand caught up with supply in the 1970s; but then, as already noted, college enrollment nearly doubled in the early 1980s in response to popular pressure for improved access to higher education. Thus, intellectual employment again became a problem. Only slightly over half of the university graduates of 1985 had found jobs by the end of the year (although some others continued into graduate school).[17] Demonstrations also involve a certain element of generational change. With no personal memory of the Korean War, and therefore no direct experience to fuel their hatred of the north Korean regime, through the years students have been less and less willing to accept the anticommunist dogma of the south Korean regime, especially when anticommunism has been so flagrantly used to mask abuses in the south Korean system such as the army massacre in Kwangju in May 1980. While activism of the shouting, rock-hurling variety was a way of life to a minority of students in the 1980s, these students were the only ones who found a voice to protest the Chun Doo-hwan dictatorship, and their activities, disruptive though they were, kept pressure on the government by exposing the regime's repression.

The activists sometimes succeeded in recruiting many more moderate students to their cause, and at certain times of the year such as the anniversary of the Kwangju massacre or the April 1960 uprising against Syngman Rhee these mass actions were significant, drawing busloads of riot police in padded uniforms firing tear gas from shotguns and "Black Maria" tear gas vans. These encounters sometimes even acquired an aspect of ritual; that is, they were predictable, ran a prescribed course, and did not (with some notable and regrettable exceptions) result in serious injuries. They did, however, make the political point, filling neighborhood streets with tear gas and forcing the government to engage in frequent public acts of repression.

The nonparticipating majority of students have mostly gone about their regular business during such demonstrations; a few watched from a distance. Nevertheless, there is a body of fairly widespread student sentiment that focuses on poor wages and working conditions, maldistribution of wealth, political corruption, American hegemonism, and to some extent, the capitalist system generally. Other causes are student issues such as tuition increases, campus elections, the quality of campus facilities, and military training. Demonstrations with nationalist themes often stress the ethnic identity of Koreans as an ancient race, using unique Korean cultural symbols such as music and dancing from shaman rituals and farmers' festivals. These expressions have a strong subtext of social criticism aimed at the corruption of contemporary society by modern—including West-ern—forces.

The Reaction: Control and Reform

Over the years, the south Korean government has responded to student activism in a variety of ways, both academic and political. In the academic realm, the gov-ernment has moved to improve the educational system by instituting a national examination; by promoting the growth of scientific and technical institutions on both college and high-school level, including schools of business administration, to ensure that the supply of college graduates better meets the changing social de-mand; by ending the lifetime tenure system of professors (a move attacked as a device for getting rid of politically unpalatable teachers, which was also a result); and by requiring student attendance at classes as a condition for evaluation. Pro-fessors' salaries have also been brought somewhat closer to parity with their high social status to promote excellence, and tuitions have increased as a result (al-though the most prestigious institution, Seoul National University, is state oper-ated and charges low tuition).

Successive south Korean governments have also applied direct political means to control student activism. Demonstrations outside college campuses, and some-times inside them, have been suppressed by force—usually without major injury, clubs and tear gas being the principal weapons, as noted earlier. Student govern-ments and campus organizations were disbanded, to be replaced by paramilitary organizations controlled by the Home Ministry through the college administra-tors. Under the Park and Chun regimes, college presidents and administrators were required to suppress student activism—through suspension, expulsion, and other means—and were discharged if they failed to do so. Student activists them-selves—mostly those involved in violence—were apprehended and given severe exemplary prison sentences; expelled students were, by prevailing practice, imme-diately subject to military draft. These controls began to wane in the mid-1980s, and by 1990 there was a notable change in the mood on campuses. Though they were still under heavy police surveillance, campuses were places where posters with politically incorrect ideas could be posted and rallies and debates could occur quite freely.

Art and Literature

Korean aesthetic expression has a tradition going back thousands of years, as evi-denced by Paleolithic and Neolithic remains. Most surviving evidence of artistic activity, however, dates from and after the Three Kingdoms period (roughly, the fourth to the seventh centuries A.D.). Tombs of royalty and nobility in each of the three kingdoms have been excavated to disclose remarkable wall paintings, cere-monial vessels of both metal and clay, tableware, gold crowns, weapons (many of them apparently ceremonial rather than for actual combat), costumes, and orna-ments. The conception and workmanship of these objects is impressive.

Buddhism came to Korea in the fourth century A.D., bringing with it the rich inspiration of Indian and Chinese art forms depicting the Buddha and the many scenes and personages from Buddhist scripture. The Koreans adapted these forms to their own tastes—they preferred carving in stone, for example, to wood. Few examples of Buddhist graphic art survive from the Three Kingdoms period, but there are a number of extant sculptures and monuments as well as remains of temple foundations.

The oldest known Korean written work is a stone monument commemorating the victories of King Kwanggaet'o of Koguryo (A.D. 391–413), erected at his tomb north of the present Korean border in Manchuria. The inscription is in Chinese characters; the Koreans, as already noted, did not develop their own writing sys-tem until the fifteenth century, although earlier use was made of a phonetic adap-tation of Chinese.

The earlier part of the United Silla period (668–936) saw a flowering of art forms. Buddhism was now in the ascendancy; great temples were built, although only the foundations survive (the great temple of Pulguk-sa, at the Silla capital, was burned by the Japanese in 1592). Perhaps the most impressive survival from this period is the heroic granite statue of the Buddha in an artificial stone grotto atop a hill near Pulguk-sa (Fig. 3.2); the statue is surrounded by a series of splen-did stone reliefs depicting Buddhist scriptural figures. Some temples and palaces had immense bronze bells; among those surviving today the most notable is the so-called Emille Bell, now kept at the state museum in Kyongju.

The Silla kings were buried in huge and relatively theft-proof mounds in the vicinity of Kyongju; a few of them have been excavated, yielding a rich collection of gold, silver, bronze, and ceramic artifacts that show the grandeur of the pe-riod—rich and delicate, yet with an exuberant touch. Poetry, calligraphy, paint-ing, and writing flourished. Only stone inscriptions and secondary references re-main today, but sung poems of the period, called *hyangga,* have survived in the oral tradition.[18]

The Koryo period (936–1392) is best remembered for its lovely celadon pot-tery—graceful in shape, with a blue-green glaze that has never been reproduced with total success. Another famous Koryo achievement is the carving of wood printing blocks for the entire Buddhist scripture. These were destroyed during the Mongol invasion, but were redone in 1251; all 81,258 of them are preserved at the Buddhist temple of Hae' in-sa.[19] Since Buddhism was the dominant religion, many temples were built, but only a few of them have survived the ravages of time and foreign invasion. (The oldest surviving wooden buildings in Korea are two at the Buddhist temple Pusok-sa, dating from about 1350; a wooden image of the Buddha in the temple's main hall also survives.) Metal and stone images and stu-

FIGURE 3.2   Statue of the Buddha at the Kyongju stone grotto in Sokkuram (photo courtesy of Korean Information Office, Washington, D.C.)

pas remain. The art of painting flourished and—like pottery—was influenced by Chinese Song Dynasty techniques; but few examples of the graphic arts from this period survive.

The earliest extant Korean literature dates from the Koryo period. Most notable is Kim Pu-sik's *Samguk Sagi* (Historical Account of the Three Kingdoms). This work, written in 1145 (in Chinese, like all Koryo-period literature) is the earliest indigenous source of Korean history still in existence, although it quotes earlier documents. Two other histories also survive, adding insights on ancient folkways and traditions. New forms of poetry made their appearance, among both aristocrats and common people. Wood-block printing, of which the greatest example was the Buddhist scripture already mentioned, was also used for other works; and by 1240, Korea had independently developed movable metal type. Korea's first medical treatise was published in 1236.

The Choson Dynasty (1392–1910) saw an early flowering of artistic and literary work. The creation of the Korean phonetic alphabet (*han'gul*) in 1446 has already been mentioned. Movable type was improved, making possible wide distribution of works on history, geography, medicine, and agricultural technique. Most books, however, continued to be written in Chinese because of the preference of the intellectuals, and *han'gul* was used chiefly in works by or for women or the common people—except for military treatises to be kept secret from foreigners. Most of the prose writing was on serious subjects until the latter part of the period, but there was some anecdotal material and poetry.

By the sixteenth century, two poetic forms had evolved, distinct from the Chinese-style poems of the late Koryo and early Choson literati: the *kasa,* a brief form of prose-poetry usually focused on the beauties of nature; and the more philosophical *sijo,* written in the Korean language (although often including Chinese characters), which became a major form of literary expression. (The origin of the *sijo* can be traced to the late Koryo period, but it came to full flower at this time.)

The *Sirhak* reformist philosophical movement of the sixteenth to the eighteenth centuries gave rise to new literary forms, including fiction. Authors of non-*yangban* status grew in number (many of them illegitimate sons of the aristocracy or of the intermediate *chung'in* class). Some of these indirectly attacked the parasitic status and lifestyle of the *yangban.* Other materials transcribed oral folklore. Much of the work from this time appeared in *han'gul*[20] to appeal to the general public. Some of the fiction dealt with historical or moral themes, but romantic love was uppermost in those most widely read. *Sijo* poetry also came to be written by non-*yangban,* who—like the professional painters—often did not sign their works.

The disestablishment and official discouragement of Buddhism led to its decline as a cultural force, although its impoverished temples and monasteries continued. Thus Confucianism governed social life, particularly among the upper classes; Buddhist themes diminished in the art forms of the time, and although the monks continued to produce works centered on these themes, the quality diminished.

Graphic art became clearly divided between amateur "literati paintings" of the aristocratic scholars, often exceedingly well done, and the paintings of professionals, which were beneath the dignity of the *yangban*. Many were done on commission by government artisans—both landscapes and portraits of the status-conscious aristocrats. Calligraphy, in contrast, was a province of the scholars. Korea's famed eighteenth-century calligrapher and painter, Chusa (Kim Chong-hui), was hailed in China as well as at home for his distinctive style. From the seventeenth century on, landscape painting became more realistic and centered more on Korean scenery in preference to the traditional Chinese scenes. Paintings of daily life—of workmen, peasants, or partying *yangban*—also flourished.

Chinese models continued to exert their influence, but distinctive touches in painting—a certain freedom and vitality—distinguish most Korean painting from contemporary Chinese or Japanese work in the eyes of experts. Art historian Evelyn McCune wrote:

> A growing appreciation of Korean art has accorded it recognition for certain qualities which have set it apart in the museums of the world. . . . Korean artists were obliged, more often by their poverty than by their neighbors, to rely upon beauty of line and shape rather than upon costly materials. The resulting works of art were marked by elegance and refinement during periods of political stability, but during periods of war they were rustic and careless. In both extremes of refinement and rusticity, however, were to be found strength and an attractive honesty that were much admired in China and Japan—in particular by the Japanese, who imitated them.

She went on to say that Korean art reflected attachment to the land and tradition, love of nature, adaptation of foreign influence, respect for learning, and a "cult of weakness" deriving from Korea's vulnerable location.[21]

The leading archaeologist and art historian Kim Won-yong once wrote, "Anyone who has some knowledge of Asian art can easily discern Korean art from Japanese or Chinese art. But it is not easy to explain the difference. . . ." He quoted Professor Seckel, who suggested two basic elements of "Koreanness": "(1) The decomposition of form-complexes into small elements like a mosaic work; (2) Flat in volume and graphically linear in surface design." The underlying characteristics are "vitality, spontaneity and unconcern for technical perfection (nonchalance)."[22]

Choson Dynasty Confucian literati tastes turned away from the celadons of the Koryo period—first to a cruder, but freer, brownish or grayish *punch'ong* ware (which is popular with Japanese today), then to white and blue-and-white true porcelains. Although the latter were similar in some ways to the porcelains of the Ming Dynasty in China, they were simpler and freer in expression.

A simple, uninhibited folk art emerged during this period in both graphic and performing fields. Paintings of tigers and other creatures, some of them illustrating shamanistic themes or ideas from Chinese folk Taoism, were popular among the people. The artists rarely signed their work, so they remain unknown. Until very recent times, these works were ignored by the ruling classes; their develop-

ment may have been encouraged by the growth of a small commercial and manufacturing class from the mid–seventeenth century on. Their merit is now recognized, partly through the pioneering efforts of the privately sponsored Emillle
folk-art museum of Zozayong (Cho Cha-yong).

Traditional folk music (*nong'ak*) of the countryside, played by amateur farmer
musician-dancers, has a spontaneity and gaiety lacking in the formal Confucian
court music (*a-ak*); the folk music, too, has lately become recognized. A form of
folk story with song, called *p'ansori,* emerged among the people, responding to the
oppression of the ruling *yangban;* its often humorous repertoire ridicules the life of
the aristocracy and priesthood and extols the traditional Confucian virtues. *P'ansori* also absorbed some of the shaman practitioners' ritual themes and techniques.

Western artistic and literary influence had no more than started to affect Korea
when the Japanese established their rule. The colonial era inhibited Korean national self-expression, but nationalistic themes nonetheless appeared in novels
and poetry, many of these works quite Western in form. Use of *han'gul* by the foreign missionaries in widely circulated Bible translations and religious tracts
helped to overcome the traditional bias against it. A society for the study of the
Korean language became a focus of nationalist sentiment under the Japanese,
who eventually suppressed the group—and from 1938 on, endeavored to suppress the language. Before this happened, however, the society had developed a revised system of spelling that reflected the structure as well as the sound of the language. After substantial controversy in the early post-Japanese years, the new
system became standard for both north and south Korea. (For a discussion of the
Korean language, see Appendix B.)

South Korea since 1945 has demonstrated enormous talent for Western art
forms, particularly music. Both classical and modern Western music are extensively played and enjoyed; there are two national and several civic symphony orchestras, some of which have been acclaimed on international tours. Music appreciation is stressed in the schools. A recent survey showed that nine out of ten
professors of music had studied abroad for two to seven years—40 percent of
them in the United States. Korean instrumentalists have played with distinction in
European and U.S. orchestras.

In the graphic arts, traditional styles continue in vogue, executed in black and
colored ink on paper or silk, sometimes including modern themes. All Western
schools of graphic art are represented among contemporary Korean artists, whose
use of oil, acrylic, and water-color techniques is fully up to international standards. Some artists' works command exceedingly high prices. Nam June Paik is
undoubtedly Korea's best known modern artist. In 1994 Paik headlined an international cast of artists and performers in the "SeOUL-NyMAX" celebration of
"Arts Without Borders," which featured Korean themes as well as Fluxus installa-
tion art.[23]

Both fiction and nonfiction books and magazines abound, as do bookstores.
Koreans are voracious readers, and some of the busiest places in Seoul are book-

stores and the used-book sections of the city's big markets. In downtown Seoul there are several huge bookstores that are thronged throughout the day. Most books are domestically produced, but with the easing of restrictions on imports there are many more foreign publications each year.

The press in Korea has developed under adverse conditions. Throughout most of south Korea's history it has been subjected to restrictions imposed by the country's austere economic situation (e.g., shortages of newsprint) and, more importantly, political controls that have amounted to censorship and even, at times, requirements that certain pro-government things be published daily—such as a photo of President Chun Doo-hwan's activities of the previous day in each day's newspaper, in a particularly prominent location.[24] Some of the journalistic tradition of Korea reflects the colonial experience with Japan. Indeed, the Koreans, like the Japanese, are fond of thought magazines, popular monthly journals such as *Wol'gan Choson* and *Shin Tong'a,* published by newspaper companies but carrying long analytical articles about national and world trends. Much of Korea's intellectual discourse circulates in monthlies of this type and in shorter weekend magazines more along lines of the American *Time* or *Newsweek* that are always full of articles by the country's opinion leaders. At the end of 1992 there were two news agencies, 114 daily newspapers, 1,847 weekly publications, and 2,910 monthly magazines reflecting a proliferation of special-interest titles on computers, fishing, parenting, and many kinds of entertainment.

Radio and television, like the press, offer mass-market attractions and are primary media for commercial advertising. Until the early 1990s south Korea's television channels were government owned and controlled. The only alternative was the U.S. Army's television channel, which broadcast American fare—good, bad, and indifferent—twenty-four hours a day. With the advent of satellite television and what one Korean observer calls "CNN-ization," Koreans now have access to worldwide sources of broadcast information. Furthermore, the computer era has brought the Internet to Korea. In 1993 Korea had a few gopher sites. At the end of 1994 there were a few Korean sites on the World Wide Web. However, by the end of 1995 every significant Korean institution had electronic mail, there were thousands of Web sites, and Koreans were full participants in the exponential growth of worldwide computer communications. Not only was it possible to read tomorrow's Korean newspaper today in the United States, but also Koreans likewise could read documents of every conceivable type from all over the world. Under the circumstances, it seems safe to say that traditional-style information control is a thing of the past in south Korea.

North Korea, far behind the south, is also undergoing a certain information evolution. Direct-distance-dialing is now possible from overseas, with voice and fax capabilities. Information access, however, is still strictly controlled. South Korean and Japanese television, using the NTSC format, is not compatible with north Korean television, which uses the Chinese/Soviet/Eastern European PAL format. Radio transmissions from abroad continue to be jammed, and radios are pre-set to government-approved broadcast frequencies. It can be said that every traveler from abroad who enters north Korea, and every north Korean who travels abroad, opens the door a tiny bit; but the kind of information that could drive significant change in north Korea is still safely kept outside the country's borders.

In the north, contemporary literature and other art forms reflect the same general quality of "socialist realism" as was typical of the old socialist bloc. All forms of art are expected to promote the goals of state and Party. Western influence is apparent, but it is more controlled—for example, modern popular Western musical forms are apparently not tolerated, nor abstract graphic art. Architecture is heavy and grandiose. Nevertheless, north Korea has produced spectacular artistic performances, some of which have gone on foreign tour. There seems to be an active publishing industry. Many north Korean motion pictures are technically of high quality, although their themes are usually somewhat labored and circumscribed. Observers who compared north and south Korean performances during the exchange of September 1985 thought the south was in the lead in terms of artistic quality.[25]

Religion

Four main streams of religious and philosophical experience have shaped Korean culture: the indigenous shamanism, with its roots in east-central Asia; Buddhism, which entered Korea in the fourth century A.D. and was firmly established by the eighth century; Confucianism, probably first brought to Korea through the Chinese colony of Lolang until the fourth century A.D., and thereafter through diplomatic and trade exchanges with China; and Christianity, which first entered Korea from China in the eighteenth century and was promoted by foreign missionaries from the late nineteenth century on, until it became self-propagating fifty years or so later. Chinese Taoism has had influence in Korea, mostly as a leitmotif in shamanism and the other main philosophies (except Christianity). There is also a native Korean church called *Ch'ondogyo,* which inspired the *Tonghak* revolt of 1894 and still endures, although it is diminishing.

It is important to recognize, in discussing these various religious and philosophical currents, that Koreans and other East Asians are not exclusive in their religious beliefs. Christians are a partial exception; but in general, the various religions are seen to complement rather than contradict one another. Moreover—with the exceptions of Christianity and *Ch'ondogyo*—the Asian religions are not congregational but a matter of personal communion with the eternal. Temples, images, scriptures, and clerics are means of attaining this communion at the option of the believer. Affiliation with a religion is more a matter of attitude and faith than of formal indoctrination and membership, unless one enters the priesthood.

In north Korea, as in most other Communist states, religion has been proscribed as "the opiate of the people." The proscription specifically includes Confucianism. Vestiges survive: After years of neglect, some historic Buddhist temples are being restored at state expense, and approved Christian groups are permitted to function. How much religion exists in private is as yet unknown; it must struggle against the officially promoted Marxist-Leninist and *juch'e* philosophies, which in north Korea are supposed to respond to all people's spiritual as well as physical and social problems.

Shamanism

In south Korea, shamanism—earliest among Korean religions—continues to have a large number of adherents, often in combination with other beliefs. Shamanism recognizes a myriad of spirits who can work for good or ill. They must be propitiated to avoid evil, cast out if need be, and solicited to ensure success and fortune. Families, houses, natural objects all have spirits. Many ancient customs have to do with winning the spirits' favor or averting their wrath. In Korea (unlike in Japanese Shinto, which in some other ways is similar), there are few large shamanistic shrines or groups of practitioners. However, Buddhist temples typically have a small building dedicated to the "mountain god," implicitly a shaman deity, and some villages and families have modest shrines.

The adepts of shamanism are mostly women, known as *mudang* or *manshin*, who inherit their profession or otherwise demonstrate special communion with the spirits; they are retained by individuals or families in time of special fortune or special trouble. Often they perform a lengthy ceremony called *kut*, including costumes, song, and dance, to communicate with the spirits and sometimes to be possessed by them.

Shamanism was officially discouraged as primitive in south Korea until the 1980s, when it gained great popularity as part of the search for authentic Korean cultural roots. Shaman rituals were part of campus demonstrations. They became a part of opening ceremonies of all kinds: It became common to open businesses, from bars to banks, with dedication rituals that featured the shaman *kut* with all its symbols. Shamanism thus evolves as a community ritual as well as a religious expression.

Buddhism

Buddhism claims the largest number of Korean believers among the five main religious groups (roughly 11.9 million, or 27.6 percent of south Korea's population, according to south Korean government figures). It is divided among eighteen sects, principally according to the priority given to meditation and inspiration and to the priority given to various portions of the enormous volume of Buddhist scripture. More mundane issues in recent years have been the organization of the clergy, control of temples and temple property, and the question of whether priests should be married.

Korean Buddhism, like that of Japan and China, is mainly of the Mahayana school, emphasizing attainment of eternity through faith. The original Gautama Buddha, a historical north Indian figure of the sixth century B.C., taught that the pain of life is due to earthly desire and that the attainment of Nirvana, or deliverance from life's bondage, is to be sought through the elimination of desire, through many reincarnations, followed by enlightenment. The three great foundations of the Buddhist faith are the Buddha himself, the body of scripture, and the clergy, whose conduct is guided by an Eightfold Path of right living and right thinking. Ordinary people are expected to live and improve themselves according to standards of righteous life but cannot expect to attain Nirvana within their lifetimes. Salvation is an individual matter, and the emphasis is on withdrawal more than on social action. This does not mean, however, that Buddhism is not socially conscious; love and charity toward all sentient beings are a dominant part of it.

Over the years, Mahayana Buddhism has evolved a pantheon of luminaries. The Buddha himself is believed by some to exist in many forms and persons. Some sages, having attained enlightenment, restrain themselves from entering Nirvana in order to help enlighten others; these are called Bodhisattvas. Disciples and priests of eminent virtue are recognized. Temples contain images of the Buddha, Bodhisattvas, and sometimes many of the disciples. They also contain murals illustrating scenes from the Buddha's life and other scriptural messages, for the benefit of the faithful who go for prayer, meditation, and guidance.

Confucianism

Confucianism is a philosophy rather than a religion. Confucius did not deny metaphysics but rather took it for granted, on the basis that it was people's main business to run their own world in a way that would please Heaven. If human affairs were properly ordered, this would enhance the universal harmony; if they were not, nature might be disturbed, and the ruler might lose the Mandate of Heaven.

Although Confucius was the first and the greatest thinker of the philosophy that bears his name, his ideas were shaped and modified by others after him, particularly Mencius, a century or so later, and Zhu Xi around A.D. 1100. Zhu Xi enhanced the metaphysical content of Confucianism and shaped it in such a way that it became a potent instrument of rule in both China and Korea. As interpreted over the centuries, Confucianism holds that man is basically good, but malleable; that human affairs should be ordered by those who earn authority through superior wisdom and benevolence, attained through study of the classics and of the ancient Golden Age they describe as a model. In addition to teaching principles of right social action—including a version of Jesus' Golden Rule, expressed negatively—Confucianism emphasizes the importance of doing things in the right way. Thus ceremony becomes important, as well as substance. Family plays a central role in social life, and its extent over space and time is emphasized.

It is clear from these brief descriptions that Confucianism and Buddhism complement each other. Buddhism fills the spiritual void of Confucianism; Confucianism puts its emphasis on interpersonal relations rather than relations with the eternal. The Western advent, however, challenged the structure of both beliefs because they took for granted an essentially static world of suffering, ruled by specially qualified authority entitled to unquestioning respect and obedience from the common people. In the rapidly changing Western world, however, old relationships did not work, and new horizons of earthly progress and of equality among men were opened.

Christianity

For many Koreans, Christianity seems to have filled the void created by intellectual stagnation and peasant impoverishment and by the impact of social change. It took hold among a few reform-minded aristocrats in the late eighteenth century and quickly spread, until it was suppressed by the royal authorities.

The treaties of the 1880s brought Western representatives to Korea. Horace Allen, a physician-missionary attached to the U.S. legation, opened the way for missionaries when he saved the life of Prince Min Yong-ik after an attempted coup d'état in 1884. Korean Protestantism dates from Allen's arrival, though because of his affiliation with the legation it is more correct to date it from the arrival of the American Methodists Henry and Ella Appenzeller and the Presbyterian Horace G. Underwood, on Easter Sunday 1885. In 1984, roughly at the same time that the Protestants celebrated their centennial with commemorations of Allen's arrival and the landing of the Appenzellers and Horace Underwood, Korean Catholics celebrated their bicentennial with a mass conducted in Seoul's Yoido Plaza by Pope John Paul II. During the pope's visit, 103 Korean and French martyrs—sacrifices to nineteenth-century pogroms against outsiders and foreign ideas—were canonized.

Christianity took hold slowly at first, since it was officially suspect and the *yangban*, particularly in the hinterland, opposed its spread. However, by the early twentieth century Catholic and Protestant mission stations had sprouted in all corners of the country, planting churches and starting schools and clinics, demonstrating the traditional "triad" of mission work. Around the time of Korea's fall to Japanese colonial control, the Christian community, especially Protestants, began to undergo exponential growth. Under Japanese rule Christian associations, schools, and churches seemed to offer an alternative to colonial institutions, and Christianity took on a certain association with nationalism, especially when the church tried in the 1930s to resist Japanese demands that Christians worship Japanese spirits at Shinto shrines. The Christian population lost many members during World War II, mostly because of Japanese repression but also because most of the missionary community withdrew. During the war years and immediately after 1945, the Christian church operated under its own leadership; and although missionaries returned in large numbers to assist with reconstruction after the Korean War and helped to revive the momentum of church growth, they did not long keep their mentor position. By the 1970s almost all Christian churches and institutions were under Korean leadership.

With its message of human salvation through faith and its programs of social action, including education, health, and welfare activities, Christianity has grown steadily and rapidly; Christians now number over 1.5 million Catholics and 8 million Protestants—nearly a quarter of the south Korean population. Among these are many Christians from the north who fled from Communism, and their descendants; north Korea originally was more Christian than the south.

Like the Buddhists, Christians—especially the Protestants—have proliferated in divisions as well as adherents. The early divisions were brought by the missionaries themselves, dividing the Koreans from the start into Catholics and several sects of Protestants. The Protestant sects, however, have divided and subdivided. Additionally, they have spawned new religions and new interpretations of Christianity, responding not only to doctrinal differences and the tensions of social change but also to the individual ambitions of some clergymen. There are now seventy Protestant denominations in south Korea, forty-six of them Presbyterian. There is also a small Eastern Orthodox congregation in Seoul, which began in the days of Russian ascendency in the late nineteenth century and was given new impetus by the Greek forces in the United Nations Command during and after the Korean War.

Christianity brought modern social values of freedom, equality, and human rights to Korea and was associated with movements for independence and democracy. This history, coupled with the greater organization of the Christian churches, has impelled some clergy and lay leaders to play active roles in movements for social reform (such as the Urban Industrial Mission, to improve wages and working conditions among poor urban workers) and to speak out on political issues. Like student activists, such leaders do not necessarily represent the majority of Christians, but they do reflect, in extreme degree, attitudes that are more widely held. Also like the students, some Christian activists have been arrested, tried, and sentenced for alleged subversive activity under both President Park and President Chun. The Reverend Mun Ik-hwan, for example, was indicted in June 1986 and subsequently imprisoned for his alleged encouragement of student activists at Seoul National University and his leadership in the protest riot at Inch'on in May of that year. Mun was released in an amnesty for political prisoners in mid-1987, after which he resumed his challenge to the government. He traveled to north Korea and met with Kim Il-sung in an effort to promote national reconciliation. Upon his return he was jailed again, then released just before his death in 1994.

Ch'ondogyo.   In 1860 a native Korean religion known as *Tonghak* (Eastern Learning) was founded in southwestern Korea as a conscious reaction against the introduction of alien Christian doctrines. Its originator, Ch'oe Che-u, was executed three years later. Nevertheless, its appeal spread rapidly in response to economic and political oppression, and its adherents formed the core of the *Tonghak* rebellion, which captured much of the two Cholla provinces in 1894. Although the rebellion was crushed, the religion survived under the name *Ch'ondogyo* (Religion of the Heavenly Way).

The *Tonghak* or *Ch'ondogyo* principles incorporate neo-Confucian, Buddhist, and Taoist ideas and reflect some Christian influence (such as congregational worship). A central *Ch'ondogyo* theme is that every person has the eternal within him and is therefore equal to everyone else—a revolutionary idea in a Confucian society. Other elements of Ch'oe Che-u's doctrine include incantation, meditation, use of a talisman to cure sickness, and revelation of truth. "The teachings of Ch'ondogyo assert that through self-discipline and cultivation one can obtain the divine virtue of being able to influence everything without conscious effort or volition."[26] *Ch'ondogyo* leaders distinguished themselves by signing the declaration of independence against Japan in the 1919 independence uprising, along with Christian and Buddhist leaders. *Ch'ondogyo* had 600,000 followers in 1992, according to government estimates.[27]

Since 1945 a variety of religious sects have sprouted, some of national extent but most locally organized. These include *Taejonggyo,* organized around the worship of Tan'gun, mythical founder of Korea; it had 325,000 adherents in 1983. The Unification (*T'ongil*) Church of Rev. Sun Myung Moon (Mun Son-myong) is now perhaps more influential in the United States than in Korea. A former Presbyterian elder organized the so-called Olive Tree Sect shortly after the 1945 liberation; his adherents, concentrated in their own villages, operate a number of factories and collectives. Turkish troops in the Korean War brought Islam to Korea, and subsequent Korean contact with the Middle East reinforced it. A mosque now overlooks the south-central part of Seoul along with innumerable Christian churches. A total of 538 sects of all religions were reported to be in practice in Korea in 1985.[28]

Social Welfare

In Korean tradition, the state is responsible for social regulation rather than social welfare, the latter being a family and community responsibility. (It is often forgotten that this was the tradition of all governments, including those in the West, until the mid-nineteenth century, although charity by religious and private institutions was perhaps more common in Europe.) Modern social welfare programs began in Korea with the Christian missionaries. During the Japanese period, relatively little was done for the Koreans, although such institutions as state-operated hospitals were established. However, the spread of Western social welfare ideas inspired their inclusion in the platforms of all groups aspiring to political power after 1945.

If state responsibility for individual needs is the basis for judgment, then north Korea has moved far ahead of south Korea in social welfare. Limited observation by foreigners suggests that there is no abject poverty. Although north Korean wages and living standards are believed to be considerably lower than those of the south, there is a universal system of health care, subsidized housing, and food rations, as well as a system of worker vacation resorts. The state professes to ensure work for everyone, although not at the choice of the worker, and to provide for support of the aged. Education through the ninth grade is universal, free, and compulsory. Whether these programs truly meet popular aspirations, and whether they are actually carried out in accordance with the claims of the regime, cannot be determined.

South Korea has had to cope with twice the population density of the north. Until the mid-1960s, its economic development was slow and its resources poor. Accordingly, it is only in recent years that state-sponsored social welfare programs have spread to large parts of the public. Although the concept of state responsibility for the needy was recognized in legislation, most action was left to individual families—the traditional source of welfare—and to private organizations. A separate Ministry for Health and Social Affairs was established in 1948, but less than two years later its efforts had to be directed wholly toward wartime and postwar relief for refugees, widows, orphans, and disabled soldiers and civilian casualties of the Korean War. Only massive U.S. government and private support—largely in food, clothing, and consumer goods—averted widespread starvation in the war and immediate postwar period.

Given the state of the south Korean economy and the pressure of population, there was little more the government could do in the ensuing decade, even had there been a tradition of state social responsibility. South Korea in the postwar period was supporting 1.5 million returnees from the Pacific, 3 to 4 million refugees from north Korea (before and during the Korean War), and a population growth rate of nearly 3 percent a year, while the economy was growing at only a slightly higher rate (around 5 percent).

Since the mid-1960s, rapid south Korean economic progress has made more social welfare programs possible in response to continuing public demand. In the private sector, earlier foreign missionary enterprises in such areas as hospitals, leprosy colonies, and orphanages were supplemented and often taken over by indigenous Christian and other groups, whose activities broadened. The Government also increased its concern for social programs, particularly for disabled veterans and widows. A separate Ministry of Labor was established, taking the former Office of Labor from the Ministry of Health and Social Affairs. Most recently, a Ministry of Sports was created. The New Community Movement, launched in 1971 in the rural areas, had a welfare component. Provisions of existing laws, such as employers' payment of one month's separation pay on dismissal for each year of work, were better enforced.

The Fourth and Fifth Five-Year Plans for the economy included emphasis on social welfare—particularly the extension of health insurance programs financed by employers, workers, and government. Such programs now cover over half of all workers and are scheduled for near-universal application. More attention is being given to working conditions. The Government and some large firms now have pension plans, and a minimum wage was established in 1988. Employment information centers were established by the mid-1980s to help workers find jobs. The 1990 budget allocated substantial amounts for rental housing, aid to low-income workers, education, and medical insurance.

South Korean government policy differs from that of north Korea, however, in placing emphasis on economic growth and a strong family system as the bases for social welfare rather than centralized state allocation of the individual's economic share. The consequence for the individual is more opportunity but less security in south Korea than in north Korea. The comparative evidence since 1980 or so suggests that the south Korean formula is more conducive to economic growth. Nevertheless, intellectuals, students, and religious leaders have shown increasing concern for what they see as an unfairly skewed apportionment of wealth and income.

Although medical care in south Korea has improved, it still has not reached the level of industrialized societies. Official statistics in 1994 indicated that there was one doctor per 786 persons, compared with one to 400 or 500 in Europe or the United States. Statistics for nurses and dentists showed similar gaps. However, the delivery of health care services to the countryside has improved dramatically since the 1960s, when the government instituted mass inoculation programs and programs in tuberculosis and communicable disease control. The development of medical insurance programs for working people and the establishment of health care stations in rural areas as well as cities has made medical care a virtual entitlement for nearly all south Koreans.[29]

Environment

Korean culture lays great emphasis on the country's natural environment. The national anthem celebrates the beauties of seas, rivers, and mountains; the country's art and literature extol the splendors of nature. Yet the pressures of poverty, the destruction of war, and the drive for rapid economic development have taken a heavy toll on Korea's environment—particularly in the south, where both population density and the rate of economic growth are higher than in the north. South Korea has become one of the most polluted areas in the world.

One shining exception to south Korea's environmental degradation has been the renewal of its forests. Poverty, dating from even before the nineteenth century, had driven many farmers into using slash-and-burn agriculture and much of the population into the forests in search of fuel and food. During World War II, the Japanese occupiers further depleted the forests. After liberation in 1945, deforestation and erosion were accelerated by the continuing poverty and unaccustomed freedom from controls, and the Korean War exacerbated the problem. Most of south Korea's landscape other than farmland became bare, brown, and eroded. The loss was so great that some believed the forests could never be restored.

President Rhee inaugurated a reforestation program, celebrating Arbor Day each year with the planting of trees, but progress was largely symbolic until 1961. Thereafter, the military regime and succeeding governments brought both discipline to enforce the protection of forests and economic growth to lessen poverty. Prohibition of woodcutting was enforced, and new fuels were developed to replace firewood—first the famous coal briquettes called *sipkukongt'an* (for the nineteen ventilation holes molded in the coal-and-clay cakes) and, in more recent years, bottled gas. As a result, trees again cover the hills, erosion has been moderated, and the countryside has regained much of its earlier beauty. In the 1970s, south Korea developed a national park system for both recreation and forest conservation. Restoration of tree cover has also contributed to flood control. However, south Korea can never be self-sufficient in wood production; the great majority of its requirements are imported.

In other respects, as the number of people and their standard of living increase, growing problems threaten the Korean environment. The city of Seoul is one of the most polluted in the world. In 1989, its air contained 0.056 parts per million (ppm) of sulfur dioxide. Its tap water was not considered safe to drink. South Korea as a whole produced 60,000 metric tons of household waste per day, of which 95 percent was dumped in surface landfills—along with 75 percent of the industrial waste. Industry produced 733,000 metric tons of hazardous waste in 1988. The surrounding seas were being polluted by untreated waste, particularly on the south and west coasts, with resulting damage to marine life. At the southeastern port of Masan, chemical oxygen demand (a measure of water pollution) reached 6.1 ppm, higher than any other port area in south Korea.[30]

The drive for rapid economic development overshadowed the pollution problems until the mid-1970s. Growing environmental concerns, however, led to the inclusion of environmental provisions in the Constitution of the Fifth Republic in 1980 and establishment of a central government Environmental Agency in the same year. Although this agency has been underfunded and understaffed, it has led the way in the enaction of strict environmental regulations. Environmental impact statements have been required of development projects since 1982, and penalties were imposed beginning in 1983. The Sixth Five-Year Plan (1987–1991) allocated the equivalent of nearly US$6 billion to water protection, air protection, and solid waste management. The Environmental Agency was elevated to cabinet level in December 1989. Its long-term plan (1987–2000) contemplates public and private investment equivalent to $21 billion over the plan period. Environmental laws have been toughened, and south Korean industry is paying increasing attention to its environmental responsibilities. However, "the predominant business attitude toward the environment is still one of apathy or disrespect."[31] There are visible results. Although Seoul is still choked with refuse and dirty air, a dramatic increase in the use of liquid propane gas (LPG) for vehicles and low-sulfur fuel for heating led to a dramatic drop in sulfur dioxide in the air to 0.023 ppm in 1993, the outer limit set by the World Health Organization. Progress remained slow, however, because of diesel-burning trucks and buses, and because the steadily increasing numbers of private cars that continue to burn gasoline are not always well maintained. The number of automobiles on the streets of Seoul in 1989 was 910,000; between 1992 and 1993 the total number of private automobiles in south Korea jumped from 3.2 million to 4 million, a jump of 20 percent in a single year.

Development of nuclear power generation in south Korea was originally motivated by the desire to reduce dependence on petroleum imports, but it was given added impetus by the pollution problem. As noted in Chapter 6, south Korea's nine operating nuclear plants produce nearly half of the country's electric energy; two more plants are under construction, and three more are planned. There is an antinuclear movement in Korea, which has added its concerns for plant safety and waste disposal to its opposition to nuclear weapons.

Sports and Recreation

Koreans traditionally put less emphasis than Western societies on physically strenuous sports and games, and more on socializing, for recreation and amusement. Moreover, games tended to involve individuals and small groups rather than team confrontations. (However, there were intervillage contests such as tugs-of-war and rock fights.) Much of the recreational activity followed the holidays of the Chinese lunar calendar, with sports and games appropriate to certain holidays. Men and boys sought their group recreation separately from women, particularly in the upper social levels, although female entertainers were a standard feature of male parties. Weddings, funerals, and other celebrations of life-cycle events, such as a man's sixtieth birthday (*hwan'gap*) and a child's first year of life (counted as his second birthday), were great social occasions, offering entertainment and relaxation as well as expressions of joy or sorrow.

Forms of Recreation

Traditionally, men and women sought their recreation separately. Men relaxed with friends of the same approximate age, leaving children in the care of their wives. Men with enough money had a separate room in their houses (the *sarang-bang*) for entertaining their friends. Among the upper classes, parties in eating and drinking houses or in outdoor pavilions might involve poetry reciting, singing, dancing, and listening to performances by trained women entertainers (*kisaeng*). Calligraphy, board games, or just conversation or strolling might be the focus of male gatherings. Women, in the old days, were far more restricted. The phrase "gathering mulberry leaves" refers to the device of young women for getting out of the house to see a friend by pretending to gather leaves for the silkworms.

Today, the recreation picture is greatly changed. Young men and women enjoy dates together; there is still some separation of sexes for relaxation, but women, at least in the cities, have the same access to entertainment as men. Television is almost universally available. Cities and good-sized towns have movie houses featuring both foreign and Korean films. There are innumerable eating and drinking places; tea houses (which usually serve coffee today) are particularly popular, and U.S.-style fast-food restaurants have made their appearance. Billiard halls, electronic game rooms, golf driving ranges, and other blessings of advanced civilization are everywhere. National parks have greatly developed in recent years. Koreans are very fond of nature and take full advantage of such facilities. In Seoul, the old royal palaces and other monuments to the past are open to the public; museums, art exhibits, and concerts are available and quite well attended. Theme parks are wildly popular. Travel is a favorite Korean recreation and has become available throughout the country by means of local and intercity bus service, railroads, and—for a growing number of people—private automobiles. The expressways leading in and out of Seoul are more like parking lots at peak times on weekends.

Traditional Athletics

Until the nineteenth century, sports consisted primarily of martial arts (including archery) and the Korean version of wrestling (*ssirum*). The martial arts were pursued more for spiritual and physical training and military readiness than for relaxation or enjoyment. Physical exertion was considered beneath the aristocrats' dignity; they left it to the soldiers, the women, the peasants, and the children.

The Korean sport most widely recognized in other countries is *t'aekwondo,* a disciplined form of person-to-person combat without weapons. One book on the subject describes *t'aekwondo* as "essentially discipline: discipline of the mind, the body, and the spirit. The physical manifestations . . . simply provide a measure of progress. . . . The lethal aspects of Tae Kwon Do attack come about just because one hopes it will be there. . . . It must be developed. Also, the individual must have certain mental, physical, and spiritual resources in the first place. . . ."[32] Totally unlike boxing, *t'aekwondo* involves periods of waiting and inward preparation, followed by quick and brief physical contact in forms carefully planned and practiced in advance.

T'aekwondo participants go through stages of training and practice. Completion of each stage, as demonstrated to a master, is marked by the award of a colored belt, a different color representing each level, to be worn with the traditional fighting garment; black is the highest level. In training and exhibition, physical injury is neither contemplated nor allowed, but the techniques are intended to subdue and if necessary incapacitate or kill an adversary in real-life situations.

Hwarangdo, a less widely known combat form, is similar in basic concept to *t'aekwondo* but makes use of the sword and other weapons. Its origin is traced to the young *hwarang* warrior-aristocrats of the Silla dynasty. Its discipline incorporates Buddhist spiritual elements. *Yudo* (judo) is another similar art, weaponless like *t'aekwondo;* usually associated with Japan, it is believed to have a Korean origin. *Ssirum* is somewhat similar to Western wrestling and is primarily a spectator sport. The wrestlers are specialists, with large, heavy bodies. (Japanese *sumo* is similar.)

Archery and horsemanship were traditionally essential in Korean military readiness. Practice of both was encouraged, particularly among the military, until the end of the Choson Dynasty. Archery is still popular but is becoming increasingly Westernized.

A succession of festive and solemn days throughout the lunar year enriched the lives of traditional Koreans, and some of these celebrations survive today. On festive days, the people of agricultural villages had group competitions such as tug-of-war. There were also rock fights between the young men of competing villages. A major form of village relaxation was impromptu dancing, often to the *nong'ak* music of a farmers' band. Swinging and seesawing are traditional women's games, engaged in particularly on festive days (New Year's, for seesawing; *tano,* fifth day of the fifth lunar month, for swinging).[33] The famous romantic story of Ch'un-hyang, a commoner woman loved by a young aristocrat, begins with a scene in which the hero spots Ch'unhyang swinging near the pavilion where he is relaxing. Kite-flying is a traditional and still-popular boys' sport, particularly at the New Year; there are national kite-flying contests. The traditional forms are still enjoyed in regional and national folk celebrations and in some agricultural villages. They have had a recent comeback on college campuses, accompanying the growth of nationalist spirit.

Traditional Games

Adults and children alike play a game of Korean origin called *yut,* which uses a set of four sticks tossed in the air by each of several players in turn. The sticks are semicircular on one side, flat on the other; the number that land flat side up determines the score. Players advance scoring markers around an impromptu board; the first to complete the circuit wins.

Far more intellectually serious are the games of *paduk,* a kind of checkers that is the same as Japanese *go,* and a form of chess called *changgi.* Both are board games for two people. International *paduk* competitions are held, featuring mostly Japanese and Korean players. Like their Western counterparts, these games call for intense mental concentration and may go on for hours.

Traditional card games use decks of forty to sixty cards of a different design from those in the West. They are very popular and are frequently the basis for gambling. Western poker has become a favorite activity among Koreans, who frequently play for very high stakes; an apocryphal story has it that a player once bet his entire business on a single hand and lost. Mahjong is also popular and is another means of gambling.

Modern Sports

Team sports were brought to Korea by Europeans and Americans and were incorporated into the programs of modern schools and other institutions (such as the Young Men's Christian Association). Soccer, for example, the most popular team game in Korea, was introduced by the crew of a British warship in 1882. Until recently, team sports were mainly thought of as physical and mental training rather than recreation. Such ideas as pickup teams and sandlot softball are very new. Nevertheless, as the world is coming to realize, Koreans—both north and south—are demonstrating high skill in the new sports forms. South Korea first entered a national team in the 1948 Olympics and has steadily improved the country's showing. North Korea has fielded its own teams in international competitions and scored significant victories: Its athletes won medals in boxing, wrestling, and weight lifting in the 1976 and 1980 Summer Olympics (the latter boycotted by south Korea along with the United States). In the 1984 Olympics (boycotted by north Korea along with the Soviet Union), south Korea was tenth among competing nations in medals won (six gold, six silver, seven bronze).

South Korea has scored major international competition successes in soccer, wrestling, boxing, and basketball. As long ago as the 1936 Olympics at Berlin, Son Ki-jong won a gold medal in track as a member of the Japanese team. (At over seventy years of age, Son carried the Olympic torch into the stadium for the 1988 games.) A National Sports Festival, held each October in various major cities, includes twenty-seven categories of sports; there are also junior and winter meets. Professional or semiprofessional leagues play soccer and baseball (baseball is second in popularity to soccer); leading professional players command very high salaries. There are a number of skilled amateur teams sponsored by Korean business enterprises. Volleyball is another popular team sport. Western-style boxing was introduced in 1912. Tennis and golf are widely played, as is table tennis. Swimming, skating, roller-skating, and mountaineering have their followers; a Korean mountain climbing team reached the top of Mount Everest in 1977.

The 1988 Summer Olympic Games

South Korea now has hosted a series of major world sports spectaculars, but nothing tops Seoul's hosting of the XXIV Summer Olympiad from September 17 to October 2, 1988. The tremendous political significance of the event is discussed in Chapters 4, 7, and 8. Suffice it to say that the 1988 Olympic Games were generally regarded as the most successful in Olympic history from the standpoint of the number of sports events, the number of participating national delegations and athletes, the records established, and the peaceful atmosphere. (The tranquillity of the Games' environment owed much to extraordinary security efforts by the Republic of Korea, supported by the United States. Once north Korea's efforts to participate in or obstruct the Games had failed, it apparently did not challenge the security arrangements, despite fears to the contrary.)

The Korean athletes won 12 gold medals of a total of 241 awarded, placing the Republic fourth after the Soviet Union (55), East Germany (37), the United States (36), and ahead of West Germany (11). Altogether, Koreans won 33 medals, including 10 silver and 11 bronze. (West Germany's total of 40 medals in all categories exceeded Korea's.) The Koreans excelled primarily in archery and contact sports such as boxing, wrestling, and judo; but Korean women surprisingly captured the gold medal in handball—not a common Korean sport. For the first time in the Olympics, medals were awarded in table tennis, and the Koreans won gold medals in the men's singles and the women's doubles.

All told, 160 nations participated in the 1988 Games; for the first time in twelve years, both the Soviet Union and the United States competed in the same Olympiad. There were over 39,000 participants in 1,030 events, including 13,300 athletes and officials, plus umpires, administrative personnel, and media representatives. Thirty-three world records were set and five tied, plus twenty-seven Olympic records set and forty-two tied. The chairman of the Seoul Olympic Organizing Committee estimated that 2.5 billion people throughout the world watched the Games on television. Attendance totaled approximately a quarter million (somewhat less than anticipated, because of public fears for security). Nevertheless, the Committee concluded its operations with a profit of $349 million, which was to be used for future support of sports.

Under a system adopted in 1975, the seventy-seven Korean medal winners from this and other international competitions won lifetime pensions, with the amounts proportioned to the type of medal and event. Kim Soo-myung, the woman who won two archery gold medals in the 1988 Games, was awarded the maximum pension of 1,100,000 won (about US$1,600) per month.

Notes

1. Material in this chapter is based chiefly upon the author's experience and observations, as verified by Korean and U.S. colleagues. Relevant sources include Vincent S.R. Brandt, *South Korean Society in Transition* (Elkins Park, Pa.: Philip Jaisohn Memorial Foundation, 1983); Paul S. Crane, *Korean Patterns* (Seoul: Hollym Publishing Co., 1967); Sung Chick Hong, *The Intellectual and Modernization: A Study of Korean Attitudes* (Seoul: Social Science Research Institute, Korea University, 1967); Ki-Hyuk Park and Sidney D. Gamble, *The Changing Korean Village* (Seoul: Shin-hung Press for the Royal Asiatic Society, Korea Branch, 1975); Man-gap Yi, *Sociology and Social Change in Korea* (Seoul: Seoul Na-

tional University Press, 1982); and Hagen Koo, *State and Society in Contemporary Korea* (Ithaca: Cornell University Press, 1993).

2. On the Korean contribution to Confucian philosophy, see William T. de Bary and JaHyun Kim Haboush, eds., *The Rise of Neo-Confucianism in Korea* (New York: Columbia University Press, 1985), p. xvii. Professor Michael Kalton has also done much to put Korean Confucian theory into the mainstream. For example, see his edited translation of Yi T'oe-gye's "The Ten Diagrams on Sage Learning," *To Become a Sage* (New York: Columbia University Press, 1988).

3. The twelve most common family names in Korea, in McCune-Reischauer romanization (with variant spellings in parentheses) are Yi (Lee, Rhee), Kim, Pak (Park), Chong (Chung), Yun (Yoon), Ch'oe (Choi), Yu (Yoo, Ryu), Hong, Sin (Shin), Kwon, Cho (Joe), Han (Hahn), and O (Oh, Auh). Individuals adopt their own romanized spellings, which may vary considerably. For example, a former prominent political leader, Cho Pyong-ok, spelled his name P. O. Chough. See Bruce Grant, *A Guide to Korean Characters: Reading and Writing Hangul and Hanja,* 2nd revised edition (Elizabeth, N.J.: Hollym International Corp., 1982), p. 335.

4. I am indebted to Professor Lee On-Jook for this and several other points in this chapter.

5. William E. Henthorn, *A History of Korea* (New York: Free Press, 1971), pp. 161–162.

6. On the New Community Movement, see Vincent S.R. Brandt and Ji Woon Cheong, *Planning from the Bottom Up: Community-Based Integrated Rural Development in South Korea* (Essex, Conn.: International Council for Educational Development, 1979). I discuss the New Community Movement also in Chapter 4.

7. *Korea Times,* March 4, 1986; *Korea Annual 1994* (Seoul: Yonhap News Agency, 1994), p. 177.

8. The Western term "block" does not precisely explain the equivalent Korean area but is the best approximation.

9. For an overview of contemporary women's issues in south Korea see Chungmoo Choi, "Korean Women in a Culture of Inequality," *Korea Briefing 1992* (Boulder: Westview Press, 1992), pp. 97–116.

10. For a scholarly summation of Korean ethical values, see Michael Kalton, *Korean Ideas and Values* (Elkins Park, Pa.: Philip Jaisohn Memorial Foundation, 1979). See also Steven R. Brown, "Values, Development, and Character: Appraising Korean Experience," *Korea Fulbright Forum* 1 (Winter 1984):33–66.

11. North Korean scholars, because of their Marxian theoretical framework, are at pains to point up the emergence of "capitalist" enterprise in Korea at this period. One example is a paper by north Korean scholar Ch'oe Chin-hyok, "*Chosen minjujui inmin konghwagukeso-ui rijo sigi-ui ryoksa wa munhwa yon'gu-e taehayo*" (Regarding Research on the History and Culture of the Yi Dynasty in the Democratic People's Republic of Korea), delivered at the annual conference of the Mid-Atlantic Region, Association for Asian Studies, October 1985.

12. Republic of Korea, Ministry of Education, *Education in Korea 1985–1986* (Seoul, 1985), pp. 30 ff; conversations with Korean professors.

13. *Education in Korea 1985–1986,* pp. 41–42.

14. Enrollments are from Yonhap News Agency, *Korea Annual 1994,* p. 191; distribution from Korea Overseas Information Service, *A Handbook of Korea* (Seoul: Korea Overseas Information Service, 1993), p. 452.

15. Andrea Matles Savada, ed., *North Korea: A Country Study,* 4th ed. (Washington, D.C.: Government Printing Office, 1994), pp. 92–96.

16. *Kodae Sinmun* (Korea University News), June 21, 1983, pp. 6–7, and September 16, 1985, p. 6.

17. Figures from Korean newspaper reports.

18. Evelyn McCune, in *The Arts of Korea: An Illustrated History* (Rutland, Vt.: Charles E. Tuttle, 1962), p. 90, has stated that a work of the great Silla scholar-official Ch'oe Chi-won (858–910) called "Pen Scratchings in a Cinnamon Garden" still exists. See also Henthorn, *A History of Korea*, p. 76.

19. Paik Nak Choon (L. George Paik), "Tripitaka Koreana; Library of Woodblocks at Haein Sa, Korea," *Transactions of the Royal Asiatic Society, Korea Branch*, 32 (1953):62–78.

20. Appendix B on the Korean language includes examples of the *han'gul* phonetic script.

21. McCune, *The Arts of Korea*, pp. 19–20.

22. Won-yong Kim, "Spontaneity Defines Korean Art," *Korea Newsreview*, March 14, 1987, p. 23. See also the same author's "Philosophies and Styles in Korean Art," *Korea Journal* 19(4):8.

23. The internet address for the SeOUL-NyMAX festival is http://www.panix.com/fluxus/MedialeMenu.html.

24. For details of Chun-era press controls see "South Korea: 'Guiding the Press,'" *Index on Censorship*, 16(5) (May 1987):28–36.

25. See Marshall R. Pihl, "Contemporary Literature in a Divided Land," in *Korea Briefing 1993*, ed. Donald N. Clark (Boulder: Westview Press, 1993), pp. 79–98.

26. Susan S. Shin, "Tonghak Thought: The Roots of Revolution," *Korea Journal* 19(9) (September 1979):11–20.

27. Korea Overseas Information Service, *Handbook of Korea*, 9th ed. (Seoul: Korea Overseas Information Service, 1993), p. 142.

28. *Korea Annual 1986*.

29. Korea Overseas Information Service, *A Handbook of Korea*, 9th ed. (Seoul: Korea Overseas Information Service, 1993) pp. 476–478.

30. John Song, "Too Much Rubbish," *Korea Business Month*, October 1989, pp. 25–28.

31. Song, "Too Much Rubbish," p. 26; Richard A. Ellis and Mary M. Walker, "U.S. Pollution Control Technology Marketing Opportunities for the Republic of Korea," undated paper submitted to roundtable discussion, "Exporting U.S. Pollution Control and Waste Management Equipment, Technology, and Services to Korea," International Business Development, Northwestern University, Evanston, Illinois, February 28, 1989.

32. Duk Sung Son and Robert J. Clark, *Korean Karate: The Art of Tae Kwon Do* (Englewood Cliffs, N.J.: Prentice-Hall, 1968), p. 5.

33. A description of traditional holidays is in Sang-su Choe, *Annual Customs of Korea* (Seoul: Seomun-dang Publishing Co., 1983). They are observed according to the lunar calendar and thus vary every year. The major ones are New Year's (observed for three days); the spring and fall Confucian shrine ceremonies; *hansik* (cold food day), the 105th day after the winter solstice, on which people visit their ancestors' graves; *chop'a-il*, Buddha's birthday, the eighth day of the fourth month; *tano*, fifth day of the fifth month; *chusok*, the fifteenth day of the eighth month, a harvest festival and a day for honoring ancestors' graves; *kaech'onjol*, third day of the tenth month, birthday of Tan'gun, the legendary founder of Korea (now a modern holiday, celebrated as south Korea's national day on October 3 of the Gregorian calendar). For each of these holidays and a number of additional ones, there are traditional foods, games, social activities, and ceremonies.

4

Politics and Government of the Republic of Korea (South Korea)

Introduction

The political system of Korea is a fascinating study in the interplay of four different traditions. Strongest of the four, even today, is the Chinese Confucian pattern of institutions and behavior, with its emphasis on hierarchy, virtue, and proper form. The Western European and U.S. political model of liberal democracy, although long admired by Korean intellectuals, is only beginning to penetrate below the surface (although Western organization and management techniques have had greater impact). The Marxist philosophy, as systematized by Lenin and Stalin, was transplanted and fostered in north Korea; the gentler socialist version colors political attitudes in the south as well. Beneath all these traditions lie Korea's own native ways, giving a distinctive Korean cast to political life.

A good way to approach the study of Korean politics (or any politics, for that matter) is to think of government, as well as related political institutions, as a kind of mechanism within society. This mechanism responds to basic needs and wants of the people for security, order, livelihood, fair sharing of resources, and national pride. The government does this by listening to popular demands, choosing those that are most important, making plans and policies for meeting the chosen demands (in the form of laws and programs), and applying national resources to carry out the plans and policies. The people support the system by providing taxes, military service, respect, obedience, and votes. This support provides the government with the authority and resources it needs to make and carry out decisions. It also enables the government to use force against those who do not follow its directions or obey its laws.

In a democratic system, when the people dislike the government, they vote the leaders and ruling party out of power in favor of a new group. In an autocratic system, the government tells the people what the limits of their demands are and gives the people what it thinks they should have. The political system can be stable under either democracy or autocracy—or some in-between arrangement—so long as the people accept it or the government has the necessary force and efficiency to make them accept it.

Although it may seem strange to people with a democratic tradition, many people in the world—including the Koreans, until recently—live without protest in an autocratic system as long as its leaders govern effectively and with reasonable concern for the public welfare. Most governments in the world throughout history have been autocratic. The rulers were perceived to have divine right to rule; in some cases, as in the Roman Empire, they themselves had the status of gods. Their actions were therefore beyond the control of ordinary mortals, like floods and earthquakes.

However, if massive discontent develops in an autocracy, it boils over in rebellion, which compels the rulers to change their policies, or (if it becomes a revolution) transforms the political system. Revolution and rebellion may or may not be good things, depending upon the evils rebelled against and the practical means of doing away with these evils. The problem is that most revolutionaries have little experience in running a government; yet the problems of government are most difficult in the conditions of disorder that accompany rebellion. The resultant process of trial and error can have terrible consequences, including aggression from outside.

It follows that political stability is generally preferred to the risks of rebellion. In the words of the U.S. Declaration of Independence, "Mankind are more disposed to suffer, while Evils are sufferable." The genius of democracy, of course, is that it provides a built-in device for instant peaceful revolution by voting the rulers out of power. However, if democracy is to function, the complex rules and understandings of the democratic political game must be known, understood, and respected by leaders and people. Otherwise, it will fail, as many recent examples demonstrate.

In today's interdependent world, moreover, sovereign nations have demands and expectations of one another that also must be met. The smaller a nation is, the more important these outside expectations become, and the more they limit that nation's freedom of action. South Korea, particularly, faces such limitations: It has few natural resources yet must support a dense population on an ever-higher level and defend them against a heavily armed adversary, north Korea. Its international relations, both political and economic, are therefore of key importance in domestic stability and prosperity.

Politics involves more than the formal government structure as laid down by the constitution and laws. It also involves all of the groups and categories of people who look to the political system to meet their needs and expectations. Some of these people, individually or in groups, have more influence than others, so they may benefit more. The political system works according to a set of understandings shared by the population, most of them unwritten, that make up the political culture. The way the system really functions cannot be understood just by reading the constitution; rather, it must be learned by observing how people actually think and behave. To emphasize this point, the south Korean Constitution is summarized toward the end, rather than the beginning, of this chapter.

Political Culture

The political culture of the Republic of Korea is a blend of Korean, Chinese, and Western elements. The native element, as it existed prior to the Chinese impact, can only be guessed at. It seems to have had a strong element of aristocratic authority, based on birth and family, coupled with an equally strong spirit of individual independence. The Chinese input sank in very deep over nearly 2,000 years of exposure—particularly after Confucianism was officially adopted by King T'aejo at the beginning of the Choson Dynasty (see Chapter 2). It became an integral and dominant part of Korean political culture.

The political aspects of this culture, as it existed down to the mid–nineteenth century, included the following elements:

- belief that human society was an integral part of the whole universe, interrelated with it in maintaining order and harmony;
- acceptance of harmony, order, and consensus as major political values and purposes;
- acceptance of duty toward family and associational group (such as the court factions) as more important than individual satisfaction;
- concurrently, a strong individual drive for power and position, often manifested as a struggle among factions of rival leaders and their supporters;
- loyalty of subject to the person of the ruler, rather than to the whole state as such;
- belief that the proper model for political behavior was the ideal kingdom of the ancients, the principles of which were to be found in the Chinese classics;
- a static view of the human condition, in which nations and dynasties and families rose and fell in cyclical fashion, but life's potentialities remained basically the same;
- acceptance of hierarchical relations among people within the society, and among nations, so that everyone was inferior or superior to everyone else except for friends of the same age;
- a view of the ruler as responsible to Heaven (through China) for the order and well-being of all aspects of his kingdom—political, economic, and social—and possessing the Mandate of Heaven to rule so long as he fulfilled this responsibility;
- disparagement of industrial and commercial activity and encouragement of agriculture as the central activity;
- emphasis on form and procedure, as well as substantive performance, as key elements in maintaining order;
- preference for decisionmaking by consensus, rather than by majority vote or force of arms; yet at the same time, unwillingness to compromise on matters perceived to involve principle;
- respect and honor to scholar-officials, passers of the examinations, as a class possessing superior benevolence, wisdom, and administrative ability and therefore entitled to special status;
- self-governance of the agricultural majority of the population in their villages, except for governmental collection of taxes and labor and punishment of particularly heinous crimes;

- reluctance to involve governmental institutions in personal or family quarrels, which were settled whenever possible within families or communities.

These values were opposite in many respects to those of the West, which (at least from the late eighteenth century, particularly in the United States) emphasized progress, change, individual freedom, equality of all persons, adversary relations, government by consent of the people, separation of political from economic and social affairs, and the importance of civic duty. However, as Korea—like China and Japan—was driven to modernize and industrialize, both for self-protection and to meet the rising expectations of the people, it had to accept the Western values that accompanied the process. Attempts to be selective failed and the traditional culture resisted change.

Since 1876 (the year of the Koreans' first Western-style treaty with Japan), and even before that, Korean leaders and people have lived in a shifting cultural environment where old values crumbled but new ones were suspect. In the military and economic spheres, modern organizational values are accepted and applied (along with some traditional values). In north Korea, the political culture seems to have been drastically modified. Communist attitudes, beliefs, and values are accepted there as they have been in other Communist nations, although with some Korean variations such as the *juch'e* principle discussed in Chapters 3 and 5.

In south Korea, however, an integrated political culture is still emerging, through a much freer process. Significant elements of the traditional pattern survive beneath an overlay of Western institutional forms. Family, associational group, and factional loyalties still outweigh civic consciousness. Informal group networks, such as school and college alumni associations (notably the successive graduating classes of the Korea Military Academy) or shared provincial origins, are powerful channels of communication and influence. The sense of abstract justice and universal human rights is weak in comparison to group loyalties and duties.

The right and duty of citizen participation in voting and other political acts is still imperfectly understood among the general public, although that understanding is growing. The concept of political parties is not clearly established; parties still carry something of the contempt attached to the old court factions. The concept of loyal opposition and open debate on policy still does not fit a culture emphasizing authority, hierarchy, and harmony. Political opponents tend to be viewed by those in power as heretics and subversives, just as they were in the Choson Dynasty court, and a conspiratorial element persists in opposition political activity. The relation between the economic and political sectors of the society is currently a matter of leadership debate, in which the old tradition that included all national life within the domain of political control still seems strong.

An anecdote may illustrate Korean political style. In 1956, a newly formed opposition party was preparing for the presidential election. At that time, the president and vice president were both elected by separate popular votes. Public discontent with political and economic conditions was running high. President Rhee had angered the previously divided opposition forces into unity by forcing through the Assembly a constitutional amendment permitting him to run again. Three senior politicians, who led the main factions of the new Democratic Party, gathered one afternoon in the home of a party supporter to decide which of them would be the party's presidential and vice presidential candidates.

It was relatively easy for the three men to agree that P. H. Shinicky (Shin Ik-hui, known to foreigners as Patrick Henry Shinicky), former speaker of the National Assembly, would run for president; but Cho Pyong-ok, the Democratic Party's "old faction" leader, and Chang Myon, the "new faction" leader, each wanted to be vice president. Shinicky and Cho had been opposition leaders for years; Chang had only recently joined the party. The three men sat in solemn silence for hours. Neither man would yield, but it was not seemly to covet the candidacy openly.

Finally, in the small hours of the morning, Cho—who had a reputation for impatience—said, "Dr. Chang, why don't you run?" Etiquette required that Chang reciprocate by inviting Cho to do so. Instead, he quickly agreed.[1]

Shinicky died of a heart attack on his campaign train shortly before the presidential election, but Chang Myon, to the surprise of nearly everyone, defeated President Rhee's running mate and held the powerless office of vice president for four years. Shortly after his election, he was the target of an assassination attempt but suffered only a wound in his hand. He became prime minister after the 1960 student revolution overturned the Rhee regime and was himself turned out of office by Park Chung-hee's military coup the following year.

The Sixth Republic

The year 1988 was a watershed of political development in Korea. This was the year of the Seoul Olympic Games, a source of enormous national pride as Korea took its place on the world stage. It was also the year set by the 1980 Constitution for a peaceful transfer of power to a newly elected president—the first such transfer in the history of the Republic. During his presidency, Chun Doo-hwan repeatedly promised to be the first chief executive to hand the office over to a duly elected successor at the end of his seven-year term, and he retired as promised on February 26, 1988. Roh Tae-woo, Chun's chosen successor, was inaugurated after winning a plurality in a direct popular election. It was the first such event in the Republic's history and symbolized a new precedent for law and public opinion over personal ambition and autocratic tradition. (The election of Yun Po-son by the legislature to succeed acting President Ho Chong in August 1960 was not comparable because it simply confirmed a change that had already occurred.)

Roh's succession was a complicated process that started out in early 1987 as a foregone conclusion, given the composition of the south Korean electoral college, and ended up the ironic result of a free election by the people, who divided their votes between Roh and two opposition leaders, Kim Dae-jung and Kim Young-sam. The election process was a main issue, and the public's role in forcing the constitutional change from electoral college election to popular election was the main story.

The campaign to abolish the electoral college began in the mid-1980s with the 1985 National Assembly elections, when the opposition New Korea Democratic Party won a surprisingly large number of seats. The amendment proposal drew wide public support—manifested in large demonstrations and an opposition-sponsored petition campaign—because of general discontent with the Chun administration. The amendment controversy centered on the popular vote issue and also on debate over the structure of government—whether it should be presidential (like the United States), parliamentary (like Great Britain or Japan), or "dual-executive" (like France).

President Chun, who had previously opposed any amendment before the end of the decade, agreed to consider amending the Constitution before the 1987 elections. In June 1986 the National Assembly created a committee to work out a draft; but in a year of sparring, neither government nor opposition departed from its position. Each side sought a formulation that would maximize its chance to retain or to gain power. On April 13, 1987, Chun decreed an end to the discussion, returning to his earlier position that constitutional change should come after the next presidential election and virtually guaranteeing the election of his chosen successor by the electoral college.[2] In June, the president's political party nominated Chun's candidate: party chairman Roh Tae-woo. Roh's nomination was controversial both because it represented Chun's virtual appointment of his successor and because the successor was an ex-general who had been involved in Chun's coup of December 1979 and had supported Chun all along the way, apparently earning the nomination in return. Chun had created an institutional nest for himself in the form of the Ilhae Foundation, a well-endowed organization that displayed every sign of enabling the military dictatorship to continue with Chun in the position of retired shogun. This of course made a mockery of Chun's ostentatious promises to be the first south Korean president to participate in a peaceful transfer of power. The day of Roh's nomination there were massive demonstrations in the streets of Seoul expressing outrage at this flouting of the public will. The pressure built over several weeks, with ever-larger demonstrations. A student was killed by a flying tear gas grenade. American officials conveyed to Chun Washington's unwillingness to be painted as the friend of military dictatorship in south Korea as the Korean strongman had done in 1980. Under intense public pressure Roh announced on June 29 that he supported the principle of direct popular election and favored an immediate constitutional amendment paving the way for direct popular election of the president. Chun grudgingly went along. The National Assembly approved an amendment that provided for direct presidential elections and for expanded guarantees of rights but otherwise continued the existing form of government. The amendment, which created the "Sixth Republic" (or the "5.5 Republic" as it was jokingly known), was approved by popular referendum in October 1987.

Underlying these points were questions of human rights and political participation, on the one hand, and the personal ambitions of political leaders for power on the other. Such considerations brought about a reversal of the historical positions of the government in power—which had always favored a presidential system in support of its leader—and the opposition, which had seen a parliamentary regime as a means through which to put the leader on the shelf and thus achieve power. In 1987, these considerations also brought about a split in the opposition, because neither of its two principal leaders—Kim Dae-jung and Kim Young-sam—would yield to the other.

The Roh Tae-woo Years, 1988–1993

In the election on December 19, 1987, Roh won 36.6 percent of the popular vote, against 28 and 26 percent, respectively, for the two Kims—both of whom alleged fraud, pointing to such things as pressure on voters in the military. It was therefore clear that President Chun's ostensible desire to step down would be sorely tested by the fact that his successor would almost certainly have less than majority support and would have a hard time continuing Chun's style of military rule, being forced to make common cause with civilian politicians. President Roh Tae-woo was inaugurated on February 25, 1988, as the twelfth president of the Republic (the sixth person to have held the office, but the twelfth to be elected or re-elected). Immediately upon Chun's retirement from the presidency, the stories of corruption and dictatorial excesses under his regime began bubbling to the surface. Many members of his administration and even members of his family were tried on criminal charges related to various scandals and ended up spending time in prison.

The April 1988 parliamentary election also produced a major change in the south Korean political scene by putting more opposition than government candidates into the 299 seats of the newly strengthened National Assembly. The new election law more than doubled the number of election districts and provided for single-member rather than two-member elections in each. The proportion of total seats elected directly from districts increased from two-thirds to three-quarters, guaranteeing half of the remainder (rather than the former two-thirds) to whichever party gained the largest number of popular votes and distributing the other half to other parties in proportion to the popular vote.

To the government's surprise, the new arrangement worked to the opposition's advantage. The government's Democratic Justice Party, with 34 percent of the popular vote, gained a total of 125 seats. Kim Dae-jung's Peace and Democracy Party won 19.3 percent of the vote (less than the 23.8 percent of Kim Young-sam's Reunification Democratic Party), but because of intense regional loyalty in the southwest province of Cholla (scene of the 1980 Kwangju uprising and Kim Dae-jung's birthplace), the Peace and Democracy Party claimed 71 seats to 59 for the Reunification Democratic Party. Kim Jong-pil's New Democratic Republican Party, composed largely of members of the government party of the Park administration, won 15.6 percent of the vote and 35 seats. Independents won nine seats.[3]

In the first two years following the election, a few Assembly members changed party affiliations, but the seat distribution remained essentially the same. Opposition parties were occasionally able to agree among themselves—as in electing a speaker and rejecting President Roh's first nominee for chief justice. The 1989 budget and other major legislation were passed, with modest reallocations forced by the opposition. However, despite talk of coalitions and realignments, no established pattern of collaboration emerged.

In its first two years, the revised political system of the Sixth Republic responded in part to the popular demand for more freedom and participation. This partial success was evidenced by the shift in radical demands away from the 1987 cry for democratization to a new focus on reunification and anti-Americanism. However, as was to be expected, the new system could not immediately meet the conflicting demands of newly emerging interest groups. The executive branch, which continued to be the center of government power, sought the high ground between liberal calls for freedom and conservative demands for order. The latter focused largely on the control of radical student, worker, and other dissident activity that the conservatives linked with subversion from north Korea. Both extremes remained unsatisfied.

The National Assembly, no longer cowed by a government majority, exercised its restored powers of investigation and criticism, initially with a good deal of grandstanding. Opposition forces succeeded in holding televised legislative hearings on the abuses of the Fifth Republic, culminating in a stormy day of testimony by ex-President Chun Doo-hwan on December 31, a date meant to symbolize the closing of the whole unhappy chapter of the Fifth Republic. In front of the National Assembly Chun admitted a certain limited degree of responsibility for what had gone wrong during his tenure and assigned himself to a two-year period of reflection and purification at Paektam-sa, a temple in the mountains of Kangwon Province. This quieted public demands for further prosecution—until the scandal-wracked year of 1995 when Chun was finally called to account for the 1979 coup and 1980 Kwangju massacre.

In the area of human rights, however, the Roh administration stopped short of thorough reform. Although the press enjoyed new freedom, the restrictive National Security Law and other legislation of previous regimes were still largely unchanged. The laws were vigorously enforced against student, worker, and other groups challenging the regime in power. Complaints of brutality by security agencies and unjustified arrest and detention continued. President Roh, who had promised to hold some kind of midterm referendum or evaluation of his administration, postponed it indefinitely.

Some of the anomie that afflicted the early Roh years arose from his intentional assumption of a lower profile presidency. After a generation of military strongmen, the comparatively soft touch of Roh Tae-woo was taken for indecision and weakness. He was referred to derisively as "Mul Tae-u" ("Watery," meaning "Wishy-Washy" Tae-woo), and people remarked on the disarray in the ranks of his followers in the ruling Democratic Justice Party. There was renewed talk of constitutional revision and criticism both of growing crime and disorder at the same time that there was criticism of government moves against student and other dissidents. Long-suppressed worker demands erupted during the Roh years, causing strikes and work stoppages that led to substantial wage increases, on the one hand, while threatening the economic growth rate, which had been a major element of political stability since 1960, on the other.

An important reorganization of south Korea's political leadership occurred in January 1990 when three of the country's four political parties announced a merger, creating the Democratic Liberal Party (DLP), a clear reference to Japan's ruling Liberal Democratic Party, whose faction leaders had been ruling and trading the prime ministership in Japan since the mid-1950s. The DLP was designed to command a majority in the National Assembly and to isolate the main opposition under Kim Dae-jung. Though it was ostensibly intended to increase political stability, it clearly served the political ambitions of its three proponents, Roh, Kim Young-sam, and former Prime Minister Kim Jong-pil. Kim Young-sam, who had failed in his bid for the presidency in 1987, burned some bridges when he joined forces with the government in 1990; yet in the end he turned out to have been the biggest winner as he deftly maneuvered himself into the presidency, succeeding Roh in 1993. Kim Jong-pil, older and more representative of the bygone Park era, gained much less, having to settle for the party's cochairmanship. His interest was in a constitutional amendment that would create a Japanese-style cabinet system with a prime minister representing one of the ruling party factions. This scenario, however, never developed.

During the Roh years the south Korean political institutions evolved in several significant ways. In March 1991 local elections were held for the first time to elect representatives to city, county, and district assemblies. Candidates ran ostensibly without party labels, but candidates supporting the ruling DLP were seen as having won a strong majority of the races. This took south Korea closer to the ideal of local democracy, overcoming a generation of centrally controlled appointments to local offices. The next step in the process came several years later, in 1995, when local candidates with party affiliations were allowed to run for mayor and county chief positions. Once again, government candidates won many races; however, the results highlighted a worrisome trend toward division within south Korea associating the government party with the southeastern Yongnam region and the opposition with the disaffected southwestern Honam region. Greater local autonomy, therefore, merged with endemic regional rivalries as a dynamic force in south Korean politics.

The Kim Young-sam Administration, 1993–

Kim Young-sam's (Figure 4.1) succession to the presidency in February 1993 was the second peaceful transfer of power in the Republic's history and the first one that did not involve a constitutional change. Kim's election also ended more than thirty years of rule by generals and ex-generals.

Kim Young-sam's rise to power was marked by political intrigues, particularly those surrounding the merger of his opposition party with the government's ruling party to form the Democratic Liberal Party in 1990 and the infighting and maneuvering that ensued between the 1990 party merger and the 1992 presidential election. As a DLP leader, Kim fought off challenges from the rival "T.K. faction" of North Kyongsang Province politicians from around the city of Taegu, allies of President Roh, and attempts by the Kim Jong-pil faction to revise the Constitution to create a Japanese-style "parliamentary" system in which the prime minister, not the president, holds real political power. Kim staked his career on emerging as the DLP nominee for president in a winner-take-all contest, and he prevailed. In the December 1992 election he won with a plurality of 42 percent.

FIGURE 4.1   Kim Young-sam, president of the Republic of Korea (photo courtesy of Korean Information Office, Washington, D.C.)

Kim presented himself as a reformer and practitioner of a new politics in south Korea that would address the "Korean disease," the corruption that infested every level of society. His first months in office brought the forced disclosure of financial assets of many leading officials including himself, and purges of military officials who had been involved in procurements scandals. In August 1993 Kim approved the "real name financial transaction system," requiring an end to the practice of shielding money in accounts under false names to avoid taxation and to cover up illegal profiteering. Kim also opened the way for reevaluation of the 1979 "coup-like incident" through which Chun Doo-hwan took over the defense establishment following the death of President Park, and of the May 1980 Army massacre of demonstrators in Kwangju. Kim's reforms touched election laws, political influence-peddling, and human rights aspects of the National Security Law. The new president cut his own staff, ordered tax investigations of big businessmen, and decreed the removal of vestiges of the Japanese colonial occupation, showing that his reform impulse could reach into every area of national life.

During Kim Young-sam's first three years in office he was faced with several major national problems. The biggest was north Korea's nuclear program and the breakdown in inter-Korean diplomacy that resulted when north Korea refused to cooperate fully with the international inspection regime (see Chapter 7). Another was the need for Korea to sign the Uruguay Round of the General Agreement on Tariffs and Trade (GATT) talks and subsequently to join the new World Trade Organization (WTO), over the loud protests of farmers and others who thought that freer trade would mean ruin at the hands of foreign competitors. Both the nuclear issue and the trade issue complicated south Korea's relations with the United States: the nuclear issue because the United States appeared to be going around the Kim Young-sam administration for direct talks with Pyongyang, and the trade issue because it seemed that the Kim administration was buckling under pressure, especially American pressure, to open its markets too quickly.

In the realm of domestic party politics, Kim's administration was beset by factional infighting within the ruling party, a fundamental contradiction that finally tore the Democratic Liberal Party apart in 1995. In the same year the public clamor for a definitive resolution of the lingering doubts about the 1979 Chun coup and the 1980 Kwangju massacre reached a crescendo with lawsuits demanding that Chun and others involved in the events of 1979 and 1980 be brought to justice. Kim's reluctance to press the legal case against the Chun camp no doubt was a by-product of his party's merger with the Democratic Justice Party in 1990. However, in October 1995 scandal engulfed Roh Tae-woo when it was discovered that he had accepted hundreds of millions of dollars in political funds from Korean businesses, much of it for his own personal use. Following Roh's arrest, the net closed on Chun Doo-hwan himself, arrested in December first for his role in the events of 1979–1980 and then, when the spotlight turned on his own slush fund, for an accounting of his receipt of political funds as well. By the end of 1995 it seemed that events were nearly out of control, with ex post facto laws being passed to enable the government to try Chun and Roh after the expiration of the statute of limitations. Many Koreans were embarrassed to see two former presidents behind bars and they wondered how long President Kim Young-sam himself, a veteran of four decades of participation in the political culture of south Korea, could keep his "Mr. Clean" image. As south Korea looked forward to new National Assembly elections in April 1996 and a presidential election in 1997, there was much disquiet about what kind of "new politics" would replace the discredited "old politics."

The Political Process in South Korea

Inputs: Popular Demands on Government

The demands that the Korean people make on their government are rapidly changing and growing. So are their expectations of response. Traditionally, the predominantly agrarian people asked little more than to be secure and left alone in their villages; the *yangban* sought power and prestige. If the *yangban* became too predatory, the people resorted to petitions and often to riots. During the period of Japanese rule, the prevailing popular mood was one of sullen, reluctant compliance with coercive authority. Those who learned to live with the colonial regime were condemned by the others as collaborators. The 1919 popular uprising demonstrated the demand for liberation.

In the first twenty years after liberation, security and social-economic demands took precedence over everything else. Food, clothing, shelter, education for children, economic opportunity, and equitable distribution of wealth were the primary wants. (The annual "spring hunger," when considerable numbers of Koreans ate grass and tree bark for want of grain, did not end until the mid-1960s.) Until very recently, demands for political and civil rights were generally weak except at times of crisis or political provocation. Western concepts of personal liberty and civic rights were learned in school or from the media. While these concepts were attractive in the abstract, there was little native experience or cultural support for them. An often-cited public opinion poll conducted in Korea in the mid-1960s indicated that popular demands were for rapid economic development, national security, and democratic politics, in that order.

Now the "spring hunger" is only a memory; rapid economic development has brought a dramatic rise in the standard of living for many people, and some measure of improvement for most. Health insurance programs, pension plans, and other social benefits are expanding. Thus the economic imperative is being met in gross terms. Security continues as a major concern, although many observers believe it has been overplayed by the government, and forty-two years without major hostilities have reduced the anxiety level.

Having largely been freed from extreme poverty and the threat of war and possessing a high educational level, south Koreans are throwing off the shackles of traditional deference and acquiescence to authority. As they acquire a stake in the national society, property ownership, and employment, they are demanding a greater share in political decisionmaking and a larger measure of personal freedom. As early as 1980, a public opinion poll showed a reversal of the economic and political priorities of the 1960s. By 1987 the demands of students and intellectuals for political change had drawn widespread support among the general public. It was this support, together with a newfound wisdom and flexibility on the part of government leaders, that brought about the government's remarkable capitulation to opposition demands for change in June 1987 and the considerably liberalized political atmosphere of the Sixth Republic. The election of Kim Youngsam in 1992 continued this trend, broadening political participation through local elections and uncovering new political dynamics, not the least of which was the demand by the rising middle-aged generation to claim its time for leadership.

Moreover, as Korean society becomes more modern and complex, political and social interest groups that have more complex and sophisticated needs have developed. Such matters as protection against foreign imports, women's rights, environmental regulations, financial policies, the special needs of small and medium-sized businesses, which received little political attention in the past, are now front-burner issues. The desire for reunification of the country, long overshadowed by the fear of north Korean attack, has given way to sober consideration of the means and terms by which it might come about. Foreign demands are also more sophisticated, as foreign business increasingly enters the Korean market and Korea plays a larger international role.

The demands of a radical minority, chiefly students and intellectuals, go beyond the assertion of basic individual and group needs to call for a restructuring of the entire political system, which they propose as the only way to meet the aspirations of the masses. Students, for example, call for establishment of a vaguely defined *minjung* ("mass") democracy in which all the people, not just their self-styled bourgeois representatives, make the decisions—a sort of continuous nationwide town meeting—and for radical redistribution of national wealth to benefit the poor.

Such demands are a continuation of the Marxist revolutionary thought of the 1920s and 1930s and a reaction to the oppressive policies of south Korean governments since liberation. They certainly reflect the ideas of such Western thinkers as Herbert Marcuse and the Latin American dependency theorists, and to a certain extent they may also reflect north Korean ideology. They also draw from the Kim-ilsungist ideology of *juch'e* in their protests against American hegemony and demands for immediate national reunification. But they do not appear to be shared by any substantial proportion of the south Korean people; their proponents have gained wide popular support only when they have taken the lead in opposition to generally perceived injustice and oppression, as in 1987. At other times radicals have been relatively isolated, particularly when they have used violence to dramatize their demands.

Government Effectiveness

The capability of the government of the Republic of Korea to meet its people's demands is determined by four factors: the people's support for it—including their acceptance of its legitimacy and authority; the competence of the government itself; the resources of the nation; and the ability of the government to influence the character and intensity of the demands made upon it. These factors are interrelated, but in the long run they determine the stability of the political order.

Acceptance of government authority is a function of two perceptions by the public: the government's legitimacy, in terms of tradition, law, or popular will; and its effectiveness in doing what the people want, or in forcing them to accept what they get. The Republic of Korea was first established in 1948 by general elections conducted by the U.S. military government under United Nations observation. Although up to 20 percent of the eligible voters may have withheld their support of the election because it meant the creation of a separate Korean state limited to the south, the great majority accepted the election's legitimacy.[4] They accepted the Constitution and the government it produced. Syngman Rhee, probably the most highly reputed Korean nationalist of the time, was accepted as the elected president.

Support for the legitimate political order was nonetheless weak because of traditional family and parochial loyalties, struggles for political power, and the blatant manipulation that accompanied them—especially in the fraudulent election of 1960. Poor government performance in economic development gave the regime poor marks for effectiveness (the best noncoercive substitute for legitimacy). The protests and violence that followed the 1960 election brought down the Rhee government. The ensuing experiment in open parliamentary democracy under Prime Minister Chang Myon suffered from leadership inexperience and factional infighting. It could not stand against the military coup d'état of 1961.

None of the three subsequent south Korean political regimes enjoyed the legitimacy of the First Republic. However, the extraordinary economic progress achieved by President Park Chung-hee and perpetuated at a rapid though somewhat lower rate by the successor Fifth Republic of President Chun Doo-hwan, served to maintain broad (though far from universal) popular acquiescence. In 1971, Kim Dae-jung, the opposition candidate for President, got 45 percent of the vote. Kim's near-victory contributed to the Park regime's decision to amend the Constitution to provide for presidential election by a "National Unification Board," a government-controlled body of elders created ostensibly to decide profound questions of the national future such as unification, and also to choose national leaders such as the president. Though Chun's Fifth Republic Constitution replaced the National Unification Board with a smaller electoral college, likewise government-dominated, he continued the principle of presidential election by chosen electors.

In the 1985 National Assembly election, a new opposition party won more than one-third of the seats—about as many as the government party received. This was a clear sign of popular disenchantment with Chun and the way he had come to power. Though it should also be said that the business and military elites of south Korea supported Chun, in the eyes of the public he lacked legitimacy because of his part in the December 1979 coup and the 1980 Kwangju massacre. It was for this reason that shopkeepers and white-collar workers poured into the streets in June 1987, joining the demonstrating students in creating an irresistible movement to move the country closer to democracy through direct election of the president.

Up to now, south Korea's government has had ample authority and capability to carry out its functions, based upon a combination of legitimacy, effectiveness, and, when necessary, police power. It has greatly improved the efficiency of tax collection, which in all forms at both national and local levels yields about 20 percent of gross national product. Savings for investment have reached a marginal rate of over 25 percent. Universal military conscription for males has been effectively enforced, with a little less than 2 percent of the population on full-time active duty (more than any U.S. peacetime level), not counting the millions in reserve and civil defense activity. Voting turnout has remained high. Through the 1980s, efficient police and security forces and fairly sophisticated social controls—such as formal and informal pressures on the press and social and economic institutions—enabled the government to defuse or counter those pressures that it could not satisfy through responsive actions. The events of 1987 demonstrated the limits of the government's ability to control the people by force. Since then the political process has had much more to do with the way the government relates to the people. In this respect democracy has made great strides during the Sixth Republic presidencies of Roh Tae-woo and Kim Young-sam.

The Sixth Republic's structure has the advantage of more legitimacy than its three predecessor republics, precisely because it represents a return to popular sovereignty. It has thus far dealt successfully with the severe economic challenges posed by a tightening foreign market and by the rapid wage increases resulting from greater political freedom for labor. Political freedom, however, has increased not only the demands made upon the regime but also the conflicts among these demands—freedom versus order, entrepreneurial opportunity versus redistribution of wealth, defense versus social welfare, open markets versus protection, and so on. Such conflicts are routine in mature democracies, but their resolution will certainly continue to challenge the abilities of the Sixth Republic.

Governmental Process

In mature democracies, the individual needs and desires of citizens go through a process of combination, so that the resultant aggregated demands of large groups will have more weight and meaning for political decisionmakers. This aggregation is mostly done by a wide variety of interest groups, by political parties, and by the legislature. In Korea, interest groups are only beginning to develop such a role.

The process has been more informal, personal, and hierarchical; the legislature until 1988 played a relatively small part. Aggregation of popular demands, as a practical matter, has been done chiefly by leading officials of the executive branch, responding to information they receive through both formal and informal channels.

Korean government has been heavily conditioned by the Confucian tradition, in which the officials were expected to decide what the people should have and give it to them as the officials' superior wisdom indicated. In Korean terms, it has been considered a loss of face and dignity for high government officials to appear pressured into action by citizen demands. Accordingly, even when they responded to demands, the response might be delayed or indirect. Some demands were simply ignored while others were damped down or suppressed by propaganda, official statements, or, in some cases, coercion.

To a diminishing extent, the people still accept this tradition, but with growing skepticism. (Rumors about incompetence and corruption in high places have long circulated quite freely, despite controls; even during the Choson Dynasty, folk plays mocked the rulers.) Government coercion has been applied to modify attitudes in some areas. In the early stages of the rural New Community Movement, for example, there were charges that government representatives dictated what the farmers should want to do to benefit themselves, such as replacing their thatched roofs with sheet iron.[5] Arrest and punishment of persons believed to be agents or sympathizers of the north Korean regime is another example. For decades press controls were applied to prevent stirring up political demands in sensitive areas.

The main opposition party in 1995 was the Democratic Party, successor coalition to the parties once headed by Kim Dae-jung, which metamorphosed in September into the National Congress for New Politics. The seventy-year-old Kim had run four times for the presidency, yet with the government party reeling from losses in the local elections of mid-1995 and collapsing completely in the fall (being forced to reorganize its remnants as the New Korea Party), he seemed to be facing his best opportunity in the election of 1997. However, the age issue was a serious one. Many younger Koreans were weary of the perennial presidential maneuverings of the "Three Kims" (including former Prime Minister Kim Jong-pil) over time and were still a little sour over Kim Young-sam's merger with Roh's ruling group in 1990, an act seen as cynical by many at the time. After losing the election of 1992 to Kim Young-sam, Kim Dae-jung retired from politics, apparently tagged forever with the label of "regional candidate" from Honam, the area of North and South Cholla Provinces in the southwest. Within his party there were many who breathed sighs of relief, hoping that they could now broaden their appeal.

However, political parties in Korea are not mass organizations. They are associations of followers based in the National Assembly that extend the reach of their leaders on the national scene. Though his successor as party chairman, Lee Ki-taek, objected, in July 1995 Kim Dae-jung announced that he could not stand by and allow his political legacy to be dissipated, apologized for breaking his promise to retire, and returned to claim his following in the form of the National Congress for New Politics.

Perhaps more than any other individual in south Korea, Kim Dae-jung represented regional politics in the public mind. A Honam native, a Catholic, a former journalist with impeccable party credentials from the 1960s, and a courageous fighter for human rights in the 1970s, Kim came to be identified primarily with the yearnings of Honam people when he was arrested and sentenced to death by Chun Doo-hwan's military courts for allegedly inspiring the bloody Kwangju uprising of May 1980. The tendency toward regional factions in Korean politics in the late 1980s and early 1990s was partly due to his own political group's limited appeal beyond the borders of the Cholla provinces except in Seoul, traditionally an opposition stronghold, where enough votes might be won in a popular election to offset the advantage of his perennial rivals from the Kyongsang provinces in the southeast, the home area of Park Chung-hee, Chun Doo-hwan, Roh Tae-woo, and Kim Young-sam. The issue therefore turned on Kim's ability to overcome the handicap of age, the ruling DLP's ability to field a nationally viable presidential candidate in 1997, and the issue of whether all of south Korean politics was going to be subjected to the highly destructive tendency to fracture east versus west.

Recent times have seen other trends in party politics. In the 1992 election a major industrialist, Chung Ju-yung, the founder of the Hyundai *chaebol,* used his own funds to found a political party and ran for president on its platform. Chung appeared to be a formidable contender. Though seventy-seven years old, he was an energetic campaigner; his candidacy reflected the new importance of the business community; and he was supported by a number of important political personalities. His eventual humiliation in the election—he got only 16 percent of the vote—and his subsequent conviction on tax evasion charges did not lessen the significance of the presidential candidacy of someone other than a career politician or retired army officer.

The frequent shifting of opposition groups is not a new thing. Korean political parties, including pro-government parties, have all been plagued by internal factionalism and by low levels of real influence or popular support throughout their existence. This is a function of their hazy role and the contending individual ambitions of their leaders. However, parties will be more important as the Korean political process opens up, reflecting new configurations of power in the society.

Even during the Choson Dynasty, public demands could reach government policymakers by way of politically influential groups and their family or other connections in government. This is still a primary channel for communicating demands. Its weakness is that it gives priority to the demands of those in influential positions and their supporters and families. Some of the kings recognized this problem and endeavored to meet it by a procedure for individual petitions, as well as a network of secret agents. These channels still function, in more modern form.

Popular demands also reach the government through more modern, Western-style channels, such as representatives in the National Assembly, local government leaders, the mass media, and elections. Until recently, none of these channels could bring the pressure to bear on government that counterpart institutions in mature democracies have. An additional but little recognized channel are the reports of security agencies on the state of public order. If the government ignores popular discontent, the result—as in Choson Dynasty times—is unrest, demonstrations, and riots. The most recent examples have been the labor and student unrest of 1979, which led to the assassination of President Park; the Kwangju uprising of May 1980, the crushing of which stripped the Chun regime of its legitimacy; and the demonstrations of June 1987, which brought the government to compromise with opposition forces on amending the Constitution. The 1987 "democratization" movement had its beginnings in the opposition signature campaigns and rallies in the spring of 1986 and in persistent and sometimes violent student demonstrations, signaling public discontent over questions of political freedom and participation. The aggregation of these grievances and mass political actions brought change. The same kind of mass phenomenon occurred after "democratization," when workers engaged in mass actions to win higher wages after having been controlled so tightly under Chun's Fifth Republic.

In recent years, interest groups of the kind familiar in industrialized democracies have grown in influence and importance as channels for expressing demands. Until recently, long-established associations such as the National Agricultural Cooperative Federation, the Chamber of Commerce and Industry, and the Korean Federation of Trade Unions were mainly devices for government control of the membership. This was natural in a political culture that recognized government supremacy. Recently, however, the membership in these and newer groups has, at least in part, reversed the direction of influence. The newly strengthened national legislature and its opposition majority should enhance further the effectiveness of such groups. To the degree that they are able to gain response to their members' demands through legitimate channels, these groups will reinforce the legitimacy of the liberalized political process.

There are three problems that impede the integration of modern interest groups into the legitimate political system. First is the traditional insistence on unanimity and government control, which dismisses conflicting demands as impertinent or heretical. Second is the habitual use of demonstrations and confrontation against authority by dissident groups, sometimes escalating into violence, which dates from the Choson Dynasty and was reinforced by the Japanese occupation and subsequent authoritarian south Korean regimes. Student groups have been the most conspicuous practitioners of confrontation and violence. Bravery and sacrifice in themselves have seemed to justify the process even when it brought no useful political result. The spirit of compromise and negotiation has been a scarce commodity.

The third problem for interest groups—and for political party organizations as well—is the rigid anticommunism that has dominated south Korea since 1945, which was greatly reinforced by the Korean War. Any demand that is perceived by government authorities as socialist or that otherwise challenges the prevailing order risked being branded as subversive or as providing aid and comfort to the enemy, north Korea. Many leaders in the opposition share this view.

For this reason, south Korea has not had a legitimate left-leaning political party or organization since 1948, although a few small and tame groups have been allowed to call themselves socialist. The denial of a legitimate channel for expression of left-liberal or socialist views is partly responsible for the growth of violent radical movements in south Korea. Despite the liberalization that has occurred under the Sixth Republic, little progress had been made in this area as of 1995. Though leftist ideas circulate freely and left-leaning groups form, recombine, and disperse, they are subject to harassment and detention of their leaders under the National Security Law, which remains in effect.

The Western institution that has had the most impact on Korea is the election system. Both north and south Korea have held elections at more or less regular intervals since 1946; but while elections in the north have been a virtual 100 percent endorsement of decisions already made by the elite, those in the south have been important means of registering popular discontent. Turnout has been from around 60 to nearly 85 percent (the latter figure reached in the legislative elections of 1985); only once, in the local elections of 1960, did turnout fall below 50 percent.

By 1995, there had been fourteen general legislative elections since 1946, fourteen presidential elections since 1948, four general elections of local councils, and in 1995, for the first time, elections for mayors and local officials. Each of the legislative elections was wholly or largely by direct popular vote, offered a choice of candidates (up to ten or more per district, in earlier days), and resulted in at least some opposition winners.[6] In the legislative elections of 1981 and 1985, opposition parties together received more votes than the government party, but the electoral system kept them in the minority. Following the establishment of the Sixth Republic, as already noted, the election of April 1989 gave three opposition parties a total of 165 seats in the 299-person National Assembly against a government total of 124. This was undone with the creation of the Democratic Liberal Party in 1990, which had more than a two-thirds majority, reduced to a basic majority in the election of 1992.

Of the presidential elections, eight—including that of 1992—were by direct popular vote, two by the legislature, and five by electoral colleges. Presidential elections also offered a choice of candidates, even if they were sometimes for appearances only, and in 1956 the opposition vice presidential candidate (Chang Myon) was put in office. No election has yet allowed victory to an opposition presidential candidate. That might have been the result in 1987 if opposition leaders had agreed on a single candidate; as it was, the government's nominee won only by a plurality of not much over one-third.

Since 1963, popular referenda have been used for ratification of constitutional amendments. Although their use for other purposes is provided for in the 1980 and 1987 Constitutions, they have not been so employed. The referenda have generally approved government positions by margins of 60 percent or more; turnout has ranged from about 70 to nearly 80 percent. An unprecedented 85 percent of the voters turned out in the referendum of October 27, 1987, on the newest Constitutional amendment, and 93 percent of the voters approved it.

Response to election results has sometimes been increased repression, rather than changed policies. Large-scale rigging of the 1960 election, to prevent the defeat of President Rhee and his running mate, led to the fall of the Rhee government. The near-defeat of President Park in 1971 led to the establishment of a more authoritarian government structure. Growing opposition strength, manifested in the 1978 legislative election, may have been a factor in the hard-line policies that led to President Park's assassination. Nevertheless, the process has provided a largely nonviolent channel for public displeasure—which may help to explain the relatively low level, compared to many other developing countries, of major political violence.

Decisionmaking

Basic decisions—choices between conflicting demands, and allocation of national resources—are strongly centralized in Korea. Although the president and his immediate staff do not literally make all decisions, they apparently make a very large proportion of them. The preeminence of the executive branch and surviving traditions of deference to higher authority reinforce the president's primary decisionmaking role and could even be said to force it upon him, irrespective of his own character or preferences.

The president's advisers and secretaries function as auditors of the performance of cabinet (State Council) ministers, ensuring that the president's will is executed. The president can call upon the State Council for advice in reaching decisions; the Constitution requires State Council deliberation upon sixteen specified matters. The president also has a National Security Council, amounting to a committee of the State Council, and other advisory bodies. The centralization of decisionmaking authority also makes the president a prime target for would-be assassins and plotters; thus the president has his own separate security force, comparable to the U.S. Secret Service.

Given the hierarchical nature of Korean politics and the limits on the president's time, it follows that many policies, once laid down, must be carried out in the prescribed way despite changing circumstances or negative feedback from those affected. The decision latitude of Korean government officials is therefore narrow; referral to superiors of any doubtful point is commonplace.

Moreover, matters of personal dignity and status are involved. Juniors must be careful not to preempt the decision prerogatives of their seniors or to appear disrespectful or disobedient. An added factor is the surviving Confucian emphasis on form, reinforced by the heritage of the Japanese colonial period. To practice "statecraft" in the right way, using the right language, procedures, and paperwork, may be considered as important as the accomplishment of a substantive purpose. These characteristics—centralization of authority, personal status, and formality—make for delays, insensitivity, and large amounts of paperwork and routine. Nevertheless, Korean decisionmaking has improved considerably in recent years in speed, flexibility, and responsiveness to requirements, particularly in the area of economic planning and control.

Carrying Out Decisions

Once made, political decisions are authenticated (and occasionally sidetracked) by laws enacted in the National Assembly, and by executive orders of the president or cabinet members on the basis of State Council action, in accordance with the laws (except for emergency decrees, of which there had been none as of 1995). Laws and orders are executed by the central and local bureaucracies, related governmental and quasi-governmental agencies, and to some degree by nongovernmental organizations such as banks, operating according to government instructions. Individual members of the National Assembly may introduce legislative bills, but few are passed, and those mostly on minor matters.

The government hierarchy includes twenty executive ministries, each with a vice minister and assistant ministers, under whom are bureaus, divisions, and smaller units similar to those of all modern governments. (See Figure 4.2.) There are also offices at a level between ministries and bureaus—some of them under the president or the prime minister, some attached to ministries. As governmental responsibility has grown more complex, delegation of authority down the line has increased; its high degree of centralization is often frustrating, but, even so, the effectiveness of the bureaucracy has greatly increased since the 1970s.

Geographically, the Republic is divided into nine provinces, five special cities with provincial status (Pusan, Taegu, Inch'on, Taejon, and Kwangju), and the Special City of Seoul. Each has an elected chief executive (provincial governor or city mayor) who has six or so executive departments under him. One of these, the police bureau, reports directly to the National Police Director in all matters except those peculiar to the individual province or city. Other bureaus also have close relations with their national-level counterparts as well as regional offices of national ministries. The mayor of Seoul reports directly to the president; the other governors and mayors report through the minister of home affairs.

Provinces (*to*) are subdivided into countries (*kun*) and cities (*si*). Within the *kun* are towns (*up*) and townships (*myon*), according to population and urban character; these in turn are subdivided into precincts (*tong*) or villages (*ri*). Cities are subdivided into *tong;* special cities (*chikhal si*) are divided into wards (*ku*), and those into districts (*tong*). In 1993 there were 56 special city wards, 136 countries,

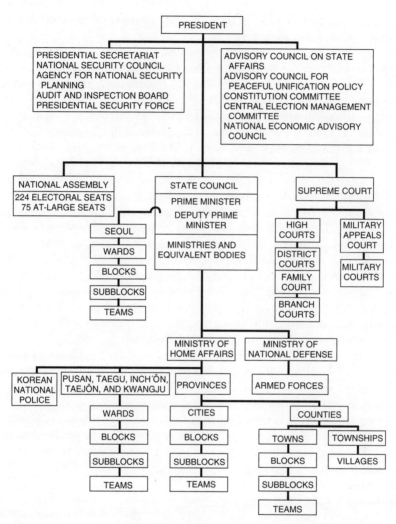

FIGURE 4.2 Chart of organization of the government of the Republic of Korea (from Andrea Matles Savada and William R. Shaw, eds., *South Korea: A Country Study,* 4th ed., Washington, D.C.: U.S. Government Printing Office, 1992, p. 208)

and 68 cities. Including the township level, there was a total of 2,589 incorporated government units.[7] At the village and town level, the head is appointed from among local residents; at higher levels, incumbents are career civil servants, and as of old, tend not to be natives of the area where they are stationed. The long-awaited reinstitution of local council elections occurred in 1991, honoring clauses in the 1980 and 1987 Constitutions, thirty years after they were abolished by Park Chung-hee's military junta. The police have an organization paralleling local administration down to the larger villages; there are also paramilitary combat police units for riot control in the larger centers.

To a limited extent, the execution of laws and regulations is subject to judicial review. Although the courts have not been truly independent of the executive branch—both because the Continental legal system is used, and because of the Korean tradition of centralized control—they do have more than nominal freedom to reach objective decisions on the law. In 1988, south Korea established a Constitutional Court expressly to exercise the power of judicial review. The nine justices are also empowered to hear human rights appeals.

Since the late 1970s, the courts have begun to levy damages against government agencies for injustices done to private citizens and groups. However, in political cases, the prosecution's view has usually prevailed. The Kim Young-sam administration claimed to have released all "political" prisoners (i.e., those who had not violated criminal laws by acts such as injury to persons or property), and it did release several internationally noted prisoners of conscience such as ex–student dissident leader Kim Kyu-t'ae and the journalist Yi Pu-yong. In 1995, however, there were still arrests of artists and intellectuals who promoted points of view that offended the National Security Law, which forbids unauthorized contact with north Korea and "antistate" speech or actions that were deemed to give aid and comfort to north Korea. Amnesty International reported that as many as 370 political prisoners, mostly prisoners of conscience, were still in prison in 1995.[8]

The Supreme Court, which has fourteen justices, is the final court of appeal. There are four high (appeals) courts, in Seoul, Kwangju, Pusan, and Taegu, and twelve district courts, with both criminal and civil jurisdiction. There are also magistrate courts for minor offenses, family courts, and other specialized courts. Judges are appointed by the chief justice for ten-year renewable terms. The chief justice and justices of the Supreme Court are nominated by the president for six-year terms (renewable except for the chief justice) and confirmed by the National Assembly. The military services have a separate court-martial system, which is subject to Supreme Court review.

Under Korea's version of the Continental legal system (originally drawn from Germany and France through Japan), the role of the prosecutors (sometimes termed procurators) is very important. These officials, organized in a fashion parallel to the courts, are under a quasi-independent office of the Ministry of Justice, headed by a prosecutor-general. They investigate all cases prior to trial; once they determine that a trial is merited, their recommendations are commonly upheld by the courts, although the courts frequently modify the recommended penalties. There are no citizen juries, but panels of three or five judges sit on serious cases, deciding by majority vote. Although defendants are entitled to counsel, the theory of equality between the state and the defendant is not recognized. The Korean Constitution provides for the writ of habeas corpus (under which the government may be required to show cause for arrest and detention), and court warrants are required for police or prosecutor arrests and searches in most circumstances.

The courts, however, have not usually been assertive toward executive branch authorities, especially in politically sensitive cases; and defense lawyers do not enjoy the social or procedural status taken for granted in the United States.

Civil suits are a small but growing part of court business—particularly in business matters. Continuing in the old tradition, individuals are reluctant to take their private or family affairs to the authorities. (Family law is still based on native Korean tradition, although changes were under discussion in 1987 to meet new social circumstances, such as increased women's rights.) Private lawyers have not traditionally enjoyed great social respect as such, although they have status as college graduates and as passers of the national examinations. This situation, however, is changing as large businesses find it necessary to seek court remedies for their problems.

Politically Important Groups

Components of south Korean society with politically relevant power or influence, or access to decisionmakers, or both—in addition to the president and his entourage—determine the performance of the political system. At present, the armed forces, the bureaucracy, businesspeople, internal security forces, politicians and political parties, mass media, intellectuals, church groups, students, labor, and farmers/fishermen are the most important.

These groups vary in organization and coherence. Several of them, in various ways, reflect the growing Korean middle class.[9] They act upon, through, and around the constitutionally or traditionally mandated governmental institutions. Each of them is discussed briefly below.

Armed Forces

The Republic's three armed services are described in Chapter 7. Among them, the Army of about 550,000 persons is politically the most significant because of its numbers, coercive power on the ground, managerial ability, and capacity to provide channels of upward mobility for the common citizen.

Before 1960, the Army's political role was chiefly a latent one. Its Counterintelligence Corps for a time was an information channel for President Rhee, and Rhee organized a nominally military Joint Provost Marshal General Command under a trusted lieutenant to enforce his political will. The organization of the National Defense College in 1956 may have encouraged the development of political consciousness among senior Army officers. However, the U.S. training of most senior Army officers in the early years of the Republic reinforced a Korean tradition of civilian supremacy. Moreover, in the early years the various factions (grouped by individual allegiance, provincial origin, or previous training and experience) tended to neutralize one another.

During most of his twelve years in the presidency, Rhee carefully played factional military leaders against one another and distributed rewards and recognition so as to minimize discontent. The Army was permitted to run a miniature economic empire of its own to supplement the miserable pay of officers and men. After the 1960 upheaval, Prime Minister Chang Myon sought to reduce the size of the Army, in part because of U.S. pressure, to reduce the economic load. Chang lacked Rhee's skill in coping with ambitious military leaders. Most of them were young, even at the highest levels; they were in severe competition for the relatively few top posts not only with one another but also with slightly younger field-grade alumni of the new Korea Military Academy, whose loyalties were by graduating class rather than faction. The resulting internal frustrations were in large part responsible for the military coup d'état of 1961, although social unrest was also a factor.

The declared purpose of the coup leaders was to reform the corrupt and economically stagnant Korean polity and strengthen it against north Korean subversion. Their six-point program of May 1961 set forth these themes and promised restoration of civilian government—a promise eventually kept, under strong U.S. pressure, two years later.

After 1961, however, it was obvious to all civilian leaders that they could not hold political power without military consent and implicit support and that Army officers' ambitions and perceptions of the national interest would have to be taken into account by utilizing their managerial talents in appropriate governmental or industrial positions. General Park Chung-hee and some of his associates resigned their Army affiliation to hold governmental office. Over time their viewpoints approached those of Korean leaders generally, although their own careers made them acutely mindful of the need for military support, and receptive to military viewpoints. Since reestablishment of civilian government in 1963, military personnel have resigned or retired before entering civilian positions.

The second exercise of military power by Army officers, in 1980, was again due in part to internal military problems. It was also due in part to the personal loyalty of certain senior Army officers to the assassinated president. The key event was Chun Doo-hwan's takeover of the military decisionmaking apparatus in his coup of December 12, 1979. In 1979, though not as clearly as in 1961, it seemed that the acquiescence of the military officers' corps in Chun's coup was motivated largely by concern for stability and the defense posture of the Republic—though it could not be said that the political situations were comparable, because in 1979 the civil government was not nearly as weak as it was in 1961. Rather, as in the earlier instance, there was an effort to disguise military rule in constitutional trappings after Chun's coup. Chun's backers retired and joined his new Democratic Justice Party, ran for office, and supported him in the National Assembly and the bureaucracy, and the structure delivered enough economic growth to purchase public toleration.

Through the 1980s, retired military officers were to be found at middle and senior levels in all areas of civilian government and in major business enterprises.

However, the 1980s saw an increasing reliance on technocrats, often graduates of American business and graduate schools, both in government and in the business sector. By the early 1990s, and especially after the election of Kim Young-sam as president, officials with military backgrounds were much less prominent. But even in the earlier period, the political role of the military was not one of day-to-day intervention in civilian affairs (except as any group in society pursues its own interests—as, for example, in budget deliberations). Rather, the military engaged in watchful surveillance, based on the power of well-organized and heavily armed soldiers backing an educated, talented, and ambitious career officer corps of around 40,000 (with a few thousand Korea Military Academy graduates at their core), which no politician could ignore. No person can enter or long remain in the office of the presidency without the acquiescence of the armed forces. Yet the president's governmental policies and administration have not recently been under military control in any direct sense. In fact, the Kim Young-sam administration, while enjoying a wave of public popularity in 1993, attacked corruption in the army, exposing a major arms-procurement scandal and purging a number of senior officers.

The Bureaucracy

The Republic's executive branch in 1993 was staffed by 878,000 civil servants, or about 1.9 percent of the population.[10] One-quarter of them were in local governments. The remaining three-quarters comprised a special category of top-ranking officials (equivalent to vice minister and above); a general civil service category of nine grades, the top five of which have presidential appointments; a separate category for administration and faculty of the public schools at all levels; and a career Foreign Service. Police personnel and those of the Agency for National Security Planning were also included, but not employees of public corporations.[11] Entry was by competitive examination. Graduates of Seoul National University had a disproportionate share of higher positions. The Ministry of Government Administration managed recruitment, training, and promotion.

Basic legislation purports to insulate civil servants from political activity or pressure and provides that they may not be discharged without cause. Civil servants do not have the right of collective bargaining under current labor laws, although recently some government workers—notably teachers—have challenged this restriction by organizing unions and even striking. Even without collective bargaining rights, however, the bureaucracy as a whole is a potent political force, both for its own interests and because of its key role in carrying out the business of government. Its members are proud of their status and still enjoy something of the public awe of officialdom that characterized the Choson Dynasty. Despite constitutional and legal provisions, the civil service acts in accordance with the long tradition of supporting the ruler and regime in power, in subtle and sometimes in blatant ways.

Politicians and Political Parties

In south Korea, the idea of using private organizations as interest groups to put pressure on the government is still very new, and the taint of factionalism still clouds the public perception of political parties and politicians. The role of parties in the political process is therefore imperfectly understood, even by party leaders, and leaders and parties alike tend to be viewed by both the elite and the citizenry as extraneous, untrustworthy, or both.

Nevertheless, the Constitution recognizes the role of political parties in elections and legislative activity, and the party role in the proceedings of the National Assembly has been well established since the early 1950s. Election to the Assembly legitimizes politicians to some extent as part of government. They can be viewed, in traditional terms, as a latter-day equivalent of the Censorate under the former monarchy, criticizing and investigating government performance and sanctioning executive proposals by enacting them into law. Moreover, opposition parties have given voice to popular dissatisfaction, although their voice has often gone unheeded.

Aside from a few short periods in postliberation history, the legislative branch of government has not been very influential. It has generally been a forum for the expression of members' opinions, which may or may not reflect those of their constituents, although Assembly members do play to their districts for reelection in ways similar to their counterparts elsewhere. The Assembly also provides rewards for politicians, even those of the opposition, through salaries and privileges. Thus the Assembly has been a significant stimulus to the creation and functioning of political parties as a supplementary means of expressing and aggregating public demands. Yet twice in the Republic's history, in 1961 and in 1980, all political parties were dissolved and their leading figures arrested or barred from political activity without greatly disturbing the political process. Party activity resumed in early 1981, and the most recent proscriptions were lifted gradually thereafter (the remainder in early 1985).

The first south Korean political parties formed under the U.S. occupation, with American encouragement (though the conservative Han'guk Democratic Party was organized even before U.S. troops arrived in August 1945). There were from 40 to over 200 of them, depending on definition, by mid-1947. By the mid-1950s, two major conservative parties were vying for power, while half a dozen smaller parties led a precarious existence—the more liberal or "progressive" among them often hounded by police. Since that time, each administration has sought to build a mass party in its support and at the same time to encourage factionalism and division among opposition ranks.[12]

The National Assembly Law and laws regulating political parties have been written since 1963 in such a way as to discourage small parties and independent representatives in the Assembly. There have usually been one or two principal opposition parties and several smaller ones, the latter typically motivated by support of a single leader or faction. The long-range trend is toward fewer, stronger, and better organized parties. In accordance with the law, even the opposition gets a modicum of public financial support, and all parties look to donations from members and from businesses, especially at election time.

In 1989, the old-line opposition to the military-backed regimes of Chun Doo-hwan and Roh Tae-woo was divided among two major parties—the Peace and Democracy Party (PDP) of Kim Dae-jung, with eighty Assembly seats, and the Reunification Democratic Party (RDP) of Kim Young-sam, with fifty-seven seats—and a few splinter parties that had no official Assembly representation, although some of the ten independent Assembly members had minor-party connections. Another significant group, the New Democratic Republican Party (NDRP), with thirty-five Assembly seats and headed by Kim Jong-pil, represented the core constituency of the late President Park. Kim Jong-pil and his party did not differ markedly in philosophy from the government, but preferred, or were forced, to remain outside Chun and Roh's ruling Democratic Justice Party (DJP). Thus they gained influence from their ability to support either the government or the opposition.

This political lineup continued the virtual exclusion of "progressive," or left-leaning, politicians and views from the main channels of political influence—an exclusion that has characterized the south Korean scene since 1948. It also continued the traditional domination of senior political figures, with their personalized operating methods. This situation, in the face of growing popular disillusionment with old-fashioned political posturing, was at least partly responsible for the emergence of a nonparty dissident coordinating group, the National Alliance for a Democratic Movement (*Chonminnyon*), associated with which are dissident student, labor, and farmer movements.

The three-party merger of early 1990 (DJP, RDP, and NDRP) restored a two-party structure, with the new Democratic Liberal Party (DLP) supporting the government and Kim Dae-jung's PDP in opposition. As a result of the parliamentary elections of March 1992, the government's Democratic Liberal Party held 149 of 299 seats in the Assembly. With government support, the DLP was continuing its efforts to organize a mass base in 1995 despite setbacks in local elections. However, the party was split among followers of Kim Jong-pil who were members of the 1961 coup generation, former Chun Doo-hwan loyalists, younger followers of former president Roh Tae-woo (the so-called "T.K. faction" from around Taegu in North Kyongsang Province), and old-line oppositionists who had joined the party with Kim Young-sam in the merger of January 1990. Kim's leadership put the party behind a reform drive that exposed corruption by some of the DLP's own members—and even members of Kim's own cabinet. In addition to the factions' incompatible origins and political traditions was their different regional bases—for example, Kim Young-sam's base was in *South* Kyongsang Province. Leaders began resigning. Kim Jong-pil left to start his own party in 1995, by which time the DLP was in disarray, with no apparent successor candidate in the wings for the election of 1997. Badly frayed, the once-monolithic Democratic Liberal Party watched its numbers dwindle in the National Assembly. With an eye on the April 1996 legislative elections, it reorganized, forcing the retirement of older politicians and representatives with ties to the former military regimes and reorganizing itself as the New Korea Party.

Internal Security Agencies

The national police, the Agency for National Security Planning (ANSP), and the Defense Security Command (DSC) are the principal internal security agencies of the Republic. Since 1980, the national police appear to be the lead agency in internal security. The ANSP was formerly called the Korean Central Intelligence Agency (KCIA); its pervasive presence and harsh methods during the Park administration gained it such opprobrium that it was renamed and its activities oriented principally toward the external threat. The DSC is responsible principally for security within the armed services, but since all south Korea is the military forces' rear area, DSC concerns include civilian subversive activities as well.

Internal security responsibilities include maintenance of public order (ranging from dealing with riots to traffic control) and protection against internal or external subversion. Many investigations in pursuit of these objectives have been criticized as intrusive, oppressive, and coercive. Repeated allegations of arrests without warrant, search and seizure, prolonged detention without trial, and torture have been voiced by both domestic and foreign observers. Government officials have repeatedly asserted that such acts are illegal and unauthorized; a few police officers have been disciplined, tried, and sentenced for them. There may have been a diminution in their frequency over the years, but their continued existence is well documented.[13]

Defenders of south Korea's human rights record point out that the country is still in a state of suspended hostilities with north Korea, and that the north has constantly sought to subvert the Republic by any means, including sabotage and assassination. Internal security is therefore a vital function of government, although its means are sometimes open to question.

The security agencies also serve as a source of information about public attitudes that—despite obvious shortcomings—has been utilized by every Korean administration, or ignored at its peril. This role as informal articulator of public demands has been particularly important because the mass media, speech, and assembly have been controlled in varying degree despite constitutional guarantees, and because those who shout the loudest may not be representative, or may be creating the very opinion they claim to represent. Even in Japanese times, the reports of the military police (*kempeitai*) seem to have provided some frank and objective information about public opinion. More recently, in late 1979, President Park was being counseled by his hard-line advisers to apply force against mounting labor and student demonstrations. The KCIA director, Kim Chae-kyu—a trusted associate of the president—was convinced, on the basis of his information, that applying further coercive measures to control dissent would not work. Frustrated by hard-liners close to the president—notably the president's security chief Cha Chi-ch'ol—and unable to put across his point of view, the frustrated KCIA Director shot Cha and President Park both, during a dinner-hour argument.

Business Groups

The business community as a political force is very new, reflecting the economic development of Korea and the emergence of the business sector as an important and prestigious aspect of national life. The greatest political clout is in the hands of chief executives of a dozen or so large industrial conglomerates, the *chaebol*. Seven of these conglomerates include general trading companies that enjoy special government recognition in international trade. Except that they do not control their own banks, the *chaebol* are comparable to the *zaibatsu* of pre–World War II Japan (the same Chinese characters represent both terms), with vertically and horizontally integrated operations. Most of them are still controlled by the founders or their sons or relatives, although they have been under government pressure to "go public" through the sale of stock. The heads of the firms are thus men of great wealth and economic power. A list of the larger firms appears in Chapter 6 (Table 6.3).

In addition to the large individual firms, the business sector speaks to government (and vice versa) through such organizations as the Korea Chamber of Commerce and Industry, the Federation of Korean Industries, the Korea Federation of Small Business, the Korea Traders' Association, and over one hundred associations of firms in various manufacturing and trading lines. There are also informal lines of communication based on shared college, military, regional, or other ties.

Intellectuals

The high status of educated persons in Korea derives from the Confucian tradition of the scholar-official. The prestige of the doctorate, particularly in the humanities, is very high, especially if it comes from a prestigious university in Korea or abroad. College and university faculty and, to a much lesser degree, teachers below college level enjoy high status, as do authors and journalists. There is some interchange of talent between government and the academic world.

To some degree, persons in these categories, and even college graduates generally, form a vaguely identified class of intellectuals whose views carry special weight with the public—particularly in the relatively few cases where there is an intellectual consensus, as there was in 1960 and 1987. The intellectuals can, to a certain extent, articulate popular demands and grievances to the political system because of their prestige. They can also create or amplify popular demands, which is the basis for governmental concern about them. The poet and social critic Kim Chi-ha evoked such a public reaction with his caustic Aesopian writings about the government that he was imprisoned for several years in the 1970s.

Intellectuals find many outlets for their ideas, and there is a lively public discussion taking place at all times in the newly liberated Korean press. During the Park era, and later when the Chun Doo-hwan regime blacklisted dissident writers, professors, and religious leaders, social criticism was muted, though never entirely silenced. After Roh Tae-woo's "June 29th Declaration" in 1987, a group of dismissed journalists started a left-of-center newspaper named *Han'gyore Shinmun* (The Korean People's Paper), financed not by advertising (which had always been subject to government control) but by public subscriptions and donations. It was an instant success, perceived as independent and fearless, and it continues to enjoy great popularity. Certain periodicals are known for pushing the political envelope: The monthly magazine *Mal* ([Free] "Speech") is known for its attacks on political corruption, materialism, and what it calls American hegemonism in Korea.

There are some intellectual organizations, as already noted, including an association for the defense of human rights. However, there is no specific intellectual consensus or plan of action, other than perhaps a general desire for more freedom of speech and behavior, more opportunities for political leadership and economic benefit, more democracy in the national political process, and more attention to human rights. Some intellectuals, particularly the younger generation, have been attracted by socialism, Marxism, and Latin American dependency theory. They favor more public ownership, worker participation, and equitable distribution of wealth. A few of them may be responsive to north Korean propaganda.

Intellectuals, together with students and church groups, were in the vanguard of growing discontent at the repressive policies of the Chun administration and the slow pace of political liberalization (Fig. 4.3). The events of early 1987 led to the emergence of an umbrella organization, the National Coalition for a Democratic Constitution, which gave voice and structure to popular opposition outside the established opposition parties. The dissident nonparty opposition group, the National Alliance for a Democratic Movement, is successor to the Coalition.

The Press and Mass Media

Traditionally, the Korean press has been as critical of government as it dared to be, beginning with *The Independent*, started by Philip Jaisohn and other young reformist leaders of the Independence Club in 1897 (see Chapter 2). However, censorship and government control are equally traditional. The degree of freedom permitted the print media has varied from the tight controls of the Japanese colonial regime to virtually complete liberty under the short-lived Second Republic of 1960–1961. During some years of Park Chung-hee's presidency, newspapers had to submit to prepublication censorship, sometimes by officials placed in editorial offices for the purpose. Beginning in the Japanese period, editors have developed a talent for conveying messages between their lines and testing the limits of government tolerance.

Government control has been all but lifted since 1990. In the 1980s, there were strict limits on the numbers of newspapers and magazines that could be printed as well as on their content. The government had a Press and Reporting Coordinating Office that issued guidelines—which were exposed in *Mal* magazine—that regulated where and how often President Chun's picture had to appear each day and what kinds of political facts and details could be published.[14] These patterns of control eased after 1987, and Korea's writers tested the sincerity of the Roh administration by publishing series on, among other things, the government's kidnapping of opposition leader Kim Dae-jung from a hotel room in Japan in 1973. The government's hands-off policy continued. New publications sprang up like mushrooms after rain: business journals, special interest magazines of all kinds, newspapers, videos, and spirited debates about politics on television, all without censorship. And although a *Han'gyore Shinmun* staffer spent 160 days in prison for visiting north Korea without permission in 1989, proving that the National Security Law was still in force, Korea's long history of press censorship seemed to have turned a corner.

Radio and, in recent years, television reach virtually every citizen in Korea. With few exceptions, however, they are government owned or closely controlled. Their emphasis, in news and commentary, on the doings of the president and se-

FIGURE 4.3 Antigovernment demonstrators in Inch'on, May 1986, charging into a police cordon with a truck they seized from police and set on fire (photo used by permission of AP Wide World Photos)

nior officials and the official propaganda line led to considerable public cynicism. In late 1985, church and student groups launched a campaign for a public boycott of "listening fees" (a tax on use of television sets) for the Korea Broadcasting Corporation's television programs. The campaign was picked up by the opposition New Korea Democratic Party. The government reacted to the campaign by appointing a commission to study the problem, rather than by launching a crackdown, and promised to reduce advertising volume (a major focus of complaint) after the 1988 Olympics. The 1987 presidential election campaign was the first in south Korea in which television played a major role; but opposition candidates accused the government-owned broadcasting companies of slanting coverage to favor the pro-government candidate—a charge with which Western journalists' observations agreed.

Since 1987 the number of publications and broadcasting organizations has grown dramatically. Yonhap News Agency continues as the biggest importer of international news. The government-owned Korea Broadcasting Service (KBS) remains the largest broadcaster. Altogether there were twenty-seven television stations and ninety-seven radio stations in south Korea in 1993. With radios everywhere and an estimated 12 million television sets, mass communications in Korea have become a primary conduit for educational and cultural information.[15] The computer also bids to revolutionize mass communications further in Korea through the Internet and the World Wide Web.

Students

Students have already been discussed in connection with education, in Chapter 3. As a political factor, students in Korea are important in five ways: They have the social status of apprentice intellectuals and the communication skills derived from their education; they have a tradition as a leading force in nationalist movements since 1919; they have the simplistic dedication and exuberance (particularly in the springtime) of youth and a sense of generation gap magnified by the rapidity of social change; they have organization and esprit de corps; and there are a lot of them. They are a key factor in the nation's future, and they know it—which adds to their frustration when they cannot find jobs in times of recession.

Students by themselves are generally a manageable political problem, so long as actions to control them do not escalate into violence and create martyrs. Their causes do not always represent broad public issues (for example, their excitement over campus problems), and hence they do not necessarily enjoy public sympathy or support. However, if they articulate genuine grievances and combine with other political groups, sharing leadership abilities and organization and communication skills, their impact can be politically destabilizing. Their importance in 1960 was that they gave voice to broad popular discontent. At times, opposition political leaders have used students for their own cause, as occurred in the anti–Japanese treaty riots of 1964 and 1965.[16]

In recent years, when labor demands for better wages have been curtailed because of the need for competitiveness in world markets, there has been apprehension over student participation or leadership in labor demonstrations. The extremist (and of course illegal) *Minmint'u* student group, which according to government sources had 46,000 members on twenty-six university campuses in May 1986, was apparently seeking linkages with labor and other groups in its campaign for "mass democracy" and anti-imperialism, but without great success—owing in part to arrests of its leaders and suppression of its activity. Even in the freer post-1987 political environment, labor-student linkages do not seem strong.

Many years of government suppression and harassment have resulted in the emergence of an organized, radical, and seemingly permanent student and ex-student opposition to the south Korean government. Two underground radical groups, *Minmint'u* and *Chamint'u*, existed in the mid-1980s, with different ideas about who was the primary enemy, the capitalist system or American imperialism. In 1987, a new umbrella organization emerged with the abbreviated name *Chondaehyop*, or All-Korea University Students' Alliance. Its leaders also were detained and prosecuted for allegedly subversive views. After "democratization" began in 1987, the students turned from democratization to reunification as their main theme, while continuing their opposition to the government and to the United States. They continued, also, to support the causes of workers, farmers, and the poor, seeking political alliances with these groups.

In the early 1990s, student activity waned for two main reasons. First, the fall of Communism in Europe discredited Marxism somewhat, though Marxist ideas and interpretations remained popular. And second, the oppression of the 1980s under Chun Doo-hwan gave way to visible liberalization across the board. But there were still plenty of issues to fuel student protests. The "corrupt" party merger of January 1990 was one. The arrest and trial of Im Su-gyong, a twenty-two-year-old French major who had traveled illegally to Pyongyang's International Youth Festival in 1989, was a cause célèbre. Anti-Americanism remained strong, peaking during trials of American soldiers for crimes against Koreans and during periods of trade pressure from the United States. And reunification remained a prime goal as students continued to accuse the government and the United States of colluding to keep Korea divided. Student activism divided into a "People's Democracy" (PD) stream, which focused on human rights issues in south Korea, including workers' rights, and the anti-American neo-Marxist "National Liberation" (NL) stream, which offended many citizens with its open avowal of the Kimilsungist *juch'e* ideology: In fact one ultraleftist NL faction called itself the "*Juch'e* Thought Faction," or *Jusap'a*.

Religious Groups

Of the three largest groups of religious adherents in south Korea—Buddhist, Christian, and Confucian[17]—only the Christians have the high degree of organization among the laity that gives them significant capability for political influence. Moreover, because of the leading Christian role in the modernization of Korea, the role of the churches as the major channel of expression and upward mobility during the Japanese regime, the association of Christianity with the nationalist movement, and the international support traditionally given to the Christians, the incentive for political activism among church members is greater than for their fellow communicants in the United States or Europe.

Accordingly, a Christian minority, including a few foreign missionaries, has been in the forefront of movements for improving labor conditions, alleviating poverty and injustice, and promoting human rights. A case in point is the interdenominational Urban Industrial Mission, whose activist workers went into sweatshops and factories to counsel workers and help them coordinate demands for more humane working conditions. Another is the part played by Cardinal Stephen Kim Su-hwan in standing up to the Chun regime during the democracy movement of 1987.

The Christian community, however, is more typically on the side of the government, both for its anticommunism and for its pursuit of economic development. A well-known example of this kind of Korean Christianity is the Yoido Full Gospel Church, the biggest church in the world with 675,000 members in the congregation, which celebrates material blessings and posits Koreans as the new chosen people, commissioned to spread the faith in other countries through a missionary force of its own that numbers more than 2,000.

Labor

The south Korean labor force of 20 million is far from completely organized. It is officially represented by the national Korean Federation of Trade Unions (KFTU), with a nominal membership of about 2 million in 1985. The KFTU was closely controlled by the government until the mid-1987 change in the political climate; it has not been in the vanguard of the effort for improved benefits. In recent years the government has sought to decentralize to the plant level such collective bargaining as law and regulation permit. Nationwide industrial unions exist in name, but they cannot organize collective action. Unions in individual plants are legally able to act on behalf of workers, including collective action, but their activities were closely restricted in practice until mid-1987.

Strikes were, for practical purposes, illegal until late 1987. There were nevertheless some significant work stoppages and sit-ins, even before the outburst of strikes in August 1987, including two in 1985 against one of Korea's largest conglomerates. Criminal action was taken against the ringleaders of both strikes. By the standards of Western industrialized nations, labor's rights and benefits have been narrowly circumscribed, and wages and working conditions are poor, especially in smaller enterprises. Labor discontent is a constant worrisome contingency, especially in times of economic adversity.

On the whole, Korean workers have acquiesced in the government's policy to hold wage and benefit increases within productivity limits. The ability to compete in world markets is the key to continued economic growth and therefore to job availability. Economic growth of at least 6 percent a year is required to absorb new members of the labor force. Toward the end of the Park regime, however, rapid inflation necessitated large wage increases to avoid labor unrest. This and other factors contributed to the recession of 1979–1980 and the concurrent political instability—in which labor unrest was a significant factor.

Under the Roh and Kim administrations, revisions in the labor laws allowed room for much more collective action. There were several violent strikes, for example, at the Hyundai shipyard in Ulsan. Subway strikes left Seoul commuters stranded on the surface, aggravating gridlock in the city. There were major gains in wages in the early 1990s, giving rise to fears that Korea was too quickly losing its competitive edge to lower-wage countries before it was in a position to take on high-tech competitors in Japan and the West. Unemployment was 2.6 percent in 1993, however, forcing wages upward. Companies responded with average annual pay increases of 8.7 percent in 1993, up from 5 percent the previous year, and the number of labor actions seemed to be falling off: There were 39 percent fewer disturbances in 1993 than in 1992.[18]

Farmers and Fishers

Industrialization in Korea has proceeded so quickly that the farm to nonfarm population ratio has reversed since 1950; now less than one-third of the south Korean people are primarily agricultural, and less than 10 percent of that number are engaged in fishing. Although recent surveys have demonstrated that farmers, as much as their urban counterparts, have acquired modern social attitudes, their political behavior continues to be more traditional than that of people in the cities. Voting turnout is greater in rural than in urban areas. Rural voters appear more responsive to government pressure and simple electoral appeals, including entertainment and gifts. They also tend to support the administration in power.

During the Rhee administration, rural support was taken for granted; but in more recent years there have been signs of erosion. Subsequent Korean governments have therefore sought to preserve good relations with the rural voters. The New Community Movement, launched in 1971 (when there seemed to be some erosion of rural support), and other steps to improve rural life and income—especially high agricultural price support levels—are prime examples. In recent years, budgetary pressures have lessened price supports, and agricultural household debt has risen to a level approaching a year's income, raising questions about future rural attitudes.

National farmers' associations have never been effective in Korea, although the government or ruling political party has sought to organize them. The National Agricultural Cooperative Federation is the principal farm organization, apart from the New Community Movement. It is a quasi-governmental association that provides farm credit, supply, and marketing facilities and speaks more for the administration than for the farmers themselves. At the local level, various types of cooperatives and New Community Movement units, as well as the local governments, respond to the farmers' interests and at the same time keep these interests under control. Beginning in the late 1960s, first Catholic, then Protestant activists helped to organize regional farmers' associations, which called for—and demonstrated in support of—better treatment for the rural sector. In the largest such demonstration, 12,000 farmers gathered in Yoido Plaza in Seoul in February 1989. This event was followed the next month by the organization of a National Alliance of Farmers, with ties to the dissident *Chonminnyon*. In another demonstration in front of the U.S. Embassy, farmers demanded a stop to U.S. pressure for Korean importation of American agricultural products. Such activity by farmers is new in Korea and is evidence of increased rural political consciousness.

Since the mid-1980s, the United States has put more pressure on Korea to import American goods, many of them farm products. In 1988, Korea started importing American cigarettes for sale, angering tobacco farmers. Shortly thereafter the Americans pressured Korea to import more beef. These and other agricultural imports are thought to threaten the livelihood of Korean farmers, and resentment of American pressure has been a major weapon in the arsenal of the political opposition.

Constitution and Formal Government Structure

The original Constitution of the Republic of Korea was adopted by a constituent assembly elected under UN observation in 1948. It has been amended nine times: in 1952, 1954, 1960 (twice), 1963, 1969, 1972, 1980, and 1987. Five of the amendments—1960, 1963, 1972, 1980, and 1987—constituted essentially new constitutions; the corresponding governments are often referred to as the Second, Third, Fourth, Fifth, and Sixth (present) Republics. The principal changes made by the 1987 amendment are to restore popular election of the president, to strengthen the role of the legislature, and to strengthen guarantees of individual rights. In other respects, the basic structure of government was essentially unchanged.

The 1987 amendment was overwhelmingly approved by popular referendum in October of that year, on the basis of a draft developed by a bipartisan legislative committee and approved by the National Assembly. As amended, the Constitution now consists of a preamble, ten chapters with 130 articles, and six supplementary articles covering the transition from the previous regime. The Constitution defines the formal, outward structure of government—within and around which the actual political process goes on. Political power realities and interrelationships do not always correspond to those specified in the Constitution. Nevertheless, the requirements of the Constitution have usually been carefully met. The main exceptions, aside from disregard of human rights provisions, were the failure to implement constitutional requirements for an upper legislative house, from 1952 to 1960, and failure from 1959 to 1960 and after 1980 to provide for meaningful autonomy of local government. The amended Constitution is briefly summarized below.[19]

Rights and Duties of Citizens

Chapter II of the Constitution guarantees basic rights and freedoms: equality; nondiscrimination; due process of law (including the right to court review of arrest or detention); freedom of movement, residence, and occupation; privacy of person, correspondence, and domicile; freedom of religion, speech, press, and petition; the rights to property ownership, education, employment, voting, and holding public office; the right to work; and the right of labor association and collective action (unqualified except for employees of government and defense industries, in contrast to the 1980 version). Most of these rights and freedoms are unconditional; they are, however, qualified by Article 37(2), which states that they "may be restricted by law only when necessary for national security, the maintenance of law and order or for public welfare. Even when such restriction is imposed, no essential aspect of the freedom or right shall be violated." (The 1987 language of this article is identical with that of 1980.)

Some of the guarantees of rights are further-reaching than those of the U.S. Constitution—such as free compulsory education, entitlement to "a healthy and pleasant environment" and "a life worthy of human beings," protection of women and the young and old, and state protection of the health of all citizens. In addition to rights, Chapter II also specifies the duty of citizens to work, pay taxes, and support national defense.

President and Executive Branch

An interesting symbolic change in the 1987 constitutional amendment was to place the chapter on the legislature (Chapter III) before that on the executive (Chapter IV), a reversal of the order in all previous versions, and a reflection of the order in the U.S. Constitution. It is quite likely that the executive will remain the preeminent branch, and so its particulars are presented first here.

Chapter IV provides that the president is head of state, head of the executive branch, and commander-in-chief of the armed forces. The president chairs the State Council; appoints the prime minister, subject to National Assembly confirmation; appoints State Council members (in practice, mostly heads of executive agencies) on the prime minister's recommendation; and appoints other public officials. The president issues decrees to implement the laws; may refer important matters to national referendum; may grant amnesty, commutation of sentences, and restoration of rights; and may award decorations and other honors.

In time of crisis, and subject to National Assembly concurrence, the president may "take . . . the minimum necessary financial and economic actions or issue orders having the effect of law, only when it is required to take urgent measures for the maintenance of national security or public peace and order, and there is no time to await the convocation of the National Assembly" (Article 76[1]). A similar provision deals with "major hostilities affecting national security" (Article 76[2]). In time of "war, armed conflict or similar national emergency" the president may declare martial law of two types, one more sweeping than the other, but must lift it if a majority of the Assembly so requests. The president may attend or address the National Assembly. Presidential power to dissolve the Assembly was removed by the 1987 amendment.

The president is to be elected for a single five-year term by "universal, equal, direct and secret ballot by the people" (Article 67[1]) and must receive no less than one-third of the votes. To be elected president, a person must have reached the age of forty years and be eligible for election to the National Assembly. The previous requirement of residence within the country for five years was deleted. If the office becomes vacant, a successor must be elected within sixty days; in the interim, the prime minister (or other member of the State Council, as provided by law) acts as president. A president may not be reelected; but "matters pertaining to the status and courteous treatment of former presidents shall be determined by law."

The 1972 and 1980 Constitutions provided for election of the president by an electoral college; this provision was the principal focus of opposition criticism. Although there are valid arguments for it, the Korean public viewed it as a device to influence voting to favor the government, since there were a relatively small number of electors (2,500 under the 1972 Constitution; more than 5,000 under the 1980 Constitution) and they did not vote by secret ballot. Electors were chosen by direct popular vote in districts roughly corresponding to townships (*up* and *myon*). Although electors after 1980 could be political party members and publicly state their preferred candidate, local officials and notables had a major say in choosing them.

The prime minister, who must be a civilian, "shall assist the President and shall direct the Executive Ministries under order of the President." The prime minister is vice president of the State Council, a body consisting of fifteen to thirty members that "shall deliberate on important policies that fall within the power of the Executive." (Article 89 lists sixteen specific categories that must be referred to the State Council.) Members of the Council "assist the President in the conduct of State affairs," and the heads of executive ministries are appointed from among State Council members. Ministries are established by law and not listed in the Constitution.

The other appointive executive branch agencies specified in the Constitution are as follows:

- an Advisory Council of Elder Statesmen, whose chairperson is the immediate past president, to "advise the President on important affairs of State";

- a National Security Council, similar to the U.S. body of the same name, to advise the president on national security policies "prior to their deliberation by the State Council";
- an Advisory Council on Democratic and Peaceful Unification, to support the president in his constitutional mandate to "pursue sincerely the peaceful unification of the homeland";
- a National Economic and Advisory Council "to advise the President on the formulation of important policies for developing the national economy";
- a Board of Audit and Inspection, composed of five to eleven members, the chairman of which must have National Assembly concurrence for his appointment and serves no more than two four-year terms. The Board's functions are roughly comparable to those of the U.S. General Accounting Office, although it is an executive, not a legislative, agency.

Legislative Branch

Chapter III of the Constitution establishes a unicameral National Assembly that must have more than 200 members (in 1989, there were 299). Members are elected for four-year terms by "universal, direct and secret ballot by the citizens." "Constituencies of members, proportional representation and other matters" are to be prescribed by law. (The new election system is described in the section "Emergence of the Sixth Republic," above.)

The Assembly convenes once a year in regular session for no more than one hundred days but may be convened by the president or by one-fourth of its members for special sessions of no more than thirty days each. Bills may be introduced either by the executive or by Assembly members. A majority of the membership constitutes a quorum, and majority vote of members present is required for decision. The president must within fifteen days either promulgate a bill passed by the Assembly or return it with written explanation; otherwise, it automatically becomes law. The Assembly can override a veto by a two-thirds vote. The Assembly must enact a budget thirty days before the beginning of the fiscal year (as of 1987, the fiscal year was the calendar year). In doing so, it may not increase the budget submitted by the executive. If the budget is not passed, the executive may make essential expenditures in conformity with the previous year's budget.

National Assembly consent is required for treaties of specified categories, such as mutual security, trade, peace, or legislative matters, as well as for declaration of war, dispatch of armed forces to foreign states, or stationing of alien forces on national territory. The Assembly "may inspect affairs of state or investigate specific matters of state affairs" and demand presentation of related documents and testimony. It may summon the prime minister or State Council members to answer questions. (This has been a frequent practice in past Assembly sessions.)

A recommendation for the removal from office of the prime minister or a State Council member may be passed by the National Assembly. Such action must be proposed by one-third of the Assembly members and approved by an absolute majority. The Assembly may move for impeachment of senior officials by the same proposal and vote; a proposal to impeach the president requires concurrence of an absolute majority of the Assembly membership, and approval of two-thirds of the total membership. Judgment on impeachment cases is by the Constitutional Court (see below).

The National Assembly establishes its own rules of procedure and elects its officers (a speaker and two vice speakers are the only ones constitutionally specified). Committees are not mentioned in the Constitution. In 1987 there were thirteen standing committees—a steering committee and twelve others charged with specific areas of government—whose officers and members were elected by the Assembly. (Much of the legislative work is carried on in committee, as in the United States.) There were four party negotiating groups (as provided in the National Assembly Law, not mentioned in the Constitution), with their own officers.

The Assembly is empowered to discipline its members and to expel members by vote of two-thirds of the membership. Members are required to "maintain high standards of integrity" and not to abuse their positions to acquire property or position. They may not concurrently hold any other office prescribed by law. They are immune from arrest or detention during sessions, except in cases of flagrante delicto or with Assembly consent, and may not be held liable outside the Assembly for opinions or votes in the Assembly.

Judicial Branch

Chapter V of the Constitution establishes a Supreme Court "and other courts at specified levels." The Supreme Court has the power of judicial review over decrees, regulations, and administrative actions; but if a court finds that a law contravenes the Constitution, the court must request a decision of the Constitutional Court. The Supreme Court has final appellate decision over both civil courts and courts-martial, but military court decisions in specified types of cases may not be appealed under extraordinary martial law (the higher of the two authorized types of martial law).

The chief justice is appointed by the president, with the consent of the National Assembly, for a nonrenewable term of six years. Other Supreme Court justices are appointed by the president on the recommendation of the chief justice for renewable six-year terms. Judges of other courts are appointed by the chief justice for renewable ten-year terms. They may not be removed from office except by impeachment or criminal punishment, nor suspended except by disciplinary action, but may be removed for mental or physical impairment. Judicial administration, procedure, and rules are established by the Supreme Court.

Chapter VI establishes a separate Constitutional Court of nine members to rule upon the constitutionality of laws, impeachment, the dissolution of a political party, and executive branch jurisdictional disputes. For most types of decisions, affirmative votes of six members are required. Three of the members are nominated by the National Assembly and three by the chief justice; all are appointed by the president for renewable six-year terms. Members may not join political parties or engage in politics.

Election Management

A separate Chapter VII of the Constitution establishes a Central Election Management Committee and subordinate committees for "fair management of elections and national referendums, and dealing with administrative affairs concerning political parties." The Central Election Management Committee has nine members: three appointed by the president, three selected by the National Assembly, and three nominated by the chief justice. The members elect the chairperson from among themselves. All have six-year terms. They may not engage in politics.

The election management committees, within the limits of laws and decrees, establish regulations for election management and political parties and manage elections. "Except as otherwise provided by law, expenditures for elections shall not be imposed upon political parties or candidates." In law, election campaigns are rather strictly circumscribed, and much of the expense is provided from government funds, but large sums are spent by candidates and parties for entertainment and favors.

Local Government

Under Chapter VIII, local governments "shall deal with . . . welfare of local residents, manage properties and may enact provisions relating to local autonomy, within the limits of laws and regulations." The Constitution specifies that local governments shall have councils, organized and elected according to law, and provides for election of heads of local government bodies. Local councils were also provided for in the 1980 Constitution, but a supplementary provision (deleted in 1987) stated that they were to be "established on a phased basis taking into account the degree of financial self-reliance attained by local governments." In 1991 there were elections for local councils in the towns and townships, and in 1995 there were elections for mayors and governors.

Economic Provisions

Chapter IX provides a mixture of provisions accepting respect for "freedom and creative ideas of the individual in economic affairs," coupled with state regulation "in order to maintain the balanced growth and stability of the national economy to ensure proper distribution of income, to prevent the domination of the market and the abuse of economic power and to democratize the economy through harmony among the economic agents." The clauses concerning state regulation have been somewhat changed from the 1980 version, clearly reflecting the populist themes of Kim Dae-jung.

Article 127 states: "Private enterprise shall not be nationalized or transferred to ownership by a local government, nor shall their management be controlled or administered by the State, except in cases determined by law to meet urgent necessities of national defense or the national economy." Natural resources may be licensed for exploitation "for a period of time"—implying state ownership of them. "Land and natural resources shall be protected by the State." The state is required to plan for appropriate utilization of natural resources.

According to Articles 121 to 127, the state is required to protect and foster agriculture, fisheries, and small and medium-sized enterprises; "guarantee the consumer protection movement"; foster regional economies "to ensure the balanced development of all regions"; foster foreign trade, with the power to regulate and coordinate it; and "strive to develop the national economy by developing science and technology, information and human resources and encouraging innovation." Tenant farming is prohibited, and "the State shall endeavor to realize the land-to-the-tiller principle," but leasing and management are recognized for efficient utilization of farmland.

Amendment

According to Chapter X, amendments to the Constitution may be proposed either by the president or by a majority of members of the National Assembly. They must be put before the public for at least twenty days, adopted by two-thirds or more of the total Assembly membership within sixty days, and approved in a national referendum not later than thirty days after Assembly action by majority vote of more than one-half of the eligible voters. No amendment may change the term or eligibility for reelection of the president who is in office when it is proposed.

Performance of the Political System

Since 1945, the south Korean political system has virtually completed the destruction of the old concentration of wealth and power in the hands of the *yangban* aristocracy—a process that had begun under the Japanese. The Korean War accelerated the process through massive population movement, physical destruction, and inflation. Effective land reform, begun by the U.S. military government and completed by 1952, virtually eliminated landlordism. Growing emphasis on merit and competence in government and industry has greatly reduced family influence and favoritism in filling government positions, and greater access to education has improved career opportunity for the average citizen.

Although elites, including the newly rich business class, enjoy obvious advantages, south Korea has done better than most developing countries in preventing extreme maldistribution of wealth. World Bank studies show that wealth distribution in the Republic is similar, though at a much lower level, to that of the United States. This situation is partly due to land reform, partly to inflation (which wiped out much of the former landlords' money), and partly to deliberate government policies such as the New Community Movement, price policies, a progressive income tax, and effective tax collection.

However, the World Bank study may have failed to take into account the very-high-income entrepreneur fortunes in urban centers, and there has been a tendency in recent years toward an increase in income disparity. A reduced economic growth rate and the decline in Middle East construction contracts increased unemployment, although a new spurt in economic growth in 1986 and 1987 masked this trend. The government is committed to a gradual increase in health and social welfare benefits. The government's emphasis on increasing exports has been supported by a policy of holding wages and benefits down to ensure competitiveness, thus engendering varying amounts of dissatisfaction and unrest in the labor force.[20] This dissatisfaction surfaced in August 1987 in widespread strikes, which have continued in subsequent years and have greatly increased wage rates. Whether these increases and the policies of the new government will contain the unrest, and whether the economy will be adversely affected by higher labor costs, remains to be seen.

Backed by a powerful army and headed by former Army generals, the Korean government has been highly effective at regulation of the society. Regulation is facilitated by the hierarchical tradition, by authoritarian central controls, and by efficient internal security forces. Regulative capacity has been used to damp down public demands on the political system in areas in which the leaders believed the system could not meet the demands. At times the application of coercion has been excessive and has created a backlash. Demands for increased political freedom and for higher wages and benefits are particularly prone to coercion.

Corruption.   Corruption, in the sense of illicit gain through manipulation of the political system, has been a major concern of both south Koreans and foreigners for years. The East Asian tradition of official "squeeze" swelled to intolerable proportions in the Republic's early days. Stamping out corruption was one of the main professed concerns of the military coup leaders in 1961, but some of those very leaders became mired in it themselves. It was routine in earlier years to skim off 5 percent or so of bank loans for government officials, although the proceeds were often used for political rather than personal ends. Although there can be no precise statistics, the general impression is that corruption has greatly diminished in recent years, even though rumors still abound of illicit gain in high places. Government salaries have increased, control procedures have tightened, and penalties have been made more severe. President Kim Young-sam's anticorruption campaigns led to the sacking not only of generals but also of members of his own cabinet. However, the knowledge that there was a certain amount of corruption in the system did little to prepare Koreans for the shock of discovering the extent of former President Roh Tae-woo's graft while in office. In October 1995 it was discovered that the major business conglomerates and numerous individuals had contributed almost $600 million to Roh's private political fund, part of which he had used to reward supporters (and even to help fund Kim Dae-jung's 1992 run for the presidency against his own candidate, Kim Young-sam) and part of which he had put away for himself and his family. An investigation led promptly to Roh's arrest. More importantly, since his imprisonment did away with the question of whether south Korea was the kind of place that jailed its ex-presidents, it removed one of Chun Doo-hwan's best informal protections. Before long there was irresistible pressure on the government to make Chun, at long last, pay the price for the 1979 coup and the Kwangju massacre. In early December 1995 prosecutors arrested a defiant Chun—and Koreans were faced with the prospect of punishment, perhaps capital punishment, for a second former president. For some, it was sweet satisfaction. For others it was a most disturbing prospect.

Human Rights.   The government's performance on human rights has been of more concern to observers in the United States than to the majority of Koreans. By traditional Korean standards, great progress has been made since the late nineteenth century, when criminals were routinely torn apart by oxen in front of the South Gate in Seoul. Individual freedoms today are abridged but by no means denied. Nevertheless, it is clear that Korea's human rights record leaves much to be desired. Torture and even murder were more common in the 1970s and 1980s under Presidents Park and Chun. Indeed, one of the key events that forced the Chun regime to accept "democratization" in 1987 was the public outcry over the death of Pak Chong-ch'ol, a dissident student who died when police held his head in a tub of water during an interrogation and accidentally crushed his windpipe. That case was remarkable in that it became well known; there were many others that did not.

The government maintained that such action is contrary to instructions and sternly punished. The courts in February 1985 awarded damages to a woman acquitted of murder whose confession was found to have been extracted by torture. In 1986, two policemen were disciplined after a woman worker charged them with sexual assault while she was under detention. In early 1987, when the government acknowledged the killing of Pak Chong-ch'ol, several policemen were charged with complicity in the case and several high officials resigned, including the minister of home affairs. Use of excessive force by the police has always been a pervasive and apparently ingrained problem.

A central part of the human rights issue in south Korea is the continued maintenance of the National Security Law, which punishes actions that undermine south Korea's ability to resist the north. South Korea has had something like it on the books since the 1940s, and it has often been used to punish political opponents, not for sedition or treason but for democratic expression. In a "national security state" like south Korea, the regime is in a position to call almost any act of political challenge or opposition an "antistate act" since it complicates the regime's job, and in south Korea successive regimes have used national security as the reason to crack down on political challengers as betrayers rather than simply critics. There have always been voices calling for an end to the National Security Law. There were hopes for a revision, at least, after "democratization" in 1987. Roh Tae-woo said in his inaugural address that "the day when freedoms and human rights could be slighted in the name of economic growth and national security has ended." However, in 1989 there was a rise in the number of prosecutions under the law. International monitoring organizations continued to criticize south Korea for holding political prisoners, and even under the Kim Young-sam administration the law continues in force and appears likely to remain so at least until the security situation on the peninsula removes the last excuse for its enforcement.

A major south Korean policy goal in recent years has been to increase the self-confidence, pride, and patriotism of the people and to overcome the shame and humiliation of the Japanese period. This effort is in contrast to attempts during the Rhee regime to motivate the people through the negative appeal of anti-Japanism and anticommunism (although anticommunism continues as a major theme). The new spirit, coupled with the evident economic success of the nation, has resulted in a material change in public attitude. The Korean armed forces and their impressive displays are a source of national pride, as well as concern. The 1988 Summer Olympic Games, aside from their economic and diplomatic payoff, were also important as symbols for the Korean people of their heightened status in the international community.

The ultimate test of political performance is the maintenance of political equilibrium. Thus far, the south Korean political system has been very effective in maintaining a relatively stable political process. Even the major political crises of 1952, 1960–1961, 1979–1980, and 1985–1987 involved violence on a scale that was minor indeed in comparison with the general experience of Third World countries. In the face of constant attempts from north Korea to weaken and subvert the system, south Korea has managed the demands upon it either by responding to them (albeit often partially or belatedly) or by controlling or suppressing them through various combinations of persuasion and coercion, with remarkably little large-scale internal violence or rebellion. The Kwangju uprising of 1980 was a conspicuous exception. Government operation, ever since 1945, has had much more continuity and evolutionary improvement than upheaval. This record provides a basis for hope that equilibrium will also be maintained in the years ahead.

The legitimacy of the UN-sponsored Republic and its respected nationalist leader, Syngman Rhee, were the primary basis of south Korea's stability in the first fifteen years after liberation. Strong U.S. security and economic support were also important factors. Since 1961, no south Korean government has had the same degree of legitimacy. Economic progress and firm control have been the main forces for stability, with U.S. support a continuing but diminishing factor. For the future, the prospects for stability—that is, effective government performance that will avoid violence, bloodshed, repression, and revolt—are somewhat less certain, but still quite good.

One of the primary bases for Korea's rapid economic development since the mid-1960s has been greatly improved tax collection and saving, permitting increased capital investment. Similarly, the military draft has been effectively implemented since the early 1960s. The New Community Movement, while primarily an instrument to mobilize and motivate the people, increased the popular contribution to the general welfare, although there are indications that it has passed the peak of its accomplishment.

As in other developing countries, south Korea until recently has taken little heed of environmental problems, except for a successful reforestation program. In recent years, however, as air and water pollution have grown increasingly serious, both the government and the public have begun to recognize the need for action on this front. As already noted in Chapter 3, the Environmental Agency was elevated to cabinet level in 1989.

An increasingly sophisticated Korean public will be less likely in coming years to accept government orders and preaching instead of performance in meeting popular demands. The demands are becoming more political and social and less centered on basic livelihood items. Economic progress cannot be maintained indefinitely at the high rate of the 1970s; therefore, there is less to trickle down, with a consequent increase in demands for equity. Thus government efficacy cannot so easily substitute for government legitimacy. Other bases must be found for popular support of government. Yet for political freedom and government responsiveness to increase, a new national consensus will have to develop, and it may not develop as fast as the demands increase.

Notes

1. This story was related to me by a reliable and knowledgeable Korean political observer, who was personally acquainted with the people involved.

2. "Gist of President Chun Doo Hwan's Special Statement on Constitutional Reform," *Korea News/Views*, No. 87-08 (Korean Information Office, Washington, D.C., April 13, 1987, mimeographed).

3. *Far Eastern Economic Review*, April 30, 1988.

4. Voter turnout in the 1948 election was about 80 percent, despite a call by dissident leaders for a boycott. Turnout in national elections has generally remained in the 70 to 80 percent range ever since. The election is analyzed in detail in Donald S. Macdonald, "Korea and the Ballot: The International Dimension in Korean Political Development as Seen in Elections, 1945–1960" (Ph.D. dissertation, George Washington University, 1978), pp. 213–224.

5. On the New Community Movement and its political dimension, see Vincent S.R. Brandt and Ji Woon Cheong, *Planning from the Bottom Up: Community-Based Integrated Rural Development in South Korea* (Essex, Conn.: International Council for Educational Development, 1979).

6. In 1946 the U.S. military governor appointed half of the members. From 1963 to 1985, one-third of the legislature was elected indirectly—in 1972 and 1978 by an electoral

college, in other years from party slates in accordance with a weighted proportion of the popular vote. Under the 1987 constitution, the proportion elected from party slates was reduced to one-fourth, and the reward for a plurality was reduced. See Donald S. Macdonald, "The 1946 Election and Legislative Assembly in South Korea: America's Bumbling Tutelage," *Journal of Northeast Asian Studies* 1(3) (Fall 1982):53–69; Chong Lim Kim, ed., *Political Participation in Korea: Democracy, Mobilization, and Stability* (Santa Barbara, Calif.: Clio Books, 1980), pp. 59–84; Ilpyong J. Kim and Young Whan Kihl, eds., *Political Change in South Korea* (New York: Paragon House, 1988), pp. 245–247.

7. *Korea Annual 1994* (Seoul: Yonhap Press Agency, 1994), pp. 134–138.

8. Amnesty International, AI Index No. ASA 25/11/95 (May 10, 1995), from the Internet, http://www.Amnesty.org/Asia95/251195.ASA.txt.

9. For an array of articles on the emerging Korean middle class see Hagen Koo, ed., *State and Society in Contemporary Korea* (Ithaca: Cornell University Press, 1993).

10. *Korea Annual 1994,* p. 109.

11. Andrea Matles Savada and William R. Shaw, eds., *South Korea: A Country Study,* 4th ed. (Washington, D.C.: U.S. Government Printing Office, 1992), p. 318.

12. For a discussion of Korean political parties, see Haruhiro Fukui, editor-in-chief, *Political Parties of Asia and the Pacific,* vol. 1 (Westport, Conn.: Greenwood Press, 1985), pp. 659–678; and *Political Change in South Korea,* pp. 75–90.

13. For a survey of human rights under the military-backed regime of Chun Doo-hwan, see U.S. Information Service, Seoul, "1985 Human Rights Report for Republic of Korea," Backgrounder, February 19, 1986; *Human Rights in Korea* (New York: Asia Watch, 1986); and *A Stern, Steady Crackdown: Legal Process and Human Rights in South Korea* (Washington and New York: Asia Watch, April 1987). Amnesty International continues to survey the human rights situation in south Korea (as it does in all countries), and current reports are accessible on the Internet at http://www.amnesty.org/Aireports.html.

14. For the Chun-era press regulations, see "South Korea: 'Guiding the Press,'" in *Index on Censorship* 16(5) (May 1987):28–36.

15. *Korea Handbook 1994* (Seoul: Korea Overseas Information Service, 1994), pp. 514–516.

16. Kwan Bong Kim, *The Korea-Japan Treaty Crisis and the Instability of the Korean Political System* (New York: Praeger Publishers, 1971).

17. Confucianism is generally considered a philosophy, rather than a religion, but it is listed in the same category by south Korean government statistics.

18. *Korea Annual 1994,* pp. 177–178.

19. The texts of the 1980 and 1987 constitutions can be found in *Korea Annual* (Seoul: Yonhap Press Agency, various years), or in *Constitutions of the Countries of the World,* ed. Albert P. Blaustein and Gisbert H. Flanz (Dobbs Ferry, N.Y.: Oceania Publications, looseleaf, various years). The official English translation of the 1987 amendment appeared in the south Korean government-owned daily newspaper, *Korea Herald,* October 24, 1987.

20. See Parvez Hasan and D. C. Rao, *Korea: Policy Issues for Long-Term Development: The Report of a Mission Sent to the Republic of Korea by the World Bank* (Baltimore: Published for the World Bank by Johns Hopkins University Press, 1979), pp. 36–43. For a criticism of the Fifth Republic's economic policies as they affected the average citizen, see Kim Dae Jung, *Mass-Participatory Economy: A Democratic Alternative for Korea* (Cambridge, Mass.: Center for International Affairs, Harvard University; Lanham, Md.: University Press of America, 1985).

5

Politics and Government of the Democratic People's Republic of Korea (North Korea)

Introduction

Since the fall of Communism in Eastern Europe and the Soviet Union and especially since the death of President Kim Il-sung in July 1994, north Korea has been undergoing its sternest test. At stake is the survival of a regime and state that claims unique historical significance in the world, and that makes claims so audacious that any failure of control, or revelation as being less than what it claims to be, will almost certainly bring about its collapse. Such is the view from the West— and yet against all odds north Korea has survived repeated predictions of its fall. It is probably not the dire military threat that some say it is; however, it is not as weak as it might seem when judged by Western standards. In this respect, at least for the time being, its claim to historical uniqueness may in part be justified.

The Korean peninsula is one of four places in the world where both Communist and non-Communist political and social systems have operated in one divided nation.[1] Given the long tradition of Korea as a single, integrated country, the contrast of the two political systems is all the more dramatic. Unfortunately, however, the Democratic People's Republic of Korea (DPRK) is one of the most closed societies in the world. The picture of north Korea must be inferred from what was known of the Korean people prior to 1950, oral and written statements from north Korean sources, the principles of Marxism-Leninism as it was received by north Korea from the Soviet Union, and the limited information provided by foreign observers.

It is well established that the Soviet political system and culture were adopted wholesale in the DPRK in the period of 1945 to 1950—much as U.S. forms were followed in the south. Proletarian internationalism, the power of the Soviet Union, and communist doctrine justified doing so; many of the people of Korea at the time were well disposed toward communism; and the doctrinaire, authoritarian approach of communism was somewhat similar to the Confucian tradition it sought to displace. Yet the foreign model was reshaped to meet Korean realities—an evolution that also occurred in the south. Outwardly, despite several purges in the 1950s, the development of the north Korean political system seems to have been carefully controlled by its leader, Kim Il-sung, and his faction, with none of the large-scale upheavals that south Korea has experienced. Yet the DPRK has had its own internal tensions. A few are known; the nature of most of north Korea's internal struggles, however, can only be guessed.

The U.S. Department of State, in its annual human rights assessment for 1994, described the north Korean regime as

a dictatorship under the rule of the Korean Workers' (Communist) Party (KWP). The party exercises absolute power on behalf of its leader, General Secretary Kim Il-sung, who is also President of the DPRK. . . . The North Korean regime is repressive and subjects the people to rigid controls. The regime establishes security ratings for each individual which determine access to employment, schools, medical facilities, and certain stores. . . .

The State directs all significant economic activity. . . . The North Korean Penal Code is draconian, stipulating capital punishment and confiscation of all assets for a wide variety of "crimes against the revolution," including defection, slander of the party or State, and possessing "reactionary" printed matter. The regime permits no independent press or associations, and little outside information reaches the public except that approved and disseminated by the Government. . . .

Political prisoners, opponents of Kim Il-sung and Kim Jong-il, and others have been summarily executed. . . . Defectors claim that North Korea detains about 150,000 political prisoners and family members in maximum security camps in remote areas. One credible report lists 12 such prison camps believed to exist in the DPRK.[2]

The Department of State's portrayal is a harsh one, but it is based on factual reports of defectors and foreign visitors and close analysis of north Korean public statements. Friendly observers who have visited north Korea have made more positive assessments, noting the lack of evident poverty and the warm support of the regime expressed by those officials and citizens with whom visitors could talk. In considering these assessments, it must be remembered, on the one hand, that visitors to China in the early years of the Communist regime there glossed over conditions that the Chinese themselves have since acknowledged. On the other hand, what appears as harsh suppression to U.S. observers may be viewed less critically by the citizens of a country without a native tradition of individual freedom. Indeed, there is every sign that the government's popular support is genuine and widespread. This is particularly true in view of the remarkable economic progress that the north Korean regime was able to achieve during much of its history and that clearly benefited the peasant majority of the population.

Political Culture

Like south Korea, north Korea's political culture is based on more than a millennium of tradition, containing native and Confucian elements. Unlike south Korea, north Korea explicitly rejected the Confucian heritage. With the establishment of a Stalinist state, north Korea adopted Marxism-Leninism as its ideology; but by 1955, Kim Il-sung had begun to emphasize the *juch'e* idea of nationalist independence and self-reliance. The *juch'e* idea has developed into a state ideology that the north Koreans represent as a higher form of Marxism-Leninism, developed to meet unique Korean conditions but suitable for the guidance of the developing world in general.

At the same time, there are indications that both aboriginal elements and Confucian ideas still play an implicit part in north Korean political culture. This culture, at present, is probably best described as a blend of all four elements—aboriginal, Confucian, Communist, and *juch'e*. The extent to which traces of Christian and European-American democratic ideas are still present—as they surely were before 1945, given the number of Christian believers then in the north—cannot be judged. Native and Confucian cultural ideas have been discussed in Chapters 3 and 4.

Communism began to attract Korean nationalists around the time of the 1917 Bolshevik Revolution in Russia. It probably was seen primarily by most nationalists as a blueprint for throwing off the Japanese yoke and secondarily as a political way of life. Early Korean communists did not distinguish themselves as Marxist-Leninist theoreticians in the way that earlier Koreans had become noted Confucian scholars. Nevertheless, under Soviet tutelage, north Korean political doctrine after 1945 hewed closely to the Soviet line.

Space permits only the briefest summation of Communist ideology, which is already familiar to many readers. It begins with the doctrine of economic determinism and the inevitable seizure of power by the proletariat. History in all countries is said to pass through stages determined by changes in the relations of the society to the means of production. Feudalism is replaced by capitalism, which ends when the workers take power from the monopoly capitalists—by violent revolution, if necessary—and establish a dictatorship of the proletariat. The proletariat, in turn, is guided by a vanguard, including qualified intellectuals who provide the necessary guidance through the Communist Party. The means of production are taken from private owners and held collectively in a socialist system, until the final stage of complete communism is reached. At that point, everyone contributes to the general good according to his or her abilities and is given whatever he or she needs. All property is owned by all the people, working through voluntary association, and the political state withers away because the new forms of cooperation make it unnecessary.

No Communist state past or present ever has claimed attainment of the stage of pure communism. On the road to communism, however, Communist governments are always on guard against the reactionary forces of the capitalists, who are still fighting from the bastions of their power, chief among which is the United States. The revolution, therefore, must continue until all capitalist remnants have been swept away; and the Communist governments must remain strong in order to lead this fight.

Moreover, the progressive forces must be totally united in their support, both within and among the Communist nations, so as to give the enemy no points of entry. The basis for unity is the doctrines of Marxism-Leninism. These doctrines have been interpreted in various ways at various times and in various countries, but the current interpretation in each country has almost the force of religion; deviation from the official line is similar to heresy—or treason, if it results from collusion with the capitalist enemy—and can be severely punished.

Not only because of its doctrines, but also because Communism struggled for power in Europe for many years before its adherents achieved control of Russia in the Bolshevik Revolution of 1917, Communism developed a conspiratorial flavor and a reputation for an emphasis on revolution, violence, guile, and deceit.[3] This atmosphere prevailed in most Communist countries until the upheavals in Eastern Europe in the late 1980s; the Communist leaders were conservative in preserving the basic structure of their regimes while espousing revolutionary themes. Although the Soviet Union and the socialist regimes in Eastern Europe have fallen and China is undergoing fundamental economic change, there continues to be virtually no observable change in north Korea.

Central to the Communist polity is the Communist Party (in north Korea, the Korean Workers' Party), which directs the policies and activities of the government in the interests of the proletariat it represents. Token parties are permitted under other names, but they have no real political significance.

A basic element in Communist political culture is democratic centralism, the doctrine that everyone should have a chance to voice his or her views and preferences, but once these views have been taken into account in Party decisions, it is everyone's duty to carry those decisions out loyally and completely, as directed by the Party leaders. Related to this is the "mass line," which makes the Party responsible both for hearing the views of the people and for educating them in Party policies, through both propaganda and personal contact. Kim Il-sung, particularly, emphasized the need for leaders and officials to get out among the people and he set the example with his numerous famous "on-the-spot guidance" visits. It is possible that Kim's personal example and his constant emphasis on government and party officials' keeping in touch with the masses contributed during his lifetime to the stability of the north Korean polity by creating at least the popular perception of leadership solicitude and responsiveness.

The Juch'e Idea

In recent years, north Korea has developed an ideology of its own, called *juch'e*. The word means self-reliance or self-sufficiency, but as an ideological term it has taken on a much broader meaning. The development of the *juch'e sasang* (*"juch'e* thought," or "the *juch'e* idea,") began by the mid-1950s, at a time when north Korea was starting to recover from the defeat and devastation of the Korean War and to face declining levels of assistance from its giant Communist allies. Kim Il-sung made his first speech on the problem of *juch'e* on December 28, 1955.[4] Since then, it has been elevated to the status of national doctrine as a new and higher stage of Marxism-Leninism.

According to Shuhachi Inoue, a Japanese apologist for the north Korean regime, *juch'e* starts from the proposition that humans are masters of all things and are uniquely endowed, among the creatures of nature, with three special attributes: *chajusong* (the spirit of independence and self-reliance), creativity, and consciousness of their own identity and potential. The doctrine is based on four "sociohistorical principles": (1) the popular masses are the subjects of social history; (2) human history is the history of the struggle of the popular masses for *chajusong;* (3) the sociohistorical movement is the creative movement of the popular masses; and (4) independent thought and consciousness of the popular masses perform the decisive role in the revolutionary struggle. However, the masses cannot succeed in their struggle without a uniquely qualified leader to interpret and give form to their aspirations and to direct their efforts. In Inoue's view, Kim Il-sung was such a leader and his son, Kim Jong-il, is uniquely qualified to succeed him because of his total loyalty, careful training, and personal qualities.[5]

The following excerpts from a 1974 speech by Kim Jong-il are quoted at some length, not only as an explanation of *juch'e* but also as a sample of north Korean ideological writings.

The *juch'e* philosophy is a new philosophy focusing on the leader [Kim Il-sung] . . . elaborated and systematized, focusing on man.

The *juch'e* philosophy made it clear for the first time that *chajusong* [concept of standing for oneself], creativity, and consciousness are the essential features of man, the social being. Thus it gave a perfect conception of man and a correct philosophical answer to his position and role as master who dominates and transforms nature and society.

The *juch'e* philosophy and human[ist bourgeois] philosophy have fundamentally different viewpoints of man. The former regards man as an independent, creative and conscious social being [who is master of everything and decides everything], whereas advocates of the latter deny man's social character and consider him to be a being dominated by his instinct, a powerless being isolated from the world. The bourgeois humanist philosophy which negates a scientific understanding of the world and revolutionary changes, inspires sorrow, pessimism and ultra-egotism.

The world is, in essence, a material entity . . . and . . . moves, changes, and develops in accordance with its inherent laws. The *juch'e* philosophy . . . elucidated a new idea of the world that nature and society are dominated and transformed by man, and thus fulfilled brilliantly the philosophical task of our time when the popular masses are masters of their own destiny and history.

Man's *chajusong* is different in quality from the simple instinct of other living matter to maintain their physical existence. It is an attribute to live and develop as a social being. . . . *Chajusong* is the main attribute of man, but . . . along with [it], creativity and consciousness constitute his social attributes. . . . *Chajusong* is an attribute of man who is desirous of living independently as master of the world and his own destiny; creativity is an attribute of man who transforms the world and shapes his own destiny purposefully; and consciousness is an attribute of man who determines all his activities designed to understand and reshape the world and himself. *Chajusong*, creativity and consciousness, though distinguishable from one another, are closely integrated.

卐　　卐　　卐

The *juch'e* philosophy newly elucidated the essential features of man and his position and role as dominator and transformer of the world, and thus raised his dignity and value to the highest level possible. This is the great achievement of the *juch'e* philosophy that no other philosophical thoughts have accomplished.[6]

The emphasis on the supremacy and independence of man seems to echo certain aspects of Christian (as well as Communist) theology, in contrast to the traditional East Asian emphasis on harmony of man with nature. However, independence in *juch'e* thought must necessarily refer chiefly to the independence of people as a national whole. The individual's independence lies in loyal obedience to leader and Party. Obedience does not rule out initiative and innovation; as a matter of fact, Kim Il-sung's statements always encouraged initiative and innovation, within the limits of doctrine and policy, and have decried bureaucratic rigidity.

Political Process

By analogy with the south, it can be assumed that the demands the north Korean people make on the regime focus upon improvement in the standard of living and quality of life, equitable distribution of income and benefits, and progress toward reunification. It can be assumed that they genuinely fear attack or subversion from the imperialists, especially the United States and south Korea (allied, they are told, in a triangular aggressive relationship with the old enemy, Japan). North Koreans probably also want greater freedom from political and social controls, but there is no way of knowing the intensity of such feelings. Given Korea's history and the insulation of the north Korean people from the rest of the world, demands for freedom may be less strong than the U.S. public might suppose.

To support their regime, the citizens of the DPRK pay no taxes under that name; taxes as such were officially abolished some years ago. On the contrary, the people benefit (particularly in urban areas) from subsidized prices for food, housing, and other items. They pay user fees for utilities. State revenues are levied as a percentage of transactions between state economic organizations and thus are indirectly collected from the citizens.

People are required to participate in various activities ordained by the Party or the government, such as indoctrination meetings in factories, farms, or localities and demonstrations of support for their leader, the regime, and its foreign visitors. Movements of individuals from one place to another are closely controlled.

Pressure on citizens to vote for representatives in local and national legislative bodies is demonstrated by official reports that nearly 100 percent of those eligible cast ballots for the officially selected candidates in all elections. Practically every able-bodied person is mobilized for defense, either in the regular armed services (which include over 4 percent of the population) or in the auxiliary services. Under the official ideology, virtually every activity constitutes support for the regime.

North Korean citizens are exposed to a heavy and sustained barrage of indoctrination as well as scrutiny by Party members, supervisors, and agents of the security services: The emphasis is on telling the people what they should do, rather than listening to what they want. Nevertheless, it appears that the Korean Workers' Party organization and perhaps the affiliated groups provide some opportunity for citizen desires to be voiced and transmitted to decisionmaking levels. Kim Il-sung always emphasized the need for government and Party officials to get out among the people and learn their problems, and his son and successor Kim Jong-il has done the same. It is also probable that the security agencies' reporting reflects citizen demands in some degree and that informal family and other group connections continue to provide a channel for articulating demands, as in south Korea.

Mechanisms for aggregation of demands, however, are weak or absent. The Korean Workers' Party is dominated by the ruling elite in Pyongyang; so is the government. The Communist ideology, as reinterpreted by Kim Il-sung, permits all dissent to be treated as subversion or heresy, to be disregarded or rooted out. As in traditional Confucian Korea, the authority of officials is paramount; Kim Il-sung's frequent criticism of "bureaucratism" is evidence. It seems evident from the record that there are policy disagreements within the leadership, but these disagreements do not seem to be directly related to public opinion.[7]

The decisionmaking process in north Korea was centralized in Kim Il-sung when he was alive, and is presumably centralized now in Kim Jong-il. The supreme leader is surrounded by members of the Politburo of the Korean Workers' Party and advised by a somewhat wider circle of senior Party and government leaders. Given Kim Jong-il's heritage, north Korean leaders are probably reluctant to differ overtly with him. Inevitably, however, he cannot simply rule by decree the way his father could. His style has yet to emerge while he is ostensibly in mourning for his father. If and when he assumes his father's formal positions, it is to be expected that his decisions will be more corporate and less autocratic.

The most visible part of the political process has to do with carrying out decisions, not making them: Party congresses and the legislature meet briefly and—by Western standards—infrequently to ratify decisions already formulated. (The Sixth Party Congress met in 1980; the First was in 1948. The Party's Central Standing Committee meets twice a year for four or five days; the Supreme People's Assembly meets annually for two or three days.) The secretive tradition of Communist politics reinforces the largely covert nature of the decision process.

Programs for carrying out decisions appear to be devised primarily by the Central People's Committee, a sort of super-cabinet; by the State Administrative Council (comprising heads of executive agencies); and by the people's committees at lower levels, acting within policy guidelines laid down by the Party and approved by the Supreme People's Assembly (or its Standing Committee, between yearly Assembly sessions) and its local legislative counterparts. The national budget and major policy legislation are presented to the Supreme People's Assembly for approval, which is virtually automatic.

Execution of programs covering the whole range of human activity—including most agriculture, industry, commerce, services, and welfare, as well as foreign affairs and external and internal security—is the responsibility of over thirty government ministries and agencies at the national level, and many more units at provincial, county, and local levels. A network of Party and state organs ensures popular loyalty to the regime and compliance with its rules.

Outwardly, enforcement of compliance is more a matter of indoctrination and persuasion than coercion; the educational and judicial systems as well as Party cells and auxiliary organizations are an important part of the enforcement process. This point can be illustrated by the experience of a south Korean schoolteacher who had a class of north Korean refugee children during the latter stages of the Korean War. The teacher was surprised when the children came routinely with tales of the misdeeds of their schoolmates. The children, in turn, were surprised to be told that tattling was not acceptable behavior, for they had been taught to report in this way.

At the same time, the testimony of defectors suggests that coercion and fear are important in enforcing compliance. The Ministry of Public Security has subordinate units at provincial, county, and local levels, closely monitored by the Party; county units may number 100 or more officers, and agents are assigned to all cooperative farms (which, in the north Korean system, are also the local political units). Citizens are encouraged to inform on each other, even within families, regarding deviant behavior; and there is reportedly an ever-present network of informers.

The north Korean judicial system is patterned after that of the Soviet Union. As in continental European states, it gives primary importance to officials of the State Procurator's Office—an executive agency—and its local counterparts. They are responsible for initiating investigations and presenting cases to the courts, which rule on the validity of the procurators' findings rather than acting as neutral referees between the state and the accused.[8]

More significantly, however, courts and procurators are subject to guidance and control by the Party and are expected to operate in support of Party policies. Thus, the declared purpose of the north Korean penal code is to suppress resistance from the overthrown classes of capitalists and bourgeoisie, counter the "people's enemies," educate the population in the spirit of "socialist patriotism," and reeducate and punish individuals for any relapse into old-style capitalistic thinking or support of the Japanese or other external powers. Political crimes (against the state and the legal order) are handled separately, with investigations conducted in secret by separate state security agencies. Political suspects can be seized, held indefinitely, and tried and sentenced in secret.

Mass media in north Korea are organized with great effectiveness to convey regime policies to the citizens. Newspapers, radio, television, motion pictures, and magazines are all operated by state or Party organs. There are also local loud-speaker networks and mobile broadcast vehicles in rural areas. Mass media are supplemented by Party and other education and indoctrination meetings and by the educational system generally. Radios possessed by the general public can be tuned only to north Korean broadcasts.

The most dramatic distinction in political style between north and south Korea lies in the fact that from the beginning of the Soviet occupation in 1945, there was an unabashed and concerted effort to persuade or, if necessary, force the entire north Korean people into the Communist philosophical and political mold, with no concern for previous tradition or alternative philosophies. Kim Il-sung and his followers (some of whom were purged for dissent) continued after independence where their Soviet mentors had left off. Since the mid-1950s, the principle of *juch'e* and other tenets of Kim Il-sung's thought have more and more displaced the original Marxism-Leninism, but the intensity of indoctrination (judging from the regime's public pronouncements) has not abated.

The Legacy of Kim Il-sung

A remarkable feature of north Korean politics is the ongoing cult of Kim Il-sung (Figure 5.1). When he was alive, the adulation accorded him in the official media was extraordinary, and his name is still invoked on all possible occasions as the source of infinite wisdom, grace, and benevolence. His father, mother, and grand-father continue to receive praise as nationalist heroes. His birthplace is a national shrine and a mecca for innumerable pilgrims. To some extent, at least, adoration of Kim is a genuine popular attitude. Its expression seems to be universal, whether because of conviction or conformity. The Kim cult lives on in his son Kim Jong-il, who stands quietly in his place, not seeming too eager to claim the mantle, but qualified to do so when the time is right by virtue of his heritage and his long apprenticeship in the Party. At that time the world will see whether the worship that was paid to the father will also be paid to the son.

Kim Il-sung's true personal background is a matter of some contention, and his official biography is not necessarily to be taken at face value. He was born in 1912 in Pyongyang, the son of a peasant couple, and named Kim Song-ju. His family moved back and forth between Korea and Manchuria while he was growing up, and he attended schools in both countries and both languages. He also may have been exposed to Christian influence as a student.[9] In adolescence he joined in

FIGURE 5.1   Kim Il-sung, former president of the
Democratic People's Republic of Korea, July 1980
(photo courtesy of Ralph Clough)

anti-Japanese guerrilla activity in southeastern Manchuria, eventually organizing
groups and attacks of his own, exploits on which his subsequent heroic image
was based. At some point he took the name of Kim Il-sung; south Koreans often
assert that he appropriated the name of a former nationalist hero-fighter, but
north Korea insists that the original Kim Il-sung was the youth Kim Song-ju all
along. In any case, Kim took charge of a guerrilla unit that mounted significant

attacks on Japanese forces in the late 1930s and then was forced to move to adjacent Soviet territory when Japanese pressure grew too intense. During World War II, Kim Il-sung became the commander of a Korean detachment in the Eighty-eighth Special Independent Brigade, an international unit of the Soviet Army's Far East Command. He married fellow partisan Kim Chong-suk, and it was in Siberia, near Khabarovsk, on February 16, 1942, that their son Kim Jong-il was born. It was by virtue of his service in the Eighty-eighth Brigade, in addition to his reputation for skirmishing and raiding along the Korea-Manchuria border, that Kim Il-sung was in a position to be brought back to Korea by the occupying Soviet forces in the uniform of a Red Army major.

Nothing in Kim's background suggests that he was highly educated or had much experience in administration before he was installed by the Soviets as a north Korean leader. His extraordinary political skill, however, was undeniable. Using his former comrades-in-arms as his base of support over a period of years, including the period of the Korean War, he managed to dispose of every other individual or group that challenged his authority.

On the one hand, they resorted to manipulation and force to maintain political control; on the other, they emphasized somewhat simplistic and otherworldly standards of loyalty, virtue, and duty, dismissing material profit as exploitation, lifting up the peasants and workers and punishing the former social elite and their descendants for their sins, irrespective of their capacities. These are Communist themes, but they were pursued in north Korea with a single-minded relentlessness that went far beyond other Communist states (except, perhaps, for China during the Great Proletarian Cultural Revolution). It seems likely that north Korean leaders will eventually modify these policies, as has already occurred in China; but the change probably will not come soon or suddenly.

The Korean Workers' Party

The Constitution of the DPRK recognizes the leading role of the Korean Workers' Party, which, as in other Communist states until recently, has more political power and authority than the traditional organs of government. It is the Party that is primarily responsible for interacting with the citizens, receiving and communicating their views to the policy level, mobilizing and recruiting the citizens to participate in the political system, and socializing them to accept and support the philosophy and policies of the state.

Party membership is awarded only to citizens who have demonstrated their eligibility through endorsement by two Party members and approval by the local and county committees. They are probationary members for one year, then may be accepted as full members. Around 10 percent of the north Korean population (about 2 million people) are Party members—the highest proportion ever in a communist state. Each belongs to a cell of ten to one hundred members in a plant, cooperative, or locality. Attendance at cell meetings and weekly study sessions is mandatory for all members.

Key Party officials at all levels are known as "cadres," selected for their special qualities of merit, attitude, knowledge of Party ideology, and absolute loyalty, to be "commanding personnel of the revolution." They are primarily responsible for educating and leading Party and non-Party citizens and ensuring that Party policies and directives are faithfully carried out. Many cadres simultaneously hold Party and government positions. (The term "cadre" is not entirely limited to Party personnel; certain essential non-Party officials and technicians are also so characterized.)

Organization of the Party is specified in its rules and regulations, revised in October 1980. It parallels and penetrates government organization at all levels. In theory, the supreme Party organ is the National Party Congress, which is supposed to be held every five years but in fact has met only six times since its foundation in 1948 (the Sixth Congress, in 1980, was the first in ten years, and there had not been another as of early 1996). There were about 3,000 delegates to the Sixth Congress, elected indirectly by and from provincial-level Party assemblies on the basis of one per thousand Party members. These, in turn, were elected by assemblies at lower levels. The Congress approves reports of Party organs and basic Party policies and elects members of the Central Committee and Central Auditing Committee; but its decisions are generally made for it in advance by the leadership and accepted with little or no debate.

The Party Central Committee of about 329 members (including alternate members) serves as the official agent of the Congress between sessions. It meets at least once every six months. It may also convene conferences of Party delegates to authenticate decisions on urgent issues or make changes in elected personnel. The Central Committee elects the Party leader (general secretary, a post held by Kim Il-sung from just after the Party's founding and left vacant after his death in 1994), secretaries, members of the Central Inspection Committee, and—most importantly—members of the Political Bureau (Politburo) and its Standing Committee or Presidium. The Central Committee includes both civilian and military leaders; the order of their listing is considered to indicate relative prestige and power in the political system.

The Politburo had twenty-four members in 1992, of whom sixteen were alternates. Its Standing Committee—the summit of political power—was composed of just three men: Kim Il-sung, Kim Jong-il, and Defense Minister O Chin-u. Kim Il-sung's death in 1994 and O Chin-u's death in February 1995 left just one: Kim Jong-il. By 1995 the top echelons of the north Korean regime in reality looked very different from their organization chart. There was no president or Party general secretary (Kim Il-sung's positions); the party Politburo had a one-man Standing Committee; and the number in the Politburo had fallen to eighteen.

Below the Politburo in the party's organization table come the Central Committee secretaries (under the general secretary). These also fluctuate in number: In 1992 there were fourteen; in mid-1995 there were six. The secretaries oversee numerous central organizations, including the Central Auditing Committee, fiscal watchdog; Central Inspection Committee, enforcing discipline; Military Commission, which directs the armed forces; and a Liaison Bureau directing clandestine activities against south Korea. The bureaucracy works through the Party organization at provincial, county, and local levels, each of which repeats in miniature the same general organization as at the center. Crucial to the operation of the Party are the doctrines of democratic centralism and mass line. The former permits rank-and-file members to express their views internally, while requiring them to carry out Party decisions without question. The mass line doctrine makes Party members responsible for getting the views of the people by going out among them and for ensuring popular knowledge and support of Party decisions.

The Party is reinforced by a number of related organizations that support its work and provide recruits to its ranks. Among them, the most important is the Socialist Working Youth League, for persons of fifteen to twenty-six years of age. (The Socialist Working Youth League and the Korean People's Army are the principal sources of Communist Party members.) There is a Young Pioneers' Corps for children nine to fifteen years old. Laborers, agricultural workers, women, scientists, and others have their organizations related to the Party. A Democratic Front for the Reunification of the Fatherland coordinates these and other nominally unrelated groups, such as political and religious organizations (including the People's Revolutionary Party, which is claimed to exist in south Korea), to ensure broad support for Party and state policies.

Constitution and
Formal Government Organization

General Principles

In contrast to the ROK Constitution, that of the DPRK, as adopted in 1972 (the first and only substantial revision of the original 1948 document), devotes considerable space to explicit definition of the nation's political ideology and to the place of the Korea Workers' Party. The state is enjoined to build a "socialist national culture." It is to be guided by the *juch'e* principle as "a creative application of Marxism-Leninism." Dictatorship of the proletariat and class struggle are recognized, as is the *Ch'ollima* Movement (a north Korean counterpart of the Chinese Great Leap Forward of the late 1950s, now largely replaced by the Three Revolutions—ideological, cultural, and technical). The familiar five principles of foreign policy supported by the nonaligned movement of Third World nations are cited, as well as the "principles of Marxism-Leninism and proletarian nationalism." The goal of the state is to realize socialism in the north, drive out foreign forces, "reunify the country peacefully on a democratic basis," and attain complete independence.

The Constitution contains an impressive list of fundamental rights and duties guaranteed to citizens, including substantially all those in the south Korean Constitution (except that there is no explicit reference to rights of legal process), and some that are not, such as the right to rest. All persons over seventeen years of age (with the usual exceptions for criminals, the insane, etc.) have the right to vote. The state is directed to provide ten-year compulsory education, universal free medical service, and preventive health care. However, the rights and duties of citizens are explicitly based on the "collectivist principle of 'one for all and all for one,' " which effectively equates the rights of the collectivity to those of the individual and thus limits freedom.

Three classes of property are recognized. State property includes "all natural resources, important factories and enterprises, harbors, banks, transport, and communications facilities." Cooperatively owned property, which is eventually to be phased out, may include "land, draft animals, farm implements, fishing boats, buildings, as well as small and medium factories and enterprises." Personal property comprises individual benefits from state and society through socialist distribution and otherwise, including the yield from "private" garden plots.

The Constitution also stipulates the methods for socialist management of industry and agriculture, based upon the so-called Tae'an work system and its agricultural counterpart, the Chongsan-ni method (initiated by Kim Il-sung in 1969 and 1970, respectively). The state is to step up technological innovation to relieve workers from drudgery, work to eliminate urban-rural disparities and worker-peasant class distinctions, and build houses for farmers in cooperatives. Work is defined as "the sacred honor and duty of citizens," to be performed voluntarily, honestly, with strict labor discipline and "a high degree of collectivist spirit."

Legislature

The Constitution defines the Supreme People's Assembly as "the highest organ of state power," although this definition is not supported in practice. The Assembly consists of a single chamber of members elected by direct popular vote for four-year terms. (In April 1990, 687 members were elected; some of these represented overseas constituencies.) It is given authority to adopt or amend the Constitution, laws, and ordinances; set the principles of domestic and foreign policy; approve the state economic plan and national budget; and decide on questions of war and peace. It elects the president and other chief officers of the state, as well as its own officers and its Standing Committee. Matters to be deliberated are submitted by the president, Central People's Committee, Administration Council, Assembly Standing Committee, or individual members. Decisions are by simple majority, established by show of hands. Members are guaranteed inviolability and immunity from arrest. Between Assembly sessions, the Standing Committee of about twenty members performs legislative functions, including interpretation and amendment of law, and conducts elections of Assembly and local council members. (A summary chart of the government organization of the Democratic People's Republic of Korea is presented in Figure 5.2.)

President

The office of president, held by Kim Il-sung until his death in July 1994 and still vacant nearly two years later, was created in 1972 (under the previous constitution, Kim as chairman of the Assembly had performed this function ex officio). The president is elected by the Supreme People's Assembly for a four-year term with no limit on reelection and no provisions for removal or impeachment. The president is formally accountable to the Assembly and is assisted by vice presidents (four in 1994), but no succession is specified. Kim Il-sung's last election by the Supreme People's Assembly was in 1990; his death created a special situation during an extended mourning period in which the consultative processes at work at the vice presidential level were virtually impossible to assess from the outside.

The general language of the Constitution empowers the president to convene and guide the State Administration Council; makes him supreme commander of the armed forces and chairman of the National Defense Commission (state counterpart of the Party's Military Commission); requires his prior consent for laws, decrees, decisions, and directives; and gives him the power to issue his own decrees with the force of law. He may grant pardons, ratify or rescind treaties, and receive foreign envoys or request their recall.

Executive Branch

The Constitution provides for a Central People's Committee, composed of the president, vice presidents, a secretary, and members, elected by the Assembly for four-year terms and subject to recall by it on presidential recommendation. The Central People's Committee is empowered to formulate domestic and foreign policies; to direct the work of the Administration Council and its subordinate entities; to direct the judiciary; to guide the work of national defense and security; and to enforce the Constitution and laws. It may promulgate decrees, establish or abolish ministries, appoint and remove Administration Council members; change administrative subdivisions and their boundaries; proclaim a state of war; and order emergency mobilization. Under it is a National Defense Commission, whose vice chairmen are elected by the Assembly, and other commissions appointed by the Central People's Committee.

Also under the Central People's Committee is the Administration Council, or cabinet, comprising a premier, vice premiers, ministers, and other cabinet-level members. The Council prepares the state budget, formulates economic development plans and implementing measures, and may countermand the orders of

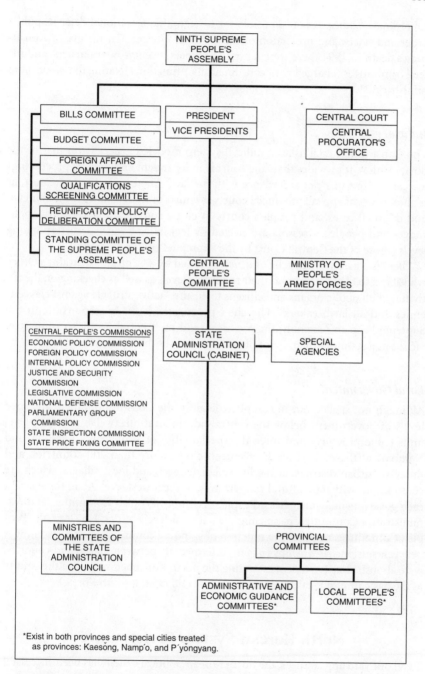

FIGURE 5.2   Chart of organization of the government of the Democratic People's Republic of Korea (from Andrea Matles Savada, ed., *North Korea: A Country Study, 4th ed.,* Washington, D.C.: U.S. Government Printing Office, 1994, p. 182)

subordinate bodies. It is responsible for foreign affairs, national defense, public order and safety, and protection of the rights of citizens. On the eve of Kim Il-sung's death in 1994 there were ten vice premiers, twenty-one ministers, and fifteen committees (charged with coordination of functions relating to two or more ministries).[10]

Judiciary

The Constitution establishes a judicial system modeled generally on that of the Soviet Union. It provides that "the court is independent and judicial proceedings are carried out in strict accordance with the law." There are a Central Court, as highest court of appeal; provincial courts as courts of first instance for major civil and criminal cases; and people's courts in cities, counties, and urban districts. Judges and people's assessors are elected by legislative bodies at corresponding levels (those of the Central Court by the Supreme People's Assembly).

There is a parallel hierarchy of officers headed by a Central Procurator's Office who act as state prosecutors at their respective levels as well as checking on the activities of all public organs and citizens to ensure "active struggle against class enemies and all lawbreakers." The chief procurator is made responsible to the Supreme People's Assembly, the president, and the Central People's Committee. He sits as a statutory member of plenary sessions of the Central Court.

Local Government

Although not spelled out in complete detail in the Constitution, there are three levels of government below the central administration: twelve province-level units (nine provinces and three the special cities of Pyongyang, Kaesong, and Namp'o) at the highest level; seventeen cities, more than 200 countries, and thirty-six urban districts, at the intermediate level; and local villages, which are coterminous with agricultural cooperatives, at the lowest level. At all three levels, each governmental entity has a People's Assembly, People's Committee, and Administrative Committee, paralleling the national-level entities. However, the People's Committees perform the function of standing committee for the assemblies between sessions. Townships (*myon*), intermediate between village and counties, were abolished in 1954, demonstrating the north Korean emphasis on the county as the basic unit of local government. (*Myon* still exist in south Korea.)

North Korean System Performance

To all outward appearances, the north Korean political system has been successful in terms of stability and order. The leadership has had substantial success in implanting its version of Communist political culture in the people—by persuasion, coercion, and denial of information about competing ideologies. In a sense, Kim Il-sung's inculcation of Communism was reminiscent of King T'aejo's inculcation of Confucianism at the beginning of the Choson Dynasty, although Kim Il-sung seems to have injected more of his own thinking than T'aejo did and to have proceeded with more speed. In both cases, there was already a group of intellectuals committed to the new ideology that facilitated its introduction. In both cases, a giant nearby power lent its weight to the new ideas. In both cases, dissident individuals and groups were ruthlessly suppressed or exiled to distant villages (although millions under Kim Il-sung voluntarily sought refuge in the south).

As a result, the north Korean political process has appeared to be better supported by popular consensus than in the south. Under U.S. tutelage, south Korea had neither the ready-made ideology nor the coercive capacity to force a political consensus and is still groping for one. However, given the northern regime's record of inflexibility, it seems likely that in the political as in the economic arena, the comparatively open, experimental approach of south Korea will have a better result, despite the confusion and occasional trauma of transitional stages.

The consensus of those who have recently visited north Korea is that there are few visible extremes of wealth and poverty, except for the privileged elite of state and Party officialdom. From the very beginning of Korea's post–World War II existence, it has been this equitable distribution—until recently, at least, a distribution more of poverty than of wealth—that has been a major basis of popular support for the north Korean regime. The relative equality is particularly attractive because of its great contrast with the maldistribution under the late Choson Dynasty and the Japanese regime. Until the Korean War, many south Korean people, and many foreigners as well, were also attracted by north Korean dynamism and egalitarian goals, which placed the uncertain south Korean regime in an unfavorable light.

However, it is clear that north Korea, after making far more rapid economic and social progress than the south, has lagged behind since the mid-1970s. Living standards on the average may be higher than China's, but they appear to be lower than those in south Korea. South Korean observers maintain that the per capita gross national product of north Korea is less than half that of the south. Most north Korean citizens are as yet only dimly aware of this disparity, if at all; thus they may be satisfied with what has been accomplished. This view may change as north Korea finds it necessary to open up to the non-Communist world.

As a Communist regime, the north Korean Party and state command all economic activity and can thus control national resources more or less as the leaders choose. North Korea has reported a balanced national account in every recent year (notwithstanding defaults on its foreign debt), which demonstrates its ability to mobilize support. However, it apparently confronts growing popular demands for consumer goods and services at a time when it must modernize its plant and import high technology in order to maintain the pace of its development. At the same time, it feels compelled to allocate 20 to 25 percent or more of its national product to defense and to keep a high proportion of its young people in uniform (see Chapter 7).[11] Communist-style central regulation of the economy has not been able to cope well with increasingly complex production and distribution problems.

The DPRK has been highly effective in regulating behavior. Dissatisfaction and unrest have been contained at levels below visibility to the outside world, except for occasional defectors, although south Korean sources from time to time have reported local disturbances. The factional struggles of the 1950s ended with Kim Il-sung and his entourage in total control. Changes in senior party and government personnel in the 1980s suggested differences over the growing role of Kim Jong-il as well as policy differences between reformists and conservatives in dealing with economic problems, but up to 1994 these had not yet had visible impact on the society as a whole.

The mantle of the Great Leader Kim Il-sung, who was made larger than life as a symbol of Korea's national status and aspirations, passed to his son Kim Jong-il in the summer of 1994. The future stability of the north Korean political system depends upon the following factors: the ability of Kim Jong-il to succeed his father as effective leader of a highly centralized, autocratic polity; the capacity of the system both to control the political and economic demands made upon it by the people and to meet these demands; the impact of the outside world—particularly south Korea—in demonstrating the potentiality for greater political freedom, economic well-being, and international status; the capacity of north Korean leaders to respond effectively to popular demands for reunification of the country; and the effectiveness of north Korea's international relations within the region, notably with China, Japan, and Russia, with the United Nations, and with its adversaries, the United States and south Korea.

North Korea's Foreign Relations in the Early 1990s

The year 1990 was a turning point in the history of north Korea's foreign relations. Throughout the 1980s, the Pyongyang government continued to present itself as a center of the world revolutionary movement, receiving visitors from the developing countries as if they were tributaries coming to pay homage at the feet of Kim Il-sung. In 1990, however, came the unraveling of Communism in Europe, followed in 1991 by the collapse of the Soviet Union. As these events unfolded, north Korea adopted new approaches in three main areas of foreign relations: with south Korea, with the United Nations, and with the United States.

In 1990 north Korea dropped its traditional refusal to meet with southern representatives on an official basis, and there ensued a series of six prime ministers' meetings, alternating between Pyongyang and Seoul over a period of two years. These encounters held promise that was more than symbolic. In December 1991 the two sides signed an "Agreement on Reconciliation, Nonaggression, and Exchanges and Cooperation Between the South and the North," and a separate "denuclearization" agreement renouncing the production or possession of nuclear weapons. The meetings broke down in 1992, however, and then were eclipsed by the shift of the diplomatic action to talks between north Korea and the United States over north Korea's alleged nuclear weapons program (see Chapter 7).

In 1991 north Korea dropped its traditional opposition to separate membership in the United Nations for Seoul and Pyongyang. The stance had always been to oppose the south as "splittist," accusing the administrations from Syngman Rhee's onward of trying to arrange permanent national division. As long as the north had assurances from the Soviet Union and China that they would veto UN membership for south Korea, the north succeeded in thwarting Seoul's attempts to join. However, when both the Soviet Union and China recognized south Korea and dropped their opposition to its membership in the United Nations, Pyongyang had no choice but to get on board. In 1991 both governments upgraded their UN observer missions in New York to full membership status and took their seats in the General Assembly.

In the 1980s there was slight movement in north Korea's relations with the United States. There were more personal contacts between American citizens and north Koreans, from the social encounters of diplomats in third countries to the occasional visits by Americans to the DPRK. In Beijing, a middle-level diplomatic dialogue began, leading to the return of American servicemen's remains from the Korean War. North Korea showed no inclination to proceed any further, however, as long as the United States maintained its troop presence in the south, carried on joint military maneuvers with the south Korean armed forces, and maintained what the north Koreans insisted was a threatening nuclear posture toward them. The United States continued to treat north Korea as a pariah state, labeling it a terrorist country and accusing it of heinous human rights violations. Notwithstanding this mutually hostile stance, however, when the world's concern over north Korea's alleged nuclear weapons program nearly went out of control in 1993, the two sides suddenly opened a direct diplomatic discussion at the subministerial level. When the DPRK threatened to pull out of the nuclear Non-Proliferation Treaty (NPT) in March 1993, a series of difficult and delicate negotiations began that continued steadily through 1995 (see Chapter 7) and resulted in several official agreements including one to exchange "liaison offices" in each other's capitals. Thus a relationship was established that had constructive potential for the future.

North Korea Under Kim Jong-il

Kim Jong-il (or Kim Chong-il), who emerged in 1974 as Kim Il-sung's chosen successor, was born near Khabarovsk in 1942, while his father was serving with the Soviet Red Army. His origins, however, have been revised in an elaborate official hagiography that places his birth at a guerrilla camp on the slopes of the sacred Mt. Paektu.[12] Kim's biography attests to a remarkable childhood about which there are many stories. As a toddler he daubed paint on a map of Japan on the very day a typhoon hit the islands. At the age of five he stood sentry duty with a wooden rifle to protect his father from the imperialists. As a child he carved still-readable revolutionary slogans on trees. These and other tales of his precocity help to establish him as Kim Il-sung's worthy heir, the son as virtual reincarnation of the father. In this he is unique.

Kim Jong-il's qualifications for leadership in the DPRK, however, though they begin with his heredity and special nurturing, amount to more than mere genetics. He was educated in Pyongyang at Kim Il-sung University and briefly in the East German Air Academy. In 1974, at the age of 32, he was given responsibility for a party-led effort to boost production, and a new term started appearing to describe him: the "party center." There is evidence that Kim Il-sung encountered resistance from within the party and even from within his own faction as he catapulted his son up the ladder of authority. By 1980, however, the opposition had been overcome. The Sixth Congress of the Korean Workers' Party promoted Kim Jong-il to party secretary, second only to his father, and a new term began appearing in the press to describe him: the "Dear Leader." The son appeared to be in full control of the party while his father was in control of the state—and, one may assume, of his son.

Kim Jong-il as Dear Leader was identified in the 1980s with several episodes that established his reputation in the outside world as an erratic and irresponsible character. One was the kidnapping of two top south Korean movie personalities, the director Shin Sang-ok and his actress wife Ch'oe Un-hi. In 1978 they were abducted from Hong Kong and taken to Pyongyang to help Kim Jong-il develop the DPRK's film industry. For seven years they were in close contact with Kim Jong-il, advising him on films and seeing him on a social basis before defecting in 1985 and returning to south Korea to tell their story. It is from their experience that the world draws much of its inferences about Kim's personal foibles and his penchant for high living.

Two other episodes were considerably more troubling. Kim Jong-il is said to have masterminded the assassination attempt on south Korean President Chun Doo-hwan while Chun was visiting Burma in October 1983. A Burmese investigation confirmed that north Korean agents planted a bomb in the superstructure of the Aung San shrine in Rangoon, timed to explode as Chun and his entourage were in the building paying respects to the Burmese national hero. Chun's entourage was waiting for him to arrive when the bomb went off, and seventeen south Koreans were killed, including several members of the cabinet and the chief presidential secretary.

The other incident, one that stamped the DPRK with the label of terrorist state for a long time to come, was the bombing of a south Korean airliner during a flight over the Andaman Sea, killing all 115 persons aboard. Two north Koreans had planted the bomb on the plane before disembarking themselves in Bahrain; one was captured and confessed to having been part of a special task force organized personally by Kim Jong-il.[13]

These gruesome facts presented the younger Kim as a sinister, perhaps even unbalanced, figure. They were supplemented by random reports of his personality quirks: his elevator shoes and not-quite-worker suits; his rotund figure and pompadour hair style; and his appreciation for liquor, women, foreign films, and parties. This caricature does not help us to understand Kim Jong-il's position in Korea much more than the "Dear Leader" caricature. Under his father's protection, Kim Jong-il spent the 1980s accumulating political experience and support. He uncovered evidence of an earlier plot against his father. He "commanded" the construction of numerous public works projects and monuments. He invented the ideological concept of "Kimilsungism," suggesting a unique Korean variant of Communism rooted in the Kim family itself. Appropriately perhaps, the sons of Kim Il-sung's own closest supporters have emerged as Kim Jong-il's closest supporters. For example, Kang Song-san, the prime minister in the mid-1990s, is the son of Kang Kon, who fought with Kim Il-sung in Manchuria and perished in the Korean War. Other supporters of Kim Jong-il are the north Korean equivalent of south Korea's "technocrats," party operatives who are skilled in economics, science, and foreign affairs. These core members of the current Korean Workers' Party constitute a succession that is more than just from father-to-son. Unlike other Communist regimes that have foundered on the rocky problem of leadership transition, the north Korean system appears to have advanced surprisingly far toward an orderly transfer of power from one generation to the next.

In the process, the emerging Kim Jong-il and his supporters have had to deal with a number of profoundly complicated problems. The most difficult from the external point of view is the security balance on the Korean peninsula, particularly as it involves the nuclear issue. But from inside the DPRK, the most difficult problem is economic. During the Cold War, north Korea enjoyed the support of the socialist bloc led by the Soviet Union, and of China, its fraternal supporter during the Korean War. These allies accepted a trading system based on barter, payment in north Korean currency, and credits that favored Korea notwithstanding the Kim regime's much-touted *juch'e* independence. Cold War considerations also kept these socialist allies from having relations with Pyongyang's southern rival, denying obvious benefits to the Seoul regime at the same time.

With the fall of Communism in Europe all that changed. The Soviet Union recognized south Korea in 1991, just before its own collapse. In the process, the Russians started demanding hard currency payments for their exports to north Korea, including the vital supply of oil. The former satellites in Eastern Europe also stopped trading with north Korea, and China followed the Russian lead by demanding hard cash in 1992. Although north Korea is comparatively rich in raw materials, it is by no means developed sufficiently to create an export-led economy on a competitive basis. The exceptional export seems to be weapons, and north Korea has a worrisome arms trade, particularly in the eyes of the United States, which sees its SCUD-type *Nodong* missile sales to Iran as a threat to peace in the Middle East. But earnings from its arms trade are not enough to fund imports on the scale that north Korea needs in order to grow its economy, which has undergone a dramatic contraction. Petroleum consumption has been slashed by as much as 90 percent according to some estimates, in order to guarantee the country's military requirements. Food shortages are such that there are said to have been food riots, and north Korea has accepted shipments of grain from the south. The economic picture—with its political implications—is therefore desperate. Economic growth, which averaged in the 2–3 percent range annually in the 1980s, turned negative in 1989, dropping by 3–5 percent annually until 1992, and then more slowly as north Korea absorbed the effects of diminished trade with Russia and China. Per capita GNP, estimated at US$1,123 in 1989, had fallen by 17.8 percent to $923 in 1994. However, the military continued to claim significant resources in the heavy industrial sector, leaving light industry and the components of the consumer economy far behind. Almost fifty years after Kim Il-sung told his people that the DPRK system's goal was one day to be able to give them "white rice with meat soup, silk clothes, and tile-roofed houses," north Korea is still not self-sufficient in food production, and visitors, even visitors to the specially maintained Pyongyang area, report much infrastructural decay.

Prospects

The north Korean military continues to be an unknown factor in the political balance with the DPRK. On the surface, Kim Jong-il's position as chairman of the Military Commission and commander-in-chief of the armed forces suggests that he exerts all necessary control. However, there are signs that the military has a certain institutional interest that hampers the civilian government's ability to wrest sacrifices from the military even though they are being made in all other sectors of the economy. One sign of this is the fact that when the north Koreans downed a stray U.S. Army helicopter in December, 1994, the Kim Jong-il government had trouble coordinating its diplomatic responses and for a time appeared to be bargaining with its own military establishment to secure the release of the surviving pilot and the body of his copilot. The significance of this particular episode, which was resolved in favor of the Americans' repatriation, remains as hard to assess as much else in the north Korean system.

In meeting popular demands, the north Korean regime faces a difficult dilemma. On the one hand, internal technical and organizational difficulties seem to be leading north Korea to look for foreign technical assistance. A mission of the United Nations Development Programme has been stationed in the country for years and in the early 1990s helped to develop the plans for a Special Economic Zone in the Tumen River area of northeastern Korea where the DPRK shares borders with China and Russia. In 1985 the regime enacted a joint venture law to encourage foreign economic participation in the north Korean economy, though there has not been an overwhelming response. On the other hand, the leadership of the DPRK appears to be ambivalent about accepting foreign assistance or foreign development planning, no doubt because of compromises that will be required but also because of the unpredictable consequences of new foreign influences. The argument over accepting south Korean technical assistance for the light-water reactors that are planned under the 1994 nuclear agreement are a case in point. North Korea desperately needs the energy but worries about the effects of having south Korean and Western technicians in the country. The demand for reunification obliges the regime to enter into at least superficial negotiations with south Korea; but as these negotiations result in concrete exchanges, such as the exchange of separated family members in 1985, north Korea's lag behind the south—both economic and political—will become more apparent.

In August 1995, tropical storm Janis dumped epochal amounts of rain on the northwest coast of the Korean peninsula, flooding out more than half of the rice crop in Hwanghae Province and leaving many thousands of people homeless. North Korea was forced to appeal to the international community for relief and emergency food supplies. The United Nations sent an assessment team, which confirmed the damage and the likelihood of famine in some parts of north Korea in 1996. Foreign agencies including Church World Service and the American Friends Service Committee sent supplies and food. The Japanese and American governments provided cash. The south Korean government furnished a certain amount of rice, but the north Koreans were so sensitive about accepting relief from their southern neighbor that the south Korean shipments generated political difficulties and Seoul ended up with the awkward choice of either not helping or being accused of exploiting north Korea's suffering. This standoff over rice relief in many ways summed up the tragedy of Korea's division over time.

As of early 1996 it appeared that Kim Jong-il and his supporters would continue to face a gap between the expectations of the north Korean people and the capacity of the system to meet them. Moreover, it will be less and less practical for the north Korean leaders to insulate their people from the rest of the world or to control the level of popular demands, as in the past. Either the political system will have to adapt itself to the new challenge, as has been happening in China, or it will have to resort to increased repression to maintain order. The former will cause confusion; the latter, eventually, anger and rebellion. Either contingency exposes north Korea to increased outside influence. The direction of north Korea's political evolution thus has everything to do with the future of both Koreas.

Notes

1. The other three places are China, Germany, and Vietnam. During the Cold War, and still today in the cases of Cuba, Vietnam, and China, countries that were referred to as

"Communist" referred to themselves as "Socialist" because none of them ever reached the state of perfect communism as defined in Marxist theory. In this book, to avoid confusion, the term "Communist" is used to describe nations that have (or had) the goal of communism as state policy, and that—unlike socialist states and parties of Western Europe—do not (or did not) permit private property ownership or severely limited it.

2. U.S. Department of State, *Country Reports on Human Rights Practices for 1994: Democratic People's Republic of Korea* (Report submitted to the Committee on Foreign Relations, U.S. Senate, and Committee on Foreign Affairs, U.S. House of Representatives by the Department of State, 1994).

3. North Korea's preoccupation with secrecy has handicapped foreign scholars by denying even the most basic information. Professor Dae Sook Suh wrote that the scarcity of materials is due, among other things, to "secrecy, backdating, and suppression of published information." He noted, for example, that the results of the 1977 Supreme People's Assembly meeting were kept secret; the date of the founding Korean Workers' Party congress was backdated from August 1946 to October 1945 (the latter date relating to a meeting before the Korean Workers' Party emerged as a separate organization); the official collection of Kim Il-sung's writings has been repeatedly and extensively revised. As another example, Suh noted that Kim Il-sung claimed that 77.6 percent of the south Korean people participated in the north Korean election of its constituent assembly in August 1948. Given the situation at the time, this figure is patently absurd. See Dae Sook Suh, *Korean Communism 1945–1980: A Reference Guide to the Political System* (Honolulu: University Press of Hawaii, 1981), pp. xi–xii, 12.

4. "On Eliminating Dogmatism and Formalism and Establishing Juche in Ideological Work," December 28, 1955, in Kim Il Sung, *Selected Works*, vol. 1 (Pyongyang: Foreign Language Publishing House, 1965), pp. 315–340; cited by Suh, *Korean Communism*, p. 6.

5. Shuhachi Inoue, *Modern Korea and Kim Chong II*, translated by Tayama Maseru (Tokyo: Yuzankaku Publishers, 1984), p. 30.

6. *Foreign Broadcast Information Service*, Asia-Pacific Daily Summary, April 10, 1984, vol. 4, pp. D16–D19, citing *Kulloja*, No. 4, 1984, reporting Kim Jong-il's speech to Korea Workers' Party propagandists on its tenth anniversary. The use of the pronoun, "man," is the translator's choice; the Korean language does not have gender-specific equivalents.

7. Although it is clear from published statements that various shades of view appear, observers have differed regarding the amount of real debate among the north Korean elite. Selig Harrison, for example, believed that both hard-line and moderate positions on foreign policy have been taken (see, for example, his article, "The Great Follower; Kim Il Sung Promotes Chinese-style Open-Door Policy," *Far Eastern Economic Review*, December 3, 1987, p. 37). John Merrill noted that north Korean economic statements "may also contain glimmers of disagreements in the leadership" that "can be read as a debate between ideological conservatives and those who advocate more pragmatic approaches" ("North Korea's Halting Efforts at Economic Reform," paper presented to the Fourth Conference on North Korea, sponsored by The Institute of East Asian Studies, University of California, Berkeley, and the Korean Association of Communist Studies, August 7–11, 1989, pp. 3–4.) Other observers however, believe, that the long-established dominance of Kim Il-sung severely limited leadership differences because those who differ have been purged.

8. "The Constitution provides that the procurators perform the functions of general surveillance, investigation, preliminary examination, and ultimate prosecution of crimi-

nals and offenders and take appropriate legal sanctions to preserve the laws and implement policies set by the party" (Suh, *Korean Communism,* p. 496).

9. See Yong-ho Ch'oe, "Christian Background in the Early Life of Kim Il-song," *Asian Survey* 26(10) (October 1986):1082–1091.

10. *Korea Annual 1994* (Seoul: Yonhap News Agency, 1994), pp. 230–233; Naewoe News Agency, *Vantage Point* 18(7) (July 1995):44.

11. Officials often compare defense spending in north and south Korea in terms of percentage of GNP devoted to the military. By this measure, north Korea's 20–25 percent defense expenditure is impressive evidence of the system's commitment to military affairs. The dollar amount, however, is estimated at around US$5 billion. South Korea commits only 3.6 percent of its GNP to defense, but the dollar amount is much greater—US$12.2 billion—because the south Korean economy is ten times the size of the northern economy. Central Intelligence Agency, *The World Factbook 1994* (Washington, D.C.: U.S. Government Printing Office, 1994), pp. 218, 220.

12. The camp is said to have been the secret headquarters of Kim Il-sung's operations against the Japanese. The choice of Mt. Paektu for his birthplace has divine overtones: It is the legendary spot where Tan'gun, the founder of the Korean race, was born.

13. The surviving terrorist was taken to south Korea, tried, sentenced to death, repented, was granted amnesty, and wrote a book: Kim Hyon-hi, *The Tears of My Soul* (New York: William Morrow, 1993).

6
Economics

Introduction

"Miracle on the Han" is an apt, if overworked, description of south Korea's amazingly rapid and successful transition from a traditional agrarian subsistence economy to a primarily industrialized one. This transition has involved social and political as well as purely economic change. In the old Confucian tradition, both industry and commerce were looked down upon, whereas agriculture (next to learning and government) was viewed as the most worthy human pursuit. It is only in the last twenty years or so that business has begun to rank with other callings as a respectable life work.

Another significant shift in attitude concerns belief in the possibility of future security and betterment. It has already been mentioned that the Korean cultural tradition assumes an essentially static human condition, in which there may be good times and bad times, but a marginal existence is the lot of most people. More than a century of economic adversity, imperialist domination, and war reinforced this attitude. Until the 1960s, there was little incentive for either leaders or people to make plans for a better future, or to lay aside resources for it, since faith in the future was essentially lacking.

A friend of mine illustrated the profound shift in south Korean attitudes with a personal experience. During a trip through a rural area of North Kyongsang Province to observe the effects of U.S. aid programs, he came upon an old farmer planting fruit tree seedlings. "Why are you planting those trees?" my friend asked the farmer. "They won't bear fruit for many years, and they're taking up space you could use for crops." "I know," said the farmer; "I'm planting them for my son. He'll be able to harvest them and profit from them." The farmer's act demonstrated the new trend: One could invest in the future with confidence.

In this chapter, we shall see how this new confidence, in combination with entrepreneurial spirit, a capable work force, able and energetic government management, foreign assistance, birth control, and a favorable world economic environment, contributed to Korea's rise from abject poverty to top rank among the world's developing nations in hardly more than a generation.

The Traditional Korean Economy

For centuries, most Koreans were subsistence farmers of rice and other grains, supplying most of their basic needs through their own labor or through barter. Markets at five-day intervals in larger towns and itinerant peddlers supplied needs the villages could not meet. Officials were compensated in grain; until late in the Choson Dynasty, the grain came from lands assigned to them for that purpose. In principle, other land was allotted to all the people in accordance with their needs and taxed for support of government activity. In practice, land gravitated into the hands of the aristocratic *yangban* class, whose members exempted themselves from taxation. Taxes grew on the decreasing base of nonexempt land, forcing many into tenancy or day labor. From the mid-seventeenth century on, money increasingly took the place of grain for taxes and purchases of goods by the court and aristocracy, although the value of the money depreciated because of deficit financing.

The simple manufactures of the period—principally cloth, furniture, cooking and eating utensils, articles of personal adornment, and paper—were largely produced by artisans of low social status in a few population centers. Many of the artisans were in the service of, or commissioned by, the court and aristocracy. Such items as hemp cloth and paper were produced for export to China on the periodic tribute missions, which also served as a principal channel of foreign trade. Other channels (apart from smuggling) included a trading station that the Japanese were permitted to maintain near the southeast port city of Pusan and some private trade with China. There were wealthy merchants and artisans, but they did not develop a financial or cultural network such as existed among their counterparts in Japan or China; rather, they tended to enter the aristocracy—often by purchasing rank.

In accordance with Confucian teachings, the *yangban* disdained commercial activity; but they nonetheless amassed wealth from the perquisites of office and the product of their estates. From the middle of the dynasty, despite efforts at reform, the gap between wealth and poverty widened, and state revenues shrank. Wealthy landlords and officials, however, did not often invest in manufacture or commerce, as did their Japanese counterparts. Although one north Korean scholar has maintained that Korean private investment in enterprise such as mining and iron manufacturing activity began as early as the eighteenth century,[1] it did not appear on a significant scale until after the Western penetration had begun, toward the end of the nineteenth century, and did not reach major proportions until the period of Japanese control, beginning in 1905. Even then, it was small in comparison to Japanese investment.

The Economy Under the Japanese

It was chiefly the Japanese who brought capitalist economic patterns of industrialization and trade to Korea. They treated Korea as an extension of the Japanese economy, principally to serve Japanese interests. A major example was the Japanese export of the Korean rice crop to Japan to fill the shortfall in Japanese rice production. Koreans had to make do with cheaper grains. Industries were established in accordance with imperial, not Korean, needs.

The result of these Japanese policies was a typical colonial dual economy, in which over a half million Japanese residents managed the modern industrial sector and enjoyed its fruits, while most Koreans—except the urban labor force—remained in the traditional agrarian economy. In this situation, it was easy for Korean nationalists to castigate capitalism along with the Japanese occupation itself. Marxist ideas spread. It was largely the minority of Koreans who kept their property and wealth under the Japanese that opposed socialist principles of public ownership and land redistribution.

The forty-year Japanese occupation brought some benefits to Korea. The Japanese built a substantial economic infrastructure of roads, railroads, and public works; they expanded the education of the Korean people at elementary-school level (from an enrollment of 20,000 in 1919 to 900,000 in 1937); they introduced factory discipline to an industrial labor force totaling nearly 200,000 by 1938 and more during the war years (chiefly in north Korea), not counting those among the 2 million Koreans in Japan who worked in industrial plants.[2]

Despite these seeming signs of progress, however, the welfare of the general public was not improved. Grain consumption per capita by Koreans, according to Japanese statistics, diminished from 2.032 *koku* in the period 1915–1919 to 1.668 *koku* in the period 1930–1933 (1 *koku,* called *sok* in Korean, is equal to about 35 liters or 5 U.S. bushels).[3] Rural starvation in the spring grew worse. Gross value of production in Korea in 1938 was 126 yen per capita, compared with 358 for Japan (the yen was then worth about US$0.50).

Although net commodity production in Korea grew at a rate of 2 percent per capita over the three decades before World War II,[4] this growth probably did not do most Koreans much good—no more than they would have gained from even an inefficient native rule. Notwithstanding Japanese efforts at educating the Koreans, 87 percent of the Korean population had less than six years of education in 1945. Perhaps the greatest contribution of the Japanese was to engender a Korean determination to equal or outdo them.

During the World War II years, the Japanese drew heavily on Korean resources (as, of course, they did on their own). Factories were diverted to military production; forested hillsides were stripped for timber and fuel; industrial plant depreciated; metals, including family heirlooms of brass, were ruthlessly collected and melted down to make ammunition. In their final weeks, when surrender appeared certain, the Japanese gave their workers a year's salary in advance and paid savings deposits and insurance policies in full, which had the effect of flooding the currency market and creating galloping inflation. The departure of all the hated Japanese expatriates at the end of the war, including the managerial elite, was politically necessary. But the Koreans were left without managers, markets, or (in south Korea) raw materials for a run-down industrial plant that was not designed to serve Korean needs.

The Korean Economy, 1945–1960

Division of Korea between U.S. and Soviet occupying forces in 1945 added further to Korean economic problems. Most of the natural resources, heavy industry (including fertilizer production), and electric power generation were concentrated in the north; the country's food-basket and center of textile and other light industry were in the south. Although trade between the two zones was not totally suspended until the Korean War, it was severely impeded. North Korea cut the supply of electricity in May 1948, depriving the south of over half of its already inadequate power. In south Korea, initial U.S. policies made the situation even worse. The U.S. occupiers, equipped only with complete faith in free private enterprise and sublime ignorance, removed wartime economic controls. Hoarding, speculation, food shortages, and massive inflation resulted.[5]

The desperate south Koreans sought fuel and saleables where they could, further denuding the already bare hillsides and actually ripping up Japanese-owned houses and factories for firewood. An influx of Korean repatriates from Japan and elsewhere and a flood of refugees from the Communist regime in the north—perhaps 4 million or more in both categories by 1951—increased the population by 25 percent. Food production was hindered by fertilizer shortage. South Korean daily caloric intake fell to less than 1,500 per person in 1946 and 1947.

Mass starvation was averted only by U.S. emergency relief under the Government Aid and Relief in Occupied Areas (GARIOA) program, intended to avert disease and unrest that might threaten U.S. forces. From 1945 to 1948, US$400 million in aid was given to south Korea, 90 percent of it in food, clothing, fuel, other consumer commodities, and fertilizer. The U.S. military government soon reversed its free-market policies, and rationalized grain collection. Some industry revived with whatever encouragement the U.S. authorities could provide.

In the final months of the occupation, the U.S. authorities made their greatest nonmilitary contribution to Korea's future: the distribution of all Japanese-owned farmland (about 25 percent of the total) to the tillers, to be paid for at the rate of 1.5 times the annual crop, spread over a fifteen-year term. This program constituted the model for eventual redistribution of Korean-owned farmland, largely completed by the south Korean government (under pressure from the United States) during the latter two years of the Korean War.

Because of the U.S. priority for negotiation of reunification with the Soviets and because of U.S. prejudice against centralized state economic planning, there was little overall thought for economic development until 1948; even if there had been, no resources were available (GARIOA money could not be used for such purposes). Nevertheless, U.S. and Korean pragmatism and ingenuity managed to keep minimum services operating and even to improve them. For example, the occupation authorities managed to import 101 U.S. locomotives in 1947, thus increasing the locomotive inventory by about two-thirds. When the north Koreans cut off the supply of electricity, the military government brought in power barges. To obtain needed trucks and other items, the military government, acting as the sovereign government of Korea, negotiated a $25 million loan to buy surplus military property (a loan that the new Republic of Korea was forced to assume in 1948, which became a bone of contention between the two governments for many years thereafter). For their part, the Koreans showed surprising capacity for improvising shoestring repairs to obsolescent equipment and maintaining family and communal existence by hook or by crook. When the Republic was declared in 1948, the departing U.S. rulers turned over to it a balanced budget and a reserve in the treasury.

The economic policies of the new Republic of Korea at first were naive, populist, undisciplined, and inflationary. Neither President Rhee nor his new senior appointees understood economics, and for nationalist reasons they were disinclined to take U.S. advice. Besides, they were preoccupied with a large-scale guerrilla challenge to their political control. It took eighteen months of sad experience and a stern U.S. diplomatic démarche (based on the leverage of economic aid, long-delayed but finally enacted) to turn things around.[6] Nevertheless, there were good harvests in 1948 and 1949. A U.S.-financed consultancy firm produced a rudimentary economic development plan, stressing coal, electric power, and fertilizer production. Industrial production rose by 50 percent in 1949 and 1950; coal, by 40 percent; electric power, 33 percent. "For south Koreans as a whole, 1949–1950 was probably the best year they had had in a decade." Despite formidable obstacles, the south Korean economic outlook in the spring of 1950, in the eyes of U.S. observers, was reasonably bright.[7]

Meanwhile, north Korea was following a very different economic path. The Soviets, acting through the Korean administration they had established, expropriated all land from former owners—Japanese and Korean—in 1946 and distributed it free of charge to the tillers. All large industry (most of it Japanese-owned) was nationalized,[8] but smaller businesses were not initially seized. These moves were popular with the majority of the population, and the apparent progress and reform were attractive to many people in south Korea as well (notwithstanding the exodus of many north Korean property-owners and professionals to the south). Preparations were made for movement toward collectivization of agriculture and for Soviet-style centralized economic management.

The Korean War shattered the economy of both south and north Korea. In addition to the millions of people killed and injured, physical loss in the south alone was estimated at 400 billion hwan (the unit of currency at the time, officially worth about US$0.02) at 1953 prices, nearly the equivalent of the Republic's gross national product for that year.[9] Because of U.S. saturation bombing, the north Korean economic plant was almost totally destroyed, and human casualties were enormous. In addition, north Korea lost many of its most qualified people in waves of terror and counterterror as refugees to the south, both before and during the war.

Reconstruction began in both halves of Korea after the 1953 armistice—hindered on both sides by the burden of maintaining huge armed forces (over 700,000 in south Korea, and about the same in the north, in the early post-Armistice years). The United States committed US$1 billion in grant aid over three years for south Korea, in addition to about $600 million through the United

Nations Korea Reconstruction Agency (UNKRA). Total external economic aid to south Korea from 1953 to the mid-1970s, when concessionary U.S. aid ceased, amounted to about $6 billion, not counting the economic impact of an additional $7 billion in military assistance.[10] Exact comparable figures for north Korea are not available, but it is estimated that grant economic aid to the Democratic People's Republic of Korea (DPRK) from the Soviet Union, Eastern European countries, and China totaled about US$1.4 billion from 1946 to 1960, after which it dropped sharply.[11]

The patterns of economic development in the two halves of Korea, which were already divergent before the war, moved rapidly in the direction of capitalism in the south and Communism in the north. In the south, what was left of the industrial plant was mostly turned over to private owners—some of whom, however, were chosen as much for political loyalty as for business acumen. Although there was some investment in import-substitution industries and textiles, primary emphasis was on food and other consumer goods to meet minimal living requirements. With revenues from foreign aid supporting over half of the Republic's government budget (including defense costs) and constrained by foreign advisers to exercise financial discipline, the south Korean economy had fairly well stabilized by 1957, and living standards had recovered to pre–World War II levels.[12] Yet the diet of most south Koreans in the late 1950s was no more than the minimum requirement, and below that for many.

President Rhee and his supporters had scant understanding of economics. Their strategy was to maximize foreign aid, overvalue their currency, meet the government deficit by printing money and bonds, keep interest rates artificially low, and focus on import substitution for economic growth. Business loans and titles to former Japanese enterprises often were granted for political rather than economic reasons. The result was inflation, speculation in land and goods, and discouragement of saving and investment. Although U.S. advice mitigated some of the economic naivete and misdirection, much of it was resisted by the Koreans—as it had been since 1948—for reasons of both principle and political expediency. Moreover, not all U.S. advice was sound, from the Korean point of view. For example, U.S. agricultural representatives pushed wheat sales to the detriment of Korean rice farmers.

Korean reconstruction was also hampered by the U.S. prejudice against national economic planning and by policy disputes among U.S. agencies and between officials of the United States and those of the United Nations Korea Reconstruction Agency. Moreover, it was not until late in the 1950s that U.S. officials and scholars began to understand the problems of the developing world. From 1958 to 1960, the approaching south Korean political crisis inhibited and distorted the economy, at the same time that foreign aid was being reduced in response to domestic U.S. pressures. The situation was worsened by poor crops. The resultant popular frustration at the lack of economic progress was a contributing factor in the political upheaval of 1960. The brief ensuing experiment in free parliamentary democracy of 1960–1961 further unsettled the economy, although it did bring the beginning of Korean multiyear development planning.

Under these conditions, the south Korean economy showed approximately a 4 percent average annual real economic growth rate for the period 1953–1962. (In comparison, the Philippine economy grew by 5.4 percent and Taiwan 7.0 percent during the same period.)[13] Population growth of nearly 3 percent a year absorbed most of the economic growth. The remaining per capita increase of around 1 per- cent—probably dropping to zero or less in the last Rhee years—was not enough to meet popular expectations. In these years, U.S. grant aid was becoming coun- terproductive by fostering dependence and by discouraging Korean agricultural and industrial growth.

> [President] Rhee used this massive grant assistance as a protection against the neces- sity of policy changes that would have made the economy more productive and self- supporting and against normalization of relations with Japan. . . . As in so many recorded instances in USAID [U.S. Agency for International Development] relation- ships, it was the weaker power that held the whip hand.[14]

South Korean Economic Development, 1961–1995

Following their seizure of political power in 1961, General Park Chung-hee and his military associates clearly recognized the importance of rapid economic progress and committed themselves to bring it about. At first, however, they em- barked on a series of rash and ill-advised economic policies—born of naive pop- ulism and a desire to raise political funds—including deliberate rigging of the stock market, a purge of leading businessmen, manipulation of the banks, and an abortive capital levy in conjunction with currency reform, which brought about further confusion and confrontation with U.S. aid officials.

Nevertheless, the military government learned quickly from its mistakes. Tak- ing the plans of the short-lived Chang Myon administration as a base, it devel- oped a five-year plan for rapid, export-led development, with the assistance of the United States (the Kennedy administration accepted new ideas on economic de- velopment). The military leaders stabilized the economy and under U.S. pressure brought their budget under control. They managed the economy with far more energy and effectiveness than any previous south Korean administration, utilizing the expertise of U.S.-trained civilian economists.

Domestic savings increased as a result of increased interest rates and stability. Production for export was spurred by an improved foreign exchange regime: The new unit of currency introduced by the Park regime, the won, which had had var- ious exchange rates for different purposes, averaging around 130 won to the dol- lar, was devalued to 260 to 1, and a single exchange rate was established. Export regulations were simplified. Preferential credit was extended to firms with good export performance. Family-planning programs, begun in the 1950s, were energetically and effectively pushed. In 1965, encouraged behind the scenes by the United States, the south Koreans normalized relations with Japan, bringing an assistance package of $800 million in various forms of grants and credits. These measures permitted full advantage to be taken of elements of strength that had been accumulating, almost unnoticed, since 1945. They also made the economy creditworthy, permitting the induction of foreign investment capital for expansion.

By 1965 south Korea was well launched on a course of rapid, sustained economic growth, in accordance with its successive five-year plans. As annual population growth fell to about 1.5 percent, the per capita share of economic growth increased. Real GNP growth averaged 10 percent per year until the second oil shock of 1979; growth was negative in 1980, but it resumed in 1981 and averaged 9.3 percent from 1981 through 1988.[15] (Between 1964 and 1985, there were three cycles of high growth followed by recession.[16] Exports grew from $30 million in 1960 to $30 billion in 1985—a thousandfold increase at current prices, despite oil shocks and world recession. From 1962 to 1985, real GNP per capita tripled; in 1990 it reached $5,883, and in 1994 it was just short of $8,000 (roughly one-third of the level of the United States.) This performance is a principal factor in the restoration of Korean political stability and of Korean pride and self-confidence as a nation.

As the south Korean economy has grown, it has drastically altered in nature from a basically agrarian to an industrialized one. Agriculture made up 50 percent of domestic product in the period 1953–1955, but dropped to 30 percent by the 1970–1972 period, while the industrial sector's share rose from 11 to 35 percent. Since then, agriculture's share has continued to decline, but in later phases it is the service sector that has expanded most. It is noteworthy that although a similar shift occurred in such countries as Japan and Sweden, it took forty to forty-five years, compared with twenty for Korea.[17]

Income distribution, along with per capita averages, is an important indication of economic performance. In this respect, south Korea has done much better than most developing countries. A World Bank study published in 1975 showed an inequality between the top and bottom 20 percent of the population roughly comparable to that of the United States, although at a much lower level.[18] Inequality increased during the late 1970s because of emphasis on heavy industry, inflation, land speculation, and the unequal impact of rural support programs. The Third and Fourth Five-Year Plans addressed the rural-urban gap in living standards by means of the New Community (*Saema'ul*) Movement, which pushed electrification, transportation, credit mechanisms, and community development in south Korea's villages and hamlets. The New Community Movement, though marred by scandal in the 1980s when it was run by President Chun Doo-hwan's brother, made a considerable difference in farm incomes, productivity, and overall quality of life. However, the 1980s also brought an accelerated trend toward concentration of wealth (as opposed to income) as fortunes were made in real estate and other boom sectors of the economy. A 1988 survey of 2,500 households indicated that the wealthiest 10 percent controlled 41 percent of total privately held assets, while the poorest 30 percent controlled 0.4 percent of the country's wealth. Though it may be said that south Korea's income distribution record continues to be better than those of most other comparable countries,[19] the fortunes being made through real-estate speculation and other forms of corruption are a festering source of political anger. People who do not own urban land and cannot take advantage of the land boom know that they are at a dramatic disadvantage.

Until 1982, a high rate of inflation (from 15 to over 30 percent per year, averaging an annual 20 percent) had characterized the south Korean economy in most years since 1945. After 1963, inflation was both a means and a cost of rapid growth. In part, it reflected the world situation as well as internal social pressures for higher wages and more social services; in part, it was due to inflationary expectations; and in the late 1970s, it was aggravated by overemphasis on investment in heavy industry for greater economic and military independence and export growth. However, new government policies restricting credit and the money supply brought inflation down to single-digit figures in 1982 for the first time since liberation. Consumer price increases were 3.0 percent in 1985, and between 1987 and 1994 they averaged 6.3 percent.[20]

A comprehensive Harvard University study of Korea's economic development sought to determine the reasons for south Korea's extraordinary economic performance. It listed the following factors:

- a work ethic, probably derived from the Confucian tradition, comparable to the Protestant ethic of Western Europe;
- the residue left by Japan, including access to technology and management;
- social mobility and destruction of the traditional structure by liberation, division, social confusion, war, and the return of overseas residents;
- cultural homogeneity;
- foreign financial and technical assistance;
- a rapidly expanding educational system.

These factors, according to the study, produced a disciplined and well-educated work force; an influx of added workers as agricultural productivity increased; access to investable funds from abroad; increased domestic savings; an expanding stock of entrepreneurs; and access to foreign technologies. Additional factors were basic political stability and the shift in government policies from inward-looking import substitution to outward-looking export orientation.[21]

In my opinion, the following additional factors can be listed:

- the assurance of national security by the presence of an American shield;
- Korea's earnings from contribution of men and supplies to the United States in Vietnam;

- improved nutrition levels;
- a reduced birthrate;
- the precipitous drop in chronic intestinal and other infections that had for centuries drained the Korean people's energy;
- improvement in the quality of government administration.

South Korea's Current Economic Situation

Overview

The gross national product of the Republic of Korea in 1994 was the equivalent of US$355.9 billion, based on an average exchange rate of 803 won per dollar, or $7,981 per capita—an 8.2 percent real increase over the previous year. South Korea ranked eleventh among the world's nations in gross national product and thirty-sixth in per capita GNP. (A tabulation of south Korean major economic indicators is presented in Table 6.1.)

The largest component of the total national product (based on 1994 figures) was services, at 52 percent, followed by manufacturing and mining at 40 percent. Agriculture, including fisheries and forestry, accounted for only 8 percent of the GNP, down from 13.5 percent in 1988. These numbers reflect the dramatic growth in the industrial sector in recent decades more than a decline in actual agricultural output, which actually has posted modest increases in productivity in most of the past fifty years. Exports and imports in 1994 were each around 28 percent of GNP (exports were $96.2 billion; imports were $102.3 billion).

The international current account ("balance of payments"), which includes "invisible" exports and imports such as tourism, showed a deficit of $6.1 billion in 1994. This was the fifth straight year of trade deficits for south Korea following a series of surpluses between 1986 and 1989. Cumulative foreign debt, which peaked at nearly $47 billion in 1985 and had fallen to $24 billion in 1988, was back up to $42.5 billion in 1994, a figure that would have been more alarming if the GNP had not nearly quadrupled in the intervening decade. One reason for this trend was Korea's emphasis on the domestic market and policies of import liberalization in the early 1990s. Another was the combined effect of the "Three Blessings": the collapse of world oil prices, low international interest rates, and the devaluation of the U.S. dollar against the Japanese yen—which helped Korean exports compete with Japanese goods.

South Korea's economic system, still in evolution, is intermediate between state capitalism and free enterprise. Government economic powers—both formal and informal—are pervasive and are facilitated by a long tradition of political supremacy over economics. Public ownership (chiefly utilities, fertilizer, iron and steel, chemicals, and other heavy industry) has been as high a percentage of Korea's industrial plant as in India, which calls itself a socialist state but has a large private sector.[22] The government sets overall goals, both in successive five-year plans (the Seventh Five-Year Plan began in 1992—see below) and in yearly pro-

TABLE 6.1   South Korean Economic Indicators: South Korean Economic Development,
1986–1996

		Target		
	1986	1990	1994	1996
Socioeconomic Indicators				
Population (millions)	41.6	43.1	45.5	N/A
Population growth rate (percent)	1.2	1.2	1.04	N/A
Economic Indicators				
GNP ($ billions)	102.7	204.6	355.9	492.6
Real GNP growth rate (percent)	12.9	9.3	8.2	7.0
Per capita GNP ($)	2,548	4,754	7,981	10,908
Consumer prices (percent change)	1.4	9.4	5.6	3.6
Employment (millions of workers)	15.6	18.0	20.0	N/A
Unemployment rate	3.8	2.9	2.0	N/A
Investment/GNP ratio (percent)	28.9	37.1		
Government budget ($ billions)			63	81.9
Balance of Payments				
Balance of trade	+4.206	−2.15	−6.1	+4.8
Current account balance ($ billions)	4.6	−2.8	−4.7	2.1
External Finance				
Foreign exchange reserves ($ billions)	8.0	14.4	N/A	N/A
Average won-dollar exchange rate	881	716	803	N/A
Total foreign debt ($ billions)	44.5	31.7	42.6	N/A

SOURCES: Korea Economic Institute, *Korea's Economy 1995,* vol. 11 (Washington, D.C.:
Korea Economic Institute, 1995), p. i; U.S. Central Intelligence Agency, *The 1995 World Fact
Book;* Internet: http://www.odci.gov/cia/publications/95fact/ks.html, October 27, 1995);
OECD Economic Surveys, 1993–94: Korea (Paris: Organization for Economic Cooperation
and Development, 1994, *passim; Korea Newsreview* 24(40) (October 7, 1995):21, 33; *Korea
Focus,* 3(4) (July-August, 1995):58; Economic Fact Sheet, U.S. Department of State, October
24, 1989, from statistics of the International Monetary Fund, Data Resources Asia Review,
U.S. Embassy [Seoul] reports, and State Department EAP/EP estimates.

grams, and it guides industry by means of export and production targets, the control of credit (probably its most powerful lever), and various informal means of
pressure and persuasion, as well as the usual fiscal and monetary controls of the
economy as a whole.[23] Thus the Korean government plays a major role in the national economic enterprise and is, in effect, its senior partner.

Nevertheless, south Korea has basically a market economy, and its government
planners are committed to liberalization. They recognize that Korea already has
such a highly developed and complex economy that market forces, rather than
government fiat, must be the primary regulator. Private industry has growing latitude to develop products, processes, and markets. The expanding economic
power of the leading industrialists gives them increasing independence of action

and capacity to influence government policies—several of the Korean conglomerates are listed among *Fortune* magazine's top 500 firms of the world. Business has become socially respectable in recent years and now attracts the best talent. Commercial banks have been returned to private ownership (although they are still closely controlled through the Monetary Board and Ministry of Finance). Restrictions on foreign trade and investment are being relaxed, both to improve domestic industry by foreign competition and to meet complaints from the United States and other trading partners.

The Economic Planning Board (EPB), headed by a deputy prime minister, was for more than thirty years the main locus of government economic planning and direction, until President Kim Young-sam combined its functions with the Finance Ministry in 1994 to create the Board of Finance and Economics (BFE). When it was created under President Park Chung-hee in the 1960s, the EPB became the main coordinating agency for five-year plans, deciding what industries would get government support and directing the flow of credit. This organization had a sustained reputation for high intellectual ability and competence. Its overall charge was to function as a bootstrap agency to launch what appeared at the time to be a highly improbable Korean economic "miracle." By the early 1990s, after having succeeded admirably, its functions were better handled by the regular government ministries, and it was put out of business.

The Economic Planning Board was supported by a second agency, the largely independent Korea Development Institute (KDI), a think tank whose purpose continues to be to plot long-term trends in the economy and to recommend policies and policy adjustments. For example, in 1987 the KDI issued a report entitled *Korea 2000* with predictions for the economy at the end of the century that put south Korea in the ranks of the world's developed countries. Such projections were the basis for south Korea's bid for admission into the Organization for Economic Cooperation and Development (OECD), the "club" of the world's advanced economies.[24]

Apart from the Board of Finance and Economics (BFE), there are several other major governmental actors in the economy. One is the Office of the President (the "Blue House"), which has a senior secretary for economic affairs. Others include the Ministry of Trade and Industry, the Ministry of Labor, and the nation's central bank, the Bank of Korea, which is controlled by the BFE.

Until the 1980s, government policy favored the large combines because large enterprises had lower production costs and could be controlled more easily by the government to ensure compliance with its policy of maintaining high export growth. In recent years, however, the government has become concerned at the degree of industrial concentration. It has also recognized the contribution of small and medium-sized enterprises to employment and to innovation, despite their high failure rate—in the mid-1980s, nearly half of the small firms organized each year failed. Accordingly, more attention is being given to credit facilities through the Medium and Small Industry Bank, quotas of loans from other banks, and other means of encouragement, such as facilitation of exports (see Figure 6.1).

Industry

South Korean industry began during the Japanese colonial period with textile manufacturing, food processing, and light machinery, concentrated in Seoul and a few other cities. Japanese companies concentrated their efforts on the Seoul area and on present-day North Korea, where there were giant chemical and electric power operations, among other enterprises.

The end of the war in 1945 brought a Japanese economic withdrawal from Korea and a separation of the industrial north from the agricultural south. Industrial know-how was at a premium. A few Korean businesses were able to maintain themselves on a large scale, such as the Kim family's Kyongsong Spinning and Weaving Company.[25] Others started small and later grew. For example, Samsung *chaebol* founder Lee Byung-chul (Yi Pyong-ch'ol) started out in the 1930s with a small milling business in Masan. Hyundai tycoon Chung Ju-yung (Chong Chu-yong) started a garage during World War II, then shifted to repairing trucks for the U.S. Army after 1945. He went into the construction business in 1947, and with his brothers opened up a trucking company during the Korean War. Chung made a great deal of money building for the Americans, first in Korea, then in Vietnam. In the 1970s Chung's Hyundai "family" of companies cashed in on the Middle East oil boom. By the 1980s the Hyundai group was selling Korean-made

FIGURE 6.1   A modern south Korean factory (photo courtesy of Korea Overseas Information Service)

cars around the world, building the world's largest ships, controlling a significant part of the south Korean economy, and looking into developing north Korea (Figure 6.2). In 1992 Chung Ju-yung even ran for president.[26]

The *chaebol*, or groups—or families—of companies, are a driving phenomenon in the growth of the south Korean economy. Samsung, for example, made wigs and textiles in the 1950s and 1960s. In the 1970s, with government help, it branched out into consumer electronics, and by the 1990s it had become a major player in the worldwide computer market, leading in the manufacture of semiconductors (Figure 6.3). All the *chaebol* followed this trajectory, building themselves up with government backing and management of competition in certain sectors of the economy, then branching out into other lines of business before finally outgrowing the need for direct government assistance.

One important feature of the *chaebol* typically has been a high degree of family ownership. The Chung family and its branches owned as much as 61.3 percent of Hyundai in 1994.[27] According to economist and former Finance Minister Sakong Il, in 1992 as much as 46.1 percent of the top thirty Korean companies' assets were owned by the majority shareholder—usually the founder or his son(s).[28] Dynastic leadership structure, complete succession from father to sons and nephews, while consistent with Korean cultural patterns, is a characteristic that is widely criticized as dangerous to the long-term health and even the survival of the *chaebol*.

FIGURE 6.2   A Hyundai factory in Ulsan (photo courtesy of Korean Information Office, Washington, D.C.)

The *chaebol,* whose top ranks include Daewoo, Hyundai, Samsung, the LG Group (formerly Lucky-Goldstar), Sunkyong, and Ssangyong, are both vertically and horizontally integrated—that is, some of the units within a conglomerate produce components for other units' products, while several different units may be engaged in different industries or services, more or less independent of one another. These firms typically include various heavy industries (such as shipbuilding, motor vehicles, machinery, and chemicals), consumer industries (food processing, textiles, electric and electronic goods, and footwear), and trading companies (general trading companies for import and export, plus domestic consumer outlets and distributing agencies). They do not own banks, although they may hold substantial bank equities and may operate investment services. *Chaebol* are often likened to Japanese *zaibatsu* (the two words are written with the same two Chinese characters), but they are different in several respects: degree of family ownership, the fact that thay do not own banks, and the fact that they handle their own exports (for example, Hyundai Motors Division, with its own dealerships in the United States and Canada).

Two of Korea's biggest companies, both of them in the 1995 Fortune 500 listing, are public enterprises: the Korea Electric Power Company (KEPCO) and Pohang Iron and Steel Company (POSCO). Both are still owned mainly by the government, though there are private stockholders as well. KEPCO and POSCO

FIGURE 6.3   A Korean electronics factory (photo courtesy of Korean Information Office, Washington, D.C.)

were the core enterprises of the Park Chung-hee regime's effort to acquire energy and steel self-sufficiency as part of Korea's modernization drive. Other examples of state enterprises that were designed to strengthen the basic infrastructure were the Ulsan Petrochemical Complex and the machine-building complex at Ch'angwon.

The collusion of government and big business in Korea since 1960 helped to create "Korea Inc.," an economic juggernaut in which the state and private spheres overlap so thoroughly that at times they can hardly be distinguished.[29] Financing came first from foreign lenders, whether governments, international lending organizations, or banks. In the mid-1960s, Tokyo's promise to supply capital was an important component of the "normalization" of relations between Japan and the Republic of Korea, and companies such as Gold Star got a boost from joint venture partners like Hitachi. This was President Park Chung-hee's "late development model," an export-led strategy that sought to compete in the world economy on the basis of low wages and borrowed technologies. Because money also had to be borrowed, in the 1970s south Korea's foreign debt skyrocketed. By 1980 it amounted to 49 percent of GNP, a ratio of debt far worse than that of Brazil or Mexico (both 31 percent). American economists were appalled at this indebtedness. Some observers believe that Park's assassination in October 1979 helped to save the Korean economy from drowning in red ink. Whatever else may be said of the Chun Doo-hwan regime that followed, by the late 1980s, after several years of management by American-trained Korean economists, Koreans themselves were saving significant amounts of money, and two-thirds of total investment capital was coming from domestic sources.[30] One of these sources was the Korean Stock Exchange, which grew rapidly as well.

South Korea's construction industry made enormous inroads into the Middle East during the 1970s, when the oil-exporting countries used their high revenues for investment in local industry and social overhead. Korean construction firms, which had developed their skills as contractors for the U.S. military program in Vietnam, successfully transferred and improved these skills, mobilizing several hundred thousand Korean workers to build roads, industrial facilities, public buildings, and housing in several Middle Eastern states.

The decline in the world oil market—and producer revenues—at the end of the decade brought 150,000 Korean construction workers home and sharply reduced this source of foreign earnings. Some companies failed; others reduced their size and scope. Their skills were turned to domestic projects such as land reclamation, government and commercial office buildings, and preparations for the Asian Games in 1986 and the Olympic Games in 1988. Attention was being given to joint ventures with the United States and other countries in the Pacific Basin and elsewhere, especially the member countries of the Association of Southeast Asian Nations (ASEAN),[31] India, and Pakistan.

A period of rapid growth in electrical appliance manufacture and export (radios, watches, television sets, microwave ovens) led to protectionist obstacles, which Korean firms answered through the establishment of manufacturing sub-sidiaries in the United States. The firms also moved into more sophisticated elec-tronics, some in joint ventures with foreign concerns as a source of advanced technology. Four large Korean firms were manufacturing semiconductors in the mid-1980s; by 1989, three of them were producing advanced (one-megabyte) dy-namic random access memory (DRAM) chips, and by 1995 Samsung Electronics was the world's leading manufacturer of DRAM chips. Because Korea got a rela-tively early start in this high-technology field and had a cost advantage over the United States and Japan, it did well, although continued growth will depend upon sustained technological advance and high-quality production.

Energy

Government enterprises dominate the energy field, although there are privately operated coal mines, and oil refineries are mostly in private hands. Korea has as yet no proven oil reserves, although offshore areas on the continental shelf are being explored. The Republic's coal is insufficient and of low quality. Hydroelec-tric resources are limited and are subject to great seasonal variations because of the concentration of rainfall in the summer.

The government has therefore put heavy emphasis on nuclear power genera-tion. Nine nuclear plants were in operation in 1994, with five more under con-struction or in the planning stage. Total electrical energy generated in 1992 was 12.6 gigawatt-hours; of this amount, 44 percent came from nuclear generators, and most of the remainder was from oil- and coal-fired thermal plants. Hydro-electric plants accounted for less than 3 percent.

Armaments

In response to the post-Vietnam shift in U.S. policy, President Park stressed self-reliance in armaments, and the country built up its own weapons manufacturing capacity as well as the heavy industry to support it. In this venture, Korea had the support of the United States, which transferred large quantities of technical data. Although details are secret, south Korea has become almost self-sufficient in con-ventional weapons—including M-16 rifles, artillery, ammunition, tanks, other military vehicles, and ships. Aircraft are assembled under coproduction arrange-ments with U.S. firms. In the absence of actual combat, armaments production is approximately half of capacity; hence the nation seeks exports. The Koreans com-plain that the United States, for reasons of both foreign policy and domestic com-mercial interest, has refused some south Korean requests for export of items man-ufactured under U.S. license. (Sources in the U.S. Embassy in Seoul stated that the United States turns down no more than about 15 percent of south Korean re-quests for third-country sales, but Korean industry sources maintain that "up to 95 percent of our chances to compete on export bidding" are impeded by licensing requirements.) Korean arms exports have fluctuated, rising as high as US$975 million in 1982 and declining to only $50 million in 1988.[32]

Agriculture

Rice is Korea's basic crop, and south Korea's yields are impressive, although rising wage levels and land values have made it costly (the retail price of rice is about twice what imported rice would cost). Korea's 1992 rice crop of 5.33 million metric tons represented a yield of 4.6 metric tons per hectare.[33] For nearly thirty years, the government has bought rice at high prices from farmers and sold it at subsidized prices in the cities to encourage production and improve the farmers' living standards. By 1983 this practice had accumulated a deficit of over $2 billion, so 1984 support was frozen at the 1983 level; however, political pressures have impelled subsequent increases in price supports, as in the United States.

Barley, grown either on upland fields or in paddies between rice crops, is the second most important crop. In recent years, the government has purchased up to 80 percent of it at support prices and distributed it in the cities, where it is often mixed with rice for eating. (To conserve rice supply, the government for some years required the mixing of 10 percent barley with rice in public restaurants.) The 1992 barley harvest totaled 315,000 metric tons. Other major crops include potatoes, wheat, maize, cabbage (used for the national dish known as *kimch'i*), and turnips. Korea imports most of its wheat and feed grains and much of its soybean requirements. Production of fruits and vegetables, both for the domestic market and for export, has increased greatly: South Korea produced more than 2 million metric tons of fruit in 1992, of which apples made up only one-third, compared with one-half of the crop in 1984. In addition to apples, pears, and peaches, Korea's mainstay fruits, the mandarin orange crop nearly quintupled between 1980 and 1992 while grapes nearly tripled, and bananas grown in giant hothouses on Cheju Island went from being a luxury item to a common daily delicacy.

Double-cropping can be practiced in the southern part of the country (usually by growing barley in rice paddies during the winter) and is facilitated by the new practice of growing rice seedlings in plastic hothouses. Double-cropping and inter-cropping (one crop sowed between rows of another) gave south Korea a land utilization ratio of 125 percent in the 1980s. To increase their incomes, farmers have been encouraged to grow cash crops such as fruit and vegetables. Greenhouses made of vinyl stretched on frames have become a common feature of the landscape, greatly extending the growing season. Animal husbandry—chiefly of pigs and chickens—has also grown. Milk has entered the Korean diet, and the dairy industry, as well as some raising of cattle for beef, has made great strides. Traditional cash crops such as ginseng, tobacco, tea, and silkworm-raising remain important. Some cotton and other commercial fibers are grown.

Korean agriculture has had to face severe problems. Despite its tradition as the peninsula's rice-basket, south Korea has not been agriculturally self-sufficient for many years. A major reason is that population and income growth have out-stripped the very respectable increase in agricultural productivity in two ways: by increasing consumption and, through urban growth, by reducing the stock of agricultural land. In recent years, also, high-yield hybrid strains of rice have proved vulnerable to pests and cold weather and have not met the taste standards of Korean consumers. There had been strong government pressure to plant the new varieties; nevertheless, some farmers have returned to the hardier but lower-yielding traditional varieties.

In addition, south Korea has had to contend with structural problems. Only 20 percent of the land is arable, and rainfall is less than that of Japan and other rice-growing countries. Farmland has been divided over the centuries into tiny plots, so that individual holdings, averaging slightly over one hectare (about 2.5 acres), actually may be divided into several noncontiguous fields. Although the land re-form of 1948 to 1953 was a brilliant political and social success, it perpetuated the fractionation of land, making cultivation relatively inefficient and lessening the opportunity for mechanization.

For some years, the government promoted agricultural improvement to offset these problems, working through the agricultural extension service, the New Community Movement, and other agencies. In addition to newly developed plant varieties, improvements included irrigation, fertilizer (of which Korea produces a surplus), mechanization, land rationalization (straightening boundaries, combin-ing small fields), and improved cultivation techniques. The ox, traditional source of power, almost everywhere has been replaced by the highly adaptable, two-wheeled gasoline tractor found powering pumps, pulling wagons, and plowing fields all across East Asia. For years, extension programs have encouraged handi-craft industry such as woodcarving and basket-weaving in farm households to supplement income. Efforts are being made to encourage location and relocation of industry in rural areas, so that farmers can augment their income without leav-ing for the city. In 1985 farmers obtained 35.3 percent of their income, on aver-age, from nonfarm sources; this proportion rose by 1992 to 49 percent.[34] The gov-ernment has commissioned extensive land reclamation projects along the west coast both to compensate for land lost to urban sprawl and to utilize construction industry resources. In 1992 the government initiated a plan to relax limits on farm size to encourage economies of scale, to expand job-training programs to help farmers make the transition to cities or start secondary business in their home villages, to stimulate rural industrialization, and to enhance welfare, in-cluding better schools, health, and social security. These steps, which were under-written by a 50 percent increase in spending for rural development, were part of the Seventh Five-Year Plan.

Services

The largest category of Korea's service sector in the mid-1980s was retail trade, most of it still in the hands of hundreds of thousands of small merchants in the nation's cities, towns, and villages, each with a modest storefront and stock. Department stores of the Western type were increasingly common, however, many of them operated by the industrial *chaebol.*

Communications and rail transportation were in the hands of government ministries or government corporations, but Korean Air Lines, sold by the government to private interests in the 1970s, and all intercity and municipal bus transport were in private hands. Tourism was a rapidly growing industry; the Koreans themselves are enthusiastic travelers, and well over 3 million foreigners came to south Korea in 1992.

Finance

Although the Government disposed of most of its equity in the five major commercial banks in the 1980s, it retained close control over their policies and operations through the Monetary Board and the central Bank of Korea, which are responsible to the Board of Finance and Economics. (A number of smaller banks throughout the country remained in private hands, but their operations were limited.) The principal government lever has been credit policy: Export growth has been promoted by favorable allocation of credit to firms with a good track record.

Korea's domestic savings, particularly public and corporate savings, are growing. In 1993 gross savings amounted to 34.9 percent of GNP and Korea (along with Japan and China) was one of the top three saving economies in the world.[35] In recent years, such savings have accounted for two-thirds or more of total investment. Business financing has always been primarily through bank loans or borrowing on the informal (and high-interest) "curb market" of private lenders; the result is that Korean corporations have very high ratios of debt to equity and are very vulnerable to changes in credit cost and availability. Among private sources of money are *kye,* informal groups of people who contribute to a pool of money that is loaned out at high interest by each member of the group in turn for an agreed period. Altogether, the scale of curb market operations is quite large because money is not readily available from banks, particularly for small-scale or venturesome operations.

The banks, too, have been in a difficult position because some of their loans have been made according to government policies rather than profitability or even creditworthiness. They thus face nonrepayment of loans and falling profits in times of economic contraction. The ability of the central bank to control the money supply through traditional means such as the rediscount rate and reserve requirements is therefore limited, making further resort to political controls rather than traditional monetary levers necessary.

Labor

In 1994 south Korea had an economically active population of 20 million people. This figure does not include approximately 2 million high-school and college students, nor many family members participating in small businesses. It also omits women not working or not actively seeking work; many of these are sure to enter the job market, in view of the growing movement for women's rights. Statistically, 300,000 young people are expected to enter the labor force each year for some years to come, until the surge from the postwar baby boom abates in the late 1990s.

In 1985 the International Labor Organization (ILO) reported that the Korean workweek was fifty-three hours, the longest in the world; it has not decreased very much since then. At the end of 1985, 8.9 percent of manufacturing workers received less than 100,000 won per month (about US$110 at that time). Of these low-wage workers, 29.7 percent were in the textile industries, which have traditionally employed young women—many of them housed in dormitories—who augment their families' incomes and save up for marriage. In other industries as well, most of the low-wage workers were unmarried women. Altogether, the wages of 300,000–500,000 workers were at or below 100,000 won per month. A minimum-wage law, promulgated December 31, 1986, inaugurated a minimum wage in 1988. In 1989 the minimum wage was set at 154,597 won ($220) per month.[36]

By 1993 industrial wages had risen dramatically, to 975,000 won ($1,214.00) per month. White collar wages were running at 1.4 million won ($1,743.00), while mining wages ran lowest, around 880,000 won ($1,095.00). Compared with the 1985 figures and allowing for inflation and rises in consumer prices and housing costs, this represented only a modest gain but a sustained rise in real incomes nevertheless.

Officially registered unemployment in Korea has been low for many years. At the end of 1994 the rate was 2.4 percent (computed according to ILO standards, which classify as employed a person who works one hour or more per week). This figure is not fully comparable with U.S. unemployment statistics—which are based on a broader definition—and probably conceals a great deal of underemployment in agriculture and small business. Nevertheless, it reflects the success of the south Korean economy, since the mid-1960s "takeoff," in harnessing its abundant human resources.

Although south Korea has had organized labor unions since 1945, they have a tradition of being more politically than economically oriented. At present, however, the officially sanctioned labor organizations concentrate their attention on economic matters. The communists used unions for political purposes from 1945 to 1948; Syngman Rhee used them for political purposes from 1948 to 1960. Since that time, organized labor activity has been severely circumscribed, both to contain the potential political threat and to prevent wage increases that would hurt Korea's export drive. Until late 1987 Korean labor laws were highly restrictive, although the Constitution guarantees the right of collective organization and action. As noted in Chapter 4, the change in political policy in the summer of 1987 was followed by an upsurge of strikes and other labor actions in support of demands for better wages and working conditions and freedom to organize. The labor laws have already been revised, and a somewhat freer climate for organized labor has resulted.

Before "democratization" in 1989, the labor laws permitted a national labor federation (the Federation of Korean Trade Unions) and sixteen national industrial federations existed in south Korea; but they were forbidden to enter into specific negotiations without government permission. In-house labor unions at individual plants might bargain collectively and in theory had the right to strike after other remedies were exhausted; but the Ministry of Labor and its constituent divisions and committees played a major role in all labor negotiations. Each plant was required to have a labor-management council, separate from the union, to deal with labor problems, including wages, other benefits, and working conditions. There were strikes and sit-ins even before the upsurge of mid-1987, such as the sit-in by auto workers at a major plant in the port city of Inch'on in early 1985. Nevertheless, the steady, if slow, growth of wages and benefits, together with government controls, was apparently sufficient to avoid massive labor unrest, except at such times as the oil-shock year of 1979 and again in 1987.

Since 1989 the situation has continued to favor company-based unions (as opposed to trade unions), and a government-supervised process of labor-management negotiations for wage increases and other benefits. The atmosphere, however, has become freer: Indeed, in 1989 and 1990 there were many strikes by company workers demanding concessions that management refused to give. The most spectacular of these were the violent strikes at the Hyundai shipyard complex at Ulsan, where riot police and workers battled with Molotov cocktails and tear gas for weeks during which production was completely disrupted. Since then, workers in larger enterprises have enjoyed better wages and benefits, both from their companies and from the continually expanding national health and social security systems. The problem now is with smaller businesses that have a more difficult time providing benefits: the subcontractors and small manufacturers that supply the *chaebol*. Unsafe and unhealthy working conditions are common, especially in the traditionally low-wage jobs taken by young, unmarried women who are understood to be temporarily in the work force until they get married. As in other industrializing countries (as well as in some industrialized nations, including the United States), they live in company dormitories, are protected and sometimes abused by their foremen, and are expected to work very long hours. The treatment they get, along with the sweatshop conditions that continue to prevail across the board in the industrial areas of Korea's major cities, has sparked a new kind of social concern among the people. One result is the effort by university students to build "alliances" with workers in an attempt to politicize them. Another is the religious communities' programs for social justice—for example, Urban Industrial Mission, which was put together, despite a government ban in the 1980s, to represent workers in confrontations with their employers and to train them in effective pressure techniques.

Under the Chun Doo-hwan regime, the government met such efforts with repression. Urban Industrial Mission's organizing efforts were flatly against the law, and the organizers from the churches were frequently imprisoned for their efforts. Laws also explicitly forbade students from posing as workers to "infiltrate" and organize factory workers. Labor actions were met by riot police and tear gas. These government policies made it difficult for south Korea to be accepted in the International Labor Organization, which it tried to join while the policies were in place. It was not until after the 1987 "democratization" and, ultimately, the fall of Communism in Europe and the elimination of Communist opposition to Korea's admission to the ILO, that the Seoul government was permitted to become part of the organization.

The International Component in South Korea's Economy

For the first twenty years of its existence, south Korea depended heavily on the United States for economic and technical aid. As its economy grew, the Republic looked to the United States for an export market and for investment and technology. Since 1965, Japan has also been a major market and investment source, overtaking the United States in some years as principal trading partner. In the early 1980s there began a surreptitious trade with mainland China via Hong Kong. It was an open secret in 1983, for example, that Korea was importing Chinese coal from across the Yellow Sea for use in power plants on the west coast; but for political reasons, because China had an alliance with north Korea and no relations with the south, and because south Korea was under strict media censorship, the nature and scale of the China trade was virtually unknown to the public. However, by the end of the 1980s the trade was obvious in any Korean marketplace. In 1992 China recognized the Seoul government and trade took off; by 1995 China had surpassed the European Union as south Korea's third-largest trading partner, with volume running at an estimated US$16 billion, up by one-third over 1994.

In 1994 the United States provided a market for 26 percent of Korea's exports, Japan took 17 percent, and 14 percent went to the European Union. The corresponding shares of imports were 26 percent from Japan, 24 percent from the United States, and 15 percent from Europe.[37] In recent years, the Republic has vigorously sought to diversify its trade, both to reduce its dependence on the American and Japanese markets and to combat growing protectionism. The president, prime minister, other senior officials, and business leaders have traveled extensively to promote trade. Although the U.S. and Japanese markets still dominate, the diversification policy has had significant results. There is continual growth in trade with the nations of southeast Asia, with the Middle East (especially Saudi Arabia), and with Australia and Canada.

During the Roh Tae-woo years, south Korea promoted trade with Communist countries as a major component of its *nordpolitik* policy (see Chapter 7). Trade with these countries as a whole rose from $1.4 billion in 1985 to $3.7 billion in 1988. As the countries of the former socialist bloc recognized the Republic of Korea one by one, they exchanged trade offices with Korea. Long before the fall of the Soviet Union, there was talk of Korean participation in the development of Siberia. In the 1990s this trade, too, shot upward, and Korean cars and consumer electronics are now commonplace in the former Communist capitals of Eastern Europe.

For most of the period since 1970 south Korea has met its capital investment requirements in a competitive domestic market and, increasingly, has done so from domestic savings. The World Bank, foreign government agencies (which are motivated more by their own trade promotion than by Korea's needs), and commercial banks have been the source of funds borrowed by south Korea. An increasing proportion of foreign investment in south Korea has been in equity capital, which by 1989 totaled well over US$1 billion. In its recent development plans, the Republic has sought and applied foreign advice, particularly from the World Bank, but has set its own policies. Foreign aid as such (i.e., grant aid) is a thing of the past. The last resident U.S. AID official left Korea in 1968.

South Korea's dependence on foreign trade means that the nation is highly vulnerable to international market fluctuations, which are largely responsible for Korea's economic cycles. The government's economic managers have coped very well with these fluctuations. Domestic demand for Korea's products is growing with the rise in income level, and thus domestic markets are a potent "second engine of growth" that can somewhat offset the effect of changing patterns of international trade. The trade-off, however, is limited by south Korea's lack of natural resources and hence its need to import raw materials, as well as by the growing need for advanced technology so that south Korea can move into more sophisticated and capital-intensive industries.

Rapid reduction of the foreign debt relative to GNP since 1987 has lessened Korea's vulnerability to international financial trends and has helped to meet the country's desire for self-reliance. Not only is it in the national interest to maximize self-reliance but there is also a feeling among Koreans, voiced largely by intellectuals and students, but more generally shared, that too much foreign penetration puts the nation's own personality and identity at risk. Farmers in particular, having had their lifeways altered by industrialization and migration to the cities, fear further dislocation because of foreign competition and are vocal in their demands for government protection.

South Korea's growing economic power and importance have attracted foreign businesspeople in increasing numbers. Most visible are the foreign banks (including several U.S. banks), which are gradually becoming competitive with domestic banks as restrictions on them are eased (but like all south Korean banks, they are subject to close regulation). In 1985 fifty-two foreign banks collectively made an estimated profit of over US$100 million on their Korean business. Larger equities, however, are held by a long list of U.S., Japanese, and other firms doing business in south Korea either as joint ventures or as wholly owned subsidiaries, including such giants as General Motors, Ford, Du Pont, and International Business Machines (IBM). Korean capital has also flowed outward, with the government's blessing, to take advantage of target countries' export quotas. By 1990 south Korea's investments abroad were running ahead of foreign investments in Korea itself. Koreans built factories in the United States, China, and around the world. In Indonesia alone, Korean-owned concerns employed more than 260,000 workers.[38]

Since the late 1970s south Korean economic planners have favored liberalization of their government's restrictions on international trade and on foreign participation in Korean business. In part, this policy responds to demands from the United States and other countries for free access to Korean markets; in part, it reflects a conviction that south Korea will benefit from foreign competition in terms of its own production quality and efficiency, as well as from availability of certain foreign goods. Above all, it is recognized that the Republic must compete internationally on a level of constantly advancing technology, the source of which is largely the industrialized countries.

In 1985 the south Korean government officially changed its control policy on foreign investment from a "positive list" to a "negative list" basis—that is, any activity not specifically restricted or prohibited was open to investment. Full foreign ownership of a business was possible in many of the areas not on the negative list. In the area of commodity trade, as well, import restrictions have been significantly eased. By the end of 1988 the south Korean government claimed that 94.7 percent of imports had been freed of prohibitions or restrictions (although not necessarily from import tariff) and that tariff rates had been reduced to an average level of less than 20 percent.[39]

Despite the evident sincerity of this liberalization policy on the part of the economic planners, the actual situation was much more complicated from the foreign businessperson's point of view. One reason was that the government was still seeking to control imports. Strong vested interests both within the bureaucracy and in business circles resisted liberalization, both on the basis of principle— avoidance of foreign economic influence—and of self-interest maintenance of traditional protection from competition from abroad. In addition, the dismantling of long-established bureaucratic controls and prerogatives is a complex and painful process. Moreover, many Koreans still believed that the United States, as a rich and powerful nation with special responsibilities toward Korea, should continue the preferential treatment of the past.

Basic differences in philosophy and practice between Korean and Western ways of doing business greatly complicate the operation of foreign business in Korea. In addition, there is a combination of die-hard nationalism, self-interest, and inertia among some influential Korean circles (including intellectual opposition to the specter of imperialist domination and opposition politicians' exploitation of the foreign trade issue to make any Korean concessions seem like toadyism). Foreign businesspeople react with indignation and frustration and call for the support of their own governments to obtain treatment more like what they would expect at home. U.S. trade with south Korea showed a negative balance of $9.6

billion in 1987—part of a trend reversing twenty years of imbalance in favor of the United States. Sustained efforts at market opening by both sides over the next several years put the trade roughly in balance by 1992, allaying fears of American reprisals under the "Super 301" provisions of the 1988 U.S. Omnibus Trade and Competitiveness Act and accusations that Korea was becoming "another Japan" to the United States.

American pressure for market liberalization centered on the service industries, where U.S. and other foreign competitive advantages tended to be high—financial services, insurance, and professional services (such as law and accounting). The Korean response was a series of market-opening steps, including access to the Korea Stock Exchange for American (and other foreign) investors. Restrictions against American agricultural imports were also eased, over the angry opposition of the farmers' federation. Another area of contention, intellectual property rights, saw progress when south Korean enacted new laws against trademark infringement and the pirating of books and software.

As the scale of the Korean economy has increased, so has Korea's position as a regional economic power. As a member of the Asia Pacific Economic Cooperation council (APEC), as a participant in the Uruguay Round of the talks on the General Agreement on Tariffs and Trade (GATT) and its successor, the World Trade Organization (WTO), and as a dialogue partner in the Association of Southeast Asian States (ASEAN), south Korea has had a voice in emerging transnational trade arrangements. As a major investor in China and the former Soviet Union and as a player in the international arrangements for development of the north Korea–China–Russia triangle, south Korea stands to improve its leadership position through the end of the century. Beyond that, speculation about possible unification of north and south Korea envisions a united country that would be a dynamic competitor for both Japan and China. The "BeSeTo system," or "BeSeTo axis" are terms used to suggest the Beijing-Seoul-Tokyo powerhouse that could dominate the Pacific economy early in the twenty-first century.

South Korean Economic Prospects:
The Seventh Five-Year Plan and Beyond

For the time being, however, south Korea is still on a development track, adjusting policies and engaging in the aggressive pursuit of the overseas markets that its structure demands. Three forces continue to affect Korea's basic development policy: first, increasing protectionism abroad, especially in its primary North American market; second, competition from other developing nations with cheaper labor; and third, growing popular pressure at home for improvement in the quality of life and social welfare. The latter factor, in its economic dimension of upward pressure on wage levels, has already reduced Korea's competitiveness in the international market as newly emerging suppliers (such as China, India, Indonesia, Thailand, and Malaysia) enter the market for traditional labor-intensive commodities.

The response of Korea's planners around 1990 was to lower the target levels for annual GNP growth to a range of 7 to 7.5 percent, as opposed to the double digit rates of the 1980s. This allowed for room to absorb large numbers of new workers entering the labor force, development of the domestic market (as opposed to the obsession with export expansion), and attention to the country's social welfare needs.

South Korea's Seventh Five-Year Plan covers the period 1992–1996, at the end of which Korea will be one of the largest economies in the world. Table 6.2 sets forth the plan's targets at the time of the plan's inception, though several of them will likely be exceeded. Per capita GNP had already broken the $10,000 barrier by the end of 1995, heading for a projected $42,550 by the year 2010. These bench-marks were cited by planners as indicative of south Korea's joining the top world economies (the OECD "club") and, by 2010, joining the ranks of countries now in the Group of Seven, the world's richest nations.

The Seventh Five-Year Plan addresses south Korea's need to move beyond the late-industrializing model to the fostering of high-tech industries with more em-phasis on research and development, and "globalization," which includes steady

TABLE 6.2   Targets of the Seventh Five-Year Plan, Republic of Korea

Item	Amount 1992	Target 1996	1987–1991 Growth Rate (percent)	1992–1996 Growth Rate (percent)
GNP (US$billion)	272.7	492.6	21.5	12.5
GNP per capita	6,316	10,908	20.3	11.5
Commodity exports ($billions)	72	140	15.6	13
Commodity imports ($billions)	81	140	20.7	11
Current amount surplus ($billions)	−10	6		
Total foreign debt ($billions)	40			
Consumer prices (percent change)	9.5	5	7.4	6
Inflation rate (percent)	18.537	20.657	3.6	2.2
Unemployment rate (percent)	2.4			

SOURCE: Korea Economic Institute, *Korea's Economy 1992* (Washington, D.C.: KEI, 1992), p. 5.

steps to liberalize the Korean market and respond to international market forces. Koreans realize that this is essential to their future in the world economy and understand that it is good for the economy as a whole, but they fear the concentrated impact of "globalization" on certain economic sectors, especially agriculture. Making Korea more a part of the world market means that agriculture must continue to decline as a relative part of the national economy. Industry is also facing new challenges from foreign competition and from new domestic legislation aimed at environmental protection. These characteristics of the plan, however, have to do with increasing the quality of life in Korea. They include provisions for expanding the welfare system and stopping the "inheritance of poverty" by children from their parents, through better education and job training and opportunities.

One burning issue in Korean politics is the relative imbalance in the benefits of industrialization between regions of the country. It is a grievance in the southwestern Cholla provinces that the southeastern Kyongsang provinces enjoyed a greater share of the Korean "miracle" under Presidents Park, Chun, Roh, and now Kim Young-sam, all of whom were themselves natives of the southeast. The Seventh Five-Year Plan encourages expansion of industrial plants in the provinces, especially the Chollas, and the relocation of enterprises from Seoul into the provinces. Some major investment plans continue to favor the already favored, such as the "bullet train" begun under the plan for the Seoul-Pusan corridor, and the Yongjong Island international airport that is intended to lure trans-Pacific air traffic away from the new Kansai Airport in Japan and the overloaded Tokyo airport at Narita.

Evolution of the North Korean Economy

The Democratic People's Republic of Korea, since its establishment in 1948, has sought to maximize the individual and collective welfare of its citizens by doing away with what it considers the evils of capitalism and enforcing the doctrines of Karl Marx, as interpreted by Lenin and Stalin in the Soviet Union. Unlike China and former socialist states of Eastern Europe, which also became Communist during Stalin's time, north Korea has adhered to the rigid authoritarianism and state planning of the Stalinist model more closely than did the Soviet Union itself. However, north Korea under Kim Il-sung made its own modifications in both ideology and practice to meet its own conditions. The desire for an independent national personality, and probably the impact of reductions in levels of support from the Soviet Union and China in the early 1960s, gave birth to the doctrine of *juch'e* (self-reliance). *Juch'e* ideology calls for an autarkic economy; however, in practice, special economic support from China and the Soviet Union was always essential to Kim Il-sung's survival and north Korea suffered greatly when these special supports (barter trade, credits, and grants-in-aid, for example) were removed or reduced in the early 1990s.

Economic Theory and Organization

In accordance with Marxist doctrine, private ownership in north Korea is limited to personal and household possessions. All means of production are owned either by groups of citizens organized as cooperatives or by various organs of the state at national or local level. No Communist state, past or present, has ever reached the stage of communism as envisaged by Marx. North Korea is still short of this stage because the state (which is to wither away when true communism is practiced) still exists and because ownership of most agricultural land is still in the hands of individual collectives, rather than of the people as a whole. Kim Il-sung himself said during his lifetime that the communist stage was far in the future because reactionary capitalism was still obstructing development and class enemies still existed even within the country. Thus north Korea still styles itself a socialist state, albeit with a form of socialism that differs greatly from the democratic socialism of such countries as Sweden, in which the economy responds to the laws of the market rather than to central government plans.[40]

The economic and political structures of north Korea, for practical purposes, are one and the same. By far the largest proportion of government agencies and personnel are devoted to the management of manufacturing, agriculture, finance, trade, and related services and activities; only such ministries as Foreign Affairs, Security, and Justice, of the thirty-odd agencies represented on the State Administrative Council, are political in nature. The ministries—in coordination with interministerial committees—control the largest plants and state farms directly; smaller enterprises are administered by provincial and local agencies. Agricultural collectives are controlled by county officials.[41]

Key economic decisions are centered in the State Planning Commission, a cabinet-level agency that sets production and activity levels for all economic entities. In the absence of a competitive market, the requirements and outputs of all economic units must be matched against one another and against estimates of overall needs. Quotas are assigned to each mine, factory, and farm for the complex process in which mines produce for factories, factories produce for other factories and farms, and the whole structure then produces consumer goods for the people, the government, and the armed forces. Actual performance is monitored and adjustments of quotas are made as necessary. Prices at all levels are set on the basis of costs of production, and wages are set on the basis of the cost of living, with some recognition for superior skills and service.

In carrying out its task, the State Planning Commission draws upon the recommendations of the individual plants and farms, the national ministries, the provincial and local government agencies (which themselves handle some of the planning process at their levels), the experience of previous years, and the goals of the overall multiyear plans. Once the quotas are assigned, they are enforced by the various operating ministries and local government agencies. Broad overall policies and goals are determined (on behalf of all the people) by the senior officials of the Korean Workers' Party, which monitors the work of the Commission and other government agencies through its members' presence in them (the Party has its own bureaucracy, paralleling that of the government), and through the agencies' reports.

This, in the view of Communist thinkers, is a better way of operation than capitalism because no unit makes a profit (surpluses revert to the state, a system that made it possible for north Korea to abolish taxes); nobody pays interest to parasitic moneylenders; and all benefits generated from the national economy accrue to the people as a whole, since the people own everything. Moreover, the workers and peasants, since they are all working for themselves and for their comrades, are expected to do their best for the common good, without the motive of selfish personal gain that leads to inequality and injustice under capitalism. (Exhortations to workers and peasants for redoubled unselfish devotion to work are daily fare in north Korean leaders' statements and in mass media, and many hours are devoted to public education along these lines.) In a capitalist system, benefits would accrue to a small handful of monopolistic entrepreneurs and moneylenders, manipulating the entire system for their own selfish profit. In the Marxist-Leninist-Kimilsungist system, benefits are supposed to be distributed equally among all the people. This supposition is, of course, based on the assumption that the leaders use their power only to make the system work and not to benefit themselves (an assumption similar to that concerning scholar-officials in the traditional Confucian state).

Historical Experience

In earlier years, the theory—supported by strong central planning and centralized, vigorous, authoritarian administration—seems to have worked well. Starting from a completely shattered economy in 1951, with the benefit of foreign aid for the first few years, north Korea scored very impressive gains that far outdistanced south Korea's then-stagnant economy. Yearly growth in national product reached as high as 20 percent.[42]

These gains did not necessarily produce a proportionate improvement in general living standards, because Communist economic doctrine gives priority to heavy industry, deferring consumer benefits until the basic industrial structure is in place (whereas in south Korea the emphasis was on meeting basic individual needs first). However, the north Korean people, comparing their lot to their experience under Japanese domination and virtually cut off from the rest of the world by a totalitarian regime, seem generally to have accepted what they got, although there may have been a leadership dispute over the priority given heavy industry at the expense of consumer goods. A Five-Year Plan for economic growth was apparently completed a year ahead of schedule, in 1960 rather than 1961, although it took a forced-draft *Ch'ollima* (Thousand-League Horse) Movement, similar to China's Great Leap Forward, to do so.

Subsequently, however, the north Korean economy seems to have run into trouble. The government stopped publishing quantitative production statistics in the mid-1960s and has never resumed doing so except for individual products at various times—announcing results only in terms of percentage increases. The First Seven-Year Plan (1961–1967) had to be extended three additional years, to 1970. There have been two subsequent multiyear plans—the Six-Year Plan (1971–1976) and the Second Seven-Year Plan (1978–1984); but during this period there have been internal readjustments in organization and method and constant exhortations for redoubled effort by workers, particularly in apparent bottleneck areas such as mining and transportation, coupled with criticisms of bureaucratism. Analysts estimate that the falling north Korean economic growth rate intersected with the rising south Korean growth rate around 1975.[43] The Central Intelligence Agency puts the south's gross domestic product at over twenty times the north's, or nearly eleven times as large on a per capita basis.[44]

Given the lack of reliable information on north Korea's economy, the reasons for the economic slowdown cannot be precisely identified. The north Koreans themselves attributed it to the burden of a defense buildup; they put their military expenditures around 15 percent of their national budget (the budget itself constitutes about 80 percent of the national economy). Other estimates of military expenditure run as high as 25 percent of national product.

In addition, external aid declined steeply—first from the Soviet Union under Khrushchev in the late 1950s, and then from China during the Great Proletarian Cultural Revolution. Furthermore, north Korea has always suffered from a labor shortage, both from wartime losses by death and defection and from the high proportion of men under arms. It was presumably for this reason that north Korea persuaded 100,000 Korean residents of Japan to immigrate[45] in the late 1950s and has encouraged a high birthrate (23.31 births per thousand population compared to 15.63 births per thousand in the south).[46]

The tone of north Korean internal propaganda, together with some apparent decentralization of controls to lower governmental levels—including an accounting system that makes individual plants responsible for balancing their costs and revenues—suggests that the highly centralized economic control system is working less well as the economy grows more complex. It presumably suffers from the usual problems of inertia, time-serving, and assertion of status that are common to large established bureaucracies and has had trouble in controlling the many variables of the economic system without the discipline of impersonal market forces.

Moreover, the north Koreans have increasingly resorted to financial incentive devices, as well as nonmaterial awards, to promote worker and management productivity, suggesting that notwithstanding Marxist theory, Communist principles have not yet found altruism to be a driving force equal to old-fashioned monetary benefits in practice. Farmers are allowed, for example, to cultivate "private plots" of up to about 100 square meters (1,076 square feet), the crops from which can be sold at periodic peasant markets at uncontrolled prices. Both industrial and agricultural enterprises can distribute some earnings above quota, and work teams can earn extra financial benefits if their quotas are exceeded.

A major administrative reform was inaugurated in 1960. Kim Il-sung, in the course of one of his many "on-the-spot guidance" visits around the country, called for a new form of agricultural collective organization in which a local Party committee worked with the administrative manager to set policies and itself had responsibility for ideological work. This dual directorate, called the Chongsan-ni method (named after the place it was announced), was extended the following year to industry in a similar visit by Kim Il-sung to a factory at Tae'an.

In the early 1970s, notwithstanding their heavy emphasis on self-reliance, the north Koreans sought to import Western plants and techniques to upgrade their own obsolescent industry. This move backfired partly because of the 1973 oil crisis; the government was unable to discharge its debt obligations, totalling over US$2 billion, and has been more or less in default ever since to Japan and several other countries, including Sweden, Finland, Austria, and Indonesia. Foreign-exchange problems were apparently so severe that north Korean diplomatic missions abroad were required to support themselves. Some embassies resorted to smuggling through their diplomatic pouches.

Another means of attacking north Korean problems was the campaign of Three Revolutions—technological, ideological, and cultural—launched in the early 1970s, reputedly under the leadership of Kim Il-sung's son Kim Jong-il. This campaign sought to encourage innovation and to eliminate the barriers of negative bureaucratic attitudes. It included the organization of Three Revolutions teams composed of qualified party and government officials who visited industrial sites to upgrade management and productivity. The focus on technology may indicate a recognition that north Korea's emphasis on self-reliance and its isolation from the West have caused a technological lag. These factors also may help to explain the slow pace of recent north Korean economic growth.

More recently, the Supreme People's Assembly approved a policy, promulgated as law in September 1984, for organizing joint ventures with foreign governments or concerns to promote the north Korean economy. This innovation may have reflected a similar and earlier Chinese move. The first two such ventures were a Japanese department-store chain and a French tourist hotel. In 1987, north Korea signed a joint-venture agreement with the Soviet Union, and ground was broken for the rehabilitation of a gold mine by a joint venture between Korean residents of Japan and a north Korean agency. Since then, and especially since the withdrawal of aid from the defunct Soviet Union, north Korea has had to be much more active in attracting foreign investment. In 1991 there were more than one hundred joint ventures in north Korea worth approximately $96.5 million, mostly financed by Korean residents in Japan.

In 1991, the United Nations Development Programme sponsored the first of a series of international conferences to explore development of what came to be known as the Tumen River Area Development Program. The plan was to create a Special Economic Zone (SEZ) along the lines of the SEZs on the China coast, to attract businesses from abroad to build factories that would use local labor, on either side of the Tumen River including areas of China, Russia, and north Korea.

For the DPRK, the Tumen River project looked like a way to break out of its economic isolation, using a lightly populated part of the country where foreign contamination was unlikely to have much impact. For the other partners, too, there were advantages: China was seeking ways to develop its northeastern economy, and Russia foresaw building the infrastructure without which full exploitation of its Siberian resources had always been hampered.

For several years the Tumen River project was the subject of intense discussion. Outside financing was invited from south Korea and Japan, among many other sources. North Korea, however, began to have second thoughts when it became clear that the zone under consideration was porous to travel between the three countries. Accustomed to tight restrictions on population movement, the north Koreans feared the unregulated influx of foreign influence, especially from south Koreans. The result was that the rosy prospects of 1992 waned into halfway proposals to have three separate areas each under the control of its respective national government. These and other contentious points, plus the misgivings of likely investors, slowed planning for the Tumen River Project. By 1995 north Korea was laying the groundwork for a Special Economic Zone in the Najin-Sonbong area of far northeastern Korea, but how much international investment the Kim Jong-il regime could attract remained uncertain.

Present State of the North Korean Economy

The gross national product of the Democratic People's Republic of Korea for 1994 was estimated by the U.S. government at US$21.3 billion or $920 per capita. This figure is somewhat speculative both because of the absence of reliable data on north Korea and because there is no real basis on which to establish an exchange rate between the north Korean won and the dollar.[47] The actual scale and condition of the economy is likewise difficult to assess, even in gross terms. In the early 1990s the conventional wisdom in the West was that the north Korean economy was shrinking and had undergone several years of negative growth in GNP. Foreign observers in north Korea, however, usually reported no signs of economic crisis, much less of implosion. To be sure, electric power was in short supply, and broken-down vehicles suggested a lack of maintenance. Anecdotal evidence, however, did not support predictions of collapse, at least before the disastrous floods of August 1995.[48]

North Korea's foreign trade was severely disrupted by the end of the Cold War. However, because it is less dependent on exports and foreign exchange than south Korea, the disruption had relatively less effect than such a disruption would have had in the south. Furthermore, the military protected its claim on national resources throughout the early 1990s. One hard-hit sector of the economy was energy: North Korea's crash program to finish its two new nuclear reactors at Yongbyon and Taech'on was a plausible attempt to address the shortage in electricity that has caused shutdowns across the board and cut into production in many other industries. The U.S.-DPRK agreement of October 1994 providing for creation of the Korean Peninsula Energy Development Corporation (KEDO) with its provisions of fuel oil represented an effort to meet north Korea's nonmilitary energy needs without resorting to nuclear power—and thus averting concerns about its by-product of plutonium and related strategic implications.

Official north Korean statements have promised increased attention to consumer-goods production, in terms of both quantity and quality—responding, presumably, to long pent-up demand. There is no firm statistical evidence to indicate whether such promises have been translated into action. Foreign visitors to north Korea agree that amenities are far behind those readily available in the south, though there is sufficiency: The north Koreans have succeeded fairly well in enforcing equal distribution of poverty, though upper-level government and Party officials apparently have access to special stores and other benefits, as has always been the case in Communist countries.

One reason north Korea is less dependent upon foreign trade than the south is its comparative abundance of natural resources. These commodities make a self-reliant economy more possible than in the south, and they also provide goods to trade for things it does not have. It is rich in timber and minerals, including coal, iron ore, graphite, tungsten, copper, zinc, lead, and precious metals. Self-reliance and limited foreign trade provide an economy approaching sufficiency in industry, but north Korea still must import food, and it is in no position to export finished goods that can compete on the world market. One exception is weapons, notably missiles and rifles.

North Korea's imports consist primarily of petroleum (from the Soviet Union and China—like the south, north Korea has no petroleum resources), machinery, cotton, and foodstuffs (primarily wheat). Exports are mainly minerals, processed metals, textiles, agricultural products, precious metals, and (to developing countries) military arms. Beginning in 1985, after a virtual boycott for many years, the Soviet Union again began furnishing advanced weaponry to north Korea.

The summer of 1995 brought torrential floods to north Korea, the unhappy result of a convergence of storms. In Hwanghae Province on the west coast, it was estimated that 500,000 people had been left homeless, and estimates of crop damage indicated that north Korea might actually experience a severe famine in 1996. The north Koreans themselves broke precedent and asked the international community to send food aid. Though they made it difficult for the south Koreans to contribute, no doubt for political reasons, they accepted United Nations Development Programme aid and assistance from such international relief agencies as Church World Service and the American Friends Service Committee. Even the U.S. State Department contributed a symbolic $25,000 on behalf of the American people, though the need was much greater, running in the millions. The north Koreans' reluctance to admit that they were in dire straits hampered outside efforts to confirm the extent of the need. But there was no doubt that north Korea had suffered a severe economic reversal on top of a series of political and economic disasters.

Prospects

As the foregoing summary suggests, north Korea's economic problems in recent years have apparently led to recognition of the need for opening up to the world as a means of accelerating economic growth and modernization; the growing economic gap between north and south Korea must be of great concern to north Korean leaders. Joint venture laws are a small step in this direction. In the early 1990s, especially during the 1990–1992 period, when north-south relations showed such promise, there appeared to be substantial sentiment in the ruling circles, including the political entourage of Kim Jong-il, for opening north Korea to the world in a limited way. Kim Il-sung taught that it was not inconsistent with *juch'e* thought to pursue friendly relations with foreign countries. However, the north Koreans, in their approaches to Japan and the United States, for example, attached such prohibitive conditions to the normalization of relations that talks were unable to go forward. In the case of Japan, the issue was usually some variation on reparations for the period of Japanese colonial rule in Korea, on terms the Japanese were unable or unwilling to meet. In the case of the United States, the issue was usually a variation on the theme of the U.S.–south Korean alliance, with demands for withdrawal of U.S. troops from the south before any progress could develop. It should also be said that the north Koreans seemed consistently to misjudge the political flexibility of leaders in Japan and the United States, not recognizing, for example, the restraints imposed on the American presidency by Congress.

For all the breakdown and impasse that attended north Korea's political relations with the international community in 1995, some form of economic reform, probably following the Chinese model, nevertheless seemed inevitable. In the meantime, however, the north Korean economy will continue on its present level of low growth, with continued priority assigned to heavy industry, a large defense expenditure, and high population growth. This will limit improvements in living standards, unless popular discontent reaches levels that force modification of current policies. Given what is known about north Korea today, there is little sign of any such possibility.

Notes

1. Ch'oe Chin-hyok, "Choson Minjujuui Inmin Konghwagukeso-ui Rijo Sigi-ui Ryoksa wa Munhwa Yon'gu-e Taehayo" (Regarding Research on the History of the Yi Dynasty in the Democratic People's Republic of Korea), paper delivered at the annual conference of the Mid-Atlantic Region, Association for Asian Studies, Washington, D.C., November 1985.

2. Andrew Grajdanzev, *Modern Korea* (New York: distributed by John Day Co. for the International Secretariat of the Institute of Pacific Relations, 1945); Andrew C. Nahm, ed., *Korea Under Japanese Colonial Rule* (Kalamazoo: Institute for Korean Studies, Western Michigan University, 1973); George M. McCune and Arthur L. Grey, *Korea Today* (Cambridge, Mass.: Harvard University Press, 1950), pp. 29–34.

3. Grajdanzev, *Modern Korea,* p. 119.

4. Paul Kuznets, *Economic Growth and Structure in the Republic of Korea* (New Haven: Yale University Press, 1977), p. 22.

5. Kuznets, *Economic Growth and Structure,* p. 30.

6. A Korean aid bill failed in the U.S. House of Representatives by one vote in January 1949 (*New York Times,* July 2, 1949). Later, an appropriation of $350 million for economic assistance was made, but little of it had arrived when the Korean War started; the U.S. aid program was still running largely on the remaining GARIOA funds.

7. Kuznets, *Economic Growth and Structure,* p. 32; David C. Cole and Princeton N. Lyman, *Korean Development: The Interplay of Politics and Economics* (Cambridge, Mass.: Harvard University Press, 1971), p. 21.

8. Some plants were reportedly taken by the Soviets as war reparations; exactly how many is not known.

9. See United Nations Command, Office of the Economic Coordinator, *Stabilization and Program Progress: Fiscal Year 1958* (Seoul, 1958), p. 11. The Korean currency was called *hwan* until 1962, when it was converted to *won,* the denomination used today. "Won" is the Korean form "yen" in Japanese and "yuan" in Chinese.

10. U.S. economic grant aid, except for agricultural commodities under Public Law 480, was terminated in 1968. Loans on special terms continued for several more years. Military grant aid ended in 1982, though loans for military purposes and equipment transfers under the Military Assistance Program continued into the 1990s. Andrea Matles Savada and William R. Shaw, *South Korea: A Country Study,* 4th ed. (Washington, D.C.: U.S. Government Printing Office, 1992), pp. 293–297.

11. *North Korea: A Country Study* (Washington, D.C.: Foreign Area Studies, The American University, 1981; for sale by U.S. Government Printing Office), p. 153.

12. Donald S. Macdonald, "Korea and the Ballot: The International Dimension in Korean Political Development as Seen in Elections" (Ph.D. dissertation, George Washington University, 1978), p. 418; Cole and Lyman, *Korean Development,* pp. 25–26.

13. Kuznets, *Economic Growth and Structure,* pp. 46–47.

14. Edward S. Mason et al., *The Economic and Social Modernization of the Republic of Korea,* Studies in the Modernization of the Republic of Korea: 1945–1975, Harvard East Asian Monographs No. 92 (Cambridge, Mass.: Council on East Asian Studies, Harvard University Press, 1980), p. 15.

15. Figures computed by averaging data from Economic Planning Board, Republic of Korea, *Palsimnyondae Kyongje Chongch'aek ui Chinch'ul Songkwa wa Hyanghu Kwajong* (Results of Economic Policy for the 1980s and Future Agenda), (Seoul, 1985), p. 10, and *Korea Business World,* October 1987, pp. 90–91.

16. Bank of Korea, *Quarterly Review,* March 1985.

17. Kuznets, *Economic Growth and Structure,* p. 50.

18. Parvez Hasan and D. C. Rao, *Korea: Policy Issues for Long-Term Development: The Report of a Mission Sent to the Republic of Korea by the World Bank* (Baltimore: Published for the World Bank by the Johns Hopkins University Press, 1979).

19. *Palsimnyondae,* p. 156; *Korea Business World,* October 1989, p. 18, citing the Republic of Korea Office of National Tax Administration; *Korea Business World,* September 1989, p. 74.

20. *Palsimnyondae,* p. 10; *Korea's Economy 1995* (Washington, D.C.: Korea Economic Institute, 1995), p. 1.

21. Mason, *Economic and Social Modernization*, pp. 28–29.

22. Mason, *Economic and Social Modernization*, p. 18.

23. For example, industry has been expected to provide high-level positions for retiring military personnel; the economic impact of this arrangement is probably not great, but it has caused controversy.

24. See Savada and Shaw, *South Korea: A Country Study*, p. 193. The OECD members as of 1995 were Australia, Austria, Belgium, Canada, Denmark, Finland, France, Germany, Greece, Iceland, Ireland, Italy, Japan, Luxembourg, Netherlands, New Zealand, Norway, Portugal, Spain, Sweden, Switzerland, Turkey, United Kingdom, and the United States.

25. For the story of Kyongsong Spinning and Weaving, see Carter J. Eckert, *Offspring of Empire: The Koch'ang Kims and the Colonial Origins of Korean Capitalism, 1876–1945* (Seattle: University of Washington Press, 1991).

26. Donald Kirk, *Korean Dynasty: Hyundai and Chung Ju Yung* (New York: M. E. Sharpe, 1994).

27. Kirk, p. 356.

28. Sakong Il, *Korea in the World Economy* (Washington, D.C.: Institute for International Economics, 1993), p. 186.

29. For a discussion of this theme see Jung-en Woo, *Race to the Swift: State and Finance in Korean Industrialization* (New York: Columbia University Press, 1991), especially chapter 6, pp. 148–175. During the slush-fund scandal that put former President Roh Tae-woo in prison in 1995, the degree of collusion became clearer when it was established that many millions of dollars had been donated to the president's private political fund by the heads of Korea's great conglomerates.

30. "South Korea Survey," *The Economist,* June 3, 1995, p. 10.

31. Brunei, Indonesia, Malaysia, Philippines, Singapore, and Thailand constitute the Association of Southeast Asian Nations (ASEAN).

32. *South Korea: A Country Study*, p. 160.

33. Korea Overseas Information Service, *A Handbook of Korea*, 9th ed. (Seoul: Korea Overseas Information Service, 1993), p. 410.

34. *Korea Annual 1994* (Yonhap News Agency, 1994), p. 248.

35. International Monetary Fund, *World Economic Outlook, May 1, 1995* (Washington, D.C.: International Monetary Fund, 1995), p. 74.

36. *Korea Herald*, January 29, 1986; *Korea Times* editorial, May 28, 1986; *Korea Business World*, July 1988, p. 26; Korea Economic Institute of America, telephoned information, April 1990.

37. U.S. Central Intelligence Agency, *World Factbook 1995*. Internet, http://www.odci.gov/cia/publications/95fact/ks.html.

38. David I. Steinberg, "The Transformation of the South Korean Economy," in *Korea Briefing 1993*, ed. Donald N. Clark (Boulder: Westview Press, 1993), p. 43.

39. *Korea Business World*, July 1989, pp. 28–29. The ratios for goods actually traded are lower. See *Palsimnyondae*, p. 35.

40. For a discussion of the philosophy of north Korean economic development, see Ellen Brun and Jacques Hirsch, *Socialist Korea: A Case Study in the Strategy of Economic Development* (New York: Monthly Review Press, 1977).

41. Joseph Chung, writing in the mid-1970s, stated that there were 22 farms, on the average, per county, each with 6,300 households and 10,000 *chongbo* (about 11,000 hectares

or 27,000 acres) of land. Joseph Sang-hoon Chung, *The North Korean Economy: Structure and Development* (Stanford: Hoover Institution Press, 1974).

42. See U.S. Central Intelligence Agency, *Korea: The Economic Race Between the North and South* (Washington, D.C.: U.S. Government Printing Office, 1978).

43. Sung Chul Yang, *The North and South Korean Political Systems: A Comparative Analysis* (Boulder: Westview Press, 1994), pp. 609–669.

44. U.S. Central Intelligence Agency, *The World Factbook, 1995* (Washington, D.C.: U.S. Government Printing Office, 1994), pp. 230–233.

45. The term "repatriation" was applied to this movement at the time, but many of the people involved came originally from south Korea.

46. U.S. Central Intelligence Agency, *World Factbook 1995*, p. 231.

47. "Study in Contrasts," p. 19. The U.S. Central Intelligence Agency's *World Factbook 1995* reports an exchange rate of 2.15 north Korean won to the U.S. dollar.

48. Marcus Noland, "The North Korean Economy," *Korea Economic Update,* vol. 6, no. 3 (Washington, D.C.: Korea Economic Institute, 1995), pp. 1–2.

7

Korean National Security and Foreign Relations

Introduction

The Korean peninsula is surrounded by three of the most powerful states in the world: Russia, China, and Japan. These three states are traditional rivals. Each of them, because of geography, fears that Korea may be used by the others against it. Since 1945, the United States has been a fourth major player. Although geographically distant, the United States has become deeply concerned about northeast Asia for reasons of its own national security and prosperity. Thus, Korea faces the contentious presence of these four great powers as a factor in its national destiny and its foreign policy.

Since 1948, however, Korea's view of the larger geopolitical picture has been overshadowed by the confrontation on the peninsula. The two Korean states have been, and continue to be, each other's chief security threat. The Korean War tragically demonstrated this fact. Technically, the Korean War has never ended; the Armistice Agreement of 1953 is the longest cease-fire in history, and it is still only a suspension of hostilities. Two great armies totaling 1.7 million men are poised to fight if hostilities should resume along the Demilitarized Zone (Figure 7.1) that separates them. About 3.5 percent of south Korea's gross national product, and fully 20 percent of north Korea's, is devoted to military preparedness.

The foreign relations of both Korean states are dominated by this situation. Rivalry between them for international recognition has been a principal theme for both. Despite some north-south dialogue from time to time, each state regards the other as illegitimate (although both have accepted the reality of separate statehood to the extent that they joined the United Nations separately in 1991). Each seeks international support for its security. The competitive concerns of the two separate states prevent attention to the larger and longer-range problems of the peninsula and its people as a whole.

At the same time, however, both Korean states are committed to the ideal of reunification, which is a universal aspiration of the people in both north and south. Compared to Korean history as a whole, even fifty years of division can be seen as a temporary aberration. Reunification is probable in the long run. Fixing the terms of reunification, however, poses seemingly insurmountable problems (these are discussed in Chapter 8).

Meanwhile, both Korean states need relations with other countries in meeting popular aspirations for economic and social progress. South Korea especially, with almost no natural resources beyond land and people, must look to the world for its raw materials and for export earnings to pay for them. Both Koreas

FIGURE 7.1   A typical scene at the Demilitarized Zone dividing Korea (photo courtesy of Korea Overseas Information Service)

need advanced technology and foreign investment capital, although north Korea, particularly, has encountered both foreign and domestic obstacles in getting them.

The two Koreas are also in intense international competition for legitimacy, prestige, and support. The Korean people, especially in the south, are motivated by their recent history to want not only national independence, but also national prestige. Popular perception of the Korean governments' standing in the world is therefore a factor in domestic stability. International perception of each Korean state is also a contributing factor to national security, since the perception would affect international attitudes in the event of renewed hostilities.

Current Korean attitudes toward relations with other states are strongly conditioned by two historical traditions: the "siege mentality" that has resulted from repeated invasions throughout recorded history; and the special relationship with China, which was the principal basis for Korea's national security for many centuries. A brief review of the Chinese relationship is therefore in order.

As an agricultural society living at subsistence level, Korea was essentially self-sufficient during most of its history. National security and the security of the ruling dynasty were its only foreign policy concerns. To meet these concerns, Korea accepted a "younger-brother" relationship to China, which until the nineteenth century was by far the dominant power of the region. China was not only Korea's protector but also its political and cultural "older brother," mentor, and because Chinese emperors "invested" Korean kings with their authority to rule, the ultimate source of the ruling dynasty's legitimacy. In a family-style East Asian international order, China was at the center or summit, and all other nations at various inferior levels; they were autonomous but tributary states.

The Chinese provided key support to the Koreans in driving out the sixteenth-century Japanese invaders. Thereafter, Korea closed its borders against all other powers and put all its security eggs in the Chinese basket—with little or no military power of its own—until the decline of Chinese power was made manifest by China's defeat in the Sino-Japanese War in 1895. In thus becoming a "hermit nation," Korea was following the same course as China and Japan, which also had policies of exclusion.

After the Japanese "opened" Korea with the Kanghwa Treaty of 1876, the nation was wrenched out of its attempt to isolate itself. After thirty years of imperialist rivalry, the Russo-Japanese War in 1904–1905 opened the way for Japan to colonize Korea. Thus three centuries of self-imposed Korean isolation were followed by thirty years of traumatic exposure to the outside world, and then by forty years of national eclipse, first as a Japanese protectorate and then from 1910 to 1945 as an outright colony. During the colonial period, Korean nationalists (mostly in exile) were split into opposing ideological camps on the left and the right. As in China during the same period, revolutionary visions of national liberation vied with gradualist visions of national salvation through education and cultural preservation that would protect traditional power elites. These competing orientations underlie the decades-long struggle that helped to create the mutually hostile regimes in north and south Korea after World War II, which soon erupted in the Korean War of 1950–1953 and linked the two Koreas to the opposing superpowers for the duration of the Cold War. Indeed, in terms of world politics, it may be said that the Cold War came to the Korean nationalist movement (as it came to China) before it came to the West.

The Japanese defeat in 1945 led to Korea's division into U.S. and Soviet zones of occupation. Reinforced by the ideological division between radical and conservative Korean nationalists, the split became permanent. Given Korea's history, it was natural for Koreans in the two new Korean states to transfer to the Soviet Union and to the United States, respectively, the same younger-brother relationship formerly given to China rather than to unite in opposition to both. However, as indicated in Chapter 2, both states have moved since the Korean War toward a position of greater self-reliance and independence of action—sooner and faster in the Democratic People's Republic of Korea (DPRK) in the north than in the Republic of Korea (ROK) in the south.

Foreign Relations of the Republic of Korea (South Korea)

National security, economic progress and trade, and enhancement of legitimacy and prestige are the basic themes of south Korean foreign policy. These themes are interrelated. Security is essential for economic progress; economic progress is now the primary basis for Korea's improving international reputation; and prestige enhances both security and prosperity.

In general, the Republic's foreign policy is characterized by caution, preservation of established relationships, and incremental improvement, rather than innovation. The prospect of sudden shifts in the policies of other countries, particularly of the United States, is a grave concern (as in President Jimmy Carter's troop withdrawal initiative of 1977 or in the U.S. dialogue with north Korea over nuclear issues in the period 1993–1995).

National Security Policy

Basic Policy Themes. In addition to maintaining its own powerful military and internal security forces, the security policy of the Republic centers on keeping a special relationship with the United States. South Korean dependence upon the United States for security began with the occupation in 1945 and was almost total during the Korean War. Today, however, it is as much psychological as military. The suffering imposed by the war is a vivid personal memory for older south Koreans, and the possibility of its renewal is a very real apprehension. U.S. ground combat forces stationed in Korea are a significant but marginal increment to Korea's own military capabilities; of much greater significance is the reassurance they provide. Though their presence carries with it certain problems, it demonstrates to Koreans in both the south and the north that the United States is committed to the Republic's defense, thus providing a major deterrent to north Korean attack; and it ensures that the United States would not opt out of actual hostilities. U.S. air, naval, and logistic support are of much more military importance, but their actual commitment would be less assured in the event of attack if U.S. ground forces were not in place.

Such reassurance is particularly important to south Korea for two reasons. First, the certainty of prompt U.S. military support—especially air support—is a key factor in the credibility of the "forward defense strategy" adopted in 1973, under which a north Korean attack would be stopped north of the city of Seoul.[1] Second, south Korea has good historical reason to doubt the permanent reliability of its U.S. ally. As the Koreans see it, the United States violated its commitment to provide good offices under Article I of the Korea-U.S. Treaty of 1882 when President Theodore Roosevelt accepted (many Koreans would say "permitted") Japanese hegemony over Korea in 1905. The United States also ignored Korean nationalists' appeals for self-determination in 1919, even though it was President Woodrow Wilson who championed the self-determination doctrine in his famous Fourteen Points.

Many Koreans blame the United States for the division of the country in 1945 (a complicated issue which is discussed in Chapter 8). In Korean eyes, U.S. disengagement from the Republic after its independence encouraged the north Korean attack in 1950. The Americans refused to believe that north Korea would invade the south. Equally concerned about preventing a southern attack on the north, the United States did not provide adequate equipment and training for defense; it denied the Republic an air force; and it withdrew its remaining troops in 1949 over Korean protest. Secretary of State Dean Acheson's January 1950 speech, seemingly defining a U.S. defense perimeter in the western Pacific that excluded Korea, coupled with U.S. preoccupation in Europe (the Berlin Blockade was then at its height), probably encouraged Kim Il-sung to think that north Korean military victory over the south was within his grasp. Although U.S. forces were the key to the Republic's survival in the Korean War, Korean confidence in the continuing American commitment to defend the ROK was shaken by the American defeat in Vietnam and by what many Koreans saw as the loss of American will that followed.

The presence of 37,000 armed foreigners on Korean soil, though considered necessary for security, creates both foreign and domestic policy problems for south Korea. North Korea, from which the last foreign troops were withdrawn in 1958, never tires of lashing the south Koreans as puppets of neocolonialist masters. Within the south, the visibility, boisterous behavior, and occasional crime of U.S. soldiers reinforce nationalist charges of "American imperialism" and cries of "Yankee go home!" from radicals. Until they were withdrawn in 1991, the unacknowledged presence of U.S. nuclear weapons in Korea (generally estimated to have numbered from 250 to 1,000) was also a target of criticism, both in Korea and elsewhere. Frequent ROK-U.S. military maneuvers continue to be taken as provocations by the north Koreans, who charge that the aggressive military posture of south Korea and its American ally constitute an impediment to reunification talks. Many in the south Korean opposition agree. It is testimony to good management by Korean and U.S. authorities, and to long-established Korean-U.S. friendship, that domestic criticism has thus far been limited to the margins, while most south Korean public opinion remains generally friendly toward the United States.

Because of uncertainty of future U.S. support, as well as nationalist sentiment for self-reliance, the Republic has sought to dilute its dependence on the United States. It has increased its own armaments manufacturing capability, increased the munitions reserve stockpiles within the country, and procured some weapons systems from non-U.S. (chiefly French, Italian, and British) sources. The Republic has also sought to export its own arms manufactures to other countries, both to exercise its production capacity and to increase foreign trade earnings; but its ability to do so is limited by U.S. license restrictions. In the mid-1970s, at the height of its worry about U.S. reliability, south Korea apparently considered going nuclear with French assistance, but decided against it, to the relief of the United States. (The Republic of Korea is a signatory of the nuclear Non-Proliferation Treaty and subscribes to the full-scope safeguards of the Treaty, as they apply to its nuclear plants.)

The Republic considers its military strength to contribute to the security of Japan because that strength denies the peninsula to Communist forces. During the Cold War, the military posture of the U.S.–south Korean alliance diverted considerable Soviet forces that otherwise might have confronted Japan. South Korea used this argument in seeking major economic assistance from Japan in the early 1980s, although the Japanese refused to acknowledge its merit. However, Korea does not want to accept Japanese forces as a factor in its own security. Because of past experience with Japanese aggression, the Republic does not favor any strengthening of Japanese military capability. South Korean forces nevertheless cooperate in arrangements with U.S. and Japanese forces for radar warning and communications, and there is limited consultation between Korean and Japanese military leaders.

In theory, cooperative military arrangements with other states in the region would offer Korea an alternative to dependence upon the United States. Ever since President Rhee tried in vain to promote a "Northeast Asia Treaty Organization" in the late 1940s, the Republic has been interested in promoting closer regional cooperation. The Association of Pacific Nations (ASPAC), which existed in the 1960s and 1970s, was another Korean initiative, and the promotion of the cooperative Pacific Basin organization called APEC (Asia-Pacific Economic Cooperation) is a goal of south Korea's Seventh Five-Year Plan (1992–1996). However, the Republic does not want security arrangements to include Japan, its traditional enemy. South Korea opened formal diplomatic relations with the Soviet Union in 1990 and the People's Republic of China in 1992, both of which had mutual defense treaties with north Korea at the time. Russia and the Commonwealth of Independent States no longer back north Korea; China still does. Thus there remains a military balance in the region, though it is much altered by the fall of Communism in Europe. Most observers, including Americans, seem to agree that for the time being an American presence in south Korea is a stabilizing factor in what is otherwise a fluid and perhaps dangerous situation.

The nations that contributed troops to the United Nations Command in the 1950–1953 action are still signatories to the July 27, 1953, Declaration of the Sixteen, which stated that if there should be a renewal of hostilities, they would be prompt to resist. In practice, however, it is doubtful that many of them would intervene to ensure peace on the Korean peninsula.[2]

The Security Threat. The threat faced by the Republic is a very real and serious one, notwithstanding the fact that it has often been exploited and even exaggerated to justify domestic political abuses. North Korea has made no secret of its hostility toward the south Korean regime and the United States, complaining constantly of alleged U.S.–Japanese–south Korean aggressive schemes. Since the early 1960s, north Korean military power has kept up its share of the arms race on the peninsula. As Table 7.1 shows, north Korea has larger forces and more weapons and equipment than the south, and these appear to be concentrated in forward positions. While the better training and equipment in the south offsets the north's numerical advantage somewhat, there was a sharp increase in the number of men under arms in the late 1980s to a total of more than 1 million, raising new worries about the overwhelming effect of a north Korean invasion. The discovery of four tunnels under the Demilitarized Zone, and the suspected presence of as many as fourteen more, posed new worries about infiltration efforts, manifestations of the body of political opinion in the north that seeks to touch off a general uprising in the south.

It is unlikely that the north Koreans could successfully repeat their lightning sweep of June 1950 through the peninsula. They would suffer devastation from south Korean and U.S. air attacks if they tried, in addition to the ground force casualties they would suffer. However, it is quite possible that the north Koreans, if they detected weakness in the south Korean or U.S. position, might try a blitzkrieg aimed at capturing the Republic's territory north of the Han River within a few days' time. Though this would also bring terrible retribution on the territory of the north and no doubt the destruction of the laboriously rebuilt capital of Pyongyang, the capture of Seoul as far as the Han River might be tempting; and if the north Koreans were successful in this relatively small geographical advance, thirty to thirty-five miles in the western sector of their line, they would control one-quarter of south Korea's population and nearly half of its economic capacity and would have a greatly strengthened hand in gaining international acquiescence for unification on their own terms. It is for this reason that the deterrence afforded by the U.S. presence is considered so vital: It raises the costs and reduces the possibility of success for any such lightning strike.

The north Koreans have launched thousands of infiltration operations against the south since 1945, across the 38th parallel southward through the T'aebaek mountain range, and along the seacoast. Highly trained north Korean special warfare troops continue armed infiltrations into the south; some of these are detected and many probably are not. Such operations are aimed at disturbing authority and public order, planting long-term agents for subversion and espionage, and promoting uprisings. These objectives are consistent with the apparent north Korean belief that the south Korean people are against their own government and would, if offered the chance, overthrow it in favor of unification with the north. Should such an uprising occur, in this view, the north Korean armed forces could legitimately support it.

Most notorious among the many north Korean forays against south Korea (aside from the 1976 ax murders of two U.S. Army officers in the Joint Security Area) were the attempted assassination of the president in January 1968 and the landing of 120 provocateurs on the eastern seacoast in October 1968. These and

TABLE 7.1 Comparative Military Strength and Equipment of North and South Korea, 1990 (including U.S. forces deployed in Korea)

	North Korea	South Korea	United States
Personnel			
Ground force	930,000	575,000	·27,000
Air	70,000	40,000	10,000
Naval	40,000	35,000	300
Reserves	5,000,000	4,740,000	0
Weapons and Equipment			
Tanks	3,500	1,560	150
Armored personnel carriers	1,960	1,550	100
Field artillery pieces	7,800	4,200	160
Multiple rocket launchers	2,500	140	N/A
Mortars	11,000	5,300	N/A
Surface-to-surface missiles	12	70	N/A
Total Aircraft	1,352	940	N/A
Fighters	850	503	100+
Bombers	80	0	0
Transport aircraft	280	37	N/A
Helicopters	142	435	N/A
Total Ships	560	189	0
Destroyers	0	11	0
Patrol frigates	6	17	
Amphibious craft	125	52	
Missile attack (or patrol) boats	11	29	
Patrol ships/boats	330	68	
Submarines	24	0	
Torpedo boats	175	0	
Midget submarines	24	3	
Mine warfare vessels	40	9	
Auxiliary ships	N/A	20	
Naval aircraft	N/A	10	

SOURCE: Andrea Matles Savada and William R. Shaw, *South Korea: A Country Study*, 4th ed. (Washington, D.C., U.S. Government Printing Office, 1992), pp. 343–345.

other attempts have so far been unsuccessful because of the effectiveness of the south Korean security forces and the alertness of the south Korean population, very few of whom have been willing to cooperate with northern agents.

Armed Forces

The core of the national security establishment of the Republic of Korea consists of 650,000 full-time military personnel in three uniformed services—each commanded by its own chief of staff—and a chairman of the Joint Chiefs of Staff as coordinator, under the Ministry of National Defense.[3] The president is commander-in-chief of the armed forces; he is advised by a National Security Council consisting of himself, the prime minister, the deputy prime minister, the ministers of foreign affairs, national defense, home affairs, and finance, and the director of the Agency for National Security Planning (the national intelligence agency).

The Army, by far the most important of the three services, consists of three armies and the Capital Defense Command, over twenty-one regular divisions (including two mechanized divisions), eight reserve divisions (each of which has a professional cadre), and various specialized units, including Special Forces. (There are also two Marine Corps divisions.) The First and Third Armies have frontline defense responsibilities, on the east and west respectively; the Second Army is for training, logistics, and rear-area defense. Several Korean Army divisions are assigned to the Combined ROK-U.S. Field Army, which guards the principal invasion corridor. South Korean ground forces are equipped with M-48 tanks, armored personnel carriers, artillery, missiles, and helicopters; their strength and armament are numerically less than those of north Korea, although both the quantity and the quality of equipment are increasing. Table 7.1 contains statistics on strength and equipment as of 1990; there have not been major changes since then.

The primary Air Force missions are close combat support for the Army and defense against enemy aircraft and submarines. The Air Force has a strength of about 40,000, organized into three commands for combat, logistics, and training. The ROK Air Force combat capability is integrated with that of the U.S. Air Force in the Air Component Command of the Combined Forces Command. Korean aircraft include over 500 tactical fighters, among them 36 F-16s, 294 F-5's (being produced in Korea) and 130 F-4s. Armament includes Sidewinder and Sparrow air-to-air missiles and Maverick antisubmarine missiles. The Air Force, with over 100 squadrons, also has cargo aircraft, trainers, and combat helicopters.

The Navy is responsible for coastal defense, particularly the countering of north Korean maritime infiltration. Its 35,000 personnel are divided almost equally between sea operations and the two divisions plus one brigade of the Marine Corps. There are naval reserves of 25,000 and Marine reserves of 24,000 (one division and two brigades). There is a total of 189 ships, ranging in size from destroyers to patrol ships (see Table 7.1).

The Republic has universal conscription of males from eighteen to thirty years old, who serve twenty-four to thirty months in the Army or volunteer for three years in any of the three services. College students are required to undergo military training, whether or not they participate in the reserve officers' training program.

Upon completion of military service, men enter reserve status in the Homeland Reserve Forces, with periodic call-up and training until they are thirty-five. There are eight reserve divisions, with field grade positions held by regular army officers. Since the reserves were trimmed and reorganized to make best use of the fittest and best-trained manpower, they have shrunk from nearly 3 million to 1,240,000. Supplementing these is a paramilitary Civil Defense Corps, in existence since 1975 in all communities and places of employment to protect lives and property in case of disaster or attack. Under the jurisdiction of the Ministry of Home Affairs, it has about 3.5 million members. South Korean military manpower thus is close to 5 million: 650,000 on active duty, 1,240,000 in the ready reserves, and 3.5 million in the Civil Defense Corps, a total figure roughly comparable to the manpower available in the north.

Other Security Agencies. Internal security in peacetime is the responsibility of the Ministries of Home Affairs and Justice and the Agency for National Security Planning (ANSP). In addition to the ANSP, security forces include the National Police (including the combat police), prosecutors in the Ministry of Justice, and their investigative staff (judicial police). The Defense Ministry's Defense Security Command has internal security responsibilities that extend beyond those of the armed forces. The president has a security force directly responsible to him for protection of his person and office.

United Nations Command, Combined Forces Command, and U.S. Forces Korea

Until 1994, about 40 percent of all uniformed military forces of the Republic of Korea were under the "operational control" of the senior U.S. military commander in Korea, as Commander-in-Chief of the Combined Forces Command (CFC). Most but not all south Korean combat units north of the Han River were therefore subject to American command in wartime, and their deployment in peacetime was a matter of direct concern to the American commander. This remarkable cession of sovereignty was an outgrowth of the military situation in Korea and promised useful efficiencies in case of attack, but it created increasing political problems for the U.S.–south Korean alliance, especially after 1980, when it became the crux of the accusation by many Koreans that the United States had participated in the decision to let the ROK Army use deadly force against civilians during the Kwangju uprising in May of that year.

Although the American military commander-in-chief has ceded "operational control" of all south Korean forces back to their government, he continues to be the linchpin of the military arrangements south of the DMZ. He is concurrently Commander in-Chief of the United Nations Command (CINC/UNC), Commander-in-Chief of the U.S.-ROK Combined Forces Command (CINC/CFC), Commander-in-Chief of United States Forces Korea (CINC/USFK), and Commanding General of the United States Eighth Army (CG/EUSA), the ground component of USFK.

The United Nations Command was established pursuant to a United Nations Security Council resolution in July 1950. The resolution invited UN members to contribute forces to help repel north Korean aggression and established an umbrella organization for such forces. The United States was made executive agent. A U.S. military officer (initially, General Douglas MacArthur) therefore became Commander-in-Chief of the UNC. Sixteen UN member nations, including the United States, contributed forces. The Republic of Korea itself was not a member of the United Nations; but Korea's President Rhee, by a letter of July 14, 1950, gave operational control of ROK forces to General MacArthur. This arrangement was confirmed in an annex to the ROK-U.S. Mutual Defense Treaty of 1953 (ratified in 1954). However, the non-U.S. UN presence rapidly dwindled after the Armistice and by the early 1970s consisted of a symbolic Honor Guard with members from the Republic of Korea, Philippines, Thailand, United Kingdom, and United States. (Representatives of these countries, plus Australia, Canada, France, and New Zealand, were members of the United Nations side of the Military Armistice Commission in 1986. The other original contributor nations were Belgium, Colombia, Ethiopia, Greece, Luxembourg, Netherlands, Turkey, and South Africa.)

The only current responsibility of the UNC since 1979 has been to maintain the Armistice Agreement, a function whose significance has diminished over time to one of mere symbolism. The original Armistice Agreement was designed to be enforced by a Military Armistice Commission (MAC) composed of five representatives from each side (the United Nations Command and the Korean People's Army/Chinese People's Volunteers), a secretary for each side, and staff. Since the Republic of Korea under President Syngman Rhee refused to sign the Armistice Agreement, the United Nations delegation was always headed by an American officer, with a south Korean present as an observer. This unfortunate arrangement enabled the north Koreans to point out to their evident satisfaction that the south Koreans were subject to American leadership during negotiations at the truce village of Panmunjom. It was one of many awkward aspects of the armistice arrangement. By 1989, the MAC had held nearly 500 plenary meetings, most of which were without substance; most MAC business was (and still is) is done at staff level.

The Armistice Agreement also provided for a Neutral Nations Supervisory Commission (NNSC) to oversee compliance with troop and equipment limitations, but less than two years after the Armistice the NNSC was reduced to a largely symbolic status since it was powerless to enforce compliance or even to verify the extent of the violations, as both sides were involved in an obvious arms race. Yet for nearly forty years, NNSC representatives from Czechoslovakia, Poland, Sweden, and Switzerland were maintained on the scene as NNSC representatives making occasional trips to Seoul or Pyongyang to carry out observations.

Today, the Panmunjom truce village site still reverberates with the consequences of the Korean War. Located in the middle of a jointly maintained Joint Security Area in the Demilitarized Zone almost within sight of the north Korean city of Kaesong, it functions for much of the time as a tourist destination. For many years the two sides met to discuss violations of the armistice and other issues in a temporary building that straddled the demarcation line between north and south Korea. Over the years the Panmunjom site has seen many dramatic episodes: the signing of the Armistice in 1953, the return of the crew of the USS *Pueblo* in 1968, the brutal murder of two U.S. officers on a tree-trimming detail in 1976, and the transit of former President Jimmy Carter in 1994 as he went to visit Kim Il-sung during the last days of Kim's life. However, the course of north-south contacts has passed Panmunjom by. Since the south Koreans were not a party to the Armistice, north-south talks had to take place in another venue. In the 1970s they took place between Red Cross delegations. In 1990 they took place between prime ministers. In the mid-1990s north-south contacts take place all over the world in informal and semiformal settings. The Military Armistice Commission talks at Panmunjom, meanwhile, lost their usefulness when in 1990 the UN side assigned a south Korean officer to represent the UNC for the first time and the north Koreans refused to come to the table to deal with a party that had not signed the Armistice Agreement. That refusal continues to be one element in the ongoing north Korean campaign to deal with the United States separately from south Korea.

After the Korean War and the gradual withdrawal of most of the United Nations forces, the United Nations Command became less useful as an umbrella for operational control of south Korean armed forces. For one thing, it gave insufficient recognition to the preponderance of ROK military power in the defense of the south, a preponderance that increased when the United States withdrew one of its two remaining Army divisions in 1971. Accordingly, the Republic of Korea and the United States agreed to establish a Combined Forces Command, comprising the combat forces of both countries, with a U.S. general as commander and a Korean as deputy (both of four-star rank). Established in 1978 as a means of carrying out the Mutual Defense Treaty of 1953, this is the mechanism through which "operational control" was exercised by an American over the essential defense forces of south Korea until 1994.

The controversy over operational control arose in the 1980s in the aftermath of the Kwangju uprising, when it was charged that General John A. Wickham, in his capacity as commander-in-chief of the Combined Forces Command (CINC/CFC) had been in control of ROK Army units that were used to suppress the popular rebellion. There were two attacks on the demonstrators, one on May 18 by special warfare commandos from units not included in the Combined Forces Command and therefore not under General Wickham's operational control. On May 27, however, elements of the ROK Twentieth Division were sent into Kwangju to restore central government control. These units were specifically withdrawn from CFC control for the purpose by the south Korean government on its own initiative in keeping with provisions of the CFC agreement. The question was whether General Wickham could have, or should have, refused to allow the troops to be used in suppressing the uprising. One point of view says that the American commander could not have interfered with the sovereign exercise of powers by the Seoul government. Another point of view says that General Wickham lost an important opportunity to restrain the south Korean army and to prevent further bloodshed. The passage of time has not cooled the passions on either side of this debate.[4]

The Combined Forces Command has three major subordinate commands for ground, air, and naval components. The commander-in-chief of the CFC is concurrently commander of the ground component; the air component is commanded by a U.S. Air Force lieutenant general. The naval component is commanded by a Korean Navy vice admiral. Two additional components are the Combined Unconventional Warfare Task Force and Marine Forces Korea. The whole question of command and control arrangements as they affect the U.S. presence and authority has been a topic of joint U.S.-Korean review in response to growing Korean sentiment for a controlling role in its own security and the deployment of its forces.

The main U.S. ground combat force in Korea is an infantry division (as of 1995, the Second Division), with an authorized strength of about 17,000; about 2,500 of its positions are filled by Korean soldiers as Korean Augmentation to the U.S. Army (KATUSA). The U.S. division is encamped a few miles behind the front line as reserve force for the Combined ROK-U.S. Field Army that defends the sector of the Demilitarized Zone that faces the traditional principal north-south invasion corridor. The Field Army is commanded by a U.S. lieutenant general, with a Korean Army deputy. The division's weapons and equipment, considerably more sophisticated than those of the Korean forces, are summarized in Table 7.1.

Other U.S. forces in Korea include six squadrons of fighter aircraft in the Seventh Air Force, and a variety of special combat and logistical units. There are no U.S. naval forces committed to the CFC, but there is a naval liaison unit at CFC headquarters. Joint Korean-U.S. military maneuvers are conducted from time to time to assure the effectiveness of U.S. support. Since the mid-1970s, there has been an annual exercise in the early spring called "Team Spirit," which in the mid-1980s typically involved over 200,000 military personnel from both countries in simulated defense against northern attack. "Team Spirit" exercises typically involve large movements of personnel and material by air from the U.S. and elsewhere in the Pacific, amphibious landings, and combined U.S.–south Korean exercises on the ground, all of a type that would be employed in any war with north Korea. As part of the effort to ease tensions on the peninsula, the ROK-U.S. side has canceled or scaled back "Team Spirit" in recent years, making it a bargaining chip in talks with north Korea. This has not entirely satisfied the north, especially since smaller-scale exercises have continued; nor has it been good for the readiness of the Combined Forces Command, which benefits from the training.

Although official ROK government policy continues to call for indefinite and undiminished presence of U.S. forces until the south's own armed forces have clearly established parity with the north (seemingly an ever-retreating goal), there are significant arguments for change. North Korean demands for removal of all U.S. forces, on the grounds that U.S. forces are an obstruction to national reunification, are echoed by some people in the south. In the United States, budgetary problems lead to calls for reduction of U.S. forces, or at least for a greater Korean contribution to their support. (In 1993, direct and indirect ROK support of U.S. forces, including the value of occupied real estate, was estimated at over US$2 billion.) Growing south Korean military and economic power leads some analysts to question the justification for continued U.S. troop presence. In 1990 and 1991 the United States withdrew over 2,000 noncombatant military personnel. Combat strength, however, was unaffected.

Joint ROK-U.S. security responsibilities are coordinated in the annual Security Consultative Meeting (SCM), specified in the Mutual Defense Treaty of 1953. The ROK minister of defense and U.S. secretary of defense head the two delegations, meeting alternately in Seoul and Washington. Under the SCM is a Military Committee, headed by the two chairmen of the respective Joint Chiefs of Staff, which meets in plenary session once a year in conjunction with the SCM, and at other times when necessary; it has daily oversight authority on matters of ROK-U.S. defense relations.

The rights and responsibilities of U.S. military personnel in Korea and of the U.S. civilians who support them are specified in a Status of Forces Agreement (SOFA) signed in 1965. Under the Agreement, many offenses committed by U.S. personnel while on official duty are acted on by U.S. authorities, and Korean authorities may transfer American suspects to U.S. jurisdiction. Serious crimes committed by U.S. personnel, however, are judged in Korean courts. Other matters covered by the Agreement include customs procedures, tax exemptions, vehicles, property, and local employee relations. Problems arising under the Agreement are handled by a joint committee of representatives of the Korean government and U.S. Forces Korea; but in recent years this body has had to meet only three or four times a year, since problems have been relatively few. Legal matters are handled between the Korean Ministry of Justice and the USFK Judge Advocate General. In 1990 the SOFA was modified to give the Korean side more latitude in the arrest and prosecution of American personnel charged with crimes in the Republic of Korea.

Foreign Economic Policy

South Korea's continued economic progress depends heavily on the international environment. Imports and exports each amount to about one-fifth of the gross national product; exports have risen steadily since the beginning of the Korean export-led economic takeoff in the 1960s (at current prices, from US$30 million in 1960 to $82.2 billion in 1993). Since the country is densely populated and lacking in most essential natural resources, it depends upon imports, which must be paid for through export. Such vital materials as oil, coal, iron ore, and aluminum must be wholly or largely imported. Imports make up the grain deficit.

As Korea enters the ranks of industrialized nations, it must import technology and know-how to be competitive in high-technology production. Its past industrial growth has been based largely on foreign capital borrowing, repayment and interest for which must come from export earnings; and the need for foreign sources of capital will continue. Korea also needs export markets to meet its own people's expectations as well, because it can produce better goods more cheaply when markets abroad increase the volume of its production beyond domestic demand. Moreover, a rising standard of living brings greater demand for import of goods not made in Korea. All of these factors make the Korean domestic economy highly vulnerable to international fluctuations.

Continued economic growth is an essential element in political stability. Because the government of the Republic has twice been taken over by military leaders on the basis of force rather than constitutional process, its popular legitimacy is weak. The principal basis for its acceptance is its demonstrated capacity to meet the material needs and aspirations of the people. Moreover, economic growth is essential in order to absorb the large numbers of young people coming into the labor market each year, including ever-increasing numbers of women who want jobs outside the home.

South Korea therefore has a large stake in maintaining an international climate favorable to its trade and investment. But this stake is increasingly hard to defend. Protectionist barriers are mounting in the industrialized countries that have been the nation's principal financial supporters and trading partners, especially the United States and Japan. Moreover, the Korean government confronts domestic protectionist pressures of its own as it seeks to respond to international demands for better access. It also confronts nationalistic demands for reducing what a radical minority perceives to be U.S. neo-imperialist domination of the Korean economy.

South Korean foreign economic policy in the mid-1990s contains the following elements:

- vigorous promotion of Korean products and services abroad, by both officials and private traders, coupled with emphasis on quality and cost controls;
- diplomatic initiatives against protectionist policies and actions of other countries, including support of international free-trade agreements and practices and the hiring of professional lobbyists in the United States to explain Korea's case to American government officials and legislators;
- gradual liberalization of foreign access to Korean markets for goods and services and extension of legal protection on such items as intellectual property and electronic software;
- participation in multinational commodity agreements;
- renewed attention to import substitution in areas such as machine parts that are now well within Korean industrial competence;
- promotion of high-technology export industries as a means of sustaining exports;
- induction of foreign capital investment and technology through joint ventures and, in selected cases, foreign-owned firms;

- negotiation of foreign investment loans from governments, international organizations, and banks, on the most favorable terms possible, both for continued economic expansion and for management of the existing foreign debt portfolio;
- continued controls on wage levels to hold production costs down;
- promotion of new and expanded markets in Europe, the Third World, China, the ASEAN countries, and the Americas;
- special tax and financial assistance to exporters with a proven record (a past practice that is being phased out).

As noted in Chapter 6, until 1994 the Economic Planning Board (EPB) was the central economic policymaking and coordinating organ. With the merging of the EPB and the Finance Ministry into the Board of Finance and Economics (BFE) the domestic and foreign spheres of the Korean economy were redefined and separated. Negotiations with foreign countries on trade matters are the business of the reorganized Ministry of Trade and Industry. The other ministries, including the BFE, play supporting roles.

In the case of the United States, Japan, and some other countries, there are annual joint meetings of economic ministers as well as negotiations on specific problems. The Republic of Korea is represented in the World Bank, the International Monetary Fund, and other international organizations, including the General Agreement on Tariffs and Trade (GATT) and its successor organization, the World Trade Organization (WTO). Korean diplomatic establishments overseas have attachés specializing in commerce, finance, and agriculture, drawn from the corresponding ministries.

Government activities are complemented by business groups, particularly the Korean Traders' Association (composed of selected large Korean trading firms). A Korea–United States Economic Council has both Korean and U.S. firms as members; similar organizations exist for other countries. These and other groups work closely with the Korean government in promoting effective international trade relations.

General Diplomacy

South Korea's quest for international recognition supports its security and economic concerns. Beyond those concerns the Republic is in continuing competition with north Korea for legitimacy as representative of the 66 million Korean people; for promoting its own approach to national reunification; and for enhancement of national prestige.

The United States. The United States remains the central concern of Korean diplomacy because of the U.S. role in Korean national security and its importance as a market and source of investment capital. Korea seeks to maximize U.S. support for the retention of U.S. troops in Korea and for favorable terms and allocations on armaments sales. The Republic also endeavors to hold down U.S. protectionist moves against Korean exports. For historical reasons the Republic wants to avoid dependence on Japan and to avoid Japanese economic or other manipulation, and it needs the United States as counterweight.

Beyond these considerations, the United States is of great importance to the Korean self-image. Despite growing anti-American feeling among a minority of Korean intellectuals and students, the United States continues to be a cultural and political model. Although the Republic is becoming increasingly self-confident and independent in the conduct of its foreign affairs, some vestige of the old rela-' tionship with China still clings to the relationship with the United States.

It should be recalled that during the administration of President Rhee (1948–1960), Korea's foreign policy was almost exclusively concerned with maximizing its benefits through its special relationship with the United States. The United States was the Republic's principal source of international support—diplomatic, economic, and military; concessionary economic assistance continued into the 1970s (although most grant aid ceased in 1968); and a U.S. presence is still integral to the Republic's defense. Korean concern over the possible loss of American security support, and sensitivity to American criticism of the Korean domestic political situation, led to the so-called Koreagate crisis of the mid-1970s, involving Korean attempts to influence members of the U.S. Congress by favors and cash payments.[5]

American official views and public opinions are given great attention in Korea, and the amount of influence over Korean domestic affairs commonly attributed to the United States is far out of proportion to reality. Such misperceptions can lead Korean politicians to try to mobilize this or that segment of U.S. opinion for their cause, neglecting the political realities of Korean-U.S. relations. Such attempts create difficulties for the overall bilateral relationship. Alternatively, Korean dissidents can blame the United States for domestic political problems.

In formal terms, the Republic of Korea is linked with the United States by a Mutual Defense Treaty, signed in 1953 and ratified the following year; a Treaty of Friendship, Commerce, and Navigation, concluded in 1956; and numerous other treaties and agreements on specific aspects of Korean-U.S. relations. As of the mid-1990s, there were annual bilateral conferences at cabinet level on security, on economic and trade matters, and on foreign relations. Each state is represented by a large embassy in the other's capital.

Japan. The Republic's relations with Japan are based on necessity rather than choice. Japan is a traditional enemy, and the emotions created by forty years of harsh occupation still affect the two countries' relations. However, Japan is a permanent neighbor and has been an important member of the non-Communist world, and Japan's support for the Korean cause is important. The forty-year Japanese administration left a legacy of Japanese methods, equipment, and trade ties that still favor Japan as a market (despite Japanese restrictions and a severely adverse trade balance) and as a source of investment, know-how, and equipment. Japanese capital, in particular, has been important for Korea's economic development as U.S. aid was phased out. For these reasons, after many years of negotiations south Korea normalized its relations with Japan in the Korea-Japan Basic Treaty of 1965, despite popular outcry and demonstrations in both countries. Annexed agreements cover specific aspects of relations such as fishing rights and the special status of the 700,000 Korean residents in Japan. Each state established an embassy in the other's capital.

Since normalization, relations between the two countries have fluctuated between near-cordiality and distrust. A low point was the abduction of south Korean opposition leader Kim Dae-jung by south Korean security agents from his room in a Tokyo hotel in 1973, an act that caused great outrage among Japanese press and public. In contrast, in 1983, Japan responded to Korean requests for assistance by pledging US$4 billion in government and private credits for Korean economic growth. In 1984, south Korean President Chun Doo-hwan made a state visit to Japan, calling on both emperor and prime minister and receiving expressions of regret for the Japanese occupation of Korea. Treatment of the Korean minority of 700,000 in Japan has caused diplomatic problems between the two countries— most recently over the Japanese policy of fingerprinting aliens. The continuing trade imbalance is a source of controversy. Nonetheless, the long-term trend is toward improvement of relations that have been advantageous to both sides.

A continuing source of difficulty is Japanese policy toward north Korea: Although Japan does not recognize the Democratic People's Republic of Korea, it permits private economic and social contacts of considerable magnitude, such as the emigration of 100,000 Korean residents in Japan to north Korea under Red Cross auspices beginning in 1959 (a flow that practically ceased within a very few years) and the conclusion of a fishing agreement between Japanese and north Korean "private" groups.

Relations with Communist Countries.   Syngman Rhee's rigid anticommunism, which was enthusiastically supported by the United States and reinforced by the Korean War, prevented any contact with Communist states during his presidency. Those states, which supported the north Korean regime, thoroughly reciprocated Rhee's hostility. Anticommunism remained a basic element of south Korean foreign policy for a decade after Rhee's departure.

The shift in the international power balance during the 1960s and 1970s, highlighted by the Vietnam War, the U.S. opening to China, U.S. détente with the Soviet Union, and north Korea's growing acceptance on the international scene, led President Park to explore contacts with the Soviet Union and other members of the Communist bloc and to suggest the idea of cross-recognition—that south Korea's allies might recognize north Korea if north Korea's allies would recognize the south.

Contacts with the Soviet Union remained tenuous until the mid-1980s. China, however, decided in 1983 to let middle-level officials negotiate with south Korean authorities on the return of a Chinese airliner, and later on the return of a Chinese ship, both hijacked to Korea. Exchanges of visits followed as well as steadily increasing trade—mostly through Hong Kong, but some directly between China and south Korea (see Chapter 6). China's participation in the 1986 Asian Games in Seoul and in the 1988 Olympics was further evidence of growing relations. Soviet representatives participated in the pre-Olympic conference of national committees in Seoul in 1986, and delegates of each nation were permitted to attend conferences in each other's capital. Both China and the Soviet Union, however, continued to support north Korea's positions on north-south relations.

The success of the Olympic Games added to south Korea's economic progress, and its increased effort to improve relations with Communist countries (an effort known in Korea as *nordpolitik*, a paraphrase of West German Premier Willy Brandt's *ostpolitik* of the 1970s) seems to have convinced the Soviet Union as well as China of south Korea's importance. Resident trade missions were exchanged with the Soviet Union; there was talk of south Korean participation in developing eastern Siberia; Kim Young-sam visited Moscow in mid-1988 as an opposition leader and again in early 1990 as a leader of the newly merged Democratic Liberal Party.

The year 1990 was a watershed year in south Korean diplomacy, for *nordpolitik* paid dividends beyond south Korea's wildest imagination. In June, President Roh Tae-woo journeyed to San Francisco to meet briefly with Mikhail Gorbachev, and in September the Soviet Union recognized south Korea, paving the way for Korean economic assistance and investment in Siberia. By this stroke the Roh government was able to defeat the scheme of cross-recognition: He had achieved it without conceding Japanese or American recognition to north Korea. Relations between north Korea and the Soviet Union turned frosty: Their military treaty was broken, and post-Soviet Russia began to demand cash for their exports to north Korea instead of letting Pyongyang pay for them with commodities or north Korean currency.

South Korea's opening toward China moved more slowly, complicated by Seoul's diplomatic ties with Taiwan. Trade, however, blossomed, with south Korean exports to "Greater China" running at US$10 billion by 1992 and $16 billion with the People's Republic of China alone in 1995. In 1991 China dropped its opposition to south Korean membership in the United Nations, and in August 1992, after a symbolic break between south Korea and Taiwan, Beijing "normalized" relations with Seoul and recognized the Republic of Korea.

South Korea's motives in pursuing relations with the former Communist world went beyond the desire to squeeze north Korea. With portentous changes in the world trade environment—notably the rise of the European Economic Community (EEC) and the North American Free Trade Agreement (NAFTA), Koreans were anxious to diversify their markets and find new trading partners. They found willing negotiators in China and southeast Asia, where Korean technology was particularly suited to the stage of development and market conditions. Even in Vietnam, where Korea fought alongside the United States against the Ho Chi Minh regime, Koreans found fertile possibilities for investments and profits.

The United Nations.   The United Nations, once of great significance in the Republic's international affairs, has receded in importance over the years. The Republic came into being through elections observed by a United Nations commission in May 1948 and was recognized as the only duly constituted government in (not of) the peninsula by a UN General Assembly resolution in January 1949.[6] UN Security Council resolutions called for assistance to the Republic in defending against north Korean attack in 1950 and established the United Nations Command to lead the defense. UN commissions, composed of seven UN member nations, resided in Seoul from 1948 until 1973. From 1950, the group was known as the United Nations Commission for the Unification and Rehabilitation of Korea (UNCURK). Although the UN representatives could do nothing to further the cause of reunification, they regularly observed south Korean elections and political developments and reported annually to the UN General Assembly.[7]

For several years after the Korean War, the United Nations was the principal forum for international concern with the peninsula. The "Korean question" was debated annually until 1975, and until that year resulted in General Assembly resolutions favoring the south. North Korea accordingly sought to undermine international support of the south and to increase its own. As many new countries with radical and anti-imperialist attitudes gained their independence, the north made considerable headway among them for recognition. Beginning with the World Health Organization in 1973, the Democratic People's Republic of Korea was admitted to most of the UN specialized organizations and gained UN observer status on a par with the Republic of Korea. In 1973, UNCURK was abolished. In 1975, two conflicting UN resolutions were passed favoring each of the Koreas, one of them calling for the withdrawal of U.S. troops. After that there was no further UN debate on the "Korean question."

Both Korean states applied for UN membership in the early post–World War II years, but the applications failed because of U.S. and Soviet objections in the Security Council. North Korea publicly opposed membership for either Seoul or Pyongyang on the grounds that if either or both existing regimes joined the United Nations it would institutionalize the country's division. South Korea, on the other hand, advocated simultaneous admission of both states as a step toward unification, to create a contact point for the two regimes in New York. The issue was settled when first the Soviet Union and then the People's Republic of China dropped their opposition to south Korean membership in the UN in 1991, and north Korea was obliged to join in order to keep up. Both governments are now full members of the UN representing the ROK and the DPRK.

The Republic of Korea is a member of all United Nations specialized agencies. It is a member of the World Bank and International Monetary Fund (IMF) (whose annual meeting it hosted in 1985). It participates in the Asian Development Bank. After admission to full membership in the UN, south Korea expanded its participation by becoming vice president of the Economic and Social Council in 1993 and a member of the Security Council in 1995.

Other Countries.   Since the end of the Rhee regime in 1960, south Korea has increasingly turned its attention to the world as a whole to diversify its markets and its sources of security and support. Its major targets are Western Europe, the Middle East, and the Pacific Basin, but it also promotes relations with the Third World generally. On the basis of its remarkable record of economic progress and through its diplomatic skills, the Republic has gained formal recognition from 130 states of a total of about 165 in the world (compared with 103 for north Korea) as of 1995. The attempted assassination of President Chun in Rangoon in 1983 gave the country a boost in the competition for recognition, since Burma, a nation with impeccable nonaligned credentials, officially found north Korea responsible for the act. South Korea maintains resident embassies in over 80 states and hosts resident embassies of more than 50 states in Seoul.[8]

A number of major international conferences have been held in Seoul, including that of the Interparliamentary Union (IPU) in 1983—a meeting that north Korea exerted great but unsuccessful effort to move elsewhere. In 1985, the Republic successfully hosted the large annual conclave of the World Bank and International Monetary Fund, as noted earlier. In 1989, the Republic hosted the annual world convention of Rotary International, a major service organization for businesspeople with over 22,000 clubs and 1 million members in 160 countries. Of these, over 30,000 members attended the convention. Biggest of all have been sporting events, particularly the Asian Games in 1986 and the Summer Olympics in 1988. The Olympics brought teams from 160 countries and a quarter million participants and visitors. For a people who long had resented the *M*A*S*H* syndrome, by which Korea was portrayed as late as the 1980s as a war-torn, poverty-ridden country, it was a matter of great satisfaction to show the world that theirs was a rapidly advancing economic power. By 1990 the *M*A*S*H* syndrome had given way to images of steel mills, automobiles, and consumer electronics.

Relations with Third World countries have also been promoted through modest technical assistance programs—some of them centered on south Korea's New Community Movement—and provision of doctors and nurses. In 1985, for example, south Korea invited ninety-three farming experts from thirty-six countries for training in rice farming, silk culture, farm machinery, and rural extension programs. In the early 1990s, the government started sending Korea Overseas Volunteers (KOVs) abroad to work in developing countries in Peace Corps–type assignments teaching construction skills, veterinary medicine, and the Korean language.

Foreign Relations of the Democratic People's Republic of Korea (North Korea)

Security Policy

The Threat.   North Korea's official view of its security situation is a bleak one. In this view, expressed almost daily in domestic and foreign propaganda, a triangular alliance of the United States, Japan, and south Korea is conspiring to repeat what north Korea claims to have been the aggression of 1950 against the peace-loving people of the Democratic Republic. (The DPRK still maintains that the United States and south Korea started the Korean War and that the north Korean attack was a defensive action.) North Korea therefore holds that it must maintain a high state of readiness to repel this aggression. At the same time, the north repeatedly asserts its commitment to peaceful means of reunification.

In normal times, allegations of American and south Korean aggressive schemes, and of what north Korea terms the U.S.–Japan–south Korea triangular alliance, reach a crescendo during joint U.S.-ROK military maneuvers. When the Military Armistice Commission was having more-or-less regular meetings at Panmunjom, the north Koreans often used the MAC forum to level charges against the American imperialists and their south Korean lackeys for everything from espionage to nuclear blackmail. The defensive theme of north Korean propaganda is constant and focuses on several objectives: the rousing of the south Korean people against their government, the demand for withdrawal of American troops from south Korea, the glorification of Kim Il-sung, and now Kim Jong-il, as the legitimate leader of the fatherland, and historical reinterpretations that hold that the south started the Korean War, and that Kim Il-sung defeated the Japanese in 1945. Liberation of the south is a favorite theme: Usually the north Koreans disavow any intention to attack, but they urge the south Koreans to liberate themselves.

Military Buildup.   In 1962, as the Soviet Union was withdrawing its support, north Korea decided to give equal emphasis to military buildup and economic development. The delay in achieving the targets of the First Seven-Year Plan (1961–1967) was publicly attributed to this policy. Nevertheless, 20 percent of the national product (even more, according to some calculations) continues to go to defense. More than the south, north Korea has built up its armaments industry for self-sufficiency. This industry is believed to be capable of supplying most of north Korea's weapons needs except for highly sophisticated systems and high-performance aircraft that it purchases from the Soviet Union. In the mid-1970s south Korean and U.S. intelligence established that north Korea had also greatly increased the numbers of its regular military forces. These estimates were again raised in recent years, notwithstanding north Korea's claim to have demobilized 100,000 troops. The official estimate in 1992 was 1,040,000.[9]

The DPRK has done a booming business in supplying weaponry, along with military training and advice, to Third World countries and national liberation movements. North Korean weapons and advisory or training personnel have been reported in several African and radical Middle Eastern countries—a division of Zimbabwe troops was trained and equipped by north Koreans—and among Tamil separatists in Sri Lanka, for example. North Korea reportedly was selling considerable quantities of arms to Iran in the 1980s for its war with Iraq.

During the Cold War years, north Korea cultivated relations with its two giant Communist allies, both for support of its military posture and for armament supply. Exchanges of visits by senior military officials with China were frequent. The Soviet Union was the main source of advanced weaponry, since north Korea's industry was probably ahead of China's in most fields at the time.

North Korea's pattern of dependence on the Soviet Union, however, was modified by the falling-out that took place between Kim Il-sung and Soviet leader Nikita Khrushchev in 1962. The Soviets withdrew their advisers and refused to upgrade north Korean armaments for a time. Relations improved in the 1980s, especially after the visit of Kim Il-sung to the Soviet Union in 1984. The Soviets started supplying MiG-23 aircraft the following year. In return, they enjoyed overflight rights and gained access to north Korean ports for naval use. This era of good feeling ended during the Gorbachev era, when the Soviet Union began dealing with south Korea. The Pyongyang-Moscow military alliance was a casualty of the Soviet recognition of south Korea. As of 1996 north Korea's only military ally is China, and its stance in any future outbreak of hostilities on the Korean peninsula doubtless would depend on the circumstances.

Armed Forces

Since north Korea's total population is about one-half that of the south, the million-plus men under arms represents a massive human commitment to military readiness—about 4 percent of the people. Another 2 percent are in the ready reserve forces, and 11 percent in the Worker and Peasant Red Guard, a paramilitary force that corresponds to the south's Civil Defense Corps. North Korea claimed in 1988 that 100,000 soldiers had been demobilized and 150,000 assigned to civil construction. There are signs that the north Korean armed forces sometimes do work that is not strictly military; that is, like the People's Liberation Army in China, they sometimes serve as a disciplined labor force for public works projects. Hence visitors reported seeing uniformed military crews working on the Nampo sea barrage in the 1980s.

Unlike south Korea, the DPRK includes naval and air forces within the Korean People's Army (KPA). The KPA is controlled both by the Korean Workers' Party, through its Military Committee (chaired by Kim Jong-il), and by the state, through a Military Commission of the Central People's Committee (also chaired by Kim

Jong-il). The two bodies have overlapping membership; the Minister of the People's Armed Forces, a Marshal of the KPA, is a member of both.

Under a Chief of General Staff, with sixteen functional staff bureaus (including a Political Bureau), there are an estimated eight corps, forty-three divisions (including two tank, three motorized, and three artillery divisions) of about 11,000 personnel each (smaller than south Korean divisions). There are six service arms: missile, armored, artillery, naval, air force, and special forces. The special forces, believed to number as many as 80,000—sometimes estimated to be over 100,000—make frequent forays into south Korea, mostly as individuals and small groups, for intelligence, subversion, and support of revolutionary movements; three of their officers planted the explosives in the Rangoon assassination attempt against President Chun Doo-hwan in 1983. As in other north Korean government organizations, there is a parallel hierarchy of Party committees and officials in military units at all levels, which oversees ideological training and propaganda. Twenty percent of platoon members are Korean Workers' Party members; the rest are members of the Socialist Working Youth League.

The Army Ready Reserve consists of 260,000 persons—army veterans less than thirty-five years old—in twenty-three divisions, which could be mobilized within a month. A Workers' and Peasants' Red Militia of 1.5 million consists of men eighteen to forty and women eighteen to thirty years old who are not otherwise committed to security functions, including students. Organized territorially and by workplace, they receive 200 hours of training per year. The 700,000 Red Youth Guards include high-school students over fourteen. Army conscription begins at age sixteen.[10]

Major items of north Korean weapons and equipment, as estimated by Western sources in 1992, are listed in Table 7.1. As noted earlier in the discussion of the security threat to south Korea, the north is far superior in quantitative terms (more and better tanks, twice the quantity of artillery, several times the number of anti-aircraft weapons, nearly twice as many aircraft—including seventy-two Hughes helicopters illegally acquired from the United States), but this superiority is increasingly offset by the qualitative improvement in the south's weapons. Much of the north's weaponry is underground or in concrete revetments.

Foreign Economic Relations

North Korea's foreign economic policy has two basic themes: self-reliance (*juch'e*) and support for economic development. Kim Il-sung often said that necessary trade with nonimperialist countries was consistent with the *juch'e* doctrine, and in his speech to the Sixth Party Congress in 1980 he called for quadrupling foreign trade during the 1980s. However, north Korea's international trade is a much smaller proportion of its national product than is that of south Korea; in 1979, exports and imports each amounted to about 13 percent of national product and by 1990 had only risen to 20.7 percent. The comparable figures for south Korea were more than 30 percent in 1979 and 56.7 percent in 1990.[11] Like south Korea, the north is totally dependent upon outside sources for petroleum. The DPRK obtained much of its oil from the Soviet Union during the Cold War years. In 1990 and 1991 when Russia and then China began to require payment in hard currency for petroleum, north Korea was forced to slash imports and consumption, a fact that some analysts believe has serious military implications as well as economic consequences.

North Korean authorities emphasize to foreign visitors the extent to which its industrial plants and machinery are domestically produced. However, technology and technical assistance from Communist countries have been important in north Korea's rehabilitation and growth. During the 1950s, for example, East Germany contributed supplies, funds, and technical assistance to rebuild the ruined city of Hamhung after the Korean War.[12]

The Soviet Union helped in the construction of a number of plants on an output-sharing basis; in the 1980–1985 period, sixteen projects were completed or in progress on this basis, with the help of teams of Soviet technicians. The Soviets contributed north Korea's first two nuclear reactors. The Chinese assisted in building hydroelectric projects along the Yalu River boundary, from which they also received power. The DPRK joined the United Nations Development Programme (UNDP) in 1979; since then a resident mission has helped in developing ports, railroads, and electronic industry.

In 1972 north Korea undertook an accelerated program of importing Western technology in the form of complete plants from Japan and industrial European countries, to be paid for through loans. That was the year in which senior north Korean officials secretly visited the south in the negotiations that led to the north-south Joint Statement. They may have been concerned by the rapid pace of south Korean progress and thus motivated to turn to the West for improved technology. This strategy backfired because the oil crisis of 1973 hurt the north Korean economy and because the planners miscalculated the difficulties and the time lag in generating exports to pay off the loans. North Korea defaulted on its payments and has been struggling with rescheduling arrangements ever since. Its international credit is therefore poor, and its hard-currency earnings remain low.

As a new approach to the problem of technology transfer, north Korea enacted a joint venture law in 1984 under which foreign enterprises could do business. (China had adopted the same policy some years previously.) There was little Western enthusiasm, however. A more promising concept was the Special Economic Zone (SEZ) planned for the Tumen River area bordering Russia and China. The idea of a special area cordoned off from the rest of the north Korean economy and society, within which foreign investment would create jobs and wealth for the north Korean people and state was attractive to the Kim Il-sung regime in the early 1990s. The UNDP conducted conferences and studies involving north Korea and its neighbors, including south Korea and Japan, to determine the feasibility of creating a Chinese-style SEZ in the northeastern corner of Korea.

The foreseeable benefits were significant; however, the north Korean regime hesitated to commit to a project that would expose large numbers of workers to foreign influence; the neighboring states noted the costs and long-term liabilities of the venture; and by 1995 the project had stalled, in effect, pending stabilization of the situation in north Korea following the death of Kim Il-sung.[13]

General Diplomacy

North Korean foreign policy, like that of the south, aims to maintain the support of its allies and friends for its defense, for its claim to be the only true government of all Korea, and for its position on reunification as well as to gain the widest possible support for its position among all nations. Under Kim Il-sung and now under Kim Jong-il, the DPRK seeks legitimacy and respect, not only to strengthen national security and domestic stability, but also from the elemental desire for world status and prestige.

The Democratic People's Republic of Korea was formally recognized by 103 states in early 1990, two dozen fewer than south Korea. (Reaction to the Rangoon bombing resulted in a reduction from the maximum of 108 that had been reached in 1982.) As was discussed in Chapter 5, the collapse of Communism in Europe, and the fall of the Soviet Union as a Communist state in particular, dealt north Korea's foreign policy a staggering blow. Having already suffered the recognition of south Korea by the government in Moscow, the north Koreans then suffered the recognition of south Korea by their other patron, the People's Republic of China, in 1992. Fearing even deeper isolation, the Pyongyang government abandoned its long-held opposition to separate admission for north and south Korea in the United Nations as well.

During the heyday of the Cold War, the north Koreans enjoyed constant contact with the countries of the socialist bloc. After the Korean War the DPRK had a difficult time establishing legitimacy in the eyes of the non-Communist world and faced little alternative to dependence on the Communist bloc. Although it did not belong to the international Communist economic organization, the Council for Mutual Economic Assistance (CMEA) or the military Warsaw Pact grouping, its defense treaties with the Soviet Union and China were as close and essential as south Korea's treaty with the United States. Thus the dissolution of the Communist governments in Eastern Europe eliminated north Korea's most potent protectors and left it with very little room to maneuver or make mistakes.

However, the history of north Korea's relations, even with its Communist allies, was never entirely smooth. After Kim Il-sung failed in his attempt to unify the Korean peninsula by military means in 1950, it was China, rather than the Soviet Union, that came to the rescue and prevented the extinction of the DPRK as a state. Following the armistice in 1953, north Korea received assistance from both China and the Soviet Union in rebuilding its shattered armed forces and economy. Chinese troops remained in the country until 1958; and in 1961, north

Korea signed treaties with both its allies, which pledged their military support; but then came the Sino-Soviet split.

When the ideological rift opened between Beijing and Moscow, north Korea was forced to play one side against the other. It needed to preserve a modicum of policy independence while maintaining relations and receiving support from both. Kim Il-sung managed this feat with considerable deftness. Though there was a low point of relations between Pyongyang and Moscow during the Khrushchev era (1955–1963), and between Pyongyang and Beijing during the Great Proletarian Cultural Revolution (1966–1971), Kim covered his tightrope act by asserting the Korean doctrine of *juch'e,* which helped him justify a kind of neutrality. One fact that is remarkable, in light of the many face-to-face meetings between successive presidents of south Korea and the United States, is that Kim rarely visited or received the leaders of his biggest Communist allies. Kim Il-sung's 1984 visit to Moscow was his first in twenty years. Soviet Vice Premier Geidar Aliyev's visit to north Korea the following year also came after a long hiatus. Kim visited China only slightly more often. His last visit, in 1992, was to persuade the Chinese to block south Korea's separate admission to the United Nations with their veto in the Security Council. He came away empty-handed.

Relations with Japan.   Japan looms large in north Korea's foreign relations for reasons of history, geopolitics, and economic opportunity. Though there is no treaty and no diplomatic relations between Japan and the DPRK, the large Korean minority in Japan has a strong affinity for north Korea and there is considerable communication and travel between Korean residents in Japan and the DPRK. Korean-owned businesses and individuals in Japan are a prime source of hard currency for the north Korean regime, and Japanese companies trade with north Korea.

In dealing with Japan, the DPRK has the levers of its strategic geographic position, its traditional support from the Japanese Socialist Party and some intellectuals, and the lure of the possibility that one day it could become a major arena for Japanese business activity. The political support from the Socialists was an element in the Japanese opposition's stance against the U.S.-Japan Mutual Security Treaty, which of course was aimed in part against north Korea. Until 1985, the Japanese Socialists did not recognize the legitimacy of the government in south Korea; indeed, a principal stumbling block in the negotiations for normalization of relations between Japan and south Korea in the 1960s was the Socialist contention that the south could not negotiate on behalf of all Korea.

Since normalization with Seoul in 1965, Japan has refused diplomatic recognition to north Korea, but has permitted varying levels of private cooperation, such as a treaty on fishing rights negotiated by a private Japanese fisheries group. A thaw occurred in 1990 and 1991 when normalization talks between Tokyo and Pyongyang were arranged. However, the north Koreans began with demands for compensation for the wrongs that Japan had committed against the Korean people during the Japanese colonial period, 1910–1945, including cash for suffering during World War II. The talks quickly broke down, and in 1992, with the development of tension over nuclear proliferation in north Korea, they ceased altogether.

The United States. As might be expected, north Korea has been strongly anti-American in both domestic and foreign policy since 1948, and particularly since the Korean War. The DPRK has repeatedly expressed its apprehension of renewed U.S. aggression. It has sponsored "Anti-American Struggle Month" from June 25 to July 27 in each recent year in as many countries as it can reach, and visitors to north Korea are routinely taken to a museum exhibiting U.S. war damage and "atrocities." The meetings of the Military Armistice Commission at Panmunjom have been dominated by north Korean allegations of aggressive designs by the United States and its south Korean "puppet," both allegedly linked with Japan in an aggressive triangular alliance.

One climax of north Korean anti-Americanism came in the late 1960s, when the United States was embroiled in Vietnam. This was also a period of heightened subversion against south Korea, including the attempted assassination of President Park Chung-hee in January 1968. Two days later the north Koreans captured a U.S. naval intelligence vessel, the USS *Pueblo,* and held it and its crew for eleven months, finally extracting a statement of guilt and apology from the United States (disavowed while it was being made) to secure the release of the crew.

The following year, the north Koreans shot down an unarmed U.S. EC-121 reconnaissance aircraft over the East Sea (Sea of Japan), with the loss of its entire thirty-one-man crew. The latter action apparently embarrassed north Korea's allies; the Soviets offered assistance in searching for survivors. The north has since shot at reconnaissance aircraft over or near its territory and has downed U.S. Army helicopters that strayed over north Korean territory.

The harshest actions against the United States since the late 1960s were the senseless "ax murders" at Panmunjom in August 1976, which took two U.S. Army officers' lives, and a firefight at Panmunjom in November 1984, triggered by the successful defection of a young Soviet visitor, which killed a Korean guard and wounded an American soldier. (The 1976 incident started with an attempt by a small detachment of U.S. soldiers to prune a tree that obstructed the view from a United Nations Command observation post in the Joint Security Area within the Demilitarized Zone—an area then open to both sides. For reasons not clearly understood, a group of north Korean soldiers set upon the U.S. soldiers and killed two officers with axes in a brutal beating. In the 1984 incident, a Soviet citizen touring the northern side of the Joint Security Area suddenly broke and ran to the southern side; he was pursued by north Korean troops, shooting as they went. UNC forces fired back. There were casualties on both sides, but the Soviet succeeded in his escape and was given asylum.)

Nevertheless, north Korea since the 1960s has continually sought direct diplomatic talks with the United States, both through propaganda and by contacts through third countries. Its stated purpose has been to lower tensions and reach a peace treaty to end the Korean War. It may also have had in mind the possibility that whether or not such talks had any practical result, they might yield, as a by-product, an increase of north Korean international stature and furtherance of its own policies. In 1984, north Korea dropped its objection to the inclusion of south Korea in such talks, proposing trilateral discussions. This proposal, somewhat like a suggestion by President Jimmy Carter in 1979, was frequently repeated by the north but rejected by both south Korea and the United States. North Korea also cultivated people-to-people relations with ethnic Koreans in the United States and a limited number of journalists. Over 700 Korean Americans visited the north in 1985 and 1986 to meet family members, returning with pictures and favorable reports of conditions.

The United States, however, being officially committed to the UN "police action" to repel north Korean aggression, maintained a near-total embargo of trade and relations. The U.S. position was that any solution of the "Korean question" was up to the Koreans themselves. In the 1970s, the United States suggested four-way talks, including China, or six-way talks, including the Soviet Union and Japan. North Korea has rejected such proposals (see Chapter 8).

A barely perceptible thaw began in the late 1980s, when the United States relaxed its ban on diplomatic contacts with north Korea and held out the possibility of limited trade in commodities such as medical supplies. This policy was suspended after the bombing of a south Korean civil aircraft in December 1987 was traced to north Korean agents, but resumed in late 1988. U.S. and north Korean midlevel diplomats met several times in Beijing since that time, and a few nonofficial north Korean visitors have been allowed to attend conferences in the United States since 1985.

The Nuclear Issue.   North Korea has had a nuclear energy program since the 1960s, when it installed a small Soviet-supplied research reactor. In 1986 it began operating a larger, five-megawatt reactor at Yongbyon. This reactor, which was of the "gas-graphite" type that had exploded at Chernobyl in the Ukraine the previous year, used enriched uranium for fuel and converted it into by-products that could be reprocessed into bomb-grade plutonium given the right kind of reprocessing facilities. Western intelligence organizations believed that the north Koreans lacked reprocessing capability, however, until 1989, when satellite surveillance detected construction of a building near the Yongbyon reactor that had characteristics of a plutonium reprocessing laboratory. In the same year the north Koreans shut down the reactor for maintenance, off-loading a certain number of spent fuel rods in the process. Because north Korea did not allow international inspections of its nuclear facilities at the time, the outside world became concerned that the north Koreans were about to reprocess the spent fuel rods into material for nuclear weapons. An additional worry was the fact that north Korea was also making its own SCUD-type missiles that theoretically could deliver a nuclear warhead into south Korea and, in the rocket's advanced version, to Japan.

North Korea's nuclear program was a direct challenge to the international community, which was trying to limit the spread of nuclear weapons through the nuclear Non-Proliferation Treaty (NPT). The treaty allows the nuclear powers to keep their weapons and to share "peaceful" nuclear technology with nations that have not yet acquired atomic bombs, on the understanding that the latter will be satisfied with nonmilitary nuclear programs. North Korea's position in the NPT system was ambiguous: It had signed the treaty in 1985 but had not ratified it. It had joined the International Atomic Energy Agency and was accepting technical assistance from abroad for its nuclear program, but it had not agreed to all the safeguards and inspections that were part of IAEA membership. In short, north Korea was positioned to become a rogue nuclear power subject to no effective international control whatever. And, as if this were not enough, the Kim Il-sung regime had two additional nuclear plants under construction and due to go online in the mid-1990s, each of which would multiply the country's ability to produce the material for nuclear weapons.

Despite the discovery of north Korea's suspected reprocessing facility, the Kim regime claimed that its nuclear program was entirely designed for peaceful purposes. Indeed, as part of its series of talks with south Korea in 1990 and 1991 it agreed to a "denuclearization" treaty for the Korean peninsula, which both sides signed at the end of 1991 promising not to make or allow nuclear weapons on Korean soil. Beyond that, it began using the nuclear issue as a lever to win long-sought political points with south Korea and the United States. In 1992 north Korea ratified the NPT and signed the IAEA Safeguards Agreement in return for cancellation of U.S.-ROK military maneuvers in the south.

Implementation of the IAEA Safeguards Agreement required the north Koreans to allow international inspectors into their country to look at all their nuclear installations. The first step, in the summer of 1992, was to furnish the IAEA with a detailed inventory of all their nuclear assets, a list that surprised the agency at first because it showed more assets than had previously been known. Under the impression that the north Koreans were being more than forthright, the first IAEA inspection team collected samples and left behind monitoring equipment. However, over the winter of 1992, further study indicated that the north Koreans had two "hot" sites near Yongbyon that looked like they contained nuclear waste. These had not been on the north Korean inventory; indeed, they suggested that the spent fuel that had been unloaded during the 1989 shutdown might actually have been reprocessed secretly into bomb material. The U.S. Central Intelligence Agency immediately issued an estimation that the north Koreans should be dealt with as if they had already produced one or two nuclear bombs, even though there was no way to prove that they had actually done so.

The International Atomic Energy Agency responded to the discovery of the two hot sites by requesting access for immediate inspection—a request the north Koreans refused to honor. North Korea reacted by accusing the IAEA of "partiality" and abuse of the Safeguards Agreement for purposes of espionage. In particular, the north Koreans said they resented the IAEA's use of satellite intelligence from the United States, which has a military alliance with south Korea. When pressed, and then when threatened with United Nations condemnation, the north Koreans shocked the world in March 1993 by giving notice that they were pulling out of the NPT completely, the first signatory ever to take that step.

Believing that it was important to keep north Korea in the international inspection system, the IAEA and the United States engaged in an intensive dialogue with the Kim Il-sung regime, trying to persuade the north Koreans to stay in the NPT before expiration of the ninety-day notice period. On the last day before the north Korean withdrawal was to take effect, American negotiator Robert Gallucci and north Korean Vice Foreign Minister Kang Sok-ju agreed in New York that the north Koreans would stay in the NPT for the time being, and that there would be negotiations to address the north Koreans' concerns.

The urgency of the negotiations in the spring of 1993 masked several significant aspects of the situation. By playing their own version of the nuclear card, the north Koreans had brought about their long-sought diplomatic dialogue with the United States in the absence of south Koreans. They had also positioned themselves to wring concessions from the West, possibly leading to economic agreements that would be substantially to their benefit. The south Koreans, noting these things, were greatly concerned that the United States was being drawn into an unsavory arrangement by extortion. To placate them the United States assured Seoul that no separate deal would be struck with Pyongyang and emphasized to the north Koreans that any positive change in U.S.–north Korean relations would have to come after a resumption of the north-south dialogue, which had been on hold since 1992.

In July 1993 the United States and north Korea established the framework for a long-term solution to the nuclear imbroglio: The United States would organize an international effort to replace the plutonium-producing north Korean reactors, both extant and under construction, with light-water reactors of a type less suitable for plutonium production. Enormous obstacles loomed, not the least of which was financing. In the fall of 1993, IAEA inspectors discovered that some of the sealed nuclear facilities at Yongbyon had been unsealed. When they objected, the north Koreans turned up the pressure by excluding future inspections, and when the batteries ran out on some of the monitoring equipment it became impossible for the IAEA to verify that north Korea was complying with the NPT.

Through the spring of 1994 there was talk of north Korean irregularities followed by more north Korean defiance. The IAEA and the United Nations threatened sanctions, though it was far from certain that these would have any effect. Talk of military sanctions brought forth a threat from north Korea that in case of war Seoul immediately would be a "sea of fire." Talk of economic sanctions always led to the question of enforcement, which meant compelling China to cease exports to north Korea, a delicate problem at best.

In May 1994 north Korea shut down the five-megawatt reactor and removed the fuel rods for storage pending disposal or reprocessing. This created the need for immediate action to control the disposition of the fuel rods. Military options were discussed in the West. News magazines ran stories with scenarios of military sanctions against north Korea. President Bill Clinton dispatched batteries of Patriot missiles to protect Seoul against SCUD attack. American senators were heard musing about the time it would take to conquer north Korea. Then suddenly in June, former President Jimmy Carter, representing no one but himself, journeyed to Pyongyang for a face-to-face meeting with President Kim Il-sung. In a tension-releasing moment Carter and Kim created what appeared to be a package: no sanctions, a return to negotiations, and a summit meeting between President Kim and south Korean President Kim Young-sam. At the time, there was a controversy about Carter's authority to negotiate on behalf of the United States. The controversy, however, was swept aside by the news of Kim Il-sung's sudden death, apparently from natural causes, on July 8.

Although the Kim-Kim summit never took place, intensive negotiations between the United States and north Korea in the summer and fall of 1994 led to a "framework agreement" in October 1994, under which the United States would organize a consortium called the Korean Energy Development Organization (KEDO) to finance the US$4.2 billion cost of constructing two light-water reactors for the north Korean power industry. Pending completion of the light-water reactors, north Korea promised to freeze its nuclear program and seal its facilities, to cease construction on the reprocessing laboratory and the two new reactors, and to hold the spent fuel rods in storage ponds pending shipment out of the country. The United States agreed to supply 500,000 tons of fuel oil per year to north Korea for nonmilitary uses, and the two sides agreed to open liaison offices in each other's capitals, quasi embassies where dialogue might be maintained more easily.

After the framework agreement of October 1994, north Korea froze its nuclear program and opened all its known nuclear facilities to continual IAEA surveillance. The United States shipped 50,000 tons of fuel oil—though it later found that the north had diverted some of it to steel production. Diplomats hunted real estate in each other's capitals, and the north Koreans opened their doors a little by accepting direct-dial telephone service and credit card sales.

The most difficult problem, however, remained the light-water reactors. The Americans envisioned KEDO as a conduit for south Korean funds: Since the south had so much to gain from the agreement their contribution was anticipated to be US$3 billion, nearly 75 percent of the $4.2 billion total cost of the agreement. For this the south Koreans insisted that they should design and build the reactors for the north; but the north Koreans, being sensitive about the technological superiority of the south and anxious not to lose face, demanded that the reactors come from the United States or Germany, neither of which was in a position to invest $3 billion in the project. At a series of meetings in Berlin, Geneva, and Kuala Lumpur in the late spring of 1995, the Americans insisted that there was no alternative to south Korean financing and construction, a position the north Koreans finally accepted.

Overseas Korean Residents
as a Foreign-Policy Factor

In addition to the 67 million Koreans living on their native peninsula, there are approximately 4 million in other countries. Of this number, 1.7 million live in China—the majority of them in Manchurian provinces bordering Korea. The United States has about 1 million (about one-quarter of them in the Los Angeles area), many of whom have taken U.S. citizenship. Seven hundred thousand Koreans live in Japan. Approximately 400,000 live in the Soviet Union, many of them in the Republic of Kazakhstan, to which they were moved from the Maritime Provinces adjoining Korea during the buildup of Japanese-Soviet tensions in the 1930s. Small but significant Korean colonies are in Brazil and other South American countries, and smaller numbers live in Europe. At the height of south Korean construction activity in the Middle East, there were about 200,000 Korean workers there; the number was greatly reduced in the 1980s. Almost all of these workers return home as their work terms expire or their jobs terminate. Additionally, many thousands of Koreans go abroad for university study, chiefly to the United States, Japan, and Western Europe from the south.[14]

The chief concerns of south Korea with ethnic Koreans abroad are to keep them from becoming an embarrassment to relations with the host countries, win their support for the government in Seoul, and prevent their being used for north Korean espionage, propaganda, and subversion. South Korean government policy is to promote emigration, especially to South America, as a means of dealing with the very high density of population at home. (Emigration to the United States has not needed encouragement.) Diplomatic and consular officials of the Republic of Korea keep in touch with the affairs of the Korean communities abroad. Cooperation and modest support are given to organizations and to schools for Korean children in the larger expatriate communities. Through information and contact, Korean officials endeavor to blunt the criticism of the south Korean government, which has long prevailed among overseas Koreans.

In cooperation with host country authorities, a watch for subversive activity is kept by south Korean security agents overseas. The concern is not unfounded. In 1974, a Korean student resident in Japan, apparently acting as a north Korean agent, shot at President Park on the stage of the principal theater in Seoul, but missed the president and killed his wife. South Korean security authorities apprehend numbers of Koreans from Japan each year for involvement in espionage and subversive activity. In the mid-1970s, concern for north Korean recruitment among Koreans in Germany led to an aggressive antiespionage campaign by south Korean authorities operating abroad that caused considerable tension in Korean–West German relations. To some extent, the same was true in the United States during the same period. North Korea has apparently concentrated its attention on the large Korean minority in Japan, although south Korea has charged that north Korea has recruited Koreans in Europe and the United States as well for espionage.

The Korean community in Japan—a survival from Korea's time as a Japanese colony—is largely composed of people in the lower parts of the socioeconomic spectrum who suffer from prejudicial attitudes of the Japanese as well as from unemployment and depressed living standards. Yet there are some Korean residents who have prospered; among these are substantial investors in enterprises in both north and south Korea. Some Koreans have taken Japanese citizenship, but the majority have not.

A series of difficult problems has arisen as to the legal status of the Koreans in Japan as Korean nationals, their eligibility for Japanese welfare benefits, and their control as aliens by the Japanese authorities. In the 1980s, concern focused on a Japanese requirement that all resident aliens be fingerprinted—a requirement strongly resisted by the Koreans.

Before the 1965 normalization of relations between south Korea and Japan, north Korea had clear majority support among the 700,000 Koreans in Japan, for whom it provided education, organization, and propaganda through an organization known by the Japanese acronym *Chosoren*. In 1959, numbers of them started moving to north Korea as repatriates under the auspices of the Red Cross societies, and before the program petered out, over 100,000 had been repatriated. This was important to north Korea as a source of needed labor and as a propaganda triumph. The Japanese welcomed the move because it diminished the size of the Korean minority in their country. Following normalization of relations with south Korea in 1965, however, the north's ascendency among Korean residents has been aggressively challenged by south Korean representatives, with considerable success. A rival pro-south residents' association (*Mindan*) has gained support about equal to the north's.[15]

A large proportion of the Koreans in China are concentrated in an autonomous district along the Yalu River in Manchuria. Since the end of the Cultural Revolution, they have won the right to govern themselves, maintain their own schools and newspapers, and use the Korean language, although they are Chinese citizens. Many of them came originally from south Korea, and recent visitors to the area report that they are more interested in south than in north Korean affairs.

In the United States, most members of the Korean community are educated, highly qualified professional and technical people. The Korean residents as a whole have been economically successful and socially self-controlled. Although their critical attitude toward the government of their homeland has sometimes embarrassed its representatives, it has not been a major problem in the two states' relations. Like many ethnic groups in the United States, the Koreans have come under occasional attack by other groups. Korean businesspeople, especially in the inner cities, have been shot and their stores firebombed. This is not a uniquely Korean problem, however; and the presence of Koreans at various levels in professional and business life throughout the United States demonstrates their capability and the degree (even if not total) of their acceptance by the U.S. public.[16]

Notes

1. See Larry Niksch, "North Korea" and "South Korea" in *Fighting Armies: Non-Aligned, Third World, and Other Ground Armies: A Combat Assessment*, ed. Richard A. Gabriel (Westport, Conn.: Greenwood Press, 1983), pp. 103–152.

2. The sixteen signatory nations (which also signed the Armistice Agreement) were Australia, Belgium, Canada, Colombia, France, Ethiopia, Greece, Luxembourg, Netherlands, New Zealand, Philippines, Thailand, Turkey, Republic of South Africa, United Kingdom, United States.

3. Andrea Matles Savada and William R. Shaw, eds., *South Korea: A Country Study*, 4th ed. (Washington, D.C.: U.S. Government Printing Office, 1992), pp. 281–288.

4. For analyses of the incident see Donald N. Clark, ed., *The Kwangju Uprising: Shadows over the Regime in South Korea* (Boulder: Westview Press, 1988). For a complete discussion of the American role in the events of the uprising and the meaning of the Combined Forces Command Agreement, see U.S. Department of State, "United States Government Statement on the Events in Kwangju, Republic of Korea, in May 1980" (Washington, D.C.: June 19, 1989). On the U.S. role in Korea in 1979 and 1980, see Tim Shorrock, "Ex-Leaders Go on Trial in Seoul," *Journal of Commerce*, February 27, 1996, p. 1A. These revelations have sparked a continuing debate on the U.S. role in Kwangju at http://www.kimsoft.com/korea/kwangju3.htm.

5. For an account of the "Koreagate" affair, see the report of the Subcommittee on International Organizations, U.S. House of Representatives, 95th Congress, 2d session, *Investigation of Korean-American Relations*, October 31, 1978.

6. UN General Assembly Resolution, December 1, 1948. For a discussion of the United Nations role in Korea, see Leland M. Goodrich, *Korea: A Study of U.S. Policy in the United Nations* (New York: Council on Foreign Relations, 1956).

7. Following referral of the Korean question to the United Nations in 1947, a temporary commission was established to observe elections. After the elections were held in 1948, a new successor commission, the United Nations Commission on Korea (UNCOK) was established and stationed in south Korea. During the Korean War, this commission was replaced by UNCURK, composed of seven member states: Australia, Chile, Netherlands, Pakistan, Philippines, Thailand, and Turkey. The commissions reported annually to the UN General Assembly; the reports are available as UN documents. Also established in 1950 was the United Nations Korea Reconstruction Agency (UNKRA), composed of UN Secretariat personnel under a director-general, which dispensed US$500 million in international development assistance. It was abolished in 1958.

8. See *Korea Annual 1994* (Seoul: Yonhap News Agency, 1994), pp. 386–392.

9. Savada and Shaw, *South Korea*, pp. 343–345.

10. Niksch, in *Fighting Armies*, pp. 113–114.

11. Figure calculated on the basis of the 1980 north Korean national budget of US$9.5 billion, assumed to be 80 percent of national income, and exports and imports of approximately $1.5 billion in 1979. See Frederica M. Bunge, ed., *North Korea: A Country Study,* 3rd ed. (Washington, D.C.: U.S. Government Printing Office, 1981), pp. xiv, 155; and Andrea Matles Savada, ed., *North Korea: A Country Study,* 4th ed. (Washington, D.C.: U.S. Government Printing Office, 1994), p. 153.

12. Rudiger Frank, "The Hamhung Project and the Development of GDR-DPRK Relations in the 1950s," paper delivered at the seventeenth Conference of the Association for Korean Studies in Europe (AKSE), Prague, Czech Republic, April 24, 1995.

13. Joseph P. Manguno, "The Tumen River Project: A Critical Appraisal," in Korea Economic Institute, *Korea's Economy 1993* (Washington, D.C.: Korea Economic Institute, 1993), pp. 44–47.

14. On Koreans overseas, see Chae-Jin Lee, *China's Korean Minority: The Politics of Ethnic Education* (Boulder: Westview Press, 1986); George Ginsberg and Herta Ginsburg, "A Statistical Profile of the Korean Community in the Soviet Union," *Asian Survey* 17(10) (October 1977):952–956; Richard H. Mitchell, *The Korean Minority in Japan* (Berkeley: University of California Press, 1967); Hyung-chan Kim, ed., *The Korean Diaspora: Historical and Sociological Studies of Korean Immigration and Assimilation in North America* (Santa Barbara, Calif.: ABC-Clio, 1977).

15. Statements about the Korean minority in Japan are based on Mitchell, *The Korean Minority in Japan;* my own professional experience and observation; and discussion with U.S. and south Korean government officials.

16. For a study of the Korean community in the United States, see Brian Lehrer, *The Korean-Americans* (New York: Chelsea House Publishers, 1988), and Eui-Young Yu, "The Korean American Community," in *Korea Briefing 1993,* ed. Donald N. Clark (Boulder: Westview Press, 1993), pp. 139–162.

8

The Problem of
Korean Reunification

Introduction

To begin the discussion of Korean reunification, it bears repeating that the Korean people have been a unified nation since A.D. 668, when Silla, one of the three early Korean kingdoms on the peninsula, conquered the other two. (To be precise, Silla unified Korea south of the peninsula's narrow waist; north of Pyongyang, a separate kingdom of Parhae, part Korean, part Khitan, existed for three centuries. The present boundaries were established during the Koryo Dynasty [A.D. 936–1392].) Koreans have thus been divided only 3 percent of their national lifetime—or 6 percent, if the fifty years or so of division at the end of the Silla Dynasty are counted.

Given the common aspiration of the Korean people for reunification and its many objective advantages, it is reasonable to expect that Korea will be reunified someday. The questions are how and when, more than whether, it will be accomplished. The demise of Communism in Europe and the democracy movement in China—though it experienced a setback in 1989—suggest that changes will come in north Korea as well. Nevertheless, the obstacles are formidable, and the trend since 1945 has mostly been away from reunification rather than toward it.

It is important to recognize that the problem of reducing tensions and confrontation on the Korean peninsula is related to the problem of reunification, but it is not identical. Reduction of tensions can be achieved without reunification; it is doubtful that reunification could be achieved without reduction of tensions. Both north and south have put forth tension-reducing proposals as well as reunification schemes. The spate of agreements at the end of 1991 calling for continuing progress in unification talks, denuclearization, and nonaggression were a postwar high-water mark in confidence-building between the two Koreas. Unfortunately, the international controversy over north Korea's nuclear program and the political reverberations of the passing of Kim Il-sung in 1994 have left the process interrupted and in doubt.

Nevertheless, the north Korean position, consistent with a revolutionary ideology, continues to be that reunification is the supreme national goal after which all other issues may be solved. The south's position, to work for reduction of tensions first, is more realistic. All the surrounding powers—China, Japan, Russia, and the United States—support the reduction of tensions whether or not they accept the risks and compromises that will be necessary for reunification.[1]

Why Korea Was Divided

Korea's strategic location in East Asia has made it the object of great-power rivalries for centuries, and particularly in the past one hundred years. After Japan defeated China in 1895, Japan and Russia struggled for hegemony in Manchuria and Korea. In 1896, Japan proposed that the two countries divide Korea into spheres of influence at the 38th parallel; Russia refused. In 1904, Russia proposed a similar division at the 39th parallel; Japan refused. The Russo-Japanese War was fought to settle the two countries' rivalries in Korea and Manchuria. Japan won, gaining total control of Korea. This control was unchallenged (except by the Koreans) until Japan went to war with the United States in 1941.

At the Tehran Conference of 1943 of Soviet, British, and U.S. leaders, U.S. President Franklin D. Roosevelt proposed an international trusteeship over Korea. This proposal followed the Cairo Declaration of a few days earlier, promising that the Korean people should "in due course become free and independent." Roosevelt initially thought in terms of a forty-year trusteeship period, having in mind the Philippine precedent. Stalin was not enthusiastic about trusteeship, but acquiesced in it, while insisting that it be as short as possible.

At Potsdam, in July 1945, the Allies stated that Japan would be stripped of all territories annexed since 1895, including Korea. Also at Potsdam, the Soviet Union—until then not a belligerent in the Pacific—was encouraged to enter the war against Japan. Up to that time, no detailed plans had been made for Korea; all attention was fixed on the defeat and postwar occupation of Japan. The Soviet Union declared war on Japan on August 8, and its forces engaged Japanese forces in Korea the next day. The impending Japanese surrender as much as a year earlier than had been anticipated by the United States (the surrender coming partly as a result of the atomic bombing of Hiroshima and Nagasaki) necessitated immediate decision on Korea.

To forestall total Soviet control of Korea, the U.S. authorities proposed that U.S. forces occupy the peninsula south of the 38th parallel and accept the surrender of the Japanese armed forces there, and that the Soviets do the same north of the 38th parallel. The Soviets accepted the arrangement. Looking backward through the prism of the Cold War it seems remarkable that they did, for their forces were pouring into Manchuria and advance units of the Red Army were already in northern Korea when the decision to divide the peninsula was made. Had the Soviets wished to occupy the entire peninsula they could have done so, for the United States would have been unable to move enough troops to Korea quickly enough to halt them at the 38th parallel if they had not agreed to the division as proposed. It is likely that the Soviets, in the early months of the German occupation experience, were still amenable to the concept of an Allied occupation by zones along lines of the German precedent. However, given their keen interest in sharing in the Allied occupation of Japan, their decision unilaterally to stop at the 38th parallel was a portentous one, permitting the Americans time to arrive in the south and allowing local political organizations in south Korea time to organize and take root.[2]

What both sides were contemplating for Korea at the time of the division was some form of Roosevelt's proposed international trusteeship. The final form of the trusteeship proposal was worked out at the meeting of foreign ministers in Moscow in December 1945. The United States, the Soviet Union, Great Britain, and China would exercise the trusteeship for five years; a transitional Korean administration would be formed by consultation between the two occupying powers, which would consult the Korean people in the process.

Public announcement of the Moscow agreement evoked wide and intense resentment throughout the peninsula. The Koreans were largely taken by surprise, although the idea had been expressed by a U.S. diplomat the previous September in a New York speech. They viewed the idea as a trick to deny them their independence. The overwhelmingly hostile Korean reaction helped to destroy any possibility that the proposal would be carried out. Instead, it became a Soviet tool in subsequent fruitless U.S.-Soviet negotiations for a united transitional regime.

Following the Moscow Declaration, the Soviets prevailed on their partisans in both north and south to support trusteeship, while in the south the United States faced a general strike by the military government's Korean employees and nationwide demonstrations. By acting as they did, the Soviets laid the basis for excluding from consultation with the Joint Commission any Korean who did not support trusteeship, which meant in effect that only Koreans who supported the Soviet point of view would be consulted. Meanwhile, Syngman Rhee, the conservative Korean nationalist who had returned from forty years of exile in the United States, pushed for a separate anti-Communist state in the south. The original temporary division, intended by the United States to avoid Soviet domination of the entire peninsula, thus became permanent.

The much-criticized trusteeship proposal, viewed in retrospect, had been a rational device. It might have protected Korea from the rival ambitions of surrounding powers while the nation developed its own political structure. However, the principal actors, the United States and the Soviet Union, distrusted each other, and the Koreans, unprepared for the idea, rejected it (except for those whom the Soviets persuaded to change their minds). It was therefore never tried.

The first conference between representatives of the U.S. and Russian military commands was held in January 1946. It resulted in minor arrangements for exchange of mail, railroad communication, and the like, but the demands and refusals of the two sides fueled mutual distrust. A formal conference of the USSR-U.S. Joint Commission, as provided in the Moscow Declaration, began in March 1946 and ended without result in August 1947. A U.S. attempt at unification under UN auspices failed, and the temporary division of Korea became permanent.

The damage done to Korea by international rivalries, culminating in its division, was reinforced by internal weakness and age-old factionalism. A thousand years ago, as the Silla Dynasty grew feeble and rent with internal dissention, rival leaders set up their own states of Latter Koguryo and Latter Paekche. In its closing years, Silla controlled little more than the capital city of Kyongju. Reunification was accomplished by Wang Kon, founder of the Koryo Dynasty, with a mixture of force and wise diplomacy. Koryo and the succeeding Choson Dynasty ruled a united country for a millennium, although Koryo was weakened by the Mongol invasion and Choson by the Japanese.

A century ago, the Choson Dynasty faced challenges far greater than Silla or Koryo could have imagined. Western nations were establishing imperialist hegemony over Asia, based on military and material superiority, and Japan was following suit. China, Korea's long-time mentor, was also under assault and in decline. Korea's first response was tighter isolation and affirmation of its traditional dependence on China. However, when China proved to be unable to furnish any protection, Korean leaders sought other alliances and then, ultimately, fell to Japan under the protectorate (1905) and then outright colonial rule (1910). For forty years Korea was denied the opportunity to move into the modern world under its own leaders. Thus, the Koreans were still weak and divided when Japanese rule ended. During that period, Korean nationalists were split by both ideology and factional loyalty. Korea's sudden liberation from colonial rule in 1945 loosed the furies of the collaboration issue as well, with Koreans accusing other Koreans of having profited from Japanese rule or having helped the Japanese to oppress their own people, as in the case of Koreans in the colonial police.

Because of this dissension, Korean factions reinforced the division of the country by the United States and the Soviet Union, rather than uniting to resist it. The Korean constituencies of rival foreign ideologies also helped to perpetuate the country's division. After Korea was annexed by Japan in 1910, nationalists—mostly in exile—continued to work for Korean independence. At first they embraced capitalism and liberal democratic ideals and sought Western support; but none was forthcoming. After the Bolshevik Revolution of 1917, some nationalists began to look to Russia and communism to support their struggle. Thereafter, the nationalist leadership was divided by the conflict between the two ideologies of democratic capitalism, preferred by the propertied conservatives, and Marxist socialism or communism, preferred by some of the intellectuals and many of the impoverished peasantry and workers.

The ideological split was reinforced by the nature of the Japanese occupation itself. Because the Japanese regime was capitalist in form, some of the hatred of Japanese domination seems to have been transferred to Western capitalism. There was considerable Marxist thinking among Japanese intellectuals, which influenced some of the young Koreans who studied in Japanese universities. Such views emerged at the end of World War II. Moreover, the Soviet Union, which has a common border with Korea and Manchuria, was able to give the nationalist cause a modicum of support and thus added to the favorable image of communism. The Western European countries and the United States did nothing for Korea, except for providing moral support at the time of the 1919 independence uprising.

All these factors—great-power rivalry, Korean weakness and internal dissension, and ideological conflict—reinforced one another and interacted with Korean nationalism. The Korean people themselves objected violently to continued outside control in the form of trusteeship. The political orientation of the two halves of Korea was already differentiated by the influence of the two occupying powers. The United States refused to recognize the left-oriented People's Republic of Korea, declared two days before the arrival of U.S. occupation forces in early September 1945 and based on rural organizations. Instead, the United States sought support among conservative leaders in the capital as they tried to organize their occupation government. In contrast, the Soviet authorities used local organizations of the People's Republic as a basis for organizing the north along Communist lines.

In the midst of the low-intensity civil war that plagued south Korea almost from the beginning of the American occupation, the Republic of Korea was finally established through UN-observed elections in 1948. The Soviet Union and its satellites recognized the Communist-led Democratic People's Republic of Korea in the north later the same year. Thus the ideological and territorial divisions came together and reinforced each other. Additional reinforcement of both factors came from the suffering and bitterness of the ensuing hot phase of the Korean civil war, 1950–1953.

Now, after half a century, the division of Korea has become a factor in itself. The existence of two separate states for over fifty years has entrenched two governments in sovereign power, each of which claims to be the only legitimate government of all Korea. Unification would require that one government absorb the other, or that both yield to a third. There are few cases in human history in which a political leader or power structure has voluntarily subordinated itself to another. Additionally, each Korean state has developed a wholly different organization. Although a common cultural heritage appears to persist on both sides of the Demilitarized Zone, differences inevitably continue to grow. For example, some of the words in the language now have different meanings in north and south. The two sides teach their younger generations dramatically different versions of modern Korean history. Reunification, therefore, must involve reconciliation of differences in Korean culture as well as politics. The longer the division persists, the greater the barrier to reunification that this cultural difference will create.

The Case for Korean Unification

From the standpoint of Korea's interests as a whole nation, the objective advantages of reunification are enormous. A united Korea, with 67 million people—three times the population of north Korea, or 50 percent more than south Korea—would be an impressive medium-sized state. With a considerable natural resource base and an internal market larger than that of many industrialized countries, it would enjoy a considerable measure of economic independence. It would have defensible natural boundaries. It would be freed from at least part of the enormous present military burden and from the threat of subversion and attack within the peninsula. It would be freed from the trauma of divided families. With the military competence that both Koreas have demonstrated, the reunited nation would be able to inflict heavy damage on its neighbors in the event of attack. Moreover, it would undoubtedly be nuclear-capable. Thus, with judicious diplomacy, Korea could look forward to a reasonably secure future as a proud and prosperous country, notwithstanding the enormous power of its neighbors.

However, there are massive obstacles to unification. All the causes of division already noted still have their effect, although Korea's weakness is now a function of its territorial division, rather than lack of energy or ability. The ideological division continues in full force, and every passing year adds to the firm entrenchment of the two rival political regimes. The mutual distrust of these regimes is so high that even the thought of reunification in the present seems ridiculous. The huge military establishments on both sides would lose their respective raisons d'être while new military considerations would have to be agreed upon for a unified national defense. The end of the Cold War has changed north Korea's power relationships; but there remain strong ties between Pyongyang and Beijing while the south maintains its alliance with the United States and, indirectly, with Japan. These are centrifugal forces; yet the end of the Cold War has at least removed any reasonable possibility that Russia or China would encourage a north Korean military move on the south. For this reason, the calculus of reunification is now changed. More than before 1989, Korean military affairs are now the internal affairs of the Korean people.

Yet the strategic location of the Korean peninsula makes its stability and security a matter of concern for its nearest neighbors and for the United States. Japan considers Korea important to its own security and would oppose the communization of the whole country. The United States wants to maintain the stability of the region because of its strategic and economic interests; it wants to balance competing political and economic challenges from Japan, and in the future China and Russia, in northeast Asia. The United States also wants to see democracy maintained and even expanded. The U.S. troop presence in Korea therefore not only deters an attempt to reunify the peninsula by force but also symbolizes America's continuing strategic interest in northeast Asian affairs.

Although the present situation in Korea is not completely to the liking of any of the surrounding powers, all of them apparently believe that the known risks and problems of the present are preferable to the unknown risks of sudden change. Thus, although all the powers pay lip service to the idea of unification, they do so in accordance with their respective national policies and interests. No outside power is likely to push for reunification, given the risks of renewed conflict. If there should be renewed hostilities in Korea short of a larger international conflict, the likely result would be maintenance of the status quo. It seems very likely that reunification will come only through the initiative of the Koreans themselves, based on the recognition in both north and south of its long-range advantages for the Korean nation, and accompanied by appropriate international guarantees.

Unification Policies and Initiatives

Basic Policies

The following general propositions characterize the whole history of Korean unification initiatives:

- Both Koreas are strongly committed to reunification. Their allies support unification in public, but attach little priority to it in private.
- Both Koreas are publicly committed to unification only by peaceful means. However, both Koreas generally have been more willing to threaten and use force than their great-power allies, at least since the Korean War.
- Both Koreas call for settlement of the unification problem by the Korean people themselves. The Soviet Union and now Russia have always supported this position. The United States has never disavowed its 1953 position that unification should be accomplished by UN-observed elections throughout Korea for representatives to determine the government of a unified state; but since the mid-1970s the United States, also, has supported the principle of unification by the Korean people themselves.
- South Korea and the United States since the mid-1970s have advocated an international conference including both Koreas, China, Japan, the United States, and possibly the Soviet Union or Russia to discuss unification. North Korea wants negotiation directly with the United States to arrange a peace treaty and withdrawal of U.S. troops. The United States traditionally has insisted that no bilateral arrangement is possible between Pyongyang and Washington unless south Korea is a party to the agreement; however, in the 1990s this position has been modified in practice by the urgent need for bilateral understandings on nuclear issues.
- Since the 1940s north Korea has envisaged a people's revolution in the south, perhaps assisted in the critical stage by the north Korean armed forces, as the stepping-stone to unification. At times, it has sought to promote the revolution with its own agents and strategies. South Korean policies have no revolutionary component.
- South Korea's approaches to peaceful unification are based on gradual, step-by-step programs of specific cooperative action, through direct contact between north and south, building up to eventual political union. North Korea has stressed major top-level meetings and "grand conferences" as the point of departure.
- South Korea traditionally favored elections and decisionmaking on the basis of "one person, one vote," which would have given it a two-to-one advantage over the north. However, since 1989 the south has accepted the principle of equality, opening the way to negotiation on a different formula.
- Since the Korean War, north Korea has demanded the withdrawal of U.S. forces, usually as a precondition for negotiations on unification (although recent north Korean proposals seem to accept U.S. withdrawal in stages

while other steps are taken to reduce tensions). South Korea, which holds that U.S. forces are present in accordance with its Mutual Defense Treaty with the United States, wants them to remain in place until enforceable agreements are reached.

- Notwithstanding various accommodations over the years and the two Koreas' admission to the United Nations as separate states in 1991, each Korean state regards itself as the only legitimate government of Korea and usually refers to the other in derogatory terms. South Korea has five north Korean provincial offices in its governmental structure; north Korea has south Korean representatives in its legislature.

- While the United States does not want to see Korean unification under Communist auspices, China would have difficulty in accepting a unification that appeared to "roll back" Communism. Thus, although the major powers support unification along the lines of their respective Korean allies, they implicitly support the divided status quo. All are apparently opposed to a military solution to the problem. Some authors believe that China, in particular, deterred Kim Il-sung from such a solution in the 1960s.

Overview of Unification Efforts Since 1945

First Phase: Early U.S. Initiatives.   The temporary division of Korea in 1945, proposed by the United States and accepted by the Soviet Union, was not initially viewed by either of them as a political division of the country. At the end of World War II, Korea was legally Japanese territory, although its people were anti-Japanese. The military occupation was a means of filling the power vacuum left by the Japanese defeat until a Korean administration could be formed. The situation was somewhat similar to that of Austria, which also had Soviet and U.S. (as well as French and British) occupation zones; it was unlike that of Germany, which was occupied for political as well as military control of a defeated enemy.

The U.S. international trusteeship proposal was intended to bring a united Korean administration into being. It failed, without even being tried, because the Koreans objected to it; because each of the occupying powers wanted to ensure that the future Korean government would be politically and ideologically acceptable, but they had incompatible standards of acceptability; and because the ideologically and factionally divided Korean nationalists could not agree on a formula of their own.

Second Phase: United Nations Involvement.   Already resolved to take its troops out of Korea, the United States in 1947 sought to solve the "Korean question" by referring it to the United Nations. The Soviet Union opposed referral to the United Nations, on the basis that Article 104 of the Charter excluded from UN jurisdiction issues arising out of World War II. This position had some legal validity, although the uncompromising Soviet stand did not win any friends. The United States had such overwhelming UN support at the time that the question was taken up anyway. The Soviet Union then submitted, in the General Assembly, its own draft resolution, which was turned around by U.S. amendments and eventually passed. The Assembly resolution, as passed, anticipated that a UN Commission would undertake consultations throughout Korea on the shape of a new Korean government. Refusal of the north Korean authorities to admit the UN commission ended all hopes that a unified Korean regime could be brought into being through peaceful negotiation. (The Soviet Union consistently referred U.S. and other authorities to the north Korean administration the Soviets had set up, although they actually held the final power until September 1948.) Separate independent states were established in the two halves of Korea, and the occupying powers withdrew their military forces.

Third Phase: Unification by Force.   After military mutiny and widespread guerrilla action in the south had failed to dislodge the UN-recognized Republic of Korea, north Korea and the Soviet Union sought unification through a quick military victory over the south. They counted upon a strong north Korean military buildup, U.S. indifference, and south Korean unreadiness. Had the United States not reversed its policies and provided massive military support under the United Nations umbrella, the attack would probably have resulted in reunification of Korea as a Communist state. Its failure led to a brief United Nations attempt to occupy north Korea and establish reunification under UN auspices, the outcome that had been a theoretical possibility in 1947 and 1948; but the Chinese intervention eventually resulted in restoration of the pre–Korean War situation. (It is worth noting that the United States in the fall of 1950 briefly adopted a policy of supporting neutral status for a unified Korea.)

Fourth Phase: Return to the United Nations.   Pursuant to a clause in the 1953 Armistice Agreement calling for a political conference, representatives of nations on both sides of the Korean War met in Geneva in 1954 to discuss Korea's future. The United States, supported by the other fifteen nations of the United Nations Command, called for elections under United Nations observation throughout Korea, in proportion to population (north Korea having at that time less than half the population of the south), to set up a conference that would decide Korea's government. South Korea's representative presented a thirteen-point unification plan, which also called for elections but upheld the legitimacy of the Republic established in 1948 as the government of all Korea.[3]

The north Koreans, supported by the Chinese and the Soviets, maintained that the United Nations was itself a belligerent in the war and that the solution to the Korean question should be left to the Koreans themselves (implicitly calling for equal status of the two Korean states). They proposed that foreign troops first be withdrawn from Korea. Free elections would then be held without foreign interference throughout Korea for representatives to a national conference, in which the two sides would be equally represented, to work out a unified administration.

The Geneva Conference broke up in disagreement, but the proposal for elections throughout Korea under UN observation became part of the subsequent UN General Assembly resolution that year. Symptomatic of the small practical value attached to this plan, it was not spelled out in the resolution—simply incorporated by reference. The UN General Assembly debated the Korean question yearly until 1975; it has not done so since. The UN role in Korean unification has virtually ceased, except in the symbolic existence of the residual United Nations Command. Instead, as separate members of the United Nations, both south and north Korea have been participants in UN international arrangements and beneficiaries of UN programs.

Fifth Phase: North Korean Propaganda and Subversion. The north Korean unification formula proposed at the Geneva Conference, with variations, underlay north Korean proposals for the rest of the 1950s. Meanwhile, the north denied the legitimacy of the Republic of Korea, vilified it as an imperialist puppet, endeavored to subvert it through its own agents, and called for popular revolution against it. After their army was defeated, thousands of north Korean soldiers melted into the south Korean hills. For nearly two years after the armistice, they continued to fight as guerrillas, based in the rugged Chiri Mountains of south-central Korea. The Republic's combat teams, according to one report, killed approximately 82,000 guerrillas in subduing the insurgency.[4] If the political violence in south Korea between 1946 and 1950 was the prologue to the Korean "hot war" of 1950–1953, this phase in the Chiri mountains was the third phase of the civil war from 1953 to 1955.

In 1954—at the same time that the guerrillas were fighting—north Korea proposed a joint conference of representatives of north and south to negotiate unification. In 1955 it proposed a nonaggression pact and in 1957 an international conference to solve the Korean question and mutual reductions of forces to 100,000 each. In this period, north Korea also advocated economic and cultural exchanges between the two Koreas. At the time, the north had the more dynamic economy and stable polity and maintained the propaganda initiative in the international arena. The south did not respond; official policy until 1960 under Syngman Rhee was *pukchin t'ongil* ("march north for unification"), with no compromises.

Sixth Phase: Confederal Republic and People's Revolution. The political upheaval of April 1960 in south Korea stimulated a new north Korean proposal. On August 14, 1960, north Korean President Kim Il-sung proposed formation of a Confederal Republic of Koryo, which would preserve the separate systems and international relations of the two states, on a basis of equality, but would set up a Supreme National Committee to handle certain matters in common. This idea, put forward again in somewhat modified and more detailed form in 1980, remains a central north Korean theme, along with proposals for a "grand national conference" of equal representation from both sides to bring it into being.

The new 1960 initiative may have been motivated by north Korean anticipation of increasing instability in the south. However, the military coup d'état of 1961 seems to have disappointed these hopes. North Korea then started its military buildup and, as the United States became bogged down in Vietnam, sought to take advantage of the situation to destabilize the south. (Its military adventures during this period have been described in the previous chapter.)

Seventh Phase: North-South Contact After the "Nixon Shock." The U.S. withdrawal from Vietnam, the Guam Doctrine on nonemployment of U.S. forces, and the U.S. opening to China as well as U.S. moves toward détente with the Soviet Union, all worried both north and south Korean leaders. In 1971, the north accepted a south Korean proposal for talks between the two sides' Red Cross societies on the plight of divided families. Concurrently, secret contacts between the two sides led to a surprise Joint Declaration of July 4, 1972, in which north and south pledged themselves to the principles of (1) independence from foreign interference, (2) unification through peaceful means, and (3) the search for "grand national unity." (These are frequently cited by north Korea as the Three Grand Principles of National Unification. North and south soon disagreed about whether "independence" excludes the U.S. troop presence.) The two sides agreed not to insult each other, to set up a South-North Coordinating Committee (SNCC) with five members on each side, to discuss unification measures, and to establish a telephone "hot line" between Seoul and Pyongyang.[5]

Preliminary negotiations went forward at both the SNCC and Red Cross levels, and one Red Cross plenary north-south meeting was held in August 1972. The first conference of SNCC cochairmen opened at Panmunjom the following October. Neither conference reached significant agreement. Talks at both levels petered out by 1973, following the establishment of the strongly authoritarian *Yushin* regime in the south in late 1972. The north Koreans from 1976 ceased to acknowledge test calls on the hot line and reverted to belligerent propaganda. Through the remainder of the 1970s the two sides periodically floated proposals for negotiations, and each time the other side raised objections. Their starting points were different: The south wanted direct political talks on unification issues while the north wanted to go around south Korea for talks with the United States aimed at a bilateral peace treaty to replace the 1953 Armistice Agreement. Consequently none of the proposals bore fruit.

Developments in the 1980s. The decade of the 1980s brought very slow movement toward an opening in north-south relations. The decade opened with an elaboration, in October 1980, of the confederation proposal that north Korea had put forward in 1960. Near the end of the decade south Korean president Roh Tae-woo announced a "commonwealth" proposal that implicitly recognized traditional north Korean positions more than any previous south Korean initiative had. Between these two initiatives came attempts at reestablishing north-south dialogue, which reached a climax in September 1985 with a token reunion of divided families in Seoul and Pyongyang, but afterward was again largely suspended. During the final months of 1989, working-level north-south meetings resumed.

In north Korea, the year 1980 brought the Sixth Congress of the Korean Workers' Party and Kim Il-sung's endorsement of his son Kim Jong-il as his successor. In the south Major General Chun Doo-hwan seized power and extended his quasi-military rule under the Fifth Republic. Chun proposed a number of promising initiatives which seemed to move south Korea toward the north Korean principle of "equality" between the two states under a confederation of some sort. However, for the most part unification issues stayed on the back burner for several years. Progress was further frustrated when north Korean agents endeavored to assassinate the south Korean president and his party in Rangoon in October 1983. Coming hardly a month after the Soviet Union had shot down a Korean passenger airliner, the Rangoon incident, which killed seventeen south Koreans but not President Chun, poisoned the atmosphere against any possible talks even though there was a promising proposal on the table for tripartite discussions including the United States.

After 1985, as criticism built up against the Chun regime in south Korea, unification reemerged as a sacred national cause. Dissidents made highly visible attempts to make contact with their north Korean brothers at Panmunjom but were stopped well short of their goal by riot police. These exercises portrayed the Chun regime and its American allies as obstacles to reunification and helped to force movement in the south toward new overtures toward Pyongyang. When Roh Tae-woo succeeded Chun as president in 1988, he announced a new openness toward north Korea, and in September 1989 he proposed a new reunification formula.

In 1981 south Korea (specifically, the city of Seoul) won designation by the International Olympic Committee as the site of the 1988 Summer Olympics. This decision, perhaps more than any other recent international event, signaled south Korea's emergence as a fully qualified player on the international scene. North Korea sought to obstruct the decision—most blatantly, by having its agents destroy a south Korean airliner in 1987—but by 1984 began to negotiate for a role in the Olympics. That spring, in spite of the hostility that the 1983 Rangoon bombing had engendered, the north proposed that representatives of the two sides discuss the formation of a joint Korean team for the 1984 Summer Olympics in Los Angeles. South Korea had made such a proposal in 1981, which the north had previously ignored. It was obviously too late to make such arrangements. Nevertheless, representatives of the two Olympic committees held two meetings to discuss the idea of a joint team for subsequent events—in particular, the 1986 Asian Games and the 1988 Summer Olympics, both to be held in Seoul. The talks were inconclusive. In an effort to move them forward, the chairman of the International Olympic Committee invited representatives of both sides to meet with him in Lausanne, Switzerland, but without tangible result.

In 1985 north Korea demanded to be co-host for the 1988 Olympics, calling for half of the games to be held in Pyongyang. The International Olympic Committee (IOC) charter does not allow co-hosting. Several talks on this subject, sponsored by the IOC, were held with the north and south in Lausanne. The IOC proposed, with south Korean agreement, that two of the 1988 games (fencing and archery) and one of the preliminary soccer matches be held in Pyongyang and that a long-distance cycling race begin there. Although the IOC eventually offered five games, with the acquiescence of south Korea, the north continued to demand that more of the games be held in Pyongyang. Discussions continued until the spring of 1988—even after the airplane disaster of December 1987—but ended without result.

In August 1984, continuing the series of offers each side had made to the other over the years, south Korean President Chun proposed south-north economic exchanges and offered to supply commodities to the north Korean people. North Korea did not accept; but in September it offered to supply relief goods to the victims of a severe flood in the Seoul area. For the first time in Korea's postwar history, south Korea accepted. The north fulfilled its promise to the letter, delivering 7,200 metric tons (7,900 U.S. short tons) of rice, 100,000 metric tons (110,000 U.S. tons) of cement, 500,000 meters (547,000 yards) of textiles, and 759 cartons of medicine by truck and ship to Panmunjom and designated south Korean destinations.

Following this unprecedented event, contacts between the Red Cross societies of both sides resumed. Full-dress plenary meetings were held in Seoul and Pyongyang, leading to visits by fifty separated family members of each side in September 1985 to meet relatives in the capital city of the other side. At north Korean insistence, cultural troupes journeyed with the family members and gave performances. Teams of reporters covered the visits. Not all visitors met their families, and the reunions had heavy propaganda overtones. Nevertheless, the exchange was universally considered to have historic significance.

Following up on an earlier south Korean proposal, discussions on economic cooperation also began in November 1984 between the two sides. Both sides designated government officials as representatives, thus implicitly acknowledging each other's government (Figure 8.1). The south advanced several specific proposals for exchange of commodities, reopening of rail links, and others. The north, however, concentrated on organization of an overall coordinating mechanism as a first step—an extension into the economic field of its usual philosophy of high-level, general agreement first. The south reluctantly agreed to much of the north's concept, accepting the formation of a committee at the deputy prime minister level; but actual economic exchange continued to elude agreement.

Also in 1984, north Korea proposed a meeting of the two sides' legislatures. Representatives of the two assemblies met several times—first at staff level, then between assembly members—to consider topics for discussion. The north wanted the joint conference to consider a nonaggression declaration. The south, pointing

FIGURE 8.1   Meeting of representatives of north and south Korea (photo courtesy of Korea Overseas Information Service)

out that this was the business of the executive branch, counterproposed discussion of a confederal constitution for a united Korea.

Talks in all four areas—sports, Red Cross, economic exchanges, and parliamentary conferences—were suspended by the north when a Soviet visitor at Panmunjom dashed across the Joint Security Area to the southern side in October 1984. The north again suspended talks during the annual joint ROK-U.S. "Team Spirit" exercise in both early 1985 and early 1986. By mid-1986 only the sports talks were continuing; north Korea turned down suggestions for resumption of economic talks.

In mid-1986 north Korea, in letters to the south Korean defense minister and the commander of U.S. forces in Korea, proposed three-way military talks aimed at reduction of tensions. The south Korean and U.S. response was that the Military Armistice Commission (established by the 1953 Armistice Agreement) offered a forum for such consultations. The 1987 and 1988 "Team Spirit" exercises led to further suspension of contacts by north Korea, although it is not clear that the south, preoccupied as it was with its own political problems, was particularly eager to see the talks reopened.

In July 1988, however, following the establishment of the Sixth Republic, south Korean President Roh Tae-woo initiated an open policy toward the north, together with a reaffirmation of south Korean *nordpolitik* (cultivation of contacts with Communist states). Also that year, the north Koreans proposed a phased and verified three-year arms reduction, which would result in armed services numbering 100,000 on each side. South Korea rejected the initiative but proposed reopening talks in the four channels previously pursued—Red Cross, sports, economic exchanges, and parliamentary conferences.

In January 1989, with the blessing of both states, south Korean business tycoon Chung Ju-yung visited his north Korean birthplace. He negotiated a joint venture agreement with north Korea to develop a tourist industry in the Diamond Mountain region, which before World War II had been internationally renowned for its beauty. Other possible joint ventures were also discussed.

Although Chung had appropriate permission for *his* visit, several dissident south Koreans with their own reunification agenda did not. In the fall of 1988 So Kyong-won, a member of the south Korean National Assembly from Kim Dae-jung's Peace and Democracy Party, made a secret visit to Pyongyang. In the spring of 1989 dissident Protestant cleric Mun Ik-hwan called on Kim Il-sung in defiance of the south Korean government prohibition against unofficial contact with the north. The meeting ended with a joint statement calling for a confederation of the two Koreas. Mun was arrested upon his return.

In July 1989 north Korea hosted a large-scale World Youth Festival in Pyongyang, using elaborate facilities it had constructed in anticipation of the Olympics. Although there was talk of a south Korean delegation, the south Korean government decided against it; nonetheless the dissident student federation *Chondaehyop* sent a representative, Im Su-gyong, accompanied by a Catholic priest, Mun Kyu-hyon. Im's pleading for Korean unity, in Pyongyang and elsewhere, was prominently featured in north Korean propaganda. Although warned not to do so by the south Korean authorities, she and Father Mun insisted on returning to the south through the Joint Security Area at Panmunjom. They were both arrested by the south Koreans.

These visits, although supported by the more radical dissidents in the south, were generally viewed with indifference or even hostility by the Korean public. Despite the unquestionably sincere intentions of the visitors, the net effect was probably to set back progress toward north-south dialogue. Their actions, together with the students' aborted plan for a march to Pyongyang, reinforced the demands of conservative elements in south Korea for firmer control of dissent, particularly when such dissent appeared to reflect north Korean themes. For example, Kim Dae-jung was indicted, although not detained, for failing to report Assemblyman So's visit and for accepting north Korean money the Assemblyman had brought back. At the same time, however, the visits dramatized the intensity of the south Koreans' desire for progress toward reunification.

The Record on Unification in the 1990s

Until 1990, the sporadic north-south contacts had never involved high-ranking officials on either side: They were always working-level contacts or contacts between explicitly nonpolitical entities such as sports representatives or Red Cross delegations. The year 1990 brought an epochal change: a series of three meetings between the prime ministers of north and south Korea during alternating visits to

Seoul and Pyongyang. As if to underscore the significance of government-to-government contact at long last, north Korean Prime Minister Yon Hyong-muk paid a courtesy call on President Roh Tae-woo at the Blue House during the third meeting in December. In terms of substance, however, the talks were less encouraging. The north Koreans had political issues on their minds, while the south wanted to discuss humanitarian and cultural issues. Prime Minister Yon, for example, proposed negotiations on joining the United Nations as a united country, on cessation of U.S.-ROK joint maneuvers such as "Team Spirit," and human rights issues sure to embarrass south Korea, such as demanding the release of Im Su-gyong and Mun Kyu-hyon as well as an end to the National Security Law under which they had been prosecuted for visiting north Korea. South Korea's counterproposals put forth an agenda of "confidence-building measures" such as cultural exchanges and communications. The two sides' approaches remained as far apart as ever, and little headway was made.

In the spring of 1991 there was significant progress on another front, when north and south Korea together fielded a single Korean team first at the World Table Tennis Championships in Japan and then at the Sixth Junior World Soccer Championships in Portugal. The Korean women won the gold in table tennis and the unified Korean team got as far as the quarter-finals in the soccer championships. These feats were accomplished under an agreed-upon flag with a blue outline of Korea as its central symbol, and the folk song *"Arirang"* was played in place of the national anthem. Significant, too, was the fact that the performance by the Korean team in Japan united the two factions of Korean residents there, the northward-leaning *Chosoren* and the southward-leaning *Mindan,* in support of their one national team.

The remarkable series of prime ministers' meetings resumed in October 1991 and resulted in a joint commitment to work toward an "Agreement on Reconciliation, Nonaggression, and Exchanges and Cooperation," a title that connoted an agreement to agree on items from both sides' agendas. The fifth round of talks in December 1991 led to a historic agreement under that title which was ratified in February 1992. In twenty-five articles, north and south Korea spelled out promises to respect each others' systems, to stay out of each others' internal affairs, to refrain from undermining each others' societies, and to work toward a peace treaty that would replace the 1953 Armistice. They agreed to promote sports exchanges, family visits, and cooperation in cultural affairs and promised to establish offices and mechanisms to facilitate cooperation. In a separate agreement on December 31, 1991, they signed a six-point "denuclearization" declaration in which the two Koreas pledged to use nuclear power only for peaceful purposes and not to test, produce, accept, store, or deploy nuclear weapons in any form, and to permit mutual inspection of nuclear facilities.[6]

These encouraging developments were followed by further steps: north Korea's ratification of the nuclear Non-Proliferation Treaty and acceptance of International Atomic Energy Agency (IAEA) inspections in the spring of 1992. However, the high hopes of early 1992 foundered on the realities of 1993 when north Korea refused to give IAEA inspectors free rein and accused the West and south Korea of using the agreements to engage in outright espionage (see Chapter 7). Over the next several years, the laborious negotiations between north Korea and the United States over the DPRK's nuclear program all but eclipsed the earlier progress in the north-south talks, and by the mid-1990s there was little to show for the agreements of 1991. The north Koreans refused to sit down with the south Korean officer assigned to represent the United Nations Command at Panmunjom. In 1994 they threatened to turn Seoul into a "sea of fire" if military measures were employed to force them to allow full IAEA inspections. In the summer of 1994 there was a brief promise of a summit meeting between Kim Il-sung and south Korean President Kim Young-sam, but it was lost when the north Korean leader died before the meeting could take place. In 1995 north Korea allowed visits by south Korean businessmen and at length agreed to let south Korean technicians help them build their new light-water reactors. When food supplies ran dangerously low because of drought and then, later, because of devastating floods, they accepted rice from south Korea and even appealed for international assistance. Each one of these openings created possibilities for better north-south relations but did not fit any systematic plan and certainly fell far short of implementing the 1991 agreements.

Unification Prospects

Considering the universal Korean desire for reunification, with its clear political, economic, and military advantages, and the risks and costs of the present military confrontation, it seems very likely that Korea will eventually be reunified. However, reunification will come about only by a united effort of the Korean people themselves. In the absence of a strong push by the Koreans, no single outside power or combination of powers will work to change the status quo except to gain a strategic advantage for themselves (such as the Soviet Union's support of the north Korean attack in 1950). Any outside power's attempt to gain such an advantage would be resisted by other powers.

Real Korean moves toward unification, as distinguished from propaganda initiatives or cosmetic gestures, are inhibited primarily by suspicion, ideology, inertia, power and status concerns, and fear of jeopardizing relations with outside powers. This suspicion itself is rooted in Korean history and culture. In north-south relations, suspicion is enormously magnified by the decade-long Korean civil war, north Korean attempts at subversion and sabotage over the years—punctuated by the 1968 and 1983 assassination attempts—and the belligerent and vituperative posture of each Korea toward the other. Each leadership group assumes (probably correctly) that the other side intends to overthrow it if possible and responds in kind. No one knows how this might change; yet change seems inevitable. No doubt over time, with continuing contact and small-scale agreements, with more and more trade and investment and gradually diminishing military tensions (apart from the nuclear issue, which could flare at any time), the suspicion may abate. Small-scale agreements and confidence-building measures seem to be the best approach for the time being. However, the situation also requires great restraint on both sides, as political constituencies within each part of Korea pressure their governments to be more assertive in north-south relations or even try to manipulate north-south issues to undermine their governments.

Complete political reunification of Korea will not automatically result from a Confederal Republic or from the German "two states, one nation" model. It is inconceivable that the more numerous south Koreans would ever accept the north Korean system for themselves; hence political unification under Kimilsungism is outside the realm of possibility. Unification is more likely to be the result of a partial or total collapse of the north Korean system, triggered perhaps by some unforeseen disaster or upheaval. It is in no one's interest to see the north Korean system implode or undergo a violent end; rather, efforts must continue to allay the fears of north Koreans, to bring them into relationships with the outside world, and to seek reunification by negotiation.

Notes

1. For a discussion of unification proposals and theories behind them in the 1990s, particularly in light of the German reunification experience, see Sung Chul Yang, *The North and South Korean Political Systems: A Comparative Analysis* (Boulder: Westview Press, 1994), pp. 797–820.

2. On the decision to divide the zones of occupation at the 38th parallel, see Michael Sandusky, *America's Parallel* (Alexandria, Va.: Old Dominion Press, 1985).

3. *The Korean Problem at the Geneva Conference, April 26–June 15, 1954,* International Organization and Conference Series 11, Far Eastern, U.S. Department of State (Washington, D.C.: U.S. Government Printing Office, 1954).

4. The operation, called "Operation Ratkiller," is described by its commander, General Paik Sun-yup, in his book *From Pusan to Panmunjom* (Washington, D.C.: Brassey's, 1992).

5. For the text of the south-north joint statement of July 4, 1972, see *Handbook on Korean-U.S. Relations* (New York: The Asia Society, 1985), pp. 375–376.

6. Byung Chul Koh, "Domestic Politics and External Relations," in *Korea Briefing 1992,* ed. Donald N. Clark (Boulder: Westview Press, 1992), pp. 22–23.

Appendix A: Glossary

A-ak. Formal Confucian court music, preserved in Korea in its traditional Chinese form.

Agency for National Security Planning (ANSP). ROK foreign and domestic intelligence agency; replaced the Korean Central Intelligence Agency (KCIA) in the 1980s.

Ajon. Locally appointed functionaries of the Choson Dynasty, who were often at their posts for life, thus providing continuity and linkage to the central government, as well as a liaison service with the agricultural villages.

Armistice. After two years of protracted cease-fire negotiations, an armistice was signed July 27, 1953, between representatives of the two opposing military commands (United Nations Command and Korean People's Army/Chinese People's Volunteers). Both sides agreed to withdraw their forces behind a Demilitarized Zone that extended two kilometers on either side of a Military Demarcation Line marking the approximate positions of the two armies, slightly north of the original 38th parallel division between north and south Korea. Prisoners were exchanged and a Military Armistice Commission established to enforce the truce.

Blue House. Colloquial English term for the South Korean presidential establishment, derived from the blue-tile roof on the presidential residence, *Ch'ongwadae.*

Cadre. Key officials of the Democratic People's Republic of Korea, usually core members of the Korean Workers' Party, who ensure that party policies are effectively carried out.

Chaebol. Large south Korean business conglomerates, engaged through their component units in many lines of industry, which have played key roles in the export drive of the Republic of Korea from the mid-1960s. Well-known examples are Hyundai, Samsung, and Daewoo.

Chajusong. Concept of standing for oneself; an inherent part of north Korea's *juch'e* philosophy.

Changgi. A Korean version of chess.

Cholla. Part of the name of two provinces in southwestern Korea: South Cholla Province (Cholla Namdo) and North Cholla Province (Cholla Pukto). The area is also known as the Honam area. The main cities are the respective provincial capitals, Kwangju and Chonju. Home region of the political leader Kim Dae-jung.

Ch'ollima (Thousand-League Horse). Term used for the economic campaign in north Korea in the late 1950s, which brought temporary rapid progress at the price of lowered quality and worker exhaustion.

Chondaehyop. Korean acronym for a national coalition of university student organizations; active in the democratization struggle of the late 1980s.

Ch'ondogyo (Religion of the Heavenly Way). Name of a native Korean religion established in the nineteenth century in reaction to Western influence and dynastic decay. Under the name *Tonghak* (Eastern Learning) it inspired the revolt that triggered the Sino-Japanese War in 1894.

Chonminnyon. Korean acronym for the National Alliance for a Democratic Movement, composed of dissident student, intellectual, worker, and farmer organizations in the late 1980s.

Choson. (1) An early Korean state in southern Manchuria or north Korea (Ancient Choson), extinguished by China in 108 B.C. (2) The name of Korea during the Choson (Yi) Dynasty (A.D. 1392–1910); also used of the reigning dynasty.

Ch'ungch'ong. Refers to South Ch'ungch'ong Province (Ch'ungch'ong-namdo) and North Ch'ungch'ong Province (Ch'ungch'ong-pukto) in west-central Korea. Main cities are the respective capitals, Taejon and Ch'ongju. Home area of the political leader Kim Jong-pil.

Chung'in. A small intermediate social class of petty officials below the *yangban* aristocracy, but above the common people, during the Choson Dynasty.

Demilitarized Zone (DMZ). A strip 4 kilometers (2.5 miles) wide and 240 kilometers (150 miles) long that separates the armed forces of the two sides in Korea. A Military Demarcation Line runs in its center. Under the Armistice Agreement of 1953, no military forces or equipment are to be deployed in the DMZ other than security patrols. In fact, the DMZ has become militarized on both sides.

Democratic centralism. A principle of north Korea's governing ideology under which all suggestions and criticisms of the people are conveyed to the decision-making center of the Korean Workers' Party, but once the decisions are made, all party members and citizens are obligated to carry them out regardless of their previous attitude.

Democratic Confederal Republic of Koryo. The name for a reunified Korea proposed by north Korea in its reunification initiatives.

Democratic Justice Party (DJP). The political party organized in 1981 by the supporters of south Korean President Chun Doo-hwan to mobilize political support for his administration. (In Korean: *Minju chonguidang,* or *Minjongdang.*)

Democratic Liberal Party (DLP). Formed by the merger of the DJP and two opposition parties headed by Kim Young-sam and Kim Jong-pil in January 1990. In its heyday the DLP commanded more than a two-thirds majority in the south Korean National Assembly. In the election of March 24, 1992, it emerged with one vote short of a majority. DLP presidential candidate Kim Young-sam won the election of December 1992; however, during Kim's administration the party began to disintegrate, and by 1995 it had gone out of business, its main element under President Kim being reconstituted as the New Korea Party.

Han'gul. The phonetic Korean alphabet created by King Sejong in the fifteenth century and in general use today—often mixed with Chinese characters called *hanja.*

Hwan'gap. A great social occasion marking a man's sixtieth birthday.

Hwarang. A society of young warriors in the Silla Dynasty (18 B.C.–A.D. 936) with a code of conduct reminiscent of Japanese *bushido* or European chivalry.

Hwarangdo. (1) The code of the *hwarang.* (2) A system of fighting similar to *t'aekwondo,* but making use of the sword and other weapons.

Hyangga. Sung or chanted poems of the Silla period.

Ibul. Quilt to cover the body for sleeping on the floor, used together with a sleeping pad (*yo*).

Joint Security Area (JSA). A circular area within the Demilitarized Zone at Panmunjom within which both sides of the Military Armistice Commission meet and have their offices.

Juch'e. (1) Roughly, "self-reliance." (2) As *juch'e sasang* (*juch'e* thought), Kim Il-sung's version of Communist ideology as applied to national development, emphasizing self-reliance and the supremacy of man over his environment; the basic ideology of "Kimilsungism."

Kasa. A brief form of prose-poetry that emerged in the late sixteenth century, usually based on the beauties of nature.

KATUSA (Korean Augmentation to U.S. Army). Active-duty Korean military personnel assigned to U.S. Army units and integrated with U.S. personnel; this arrangement began during the Korean War.

Khitan. A warlike, nomadic people from the Tungus Valley area of eastern Siberia, probably related to the Koreans, who harassed both China and Korea over the centuries and for two centuries ruled north China as the Liao Dynasty.

Kimch'i. A spicy national dish made from pickled and peppered cabbage and other vegetables, vaguely similar to sauerkraut but much spicier.

Kimilsungism. A term used to denote the variant of Communist rule that has taken root in north Korea under the leadership of Kim Il-sung and his son Kim Jong-il. Originally coined by Kim Jong-il in this spirit, Kimilsungism places primary emphasis on Korea as the center of world revolution and Kim Il-sung as the expositor of the loftiest revolutionary theory through his written works, which are thus worthy of study the world over. Kimilsungism embodies a specific narrative of modern Korean history, placing Kim Il-sung at the center of the East Asian resistance to Japanese imperialism and crediting him with the liberation of Korea (a liberation foully thwarted by U.S. imperialism) and also with victory in the great fatherland liberation war of 1950–1953.

Kisaeng. Professional woman entertainer of men at social occasions who can make intelligent conversation, recite and even compose poetry, sing, dance, and play musical instruments.

Koguryo. A kingdom constituted by nomadic peoples that dominated much of the northern part of the Korean peninsula as well as Manchuria, which thrived from the first to the seventh centuries A.D. It was extinguished by Silla in the unification of the peninsula in A.D. 668.

Koryo. Dynasty founded by Wang Kon in A.D. 936 after overthrowing the Silla Dynasty; endured until 1392. The Western name for Korea is derived from Koryo.

Ku. Subdivision (ward) of a city (also used as a suffix and sometimes spelled *-gu*); for example, Chung-gu, the heart of Seoul's downtown, the ward of the capital city where Seoul's biggest department stores and hotels are located.

Kun. Subdivision (county) of a province (also used as a suffix and sometimes spelled (*-gun*).

Kut. A shamanistic ceremony performed by an adept (*mudang*) with costume, song, and dance, to invoke or exorcise spirits.

Kwangju incident of May 1980. Also called the "Kwangju uprising," the "Kwangju rebellion," the "Kwangju massacre," and the "Kwangju Democratization Movement." A violent ten-day confrontation in May 1980 between martial law troops under the control of military strongman Chun Doo-hwan and anti–martial law demonstrators in which about 200 (by government estimates) Kwangju citizens were killed. Human rights groups typically put the death toll much higher. Fallout from the Kwangju incident hobbled the Chun and Roh regimes and ultimately led to Chun's arrest in 1995.

Kye. (1) A traditional mutual assistance group common in agricultural villages, typically composed of men in the same age group. (2) In recent times, a group of people, often women, who pool their savings for profitable investment.

Makkoli. A milky, winelike farmers' and workers' drink, brewed from rice, traditional and still popular.

Manshin. See *mudang.*

Military Armistice Commission. A body established by the Armistice Agreement of 1953, composed of five representatives of each opposing side, to enforce the provisions of the Agreement. Each side also has a secretary, duty officer, and staff.

Mudang. A shamanistic adept, usually female, who is versed in the ancient beliefs about good and evil spirits, is in communication with them, and is sometimes possessed by them in the course of shamanistic ceremony (*kut*). (Also called *manshin.*)

Myon. Rural township, subdivision of a *kun* (county).

Nangnang. A Chinese military commandery, or colony, established in 108 B.C. in southern Manchuria or northern Korea during the Chinese Han Dynasty (208 B.C.–A.D. 220). Nangnang fell to the Korean state of Koguryo in A.D. 313.

National Congress for New Politics. Political party started in 1995 by Kim Dae-jung when he reemerged from retirement. Much of the party's support comes from old-line supporters of Kim Dae-jung and the southwest Korean region of the Cholla provinces.

National Security Law. Enacted in 1958 to control the activities of "antistate" organizations in south Korea. The law's ostensible purpose is to protect national security, but it has frequently been applied selectively to punish domestic dissidents. The law was amended in May 1991 to limit offenses to those that would "endanger the security of the nation or basic order of liberal democracy," a change that human rights advocates did not regard as significant.

New Korea Democratic Party (NKDP). Political party established in early 1985, which attained the status of major opposition by winning sixty seats in the legislative elections that year, but was reduced to minor-party status by the departure of its principal organizers in April 1987. (In Korean: *Sinhan minjudang*).

New Korea Party (NKP). Political party formed by President Kim Young-sam in 1995 from the ruins of the Democratic Liberal Party that was created in 1990 when Kim merged his forces with the military-backed Democratic Justice Party of Presidents Chun Doo-hwan and Roh Tae-woo. The NKP is associated with Kim's home area of South Kyongsang Province.

Nong'ak. Traditional folk music played by amateur farmer-musicians, often accompanied by group dancing.

Nordpolitik. Term used since about 1983 for south Korea's promotion of contact with Communist countries (adapted from the West German *ostpolitik,* describing a similar and earlier policy). Among its successes were getting the socialist countries to attend the 1988 Olympics in Seoul over north Korean objections, winning trade arrangements and then recognition from the Soviet Union and the People's Republic of China, and finally winning enough support in the United Nations General Assembly to enable both Koreas to be admitted to full UN membership in 1991. *Nordpolitik* is most closely associated with former President Roh Tae-woo.

Ondol. Unique Korean house-heating system whereby hot flue gases from the kitchen fire provide heat by passing through serpentine channels among stones under the floors before escaping through a chimney.

Paduk. A popular and intellectually challenging Korean board game (called *go* in Japan), somewhat similar to checkers but more complex.

Paekche. Kingdom established in southwest Korea, which flourished in the fourth to seventh centuries A.D. and had ties to both China and Japan. It was defeated and incorporated into the united Silla kingdom in A.D. 668.

Panmunjom. A village on the outskirts of the north Korean city of Kaesong; the site of truce negotiations, 1951–1954, during the Korean War; the site of the signing of the 1953 Armistice Agreement; the site of the "truce village" where both sides' delegations on the Military Armistice Commission discussed armistice violations, etc.; the scene of several dramatic incidents, such as the north Koreans' ax-murder of two Americans who were attempting to trim a view-blocking tree in 1976; also, the only recognized gateway between north and south Korea, making it the scene of some dramatic passages: for example, the return of the crew of the captured American intelligence ship USS *Pueblo* in December 1988; the return of dissident *Chondaehyop* activist Im Su-gyong in 1989; and the return of former President Jimmy Carter after his Gordian knot–breaking visit to Kim Il-sung to discuss the nuclear issue, just before Kim's death in the summer of 1994.

P'ansori. A form of folktale with song, performed solo to the accompaniment of a barrel drum. Developed during the Choson Dynasty, its often humorous repertoire ridicules the life of the aristocracy and priesthood and extols the traditional Confucian virtues.

Parhae. Kingdom in northeastern Korea and southern Manchuria, including both Korean and Tungusic people, which was formed after the fall of Koguryo to Silla in the late seventh century A.D. and endured until conquered by the Khitan in 926. Its territories south of the Yalu and Tumen rivers (which form the present Korean border) were incorporated into Korea by the early Koryo kings.

Pukchin t'ongil. A slogan ("march north for unification") commonly voiced during President Rhee's administration in south Korea (1948–1960) expressing his desire for reunification of Korea by extending the Republic's jurisdiction—by force, if necessary.

Reunification Democratic Party (RDP). Political party formed on May 1, 1987, by supporters of opposition leaders Kim Young-sam and Kim Dae-jung, who bolted the New Korea Democratic Party and became the main opposition. The new party was split in two with the departure of Kim Dae-jung and his supporters in late 1987. (In Korean: *T'ongil minjudang,* or *T'ongmindang.*)

Ri. Village within a township (*myon*); the smallest rural Korean political unit.

Ri (also romanized as *li*). A traditional Korean unit of distance, equivalent to about one-half of a kilometer (one-third of a mile).

Sadaejuui. The principle of respect for (or subservience to) power (or greatness) that characterized Korean attitudes toward China during the Choson Dynasty. Then a reflection of Confucian morality, the term is now one of opprobrium applied to people who dance to the foreigner's tune.

Saema'ul undong (**New Community Movement**). A nationwide movement launched in 1971 by south Korean President Park Chung-hee to mobilize villagers for their own mutual benefit to improve their quality of life. Villagers were encouraged to band together for group action on public works such as housing, roads, irrigation, and community facilities as part of a nationwide organization.

Samil undong. The March First Movement of 1919—a nationwide unarmed uprising against the Japanese rulers to demand restoration of national independence.

Sarangbang. A special room in well-to-do homes where men met and entertained.

Security Consultative Meeting (SCM). Annual meeting of high defense officials of the Republic of Korea (headed by the minister of national defense) and the United States (headed by the secretary of defense) to review security matters of mutual concern. The meetings are held alternately in the two countries.

Sejong. Fourth king of the Choson Dynasty. His reign, 1418–1450, is regarded as the high point of the dynasty, and he is considered the father of the Korean phonetic alphabet, *han'gul.*

Si. Korean term for a city (generally 50,000 population or more); also used as a suffix, as in Suwon-si, city of Suwon. Seoul, the capital, is termed "special city" (*t'ukpyol si*); the cities of Pusan, Taegu, Inch'on, and Kwangju are also referred to as special cities in English but are termed *chikhwal si* (directly administered city) in Korean. All five are administratively equal to provinces. Other cities are equivalent to counties.

Sijo. A form of philosophic poetry, written in pure Korean rather than Chinese, that became a major form of literary expression during the Choson Dynasty.

Silla. Located in the southeastern part of the peninsula, Silla grew to prominence in the fourth and fifth centuries A.D. as one of Korea's "three kingdoms." By A.D. 668 Silla had conquered the other two kingdoms and ruled over most of the peninsula until A.D. 936.

Sirhak. A movement by young Confucian scholars in the eighteenth century to reform the rigid prevailing neo-Confucian philosophy. The Korean word means "practical learning."

Soju. A cheap, strong liquor distilled from rice that is popular among Korean farmers and workers.

Songgyun'gwan. The highest-level educational institution of the Choson Dynasty, a Confucian university. *Songgyun'gwan* still operates on its original site as a modern liberal arts university, but retains some of its Confucian heritage.

South-North Coordinating Committee (SNCC). Established by the Joint North-South Declaration of July 4, 1972, the Committee consists of five representatives each of north and south Korea who are theoretically charged with the negotiation of steps toward reunification. In practice, however, the Committee has seldom met except for sporadic exploratory working-level sessions.

Sowon. Academies for the instruction of young people organized by scholars and ex-officials, particularly those out of favor, during the Choson Dynasty. The *sowon* often served as headquarters for factions vying for political power; for this reason, most of them were abolished in the mid-nineteenth century.

Ssirum. Korean version of wrestling by men with large, heavy bodies; somewhat similar to Japanese *sumo*.

Suzerainty. Control exercised by one state over another's foreign affairs without destroying the latter's identity. As Korea's suzerain during the Choson Dynasty, China controlled Korea's foreign relations but in general did not interfere in its internal affairs.

T'aekwondo. A Korean martial art, famous worldwide. It emphasizes mental discipline and quick foot and fist movements, performed in a controlled manner carefully practiced in advance.

T'aejo. Reign name (meaning "great progenitor") of Yi Song-gye, a military leader who overthrew the Koryo Dynasty and founded his own Choson Dynasty in 1392. T'aejo cultivated good relations with Ming Dynasty China to reinforce his own legitimacy and modeled his government and political philosophy after that of China.

Taejonggyo. Religion of recent origin organized around the worship of Tan'-gun, mythical founder of Korea.

Tan'gun. The mythical founder of the Korean nation in 2333 B.C., a man born of a bear at the bidding of a god.

"Team Spirit." Annual large-scale Korean-U.S. joint military exercises conducted in early spring to verify the ability of the Combined Forces Command to stop a north Korean attack. In recent years the exercise has involved 200,000 or more troops of both countries and naval and air units as well as ground forces. North Korea's objections to the provocative nature of the "Team Spirit" exercises eventually led to their cancellation during negotiations over the north's alleged nuclear weapons program in 1992 and 1993, and in subsequent years. Though there have been other joint maneuvers, the "Team Spirit" exercises have either been much attenuated or eliminated altogether.

Three Kingdoms Period. A period of three or more centuries when three Korean states coexisted in the Korean peninsula—Koguryo, Paekche, and Silla. Silla unified much of the peninsula by conquering the other two kingdoms in A.D. 668, although the northeastern portion of the peninsula was controlled by a separate state of Parhae.

Three Revolutions. A campaign launched in the early 1970s under the leadership of north Korean President Kim Il-sung's son, Kim Jong-Il, to encourage innovation and eliminate the barriers of bureaucratic immobilism. The three revolutions are technological, ideological, and cultural.

To. Province, the major territorial division of Korea (often written *-do* and used as a suffix). During most of the Choson Dynasty, there were eight Korean provinces; five of these were divided in two in 1895, for a total of thirteen. North Korea has further subdivided the five provinces in its territory, for a total of nine, equal to south Korea. In addition, each Korean state has four special cities with status equal to provinces; south Korea added a fifth (Kwangju) in 1987.

Tong. Precinct; subdivision of a city ward (often written *-dong* and used as a suffix; for example, Chong-dong, Yonhi-dong, etc.).

Tonghak. A religious movement of the mid-nineteenth century that was a cause of the Sino-Japanese War. See under *Ch'ondogyo.*

T'ongilgyo. The Unification Church of the Rev. Sun Myung Moon (Mun Sonmyong), a mutation of Christianity, which has gained many converts in the United States, Japan, and other countries.

Uibyongdae. Volunteer bands who fought the Japanese invaders of the late sixteenth century and again in the early twentieth century.

United Liberal Democratic Party. Party formed by veteran political leader Kim Jong-pil in 1995 after he bolted the ruling Democratic Liberal Party. Draws support from old military factions and politicians from the Ch'ungch'ong province area of central Korea.

Up. Urban township or borough, subdivision of a county on the same level as a *myon;* often used as a suffix.

Won. The Korean monetary unit. The south Korean won is worth over onetenth of a U.S. cent; the exchange rate varies, but in January 1996 it was around

785 won per dollar. There is no real exchange rate between the north Korean won and the dollar, but it is worth several hundred times the value of its south Korean counterpart. One won is comprised of 100 *chon*.

Yangban. Scholar-officials who constituted the aristocratic or noble class of the Choson Dynasty. The majority were selected through an examination system based on the Chinese classics.

Yi Dynasty. Another term for the Choson Dynasty (1392–1910), derived from the family name of its founder, Yi Song-gye. Korean historians now prefer the term Choson for this period.

Yo. A pad, or thin mattress, placed on the floor for sleeping.

Yut. A traditional game for young and old, played with four sticks tossed in the air.

Appendix B:
The Korean Language
and Its Romanization

General Description

Korean is a language common to all 67 million inhabitants of the Korean peninsula and is an important element of Korean national identity. It is similar in structure to Japanese, Mongolian, Turkish, Hungarian, and Finnish, with which it is sometimes grouped in a Ural-Altaic family of languages. However, its phonetic structure is unique. Korean differs from the other Ural-Altaic languages even more than English differs from, let us say, Hindi, although both are Indo-European languages.

The Korean language is called agglutinative—that is, syllables are added to verbs, adjectives, and nouns to show relationships of time, place, subject to object, and social position of speaker, hearer, and person spoken about. Word order in a sentence typically puts the subject first, followed by the object, with the verb at the end. Modifiers, or adjectives, behave somewhat like verbs and can take the place of verbs. Particles (usually single syllables) known as postpositions follow nouns in somewhat the same way as English prepositions precede nouns. These differences in structure make translation from Korean to English, or vice versa, rather difficult.

The polysyllabic, agglutinative character of Korean makes it totally unlike Chinese, which is basically monosyllabic and without word inflection. Also unlike Chinese, but like English, "tones" or variations in pitch, play no part in the meaning of individual words in Korean, but do convey feeling and complement grammatical structure, distinguishing questions, statements, and commands.

Phonetically, Korean differs sharply from English in that the meaning of its consonants differs according to whether they are aspirated or unaspirated (that is, whether their articulation is, or is not, accompanied by a puff of breath). It does not matter, in Korean, whether a consonant is voiced (like the English "b" or "d") or unvoiced (like the English "p" or "t"); voicing depends on the position of a consonant in a word or phrase. This pattern is the reverse of English, which aspirates some consonants and not others without effect on meaning. Additionally, a group of Korean consonants is distinguished by an almost explosive tenseness in pronunciation, somewhat like the French "p." The Korean alphabet distinguishes fourteen consonants; at least one Korean scholar has identified twenty-four different consonantal sounds.

The Korean Writing System

Until the fifteenth century, Korea had no writing system of its own. Records were kept in Chinese or by using the pronunciation of Chinese characters to represent Korean sounds. A set of abbreviated Chinese characters, called *idu,* was developed for this purpose. The great King Sejong convened a committee of scholars who developed the phonetic alphabet now known as *han'gul.* The new alphabet was proclaimed in 1446, but despite its obvious advantages it was not generally accepted by the Korean scholarly community until the twentieth century; the official records of the Choson Dynasty (1392–1910) were kept in classical Chinese. A page from the original fifteenth-century instructions for the use of *han'gul,* intermixed with Chinese characters, is shown in Figure B.1; there has been considerable change in spelling and pronunciation since then but not much change in the manner of writing the characters. The modern *han'gul* characters, with their roman letter equivalents, are shown in Table B.1.

Han'gul is almost always written in syllabic groups, with the initial consonant at the left or top, the vowel to the right, center, or bottom, and the final consonant, if any, underneath. If there is no initial consonant, this fact is signaled with a separate character—the same one used for the "ng" sound. If there is no final consonant, it is simply omitted.

The use of syllabic groups makes it easy to combine the phonetic script with Chinese characters. Literate Koreans in the south still use Chinese characters for words derived from Chinese (which make up about half the listings in Korean dictionaries), and the schools teach a standard list of 1,900 such characters. In north Korea, the use of Chinese characters was abolished many years ago. This was an understandable gesture of nationalist assertion, and it simplified the reading and writing of Korean for the general public; but it also added to north Korea's isolation from its neighbors.

Traditionally, Korean (like Chinese) was written from top to bottom of the page, and right to left; the pages of a book were therefore in the reverse order to English. Today, both the traditional style and the Western style (horizontally, left to right) are used—the latter particularly in scholarly works where quotations from Western languages are interspersed in the text. Most publications are printed, but calligraphy is still an honored art form in Korea. It is common for noted persons to write short poems or epigrams—usually in Chinese characters, but sometimes in *han'gul*—for presentation to their followers and friends. The signboard on the Kwanghwamun, the gate in front of the old capitol building in Seoul (now a national museum), was inscribed in *han'gul* by the late President

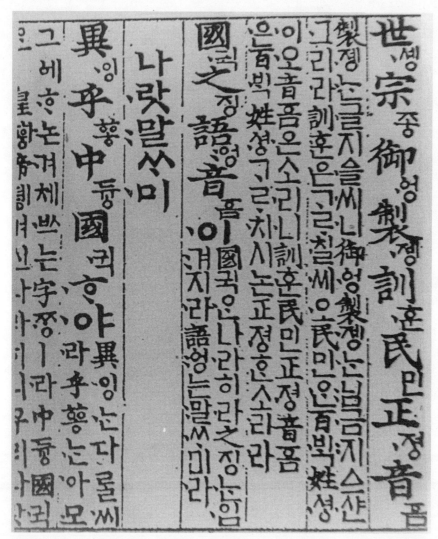

FIGURE B.1 A page of Korean phonetic script from the fifteenth-century document *Hunmin Chongum,* showing *han'gul* intermingled with Chinese characters (photo by Edward Adams)

TABLE B.1   Romanization of Korean

Han'gul	Consonants Roman (according to position)			Han'gul	Vowels Roman
	initial	medial[a]	final		
ㄱ	k	g	k	ㅏ	a
ㄴ	n	n	n	ㅑ	ya
ㄷ	t	d	t	ㅓ	ŏ
ㄹ	n, r	l, n, r	l	ㅕ	yŏ
ㅁ	m	m	m	ㅗ	o
ㅂ	p	b	p	ㅛ	yo
ㅅ	s	s	s	ㅜ	u
ㅇ	—	ng	ng	ㅠ	yu
ㅈ	ch	j	ch	ㅡ	ŭ
ㅊ	ch'	ch'	ch'	ㅣ	i
ㅋ	k'	k'	—	ㅐ	ae
ㅌ	t'	t'	t	ㅒ	yae
ㅍ	p'	p'	p	ㅔ	e
ㅎ	h	h	—	ㅖ	ye
ㄲ	kk	kk	kk	ㅘ	wa
ㄸ	tt	tt	tt	ㅙ	wae
ㅃ	pp	pp	—	ㅚ	oe
ㅆ	ss	ss	tt	ㅝ	wŏ
ㅉ	jj	jj	jj	ㅞ	we
				ㅟ	wi
				ㅢ	ui

[a]The chart does not show elisions and euphonic modifications resulting from juxtaposition of consonants.

SOURCE: Adopted from Korean Overseas Information Service, *Han'gul (Korean Alphabet and language)*, Korea Background Series, Vol. 9 (Seoul, n.d.), pp. 56–58.

Park Chung-hee; it is one of the few examples of such inscriptions that reads in the modern manner, from left to right.

Romanization—Writing Korean in Roman Letters

The spelling of Korean in the Latin alphabet for English speakers is made very difficult by differences in the phonetic systems of the two languages, which also make the Korean language difficult for English speakers to learn. After years of experimentation, both the governments of both the Republic of Korea and the United States and many Western scholars have come to accept a romanization system devised by George M. McCune and Edwin O. Reischauer in 1938. Scholarly files in the United States, including the index of the Library of Congress and most university libraries, are based on the McCune-Reischauer system of romanization.

The McCune-Reischauer system uses roman letters chosen to represent the English sound most nearly approximating the Korean. An apostrophe (') after a consonant shows that it is aspirated (e.g., p' or t'), and a double letter (e.g., pp or tt) indicates a "fortis" or explosive pronunciation. In general, an unaspirated consonant is voiced in Korean when it occurs in the middle of a word and is therefore romanized in the McCune-Reischauer system with its approximate English voiced equivalent (b, d, etc.).

Most of the vowels in Korean have approximate—but not precise—English counterparts. Two of them, which lack even approximate English equivalents, are spelled in the McCune-Reischauer system with a diacritical mark: "ŏ," a sound between the English "o" in "oh" and "u" in "uh"; and "ū," a sound like the French "u." In this book, the diacritical marks have been omitted for simplicity, so that the proper distinction in pronunciation between "o" and "ŏ," "u" and "ū," is lost. For purposes of managing the few Korean terms that appear in common U.S. use, the loss is not serious, but the reader should be aware of it. In *han'gul*, ten vowel symbols are distinguished, but they are used in combination to represent additional sounds.

Table B.1 shows the *han'gul* characters for the Korean consonants and vowels and their roman equivalents according to the McCune-Reischauer system. One special feature of the McCune-Reischauer system must be noted: the additional use of the apostrophe (') to separate "n" and "g" in cases where they are not to be pronounced together. In Korean, there is a separate single symbol for the nasal "ng" sound (as in the English word "sing"); but when this sound is romanized as "ng," it cannot be distinguished from two successive syllables, one with a final "n" and the other with an initial "g." Accordingly, whenever the two romanized consonants appear together without an apostrophe, they are pronounced together as "ng"; when separated ("n'g"), they are pronounced separately. Thus, the Han

River, *Han'gang,* has a separate "n" and "g," while "Eastern Sea" or "oriental," *tongyang,* has an "ng" sound.

Unfortunately, there has been a great deal of romanization of Korean that does not follow the McCune-Reischauer system. Before that system was devised, writers used their own phonetic interpretations. The nineteenth-century French Catholic missionaries devised a romanization system (from which the present spelling of the capital city, Seoul, is derived). The U.S. military government had its own system. The south Korean Ministry of Education established a system that was followed for a decade. Individual Koreans spell their own names according to their own preferences (for example, the former south Korean National Assembly Chairman, whose name would be Sin Ik-hui in McCune-Reischauer, styled himself Patrick Henry Shinicky; people with the family name spelled Yi in McCune-Reischauer use Lee, Rhee, Rii, Leigh). In this book, the McCune-Reischauer system is used except for proper names commonly romanized otherwise.

I have not seen any written rules for the north Korean system of romanization. However, north Korean English-language materials suggest that unaspirated consonants are represented by their voiced English equivalents and aspirated consonants are represented by the unvoiced equivalents, instead of using apostrophes. The south Korean Ministry of Education's former system employed somewhat the same principle. Some Koreans believe that this method is better than Mc-Cune-Reischauer, because to their ears it seems to make English speakers pronounce the consonants better. (The pinyin romanization system of Chinese adopted by the People's Republic of China to replace the missionary-devised Wade-Giles system also uses voiced English equivalents for unaspirated consonants, and unvoiced equivalents for aspirated ones, rather than the Wade-Giles apostrophes.) North Korean romanizations, insofar as they are known, have been used for north Korean names in this book. Thus, Kim Il-sung's son's name is spelled Kim Jong-il, rather than the McCune-Reischauer Kim Chong-il; the capital city is Pyongyang, rather than P'yongyang, in post-1945 references.

Appendix C:
Korean Studies
Reading List

The following is a representative selection of English-language materials considered suitable for undergraduate college or high-school study. Specialized scholarly works and children's books on Korea, of which there are a growing number, are not listed.

General and Reference

The Asia Society's *Korea Briefing* series, edited by Chong-sik Lee (1990), Donald N. Clark (1991–1993), David R. McCann (1996). Boulder: Westview Press, 1990–1993; New York: M. E. Sharpe, 1996. Annual collection of articles reviewing the year's events in politics, economics, and security issues, plus articles on less time-bound themes such as the press, women's issues, literature, music, dance, and law. Emphasizes south Korea but includes material on the north as well.

Bartz, Patricia. *South Korea.* New York: Oxford, England: Clarendon Press, 1972. 203 pp. The only recent geographical study of Korea; also contains a brief, although now somewhat outdated, summary of Korean history and government.

Cumings, Bruce. *The Two Koreas.* New York: Foreign Policy Association, 1984. 80 pp., paper. Brief, readable description of both Korean states, objectively and clearly written, with some historical background. Prof. Cumings, of Northwestern University, is a highly regarded scholar of Korea. (Available from the Foreign Policy Association, 729 Seventh Avenue, New York, NY 10019.)

Korea Overseas Information Service. *A Handbook of Korea.* Seoul: Korea Overseas Information Service, 1994. An encyclopedia-type compilation of narrative and statistics on all aspects of south Korean history, politics, economy, and society. Useful as a reference tool. New editions are published every few years and distributed through Korean diplomatic and consular posts overseas.

Lee, Peter H., and Wm. Theodore deBary. *Sources of Korean Tradition,* 2 vols. New York: Columbia University Press, 1996. Like the Chinese, Japanese, and Indian *Sources* volumes before it, an essential collection of primary works from Korean history, expertly translated with explanatory headnotes. Includes excerpts from classical works of history, literature, religion, and philosophy.

Savada, Andrea Matles. *North Korea: A Country Study,* 4th ed., Department of the Army Pamphlet DA Pam 550-81. Washington, D.C.: U.S. Government Printing Office, 1994. The latest edition of the U.S. Army's area handbook series, with analytical articles about history, politics, economics, society, and national security. Very useful bibliographies are attached to each section presenting titles of books and articles in English.

Savada, Andrea Matles, and William R. Shaw. *South Korea: A Country Study,* 4th ed., Department of the Army Pamphlet DA Pam 550-41. Washington, D.C.: U.S. Government Printing Office, 1992. The latest edition of the U.S. Army's area handbook series for the Republic of Korea, with the same layout as the item above.

Yonhap News Agency. *Korea Annual.* Published in Seoul by Yonhap, the *Annual* is a useful source for statistics and current events. Almost half the volume is devoted to a "Who's Who" of both south and north Korea.

History

Eckert, Carter J., Lee Ki-baik, Young Ick Lew, Michael Robinson, and Edward W. Wagner. *Korea Old and New.* Cambridge, Mass.: The Korea Institute, Harvard University, 1990. Textbook-type survey of Korean history by top historians in Korea and the United States.

Fairbank, John K., Edwin O. Reischauer, and Albert M. Craig. *East Asia: Tradition and Transformation.* Cambridge, Mass.: Houghton Mifflin Co., 1973. 969 pp. This excellent survey of East Asian history from early times to the present has two chapters on the history of traditional Korea (chapters 11 and 12, pp. 277–323), and sections of two others (chapter 20, pp. 609–618, and chapter 27, pp. 878–886) on Korea since the mid-nineteenth century.

Goulden, Joseph C. *Korea: The Untold Story of the War.* New York: Times Books, 1982. 690 pp. Thorough description of the Korean War from the U.S. point of view, with emphasis on personalities and politics. Like other American histories of the war, however, it gives insufficient attention to the south Korean forces involved.

Halliday, Jon, and Bruce Cumings. *Korea: The Unknown War.* New York: Pantheon Books, 1989. A richly illustrated, easily accessible presentation of the Korean War as a civil war whose domestic causes were overtaken by the outside forces of the Cold War.

Han, Woo-keun. *The History of Korea.* Translated by Lee Kyung-shik, edited by Grafton K. Mintz. Honolulu: East-West Center Press, 1971. 546 pp. Now republished in paperback, this is perhaps the most readable of several good English-language histories by Korean historians, published in Korea. Unfortunately, like the others it has little to say about Korea since 1910.

Lone, Stewart, and Gavan McCormack. *Korea Since 1850.* New York: St. Martin's Press, 1993. A survey that includes a useful history of the north Korean system.

Nahm, Andrew C. *Korea: Tradition and Transformation: A History of the Korean People.* Elizabeth, N.J.: Hollym International Corp., 1988. 588 pp., illustrations, chronology, appendices, bibliography, index. Comprehensive, clearly written work, emphasizing the modern period.

Suh, Dae Sook. *Kim Il Sung: The North Korean Leader.* New York: Columbia University Press, 1989. A biography that also functions as a history of the Democratic People's Republic of Korea.

Society and Culture

Brandt, Vincent S.R. *South Korean Society in Transition.* Elkins Park, Pa.: Philip Jaisohn Memorial Foundation, 1983. 50 pp. Well-written explanation of current Korean social problems in a brief paperback pamphlet available from the Foundation (60 East Township Line Road, Elkins Park, Pa.). Dr. Brandt, a social anthropologist, is one of the few recognized U.S. authorities on Korean society.

Clark, Donald N. *Christianity in Modern Korea.* Asia Society monograph. Lanham, Md.: University Press of America, 1986. 86 pp. Useful survey of the background and present position of Korean Christianity, the faith of one-quarter of the south Korean population.

Kalton, Michael. *Korean Ideas and Values.* Elkins Park, Pa.: Philip Jaisohn Memorial Foundation, 1979. 21 pp. Concise explanation of basic Korean social values, in a brief pamphlet. Available from the Foundation.

Kendall, Laurel, and Mark Peterson, eds. *Korean Women: View from the Inner Room.* New Haven, Conn.: East Rock Press, 1983. Outstanding essays on traditional and contemporary Korean women by leading academic specialists on Korea.

Koo, Hagen, ed. *State and Society in Contemporary Korea.* Ithaca: Cornell University Press, 1993. Articles by leading Korea specialists about political and social forces and the trends under way in contemporary south Korea.

Arts and Literature

Lee, Peter H., comp. *Anthology of Korean Literature: From Early Times to the Nineteenth Century.* Honolulu: University of Hawaii Press, 1981. 448 pp., paper. Good selections to give the flavor of Korean writing, with introductory explanations. A companion volume by the same author is *Modern Korean Literature* (Honolulu: University of Hawaii Press, 1990).

McCune, Evelyn. *The Arts of Korea: An Illustrated History.* Rutland, Vt.: Charles E. Tuttle Co., 1962. 452 pp., bibliography, index. For the general reader, this is still the best short survey of Korean art, although there are more scholarly and more recent works.

Shultz, Edward J. *The History and Culture of Korea*. Six sound and color film-strips with text and guide. Honolulu: University of Hawaii Press, 1985. Suitable for secondary and adult audiences.

So, Chongju. *Unforgettable Things*. Poems translated by David McCann. Seoul and New York: Si-sa-yong-o-sa, 1986. 158 pp. So Chongju is one of Korea's fore-most contemporary poets, and has been mentioned as a possible nominee for a Nobel prize. David McCann is a U.S. authority on Korean literature.

Words of Farewell: Stories by Korean Women Writers. Translated by Bruce and Ju Chan Fulton. Seattle: The Seal Press, 1989. Stories about the conflicts and choices that women face in a rapidly changing Korean society.

Politics

Clark, Donald N., ed. *The Kwangju Uprising: Shadows over the Regime in South Korea*. Boulder: Westview Press, 1988. Three thought-provoking essays on this significant event from the standpoint of anthropology, history, and literature, plus a discussion of the problem of the American connection and the U.S.-ROK Combined Forces Command.

Cumings, Bruce. *The Origins of the Korean War*, 2 vols. Volume I: *Liberation and the Emergence of Separate Regimes, 1945–1947*. Princeton: Princeton University Press, 1981. Volume II: *The Roaring of the Cataract, 1947–1950*. Princeton: Princeton University Press, 1990. The definitive study of political processes in postcolonial Korea that laid the basis for the political cultures of divided Korea; stresses the internal conflicts between left and right in Korea and the legacy of Japanese rule, "revising" the view that the Korean War was an international conflict and presenting it as fundamentally a civil and revolutionary war.

Han, Sungjoo. *The Failure of Democracy in South Korea*. Berkeley: University of California Press, 1975. 250 pp. Scholarly study of the reasons for the failure of South Korea's brief experiment with full parliamentary democracy in 1960 and 1961.

Human Rights in the Democratic People's Republic of Korea (North Korea). Minneapolis and Washington, D.C.: Minnesota Lawyers International Human Rights Committee and Asia Watch, 1988. 159 pp. Careful study of evidence available outside north Korea with critical conclusions.

Human Rights in Korea. New York: Asia Watch, 1987. 364 pp. Report of the human rights situation in Korea by a humanitarian group dedicated to observation of human rights violations worldwide.

Kim, C.I. Eugene, and B. C. Koh, eds. *Journey to North Korea*. Berkeley: University of California Press, 1983. 152 pp. Accounts by several scholars of their observations during a visit to north Korea.

Masao Okonogi, ed. *North Korea at the Crossroads.* Tokyo: Japan Institute of International Affairs, 1988. A useful Japanese view of current north Korean affairs.

Kim, Ilpyong J., and Young Whan Kihl, eds. *Political Change in South Korea.* New York: Korean PWPA, Inc.; distributed by Paragon House Publishers, 1988. 263 pp., bibliography, index. Useful analysis of recent south Korean political events and trends, including background since 1945. The authors and editors are recognized authorities.

Yang, Sung Chul. *The North and South Korean Political Systems* (Boulder: Westview Press, 1994). An encyclopedic work of comparative politics discussing theory, political dynamics, leadership, law, elites, and institutions.

Foreign Relations, National Security, Unification

Clough, Ralph N. *Embattled Korea: The Rivalry for International Support.* Boulder: Westview Press, 1987. 401 pp. Valuable survey of north and south Korean international relations, from the standpoint of their rivalry for international support and their differing positions on reunification.

Kihl, Young Whan, ed. *Korea and the World: Beyond the Cold War.* Boulder: Westview Press, 1994. A collection of essays by Korean and Western Korea-watchers on the effects of *nordpolitik* and strategies for lessening tension with north Korea.

Koh, Byung Chul. *The Foreign Policy Systems of North and South Korea.* Berkeley: University of California Press, 1984. 274 pp. Good description of how and why foreign policy is made in the two Koreas. A scholarly book, but intelligible to the intelligent general reader.

Ku, Yong-nok, and Sungjoo Han, eds. *The Foreign Policy of the Republic of Korea.* New York: Columbia University Press, 1985. 300 pp. Well-written, cogent essays analyzing Korean foreign relations.

Economics

Brun, Ellen, and Jacques Hirsch. *Socialist Korea: A Case Study in the Strategy of Economic Development.* New York: Monthly Review Press, 1977, 432 pp. Written from a viewpoint favorable to Communist north Korea, this book is useful for those who want to understand the arguments in favor of that country's centrally directed economic system. It gives little hint, however, of the serious problems that have plagued that system since the early 1970s.

Cho, Soon. *The Dynamics of Korean Economic Growth.* Washington, D.C.: Institute for International Economics, 1994. A survey by one of Korea's top economists (and mayor of Seoul in 1995), concluding with recommendations about the directions Korea should take in foreign trade.

Kuznets, Paul W. *Economic Growth and Structure in the Republic of Korea.* New Haven, Conn.: Yale University Press, 1977. 238 pp. Scholarly discussion of south Korea's economic development since the Korean War.

Mason, Edward S., et al. *The Economic and Social Modernization of the Republic of Korea.* Cambridge, Mass.: Harvard University Press, 1980. 500 pp. Summary of a comprehensive study by Harvard University's Center for Economic Development and the Korea Development Institute in south Korea of the reasons for Korea's economic success.

Moskowitz, Karl, ed. *From Patron to Partner: The Development of U.S.-Korean Business and Trade Relations.* Lexington, Mass.: Lexington Books, 1984. 234 pp. Essays by Korean and U.S. authorities discussing the evolution of the Korea-U.S. economic relationship and its current problems.

Woo, Jung-en. *Race to the Swift: State and Finance in Korean Industrialization.* New York: Columbia University Press, 1991. A study of the part played by state financing in the development of the south Korean economy, pointing to lessons learned from Japanese models and the use of American aid in the post–Korean War era.

Current Sources of Information on Korea

Daily Newspapers

Two daily English-language newspapers are published in south Korea: the *Korea Times* and the *Korea Herald.* They are privately owned and similar in coverage, the *Times* being a subsidiary of the Korean *Hankook Ilbo.* The *Korea Times* has a completely separate Los Angeles edition that is published monthly for the second generation of Korean Americans. The essential contents of the *Herald* are available daily on the World Wide Web at http://zec.three.co.kr/koreaherald.

U.S. newspapers do not give much coverage to Korean affairs except in times of crisis or disaster.

Weeklies

To keep up with Korean political and economic affairs, the best single source is probably the *Far Eastern Economic Review,* a weekly news magazine published in Hong Kong. The *Asian Wall Street Journal,* also published in Hong Kong, has a weekly edition.

For general coverage of the current south Korean scene, the best English-language publication is *Korea Newsreview,* a weekly published by the Korea Herald Company in Seoul. News bulletins and pamphlets on current topics are often available from Korean information offices attached to diplomatic and consular missions; these, of course, tend to reflect the official view.

For north Korea, there are English-language publications sponsored by the north Korean government, but they are not generally available in the United

States, and are heavy on propaganda. An alternative is the daily and weekly Asia-Pacific reports summarizing radio and newspaper stories, published by Foreign Broadcast Information Service, a U.S. Government operation attached to the Department of Commerce. These are available in metropolitan and large university libraries. The south Korean government also publishes useful materials on north Korea, although some of them have heavy propaganda overtones.

Monthlies and Quarterlies

Asian Survey, a monthly published by the University of California, contains articles covering all of East and South Asia. The January and February issues each year summarize the previous year's developments in separate articles on all Asian countries, including north and south Korea.

Bulletin of Korean and Korean-American Studies, published by Dr. Hesung Koh, East Rock Institute, 251 Dwight Street, New Haven, CT 06511.

Journal of Northeast Asian Studies, quarterly published at the Institute for Sino-Soviet Studies, George Washington University, Washington, D.C. Concentrates on China, Japan, and Korea.

Korea and World Affairs. Quarterly journal of the Research Center for Peace and Unification of Korea; has a good collection of articles on foreign affairs by recognized Korean and foreign scholars.

Korea Journal, monthly publication of the Korean Commission for UNESCO, Seoul. Articles on all aspects of Korean national life, with emphasis on history and culture. Highly recommended.

Korean Culture, quarterly published in Los Angeles under South Korean government subsidy and distributed free to teachers and others on request. Focusing on Korean art and culture, it is well written and illustrated with color reproductions.

Koreana is a beautifully produced quarterly published by the Korea Foundation in Seoul, with well-edited articles on aspects of Korean culture covered nowhere else. Recent subjects have included fabrics, food customs, eating utensils, crafts, living national treasures, and musical instruments.

Mid-Atlantic Bulletin of Korean Studies. Published three times a year at the Asian Studies Program, School of Foreign Service, Georgetown University. Reports recent publications and events relating to Korean studies.

Positions: East Asian Cultural Critique, a quarterly produced by younger scholars in the East Asian studies field, with articles strong in postmodern interpretations and social criticism. Many deal with Korea.

Transactions of the Korea Branch, Royal Asiatic Society (KBRAS). Yearly journal of the Korea Branch in Seoul. Articles are usually by speakers who have addressed the society in the preceding year, many of them noted experts. (KBRAS also publishes a quarterly newsletter for members, publishes and sells books on Korea, and conducts tours.)

About the Book, the Author, and the Editor

In this new edition, Donald Clark has thoroughly revised and updated Donald Macdonald's widely praised introduction to Korea, describing and assessing the volatile and dramatic developments on the peninsula over the past five years. Remaining true to Macdonald's original conception, Clark has reworked the existing text from the perspective of the mid-1990s to take account of the enormous political and economic changes in South Korea, the evolving relationship between North and South, and the implications of North Korea's leadership transition and nuclear capability.

The late **Donald Stone Macdonald** was research professor emeritus of Korean studies at the School of Foreign Service, Georgetown University. **Donald N. Clark** is professor of history and director of international studies at Trinity University.

Index